Risk Management for Meetings and Events

Books in the series

Management of Events Operations
Julia Tum, Philippa Norton and J. Nevan Wright

Innovative Marketing Communications: Strategies for the Events Industry
Guy Masterman and Emma H. Wood

Events Management (second edition)
Glenn A. J. Bowdin, Johnny Allen, William O'Toole, Rob Harris and Ian McDonnell

Events Design and Experience
Graham Berridge

Marketing and Selling Destinations and Venues: A Convention and Events Perspective
Tony Rogers and Rob Davidson

Human Resource Management for Events
Lynn Van der Wagen

Event Studies
Don Getz

Risk Management for Meetings and Events
Julia Rutherford Silvers

Risk Management for Meetings and Events

Julia Rutherford Silvers, CSEP

ELSEVIER

AMSTERDAM • BOSTON • HEIDELBERG • LONDON • NEW YORK • OXFORD
PARIS • SAN DIEGO • SAN FRANCISCO • SINGAPORE • SYDNEY • TOKYO
Butterworth-Heinemann is an imprint of Elsevier

Butterworth-Heinemann is an imprint of Elsevier
Linacre House, Jordan Hill, Oxford OX2 8DP, UK
30 Corporate Drive, Suite 400, Burlington, MA 01803, USA

First edition 2008

British Library Cataloguing in Publication Data
A catalogue record for this book is available from the British Library

Library of Congress Cataloging-in-Publication Data
A catalog record for this book is available from the Library of Congress

ISBN: 978-0-7506-8057-8

For information on all Butterworth-Heinemann publications
visit our web site at http://books.elsevier.com

Typeset by Charon Tec Ltd (A Macmillan Company), Chennai, India
Printed and bound in Great Britain

08 09 10 10 9 8 7 6 5 4 3 2 1

This book is dedicated to my husband Larry, who shares
my optimistic pessimism and penchant
for planning for everything that could go wrong.

Contents

The author   xi
Series editors   xiii
Series preface   xv
Preface   xvii
Acknowledgments   xxi
List of figures   xxiii
List of tables   xxv

Part One: Understanding risk management   1

1 **The role of risk management for meetings and events**   3
   Introduction   3
   Risk, management, and risk management   4
   The role and scope of events   7
   The role and scope of event management   11
   The integration of risk management and event management   17
   Summary   20
   Chapter review challenge   21
   Practical risk management exercise   21
   Key terminology   22
   Online resources   22

2 **The risk management process, tools, and techniques**   24
   Introduction   24
   The risk management process   25
   The tools and techniques for effective risk management   35
   Summary   47
   Chapter review challenge   48
   Practical risk management exercise   48
   Key terminology   50
   Online resources   52

Part Two: The scope of risk management   53

3 **Legal and ethical compliance**   55
   Introduction   55
   Legal responsibility   56
   Contracts and other legal documents   59
   Statutory and regulatory obligations   62
   Compliance management   70
   Ethical issues   72
   Summary   76

Chapter review challenge   77
Practical risk management exercise   77
Key terminology   77
Online resources   79

4 Health and safety   **80**
Introduction   80
Life safety codes   81
Public health issues   89
Occupational health and safety   93
Summary   99
Chapter review challenge   100
Practical risk management exercise   100
Key terminology   101
Online resources   101

5 Loss prevention and security   **103**
Introduction   103
Loss prevention   103
Contingency and continuity planning   106
Risk financing and insurance   108
Security   112
Summary   123
Chapter review challenge   124
Practical risk management exercise   124
Key terminology   125
Online resources   125

6 Emergency preparedness   **127**
Introduction   127
Emergency management   128
Mitigation   129
Preparedness   134
Response   138
Recovery   140
Evacuations   142
Medical emergencies   146
Summary   149
Chapter review challenge   150
Practical risk management exercise   151
Key terminology   151
Online resources   152

Part Three: Organizational safeguards   **155**

7 Administrative safeguards   **157**
Introduction   157
Time management   158

Financial management 162
Human resources management 167
Procurement management 173
Systems management 178
Summary 180
Chapter review challenge 181
Practical risk management exercise 181
Key terminology 181
Online resources 183

8 **Communications** **184**
Introduction 184
Communications management 188
Information management 199
Stakeholder management 204
Summary 208
Chapter review challenge 209
Practical risk management exercise 210
Key terminology 210
Online resources 211

9 **Marketing issues** **212**
Introduction 212
Marketing plan 213
Promotions 218
Public relations 222
Sponsorship management 227
Sales activities 230
Summary 232
Chapter review challenge 233
Practical risk management exercise 233
Key terminology 233
Online resources 235

Part Four: Operational safeguards **237**

10 **Program design** **239**
Introduction 239
Designing the experience 241
Designing the environment 246
Food and beverage service 250
Entertainment 254
Production elements 257
Summary 260
Chapter review challenge 261
Practical risk management exercise 262
Key terminology 262
Online resources 263

11 Site management 264

Introduction 264
Site selection 264
Site planning and development 270
Infrastructure management 272
Managing the logistics 280
Summary 283
Chapter review challenge 284
Practical risk management exercise 284
Key terminology 286
Online resources 287

12 Attendee management 288

Introduction 288
Attendee and participant management 289
Crowd management and control 295
Attendee care and comfort 304
Summary 306
Chapter review challenge 307
Practical risk management exercise 308
Key terminology 308
Online resources 309

Appendix A: Event concept worksheet 311
Appendix B: Risk register worksheet 312
Appendix C: Site inspection checklist 313
Appendix D: Security plan worksheet 316
Appendix E: Sample instructions for security personnel 318
Appendix F: Emergency plan worksheet 320
Appendix G: Disaster preparedness supply kits 325
Appendix H: Sample change order form 329
Appendix I: Radio protocol 330
Appendix J: Sample contact list 332
Appendix K: Sample incident report form 333
Appendix L: Stakeholder analysis worksheet 335
Appendix M: Site plan worksheet 336
References 337

Index 347

The author

Julia Rutherford Silvers, a Certified Special Events Professional, is an adjunct faculty member of the Tourism and Convention Department at the University of Nevada, Las Vegas, for whom she teaches Meetings and Event Risk Management and Meetings and Event Coordination online. She designed and wrote the *Event Management Training Program* for South Africa's Tourism Learnership Project National Certificate in Tourism: Event Support, the *CSEP Study Course Workbook* for the International Special Events Society, as well as numerous distance learning courses, instructional videos, CD ROM lectures, books, magazine articles, and award-winning research papers on event management topics. She is the originator of The Event Management Body of Knowledge (EMBOK) Project, an educational resource on her Web site that illustrates and examines the scope of knowledge and processes used in the events industry. She is a Charter Member of the International EMBOK Executive, serves on the Editorial Advisory Board for the *World Journal of Managing Events* for the World Research Organization, and is a four-time International Special Events Society Esprit Award winner for Best Industry Contribution for her event management educational programs.

Series editors

Glenn A. J. Bowdin is Principal Lecturer in Events Planning at the U.K. Centre for Events Management, Leeds Metropolitan University where he has responsibility for managing events-related research. He is co-author of *Events Management*. His research interests include the area of service quality management, specifically focusing on the area of quality costing, and issues relating to the planning, management, and evaluation of events. He is a member of the Editorial Boards for *Event Management* (an international journal) and *Journal of Convention & Event Tourism*, Chair of AEME (Association for Events management Education), Charter Member of the International EMBOK (Event Management Body of Knowledge). Executive and a member of Meeting Professionals International (MPI).

Don Getz is a Professor in the Tourism and Hospitality Management Program, Haskayne School of Business, the University of Calgary. His ongoing research involves event-related issues (e.g., management, event tourism, events and culture) and special-interest tourism (e.g., wine). Recent books include *Event Management and Event Tourism* and *Explore Wine Tourism: Management, Development, Destinations*. He co-founded and is a member of the Editorial Board for *Event Management* (an international journal).

Professor Conrad Lashley is Professor in Leisure Retailing and Director of the Centre for Leisure Retailing at Nottingham Business School, Nottingham Trent University. He is also series editor for the Elsevier Butterworth-Heinemann series on Hospitality Leisure and Tourism. His research interests have largely been concerned with service quality management, and specifically employee empowerment in service delivery. He also has research interest and publications relating to hospitality management education. Recent books include *Organisation Behaviour for Leisure Services, 12 Steps to Study Success, Hospitality Retail Management*, and *Empowerment: HR Strategies for Service Excellence*. He has co-edited, *Franchising Hospitality Services* and *In Search of Hospitality: Theoretical perspectives and debates*. He is the past Chair of the Council for Hospitality Management Education. He is a Chair of the British Institute of Innkeeping's panel judges for the NITA Training awards, and is advisor to England's East Midlands Tourism network.

Series preface

The events industry, including festivals, meetings, conferences, exhibitions, incentives, sports and a range of other events, is rapidly developing and makes a significant contribution to business and leisure related tourism. With increased regulation and the growth of government and corporate involvement in events, the environment has become much more complex. Event managers are now required to identify and service a wide range of stakeholders and to balance their needs and objectives. Though mainly operating at national levels, there has been significant growth of academic provision to meet the needs of events and related industries and the organizations that comprise them. The English speaking nations, together with key Northern European countries, have developed programs of study leading to the award of diploma, undergraduate and post-graduate awards. These courses focus on providing education and training for future event professionals, and cover areas such as event planning and management, marketing, finance, human resource management and operations. Modules in events management are also included in many tourism, leisure, recreation and hospitality qualifications in universities and colleges.

The rapid growth of such courses has meant that there is a vast gap in the available literature on this topic for lecturers, students, and professionals alike. To this end, the **Elsevier Butterworth-Heinemann Events Management Series** has been created to meet these needs to create a planned and targeted set of publication in this area.

Aimed at academic and management development in events management and related studies, the **Events Management Series**:

- provides a portfolio of titles which match management development needs through various stages;
- prioritizes publication of texts where there are current gaps in the market, or where current provision is unsatisfactory;
- develops a portfolio of both practical and stimulating texts;
- provides a basis for theoretical and research underpinning for programs of study;
- is recognized as being of consistent high quality;
- will quickly become the series of first choice for both authors and users.

Preface

Hope is NOT an Action Plan

In August 2005 a two-day risk management workshop was held in Johannesburg, South Africa that brought together representatives from the event industry and regulatory authorities to examine and discuss the obligations and opportunities for effective and efficient compliance and quality assurance in the area of safe and secure planned public events. The attendees reviewed existing legalities and the proposed legislation related to the production of public events, South Africa's Safety and Security at Events Bill, and discussed the compliance challenges faced by event organizers and the enforcement challenges faced by regulatory agencies. One of the outcomes of the workshop was a draft of a ten-point charter for a Code of Professional Conduct for Safe Events.

1. Do no harm
2. Conduct business in a safe and responsible manner
3. Meet or exceed the standard of care exemplified by best practices in the worldwide events industry
4. Identify and access all appropriate reference resources
5. Require training, research, and continuous professional development from all role players, including but not limited to staff, volunteers, suppliers, sponsors, and others
6. Cause a risk assessment to be performed by a competent person for all events
7. Require prior to the start of any live event a public announcement describing appropriate egress and evacuation steps
8. Each and every event will maintain a life safety plan
9. Life safety plans will be reviewed, updated, and communicated prior to the installation of an event
10. Continually develop and maintain currency in all of the above

This proposed Code of Professional Conduct for Safe Events illustrates that a commitment to safety must be made by everyone involved in the planning and production of the event project. Event risk management is a comprehensive process that must be fully integrated and embedded into all the event plans and throughout the event management process. It is the duty of every meeting or event organizer, producer, manager, supplier, and participant, and it involves the protection of people, property, information, and other event assets to ensure a safe, successful, and sustainable event.

This duty is being addressed by governments throughout the world and often mandated through legislation enacted to protect the health and safety of their citizenry. For example, the Australian Capital Territory (ACT) Occupational Health and Safety Council made the following recommendation in its 2005 report on the Scope and Structure Review of the Occupational Health and Safety Act 1989.

Given the whole-of-government arrangements for public events is a matter which goes beyond the issues of workplace safety and ACT WorkCover's specific responsibilities, the Council recommends the Government examine the following options:

- public events legislation;
- agency services coordination;
- guidance material or a code of practice; and
- industry accreditation of event organizers.

It is clear that the level of expected professionalism is getting higher and the penalties for not meeting these requirements will, no doubt, increase in frequency and severity. This is not to say that professional event organizers have ignored this duty; they have been actively seeking this guidance material. Risk management is consistently identified in needs assessment surveys as an area of professional weakness, and practitioner community members regularly request sample forms or checklists from each other to help them perform the risk management functions they know they should be conducting. What meeting and event management professionals need are clear, concise, and practical tools that will assist them in managing the exposure to the possibility of loss, damages, or injuries arising from uncertainties that surround their events and event operations. They want effective strategies for making and carrying out decisions that maximize the potential of favorable outcomes and that minimize the adverse effects of potential losses.

This book examines the practices, procedures, and safeguards associated with the identification, analysis, response planning, and control of the risks surrounding events of all types, and provides a solid conceptual foundation based on proven risk management techniques; effective strategies for managing the risks associated with the design, planning, and production of public and private events; and ready-to-use tools designed specifically for meeting and event organizers.

Part One lays the foundation for understanding risk management by reviewing the role of risk management for meetings and events and then examining the risk management process and the

Part One	Part Two	Part Three	Part Four
Understanding risk management	The scope of risk management	Organizational safeguards	Operational safeguards
Chapter 1 Role of risk management	Chapter 3 Legal and ethical compliance	Chapter 7 Administrative safeguards	Chapter 10 Program design
Chapter 2 Process, tools, and techniques	Chapter 4 Health and safety	Chapter 8 Communications	Chapter 11 Site management
	Chapter 5 Loss prevention and security	Chapter 9 Marketing issues	Chapter 12 Attendee management
	Chapter 6 Emergency preparedness		

tools and techniques used for identifying, analyzing, responding to, monitoring, controlling, and documenting risks within a comprehensive risk management plan.

Part Two examines the scope of risk management beginning with the legal and ethical responsibilities necessary to ensure an event operation is in compliance with all applicable statutory requirements and ethical practices. This is followed by an investigation of the health and safety issues and regulatory requirements facing meetings and events. The principles of loss prevention and security are discussed from the perspective of human and property protection, fiscal responsibility, and the effective deployment of personnel and equipment. Emergency preparedness is explored so that the proper contingency, crisis management, and disaster recovery plans may be developed.

Part Three examines the organizational safeguards that may be employed to protect the assets of an event and an event organization, and the policies and procedures that ensure effective and efficient risk management endeavors. The integration of risk management into the administrative activities and the event's organizational structure is demonstrated using project management techniques. The effective management of the acquisition and dissemination of information is reviewed so a communications strategy may be incorporated into the risk management plan and process. The role, objectives, and activities included in the marketing of a meeting or event are discussed from both a risk and crisis management viewpoint.

Part Four addresses the operational safeguards that will be necessary to make certain the risks surrounding the meeting or event program and its production are managed appropriately. The design of the meeting or event program is examined so that all its elements and activities may be properly assessed for inherent hazards or vulnerabilities that must be incorporated into the risk management plan. Site selection, inspection, layout, and development strategies are reviewed so that a safe and secure environment may be created to accommodate the audience and activities. The formulation of suitable attendee admittance and crowd management plans are discussed based on predicted and probable human behavioral patterns.

Interspersed throughout the chapters are case study examples from a variety of event genre around the world that illustrate risk situations that have occurred and emphasize the importance of risk management in the meeting and event industry. Concluding each chapter is a section providing a chapter review challenge set of questions and a practical risk management exercise that will reinforce the concepts discussed, plus a glossary of definitions and the key terminology in the chapter as well as online resources that should be useful for further investigation of the topics covered. Appendices include a variety of practical forms and worksheets suitable for immediate application to real life meeting and event projects that will serve an array of event types, sizes, and contexts.

Events of all types are produced every day for all manner of purposes and attracting all sorts of people who come together for deliberation, celebration, worship, entertainment, reunion, commerce, education, enrichment, and/or amusement. Creating and managing the environment in which these people will gather carries with it obligations – legal, ethical, and financial obligations to provide a safe and secure setting and to operate in a manner that ensures the hosting organizations or individuals achieve their objectives in a proper and profitable way.

A combination of education and experience leads to professional maturity and the ability to properly use the tools, techniques, and strategies for making good risk management decisions. It is my belief that this book will become a valuable resource for students and practitioners throughout their careers, and will inspire meeting and event management professionals to approach risk management as diligently and creatively as any other aspect of creating and producing quality events, relying on proper risk planning, assessment, response, and control practices rather than hope as their action plan for safe, secure, and sustainable events.

As event professionals we are not only creating experiences, making dreams come true; we are accepting all the responsibilities that go with that dream weaving – awesome responsibilities for the character of the dream and the care of the dreamer.

Julia Rutherford Silvers, CSEP

Acknowledgments

Learn from everyone

The collective wealth of knowledge in this industry is astounding and no single person can claim absolute expertise. Making an attempt to capture a portion of that wealth of knowledge in a book can never be attributed to a single person either. This book is the result of an amazing group of people who have shared their stories, provided their expertise, and offered invaluable guidance for this project. My deepest thanks go out to the following individuals for their contributions and unyielding support. I have learned so much from each and every one of them.

Glenn A. J. Bowdin
Beth Cooper-Zobott
Sandy Biback, CMP, CMM
Susan Deerans
Bob Estrin
Francesca Ford
Don Getz
Tyra Hilliard, Esq., CMP
Janet Landey, CSEP

Virginia Huffman
Gloria Nelson, CSEP
Errol Ninow
William J. O'Toole
Veronica Scrimshaw
Patti J. Shock, CPCE
Keith Still
Ray Verhelst
Ulrich Wünsch

I would also like to acknowledge the hundreds of thousands of individuals who have been injured or lost their lives at events, from whom I trust we have all learned the seriousness of risk management. May their sacrifice and suffering be a lesson that we take into each event we plan and produce.

List of figures

1.1	Risk cognition tree	5
1.2	The process system of the EMBOK Model	12
1.3	The phases system of the EMBOK Model	13
1.4	Sample process-phase-core value chart	18
1.5	Sample domain-class-element assessment chart	19
2.1	The risk management process	25
2.2	Response plan triggers, actions, and individuals	31
2.3	Risk monitoring	32
2.4	Risk response triggers and thresholds	32
2.5	Risk communications information flow	34
2.6	SWOT analysis	38
2.7	Ishikawa or fishbone diagram	40
2.8	Decision tree	40
2.9	Fault tree	41
2.10	Influence or relations diagram	42
2.11	Probability/severity matrix	42
2.12	Fault tree analysis exercise	49
3.1	Breach of duty of care scale	57
3.2	Dimensions of a contract	60
4.1	Fire and fire extinguisher types	86
4.2	The HACCP food safety system	94
5.1	Loss prevention process	105
5.2	Loss prevention tactics	105
5.3	Facets of a contingency plan	106
5.4	Security tactics	112
5.5	Elements of protection	119
5.6	Incident reports	122
6.1	The scope of emergency management	129
6.2	Capability assessment and integration	135
7.1	Development of a schedule	158
7.2	Activity dimension of the timeline	159
7.3	Building blocks of effective human resources management	168
7.4	The procurement process	174
7.5	Example of a MAUT decision matrix	177
8.1	The dimensions of communication	185
8.2	Communication tools	186
8.3	Typical internal and external stakeholder constituencies	191
8.4	Decentralized communications network	193
8.5	Centralized communications network	194
8.6	Illustration of an actual exit sign documented by Dr. G. Keith Still	195
8.7	The facets of information systems	201
8.8	Typical stakeholder assessment matrix	207
9.1	An overview of the marketing process	214

10.1	Functional aspects of event design	240
10.2	Experiential and operational dimension of an event	242
10.3	Potential meeting and event activities	243
10.4	Food service risk issues	251
10.5	The dimensions of audiovisual considerations	258
10.6	Typical special effects employed for events	259
11.1	The scope of event travel	273
11.2	The elements of parking management	277
11.3	Overview of event logistics	281
12.1	Factors associated with an assembly	289
12.2	Dimensions of human movement within an event	290
12.3	Public and private areas in a public assembly facility	292
12.4	Typical arrival and departure patterns	294
12.5	The dimensions crowd management and crowd control	296
12.6	Stages of crowd control tactics	302
12.7	Dimensions of police crowd control	302
12.8	Typical hierarchy of responsibility and authority for crowd control personnel	303

List of tables

1.1	Dimensions of risk	5
1.2	Typical event risk factors	6
1.3	Event genres included in the events industry	8
2.1	Risk planning benefits	26
2.2	Stakeholders to involve in risk assessment	29
2.3	Pertinent documents to review	36
2.4	Sample probability/severity matrix axis definitions and scores	43
2.5	Typical monitoring systems	45
2.6	Typical control measures	45
2.7	Typical documentation procedures	46
2.8	Typical evidentiary documents	46
2.9	Typical evaluation techniques	47
3.1	Typical laws, codes, and ordinances pertinent to events	58
3.2	Typical legal documents for events	60
3.3	Important contract clauses	61
3.4	Accessibility issues	64
3.5	Intellectual property of concern to the meeting and event industry	65
3.6	Tyra Hilliard's overview of intellectual property	66
3.7	Music licensing agencies and organizations	68
3.8	Typical compliance instruments for events	70
3.9	Event industry codes of professional conduct and ethics	73
3.10	Policies that guide and promote ethical practices	75
4.1	Distribution network for NFPA's Life Safety Code	81
4.2	Components of a life safety evaluation	83
4.3	Representative decorative materials (substrates) that should be treated with fire retardant chemicals	84
4.4	Public health hazards at events	89
4.5	Hazardous household materials	90
4.6	Sources of food contamination	92
4.7	Typical occupational hazards	96
5.1	The dimensions of loss	104
5.2	Loss prevention strategies	104
5.3	Typical types of insurance for event professionals and organizations	110
5.4	Typical security functions	113
5.5	Security survey checklist	114
5.6	Security firm assessment factors	116
5.7	Security personnel performance evaluation criteria	117
5.8	Typical security equipment	117
5.9	Typical security deployment	119
5.10	Elements of the security communications plan	120
6.1	Major emergency management functions	130
6.2	Potential threats (variable according to geographic location)	133
6.3	Emergency response planning considerations	136
6.4	Emergency action plan elements	137

6.5	Possible responders to an emergency	138
6.6	Disaster recovery activities	141
6.7	Factors of human behavior in fire	144
6.8	Warning message attributes	146
7.1	Typical financial risks for meetings and events	162
7.2	Typical hidden or unanticipated costs	165
7.3	Typical human resource risks in the events industry	167
7.4	Typical policies and procedures for event organizations	170
7.5	Typical procurement risks for meetings and events	174
7.6	Types of solicitation briefing documents	176
7.7	Typical systems used in events management	178
8.1	Communication tool issues	187
8.2	Typical communication risks	188
8.3	Typical messages for internal and external constituencies	192
8.4	Common voice procedures for two-way radio usage	197
8.5	Typical information management risks	200
8.6	Typical types of event data and documents	200
8.7	Typical event stakeholders and stakeholder groups	205
8.8	Some typical stakeholder issues	208
9.1	Some typical marketing risks for meetings and events	213
9.2	Market segmentation variables	216
9.3	Typical marketing tools for meetings and events	217
9.4	Typical public relations activities	223
9.5	Typical public relations collateral	224
9.6	Typical risk considerations for merchandising and licensing	231
10.1	Creativity techniques	241
10.2	Typical event program risks	242
10.3	Typical activity provider requirements	245
10.4	Factors influencing the perception and effectiveness of an environment	246
10.5	Typical hazards associated with event settings	246
10.6	Typical signage locations and labeling functions	250
10.7	Typical food and beverage service risks	251
10.8	Warning indicators for potential catering hazards	252
10.9	Typical risk areas for entertainment	254
10.10	Typical risks associated with production elements	257
11.1	Typical event rating attributes	265
11.2	Typical site selection criteria	267
11.3	Typical venue-specific inspection criteria	267
11.4	Typical risk management site inspection criteria	268
11.5	Local resources that might be needed during an event	269
11.6	Typical site hazards and vulnerabilities	269
11.7	Transportation issues to be considered	274
11.8	Transportation and traffic contingency plan checklist	275
11.9	Typical utility service risks for events	278
12.1	Typical risks associated with an assembly	289
12.2	Controlled access needs and strategies	292
12.3	Typical arrival and departure concerns	294
12.4	Factors included in typical crowd management and control strategies	296
12.5	Tactics for minimizing hazardous crowd movements	298
12.6	Typical crowd types, characteristics, and response strategies	301
12.7	Typical public amenities provided by events	305

Part One

Understanding risk management

Awareness is the first step

What could be risky about an event? Events are fun! They're all about gathering together to interact, celebrate, be entertained, and to learn new things. They are something to do, somewhere to go, something to look forward to. They happen everyday all over the world.

This is the typical attitude I encounter all the time from students, friends, and people I meet when they ask about my work. They go to meetings and events all the time and they don't see anything that could go wrong. But when I explain what could go wrong, the most common response is an awestruck 'I had no idea!' I then feel compelled to apologize because they will never again be able to attend a meeting or event without looking around at all the possible hazards.

Risk management is one of the primary responsibilities of event organizers, yet so often ignored or misunderstood, particularly by inexperienced planners, because, like my now-paranoid event-goers, one can't envision what one has not been exposed to – they don't know what they don't know. The two chapters in this section will show you how and why risk management is a fundamental component of meeting and event management, and introduce you to the functions of risk management within the overall field of events management and the tools you may use to perform these functions effectively.

Chapter 1

The role of risk management for meetings and events

Risk and opportunity are two sides of the same coin

This chapter will examine how to:

- **Understand the nature of risk and the risk factors typical to meetings and events**
- **Recognize and relate the goals of risk management to the role and scope of events**
- **Integrate the scope of risk management throughout the event management process**

Introduction

Risk management is increasingly identified as a priority in today's world. It is also coming to the forefront of the meetings and events industry, recognized in varying degrees as a key component of the responsibilities associated with the planning and producing of events. Some events celebrate the very pursuit of risk, seeking the excitement of potentially dangerous or lucrative outcomes, whilst others may operate without an appreciation or even an understanding of the liabilities associated with their endeavors.

Risk management is often perceived as a function that is carried out once an event has been conceived, designed, and organized. Risk management, however, should be thoroughly embedded in the event design and throughout its development and production process to ensure the risks associated with the event are managed effectively and cost efficiently.

In reality, the risk manager is often brought into the event management process after a great many decisions have been made, and his or her job then becomes finding ways to mitigate the potential negative outcomes that might arise with the event as designed. The more the risk manager knows about the event management process and the events to be managed, the more likely he or she will be included early in the process and be more influential in creating an event that delivers on expectations yet minimizes unfavorable consequences.

Armed with a thorough understanding of the risks surrounding meetings and events of all types, the risk manager will be able to provide compelling reasons and creative solutions for each event and its specific risks.

Risk, management, and risk management

Risk is the unknown, and the positive or negative outcomes that may be associated with the unknown. It is possibility – the possibility that something good or something bad might happen, the exposure to the possibility of loss, damage, or injury arising from an uncertainty. Risk is *any* condition or occurrence that *might* affect the outcome of an event or event activity and might expose an event organization to loss measured in terms of probability and consequences. Not all risk is bad. An event itself is a speculative risk; its production incurs liabilities yet has the potential for economic, political, and/or social rewards. One needs to look at the worst that can happen and the best that can happen in order to be prepared for anything in between.

- *Speculative risk*: The possibility of loss and the possibility of gain.
- *Absolute risk*: The possibility of loss and *NO* possibility of gain.

Management is the planning, organizing, directing, and controlling of resources and activities to achieve goals and objectives. Risk management is the purposeful recognition of and reaction to uncertainties with the explicit objective to minimize liabilities and maximize opportunities using a structured approach and common sense, rather than avoiding the issue (see Figure 1.1). The risk manager looks at all the vulnerabilities, including financial and professional vulnerabilities and the threats to property and life and limb (see Table 1.1), and makes and carries out decisions that lessen the effects of potential losses.

The goals of risk management include the protection of assets, to minimize legal and financial liabilities, to control potential loss, properly manage growth, and to operate responsibly (Berlonghi, 1990). The focus areas of risk management include legal and ethical responsibilities, health and safety, loss prevention, emergency preparedness, and good decision making. The tactics of risk management include exposure avoidance, loss prevention, loss reduction, contractual transfer, and exposure retention (NFPA 1250, 2000). The role of risk management is to prevent and reduce loss by '*making events as safe and secure as possible*' (Berlonghi, 1990, p. 4).

Much of the literature on risk management is presented in the context of insurance coverage and legal liability – loss prevention and loss control. While this is an important perspective, particularly to the success and sustainability of events and their hosts and hosting organizations, it is equally important, if not more so, to put this practice in the context of the health and safety of those who come together to create, operate, participate in, and attend these public and private assemblies. It is not unusual to approach the subject from the 'loss' perspective because when people are injured or killed and property is lost, damaged, or destroyed, the result is usually the

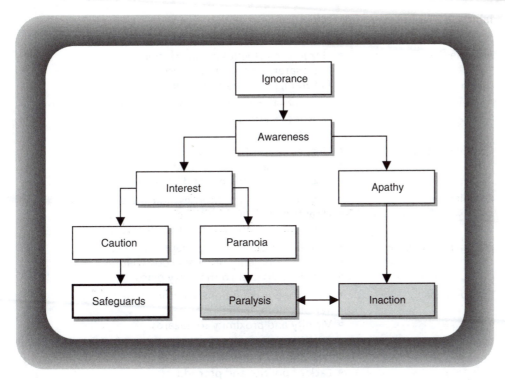

Figure 1.1   Risk cognition tree

Table 1.1   Dimensions of risk

What is at risk?	*What are the risks?*
• People	• Bodily injury or death
• Property	• Property loss or damage
• Finances	• Reduced revenue
• Systems	• Reduced capacity or capability
• Environment	• Resource availability
• Image	• Increased demand
	• Loss of goodwill or reputation

assigning of blame and the seeking of compensation. The financial assets of the event organization are protected when the potential losses are prevented or controlled.

The risk factors typical to events

The risk factors listed in Table 1.2 represent many of the risks associated with events. This list is by no means comprehensive. It does not illustrate all the risks that may occur at events, and not all of these risk factors will be pertinent to all events. In addition, the relative severity of the risks will be different in different contexts and

Table 1.2 Typical event risk factors

Activities	• Hazardous activities and attractions • Food safety and alcohol service • Program, performers, participants
Audience	• Audience demographics, history, conflicting segments • Crowd size and density • Crowd behavior
Communications	• Untried or insufficient communications • Lack of command center and control • Insufficient equipment and signage
Compliance	• Regulatory permits, licenses, approvals • Unauthorized, unsanctioned, illegal activity • Inadequate cooperation with authorities
Emergency planning	• Inadequate crisis management plans • Lack of emergency response coordination • Deficient disaster contingency plans
Environment	• Atmospheric conditions, weather dependency • Terrain, flora, fauna • Vicinity and proximity to hazards
Event planning	• Inexperienced, inadequate, or incompetent management • Oblivious to external conditions • Lack of policies and procedures
Event type and purpose	• First-time, one-time, or controversial events • Lack of admittance controls and credentials • Misrepresentative promotion
Finances	• Insufficient funding, insufficient insurance • Improper procurement practices • Vulnerable cash handling procedures/areas
Human resources	• Insufficient staffing • Untrained/inexperienced personnel • Incorrect deployment of personnel
Infrastructure	• Inadequate power, technology, utilities • Improper sanitation and waste management • Insufficient traffic and parking management
Operations	• Occupational health and safety • Installation, operation, close-down logistics • Equipment, décor, special effects
Organization	• Unclear structure of authority • Unsanctioned leadership/decision making • Insufficient/incorrect security personnel
Site	• Untried or temporary venues • Inappropriate layout, insufficient lighting • Temporary structures and staging
Suppliers	• Specialist, skilled, union requirements • Lack of supplier contact and control • Quality control, compliance and insurance
Time	• Inadequate planning and decision time • Event start and ending times, duration • Arrival and departure modes

different event genre. What should be apparent from this list is that inexperience, lack of expertise, and insufficient planning and resources has a significant impact on the level of risk associated with an event. This expands exponentially as the size and scope of the event increases.

Consider this... 1.1

Rave location via text messaging

Underground organizers/promoters of raves, all-night dance parties, are now using text messaging features to inform cohorts of the secret location of the party venue in an attempt to avoid the scrutiny and control of authorities. These high energy events, a worldwide phenomenon that originated in the U.K. and Europe in the 1980s, are often held in abandoned warehouses, empty buildings, or at outdoor locations and typically include techno music and light shows, as well as lots of alcohol and drugs, and can attract anywhere from a few hundred to ten thousand or more teens and young adults. Secrecy is required to avoid enforcement of fire codes, health and safety ordinances, liquor laws, and licensing requirements for large public gatherings. Ignoring the high numbers of alcohol and drug overdose cases requiring emergency room treatment resulting from these events, rave-goers justify this secrecy with complaints about the intrusion of government into their 'freedom of association rights' and the costs of attending commercial dance events, citing their goal of 'only wanting to have a good time.'

The role and scope of events

An event is the gathering of people at a specified time and place for the purpose of celebration, commemoration, communication, education, reunion, and/or leisure. People attend events because of the opportunity for an entertainment, educational, cultural or enrichment experience, or to satisfy social, business, or political obligations. The term 'event' refers to any public or private planned event and includes a broad range of event genres (see Table 1.3). The context of an event is the core to effective risk management (Frame, 2003). The purpose of the event will dictate the decisions about what will be included in the event and the definition of success for the event.

The characteristics of the event genres

There are considerable similarities in the way events of all types are organized and managed. However, there are significant differences in each type of event that will influence the scope and types of risks to be managed. It is important to understand the context of the event and its typical characteristics because they all have different objectives and audiences, may be different in scope and purpose, and have different characteristics and requirements that the risk manager must focus on. Each of the event genres below includes events that may be scheduled alone or in conjunction with other events, and there may be different names for each type of event depending on the corporate, geographic, or ethnographic culture.

Table 1.3 Event genres included in the events industry

• Business and corporate events	• Government and civic events
• Cause-related and fund raising events	• Marketing events
• Exhibitions, expositions, and fairs	• Meetings and conventions
• Entertainment and leisure events	• Social and life-cycle events
• Festivals	• Sports events

Business and corporate events are any event created or produced by or for a corporation that supports business objectives, including management functions, training, marketing, employee relations, and customer relations. These might include management meetings and conferences, product launch events, media conferences, company picnics or awards banquets, training programs or team building events, incentive travel programs, ground breakings or grand openings, open houses, and customer hospitality events. Corporate events typically have specific strategic objectives related to improving employee and financial performance through education, relationship building, and corporate communications. They often pose risks dealing with people, property, or proprietary information that must be protected.

Cause-related and fund raising events are created by or for a charitable or cause-related group for the purpose of attracting revenue, support, and/or awareness. These events are often long-standing traditions for their target constituencies, but may be one-time or unique events created to capture a new audience or re-energize an existing target market. They can encompass a broad range of events such as gala dinner dances, receptions, cook-offs, casino nights, auctions, tournaments, specialty tours, fun runs, walk-a-thons, and other 'a-thons'. These events are often subject to strict financial reporting regulations and restrictions, particularly for fund raising activities. As they are often organized and staffed by volunteers, risk awareness can be a significant problem as well.

Exhibitions, expositions, and fairs are events for bringing buyers and sellers together to view and/or sell products, services and other resources to a specific industry, market, or the general public. These events include trade shows for horizontal or vertical industries such as product or destination showcases, and consumer or gate shows such as sporting goods, boat, gift, hobby, or car shows, and wellness or health fairs, and arts and crafts fairs. These also include mall shows, recruitment fairs, pet shows, flea markets, and agricultural fairs. Some of these public events can be considered festivals because of their scope and annual frequency, and may attract opportunistic criminals such as pickpockets that frequent high pedestrian traffic events. Restricted-entry trade shows may be subject to industrial espionage activities. All exhibits are vulnerable to theft of the products on display and the display equipment.

Entertainment and leisure events are one-time or periodic, free or ticketed performances or exhibition events created for entertainment purposes. These include concerts, pageants, awards ceremonies, sightseeing or special interest tours, workshops or lectures, re-enactments, and parades. These will attract different audiences depending on the target market demographics, for example, a hard rock concert for young adults versus a concert by a symphony orchestra, which will affect the nature of crowd management strategies required. Sometimes these events are considered attractions in themselves or may be produced by attractions such as theme parks, biological or zoological parks, shopping complexes, schools, theaters, and museums.

Festivals are cultural celebrations, either secular or religious, created by and for the public. Many festivals include bringing buyer and seller together in a festive atmosphere. They can include seasonal or holiday festivals, music and dance festivals, ethnic or heritage festivals, food festivals, carnivals, centennials, and local or regional fairs. Festivals often evolve around a sporting or cultural event as additional activities occur or are put in place due to a large attendance, particularly in conjunction with tourism initiatives. This large attendance attracts opportunistic crime, particularly as attendees are focusing on the celebration, not their surroundings. These events are often vulnerable to financial instability and non-professional management.

Government and civic events are those comprised of or created by or for political parties or municipal or national government entities. These can include political rallies and campaign events, debates, summits, government meetings, community festivals, and official occasions such as inaugurations, investitures, state funerals, dedications, and receptions. Often involving dignitaries and sometimes controversy, these events require careful attention to protocol functions, constituency management, and the potential for confrontation.

Marketing events are similar to and include business or corporate events but are specifically commerce-oriented events to facilitate bringing buyer and seller together or to create awareness of a commercial product or service. These include exhibits or product demonstrations held in a retail outlet, familiarization and facility tours, business exchanges, publicity stunts, fashion shows, trade show exhibits and showcases, and hospitality tents, suites, receptions, or theme parties. The emphasis in these events is on interaction and current and future sales, and often represents significant investment and valuable property to be protected. The emphasis on getting consumer attention can sometimes lead to potentially dangerous activities or tactics.

Meetings and conventions are the assembly of people for the purpose of exchanging information, debate or discussion, consensus or decisions, education, and relationship building. These events are called by different names such as congresses, conferences, symposiums, colloquiums, assemblies, conclaves, study groups, or workshops. They are most often organized by and for trade or professional associations, corporate or government organizations, or social, military, educational, religious, and fraternal groups, and typically include numerous ancillary events such as receptions, banquets, trade shows, hospitality suites, companion programs, and sport tournaments. Such events may include a few hundred or several thousand attendees from local, regional, national, or international and multinational locations, and often have expansive and complex agendas. The most prevalent concerns for these events are proper contracting with hotels and other suppliers to achieve an acceptable balance of protection and risk for both the hosting organization and the service providers.

Social and life-cycle events are private events, by invitation only, celebrating or commemorating a cultural, religious, societal or life-cycle occasion. These include christenings and naming ceremonies, birthday parties and quinceaneras, bar/bat mitzvahs and confirmations, graduations, debutante balls, weddings and commitment rituals, anniversaries, funerals, social or religious gatherings organized by clubs or places of worship, and family, school, or military reunions. Aside from the hazards associated with familial and societal politics, the most common set of risks are related to the inexperience of the organizer, often unaware of the scope of responsibilities associated with event management and/or under pressure from a client with unrealistic demands.

Sports events are spectator or participatory events involving recreational or competitive sport activities. The sports event can be part of another event or a stand-alone event, and can include professional, amateur, or animal competitions, championships, matches, meets, games, tournaments, marathons, races, rallies, regattas, air shows, sports clinics, school sports, and team building events. These events often inherently celebrate risks associated with physical competition. Particular attention must be paid to audience size and potential rivalries for spectator sports events and participant abilities in participatory sports activities.

The scope of the meetings and events industry

The scope of the entire events industry is difficult to quantify definitively because there is no single source or organization collecting this data. In addition, the events industry is both horizontal (numerous event genres) and vertical (each genre using a variety of goods and services), which makes calculating total event spends very difficult. However, viewing the statistics provided in studies conducted by a variety of organizations offers a glimpse into the magnitude of the industry as a whole.

The worldwide travel and tourism industry generates in excess of $6.2 trillion (U.S. dollars) in economic activity including consumption, investment, government spending and exports, of which personal travel and tourism accounts for more than $2.8 trillion and business travel, including the meetings, incentives, conventions and exhibitions (MICE) sector, accounts for $652 billion (WTTC, 2005). The MICE industry in the U.S. represents more than $122 billion in direct spending, directly supports more than 1.7 million jobs, and is the 29th largest contributor of private-sector industries to the country's gross national product (CIC, 2005). In 2005 the United Nations recognized meeting and exhibition organizers within its International Standard Industrial Classification of All Economic Activities, adding gravitas to this industry's contribution to local and national economies worldwide (ICCA, 2005).

More than 24 percent of domestic and 77 percent of domestic business travel expenditures are credited to meetings, with an event spend of approximately 55 percent on conventions and exhibitions and 45 percent on corporate and non-convention association meetings and incentives (Krantz, 2005). Direct spending per event by individual delegate is estimated at $989, $6753 per exhibiting company, and $454 673 by the event organizer (IACVB, 2005).

There is more to consider than just the MICE sector when viewing these figures. Additional studies may be applicable to the 2.8 trillion dollar personal travel and tourism figures. Studies conducted by the Travel Industry Association of America indicate that 75 percent of the U.S. adult travelers attend cultural activities or events and 41 percent attended a festival and/or fair during their travel, 34 percent have traveled to attend family reunions, and 38 percent attended or participated in a sports event while traveling (TIA, 2005). The Association for Wedding Professionals International estimates that there are between 2.2 and 2.4 million weddings each year in the U.S. with a total event spend of approximately $85 billion, an approximate event spend of $60 billion each year in Japan, more than nine million weddings in China per year with an average spend of $19 900 per wedding, and the number of weddings throughout the world estimated at 115 000 per day (AFWPI, 2006). The International Festivals and Events Association estimates about one million regularly re-occurring events (large enough to require municipal support services) take place around the world annually and their member events alone have combined attendances of 405 million people (IFEA, 2005).

Festivals and sports events figure prominently in the sponsorship component of event marketing with sports receiving 69 percent and festivals, fairs, and annual events garnering 7 percent of the North American portion of worldwide sponsorship spending in excess of $28 billion (IEG, 2005). Promotional spending on event marketing, more than $166 billion in 2004, represents 53 percent of promotions budgets and 25 percent of total marketing spend (Joyce, 2005) and more than 65 percent of in-house corporate event or meeting organizer respondents rate the value of special events to the overall marketing plan as very important or critical (Event Solutions, 2005). Estimates indicated at least $150 million in event spend for the large scale parties surrounding the 2006 Oscars ceremony in Los Angeles alone, a figure that might be doubled when including the entertaining and event marketing activities such as social, corporate, and nonprofit events (Dubin, 2006).

It is unfortunate that the entire events industry has yet to come together, recognize its commonality and combined economic influence, and conduct the research necessary to quantify the actual number of events and their true event spends. Nevertheless, it is apparent that, as the IFEA suggests, events 'touch virtually every life on the planet' (IFEA, 2005). Besides the economic value, events have social and cultural value through the development and enhancement of business and personal relationships, facilitating fraternal and familial reunion, and increasing community pride and improving quality of life through event tourism.

The role and scope of event management

The role of event management is to facilitate the putting on of the event as well as the fulfillment of the needs and expectations of the customers or guests attending the event and the goals and objectives of its host or client. Why does the risk manager need to understand what event management is and how the event organizer performs his or her duties? In many cases the event organizer is the risk manager, and in those cases where the risk manager is a separate position, there must be a complete synergy between the two positions. In both cases a risk-aware attitude needs to be infused throughout the planning and production of the event.

The event's scope is determined through the needs assessment, specifying the *why* (the purpose and role of the event); the *who* (the audience and stakeholders); the *when* (day, date, and duration); the *where* (location and available space); and the *what* (the resources available and desired outcomes). The event organizer must determine and examine the many factors that will shape the design and production of an event, even the simplest of events. It may be advantageous to think of the scope of an event as three tents (Silvers, 2004a):

1 *Intent*: The purpose of the event; why it is being held; what the host or hosting organization wants to accomplish by holding the event (the goals and objectives).
2 *Extent*: The size of the event; the space required; the duration; the number of guests; the volumes of materials, equipment, supplies, and suppliers.
3 *Content*: The event elements and components desired or required to meet the goals and objectives of the event.

Research into the event management body of knowledge (EMBOK) suggests the scope of event management consists of phases, processes, core values, and functional areas (Silvers, 2004b, 2005; Silvers, Bowdin, O'Toole, and Nelson, 2006). The EMBOK Model (www.embok.org) proposes a knowledge framework and descriptive summary of the scope and processes that are used in the management of events. The sequential aspect of the phases and iterative nature of the processes, which are permeated with core values, allows one to approach the functional areas in a comprehensive and systematic manner. But, of prime importance is the illustration of the full scope of the responsibilities, and therefore the risk management obligations, assigned to event organizers.

The process of event management

It is useful to begin with the process system for event management (see Figure 1.2), which includes assessment, selection, monitoring, communication, and documentation, because this process system (and the proposed terminology) is based on widely accepted process models for risk management. It is a sequential and iterative system that promotes a dynamic approach to the changing nature of events (and the risks that emerge).

- *Assessment* is a two-step process of first identification then analysis. Identification is a discovery and definition process in which all the elements in each category are considered. The analytical process enhances predictive capabilities and facilitates proper prioritizing by qualifying and quantifying the characteristics of an element.
- *Selection* is the decision-making point, choosing the methods or tactics deemed most likely to achieve the goal or objective. Coupled with this decision are the assignment of resources, responsibility, and authority to carry out the tactic selected.
- *Monitoring* includes the regimented and planned tracking of the progress, status or conditions of the tactic selected, including the performance of risk control actions, and developing further options and actions as needed by reiterating the assessment and selection processes.

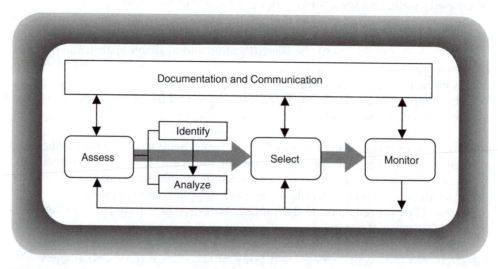

Figure 1.2   The process system of the EMBOK Model

- *Documentation* includes the recording, reporting, maintaining and archiving of assessments, analyses, response plans, monitoring and control results, and other records and documents, and provides valuable data and important evidence that leads to a robust management process.
- *Communication* is a vital component of the process system, which includes timely information acquisition and distribution plus the appropriate consultation in decision making. It is important to involve the appropriate constituents to achieve a comprehensive assessment and to foster acceptance of and support for the decisions made.

The phases of event management

The phases of event management illustrate its sequential nature, highlighting the criticality of time in any event project as it gathers momentum toward the event itself (see Figure 1.3). The progression is also cyclical, with the results of the evaluation phase contributing to the research phase of the next event. The phases include initiation, planning, implementation, the event, and closure, and are derived from traditional project management terminology (PMI, 2000). Effective event management (and risk management) relies on engagement at each juncture of this continuum throughout the life of the event project, from inception through completion.

- *Initiation* is the phase in which research is conducted and the concept is defined and validated. This is when the scope and context is set, goals and objectives are defined and the commitment of resources is established. This is also when a commitment to risk management must be instituted.
- *Planning* is the phase wherein the requirements and specifications for the event project are determined, specifying the activities that will occur, how efforts will be organized, the resources that will be required, and the context, conditions, or assumptions that affect the decisions to be made. Risk planning provides the structure for making decisions based on realistic assumptions and accepted methods.
- *Implementation* is the phase when all the goods and services are contracted and coordinated, synchronizing all the operational and logistical requirements of an

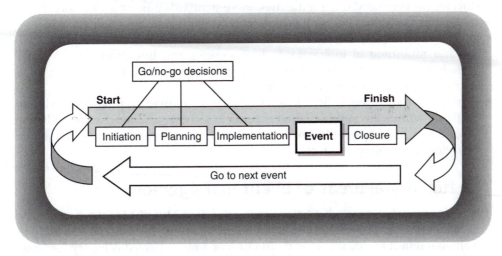

Figure 1.3 The phases system of the EMBOK Model

event project. Risk management techniques are required during this phase to ensure the proper verification and control activities are employed.

- *The Event* phase is set apart from Implementation as a distinct phase because a different and dynamic approach is required once the production begins. Although the above phases have the possibility of go/no-go decisions, once the event begins the only no-go possibility for the event is closure (or specific elements or activities included in the event). Risk monitoring and control functions are critical during this phase so that hazards or incidents are responded to in a timely and effective manner.
- *Closure* is the decommissioning phase in which the event production is shut down, dismantled, and contractual obligations are completed. This phase also includes the collection of feedback and the review of actions, activities, and decisions. This information is then evaluated to determine measurements (e.g., return on investment) or ratings against established criteria (e.g., performance critiques), reveal impacts (e.g., economic, environmental, social, and cultural), and to record lessons learned that will facilitate the effective transfer of knowledge to the next event project.

The core values of event management

The core values are those principles that must be applied to all decisions regarding every event element, phase, and process to ensure these decisions facilitate successful and sustainable outcomes. It is equally important to infuse all risk management decisions with these same fundamental values.

- *Continuous improvement* is a quality management philosophy that contends an optimized performing organization depends on the continuous and proactive improvement of all procedures, systems and, it is thereby presumed, the results rather than relying on reaction-driven planning.
- *Creativity* is regarded as essential for producing innovative and imaginative solutions and approaches to the challenges and opportunities presented throughout the management of an event project. Employing the qualities of inventiveness, inspiration, artistry, and resourcefulness are particularly important in the event industry.
- *Ethics* encompass the judgments and choices made and the actions taken that reflect and enact beliefs of what is right versus wrong. Embedded in most codes of conduct for the event and other industries, these standards guide the decisions, negotiations, and activities in a way that maintains integrity, fairness and decency.
- *Integration* reflects the critical need to coordinate, synchronize and merge the variety and multitude of interactions, dependencies and interconnected elements included in an event project to ensure decisions incorporate all the factors influencing and influenced by those choices.
- *Strategic thinking* is the ability to view and align an individual project's needs and methods within the entirety of an enterprise's short- and long-term goals and objectives in order to maintain a focus on the larger issues and impacts that should be factored into plans and tactics.

The functional areas of event management

The 35 functional areas of event management of the EMBOK Model are organized into five domains, with each domain representing an overarching area of activity, which may reflect an organizational structure or a modularized category for study and/or analysis. Within each functional area are found numerous aspects or elements (e.g., human resources: volunteers) that have specific characteristics and are affected by and subject to different objectives, procedures, constraints, and standards during the different phases and processes.

The administration domain deals primarily with the proper allocation, direction, and control of the resources used in an event project. Since resources are finite by definition, it is imperative that they be acquired, developed, and utilized in the most efficient and effective manner to benefit the event project and limit its risk.

- *Financial management*: budgets, costing and pricing, asset and cash flow management, accounting.
- *Human resources management*: organizational structure and culture, workforce recruitment–retention cycle, employees, volunteers, and contracted staffing.
- *Information management*: information acquisition, distribution, and control.
- *Procurement management*: specifications, source selection, contract administration, and change controls.
- *Stakeholder management*: client and constituency relations, strategic alliances, and power/urgency control.
- *Systems management*: physical and conceptual systems, knowledge transfer, and technology usage.
- *Time management*: activity architecture, schedule development, and schedule control.

The design domain focuses on the artistic interpretation and expression of the goals and objectives of the event project and its experiential dimensions. The elements developed within each functional area combine to create the event experience encounter that will either be enjoyed or endured, with some options considered 'risky' by their very nature or by design.

- *Content design*: topic and format selection, speaker selection, education obligations, and adult learning principles.
- *Entertainment design*: sourcing and selecting entertainment, entertainer requirement fulfillment, and performance and performer controls.
- *Environment design*: décor and furnishings, layout, functional placement, and wayfinding.
- *Food and beverage design*: menu selection, service styles, alcohol management, and catering operations.
- *Production design*: sound, lighting, visual and multimedia presentations, and special effects.
- *Program design*: activity agenda development, experience choreography, ceremonial and hospitality requirements.
- *Theme design*: theme development, cultural iconography, imagery, and branding.

The marketing domain addresses the functions that facilitate business development, cultivate economic and political support, and shape the image and value of the event project. The nature of the event as an 'experience' necessitates a thorough understanding of the unique buyer–seller relationship associated with this intangible product.

- *Marketing plan management*: target market analysis, message and medium analysis, and plan development.
- *Materials management*: printed material, collateral material, production, and delivery.

- *Merchandise management*: product development, brand management, manufacture, and distribution.
- *Promotion management*: advertising, promotional events, cross promotions, and contests and giveaways.
- *Public relations management*: image management, media relations, publicity, and crisis or controversy management.
- *Sales management*: ticketing operations, sales platforms, concessions, and cash handling.
- *Sponsorship management*: sponsorship and donors, benefits packaging, solicitation, and servicing sponsors.

The operations domain concentrates on the people, products, and services that will be brought together on-site to produce the event project, as well as the roles, responsibilities, applications, and maneuvers associated with each. Impeccable coordination is required in order to manage this symphony (or cacophony) of logistical and functional requirements and expectations.

- *Attendee management*: registration, ticketing, and housing systems, admittance controls, movement and traffic flow, and crowd management.
- *Communications management*: internal and external modes, equipment and protocols, briefing and debriefing, and the production book.
- *Infrastructure management*: transportation, utilities, sanitation and waste management, and emergency services.
- *Logistics management*: task analysis and sequencing, contractor coordination, move-in/move-out, and maintenance.
- *Participant management*: speaker and performer relations, celebrity and dignitary management, and athletic competitors and officials management.
- *Site management*: sourcing, inspection, selection, arrangement, and development.
- *Technical management*: staging and equipment, installation, operation, and technician support.

The risk domain deals with the protective obligations, opportunities, and legalities traditionally associated with any enterprise, including an event project. These areas are inextricably linked with every choice made and all activities conducted, and are increasingly mandated by stakeholders ranging from regulatory authorities to discriminating event consumers.

- *Compliance management*: statutes, codes, and regulations, accessibility, intellectual property rights, and compliance instrument acquisition.
- *Decision management*: decision framing and criteria, deliberation, collaboration, authority, and empowerment.
- *Emergency management*: medical services, evacuations, crisis management, and disaster recovery.
- *Health and safety management*: fire and life safety, occupational safety, health and welfare, and crowd behavior and control.
- *Insurance management*: loss prevention, liability, coverage requirements, and policy acquisition and management.
- *Legal management*: negotiation, contracts, licenses and authority, policies and procedures, and ethics.
- *Security management*: personnel, equipment, deployment, and command and control.

The scope of event management may initially appear overwhelming, however, these are all things most event management practitioners address everyday in their professional lives; they just may not have been itemized as discrete functions, just as we no longer itemize each task or skill required to drive our car. We just 'do it.' And if one were to really think about driving that car, there are hundreds of implications and applications that must be considered and thousands of calculations and decisions that must be made every time one starts out and for every route one takes.

Although much of this decision making becomes automatic, in order to implement the proper integration and facilitate the desired continuous improvement, the use of tools and job performance aids based on this comprehensive approach reduces the likelihood of overlooking or discounting factors (not to mention the ubiquitous 'Oh, I forgot') that may have a significant impact on the ability to manage risks associated with an event project. The chart shown in Figure 1.4 illustrates how the EMBOK Model might be used when planning an event project.

The integration of risk management and event management

Just as with the event management process, the risk management process is a sequential and cyclical one, as well as an iterative one. Each and every aspect of an event has an impact on the whole event. Each and every decision made about an event could affect how the resources will be allocated. Each and every event has various positive features to take advantage of and obstacles to overcome.

Using the process-phase-core values chart, the risk manager could scrutinize each box for potential risk factors or vulnerabilities. Using the domain-class-element model of the 35 functional areas provides a framework that compels event organizers to consider the full scope of an event project when conducting a risk assessment or a feasibility analysis. For example, the chart shown in Figure 1.5 illustrates some of the questions that might be asked about volunteer usage during the planning phase. It must be remembered that this chart only presents one question for each functional area during one phase (there are likely many more) for only one element. If one examines the true scope of decisions and considerations that may be applicable to a particular event project, probing each of these discrete functions and their elements is necessary when seeking to manage the risks surrounding the event.

The role of the risk manager

The event's risk manager must work with the event organizer to ensure that risk management is infused throughout the planning and execution of the event project and that the event organization is risk resilient – knowing the risks and being prepared to compensate for and finance them. There must be clarity for both the event organizer and risk manager (if these roles are not performed by the same individual) on the scope and specifications of the event (see Appendix A: Event concept worksheet).

Domain: administration; Class: human resources; Element: volunteers				
Assess	**Select**	**Monitor**	**Communicate**	**Document**
Initiation				
Suitability and feasibility of using volunteers Costs and benefits of using volunteers Numbers needed	Task assignment areas Organizational structure Roles and responsibilities	Need estimates Recruitment objectives	Organizational structure Recruitment policy	Need estimates Organizational structure Set up volunteer database
Planning				
Skill and knowledge requirements Recruitment sources Volunteer motives Policy requirements	Job descriptions Selection criteria Recruitment strategy	Recruitment tactics	Recruitment needs Roles and responsibilities Skill and knowledge requirements	Source projections Recruitment tactics Job descriptions Policies
Implementation				
Training requirements Staffing requirements Compensation strategy	Task assignments and schedules Training methods and schedules Volunteer benefits Orientation program	Track recruitment performance Training programs Volunteer benefit requirements	Policies and procedures Training programs Volunteer benefits	Maintain volunteer database Task assignments and schedules
Event				
Deployment and supervision requirements Credentialing requirements	Check-in/check-out procedure Credentials Policy on benefits	Volunteer turnout Deployment efficacy Supervisory tactics Benefit delivery	Task assignments Check-in/check-out procedure Credentialing requirements	Credentialing requirements Volunteer turnout Deployment efficacy
Closure				
Volunteer performance evaluation Recognition strategy Lessons learned	Recommendations for future volunteer strategies	Recognition programs	Volunteer performance Volunteer recognition	Recommendations for future volunteer strategies Recognition programs Update volunteer database
Core values guidance				
Continuous improvement	Create a volunteer handbook outlining policies and procedures Develop leadership training opportunities for volunteers			
Creativity	Develop creative recognition strategies that match volunteer motivations Find interesting ways to keep volunteers engaged throughout the year			
Ethics	Create standards of conduct policies for volunteers Distribute volunteer benefits equitably			
Integration	Ensure chain of command and channels of communication are obvious Create cross-referenced checklists for task assignments			
Strategic thinking	Develop volunteer retention and advancement strategies Seek unusual and untapped sources for volunteer personnel			

Figure 1.4   Sample process-phase-core value chart

- Type, purpose, goals, and objectives of the meeting or event.
- Dates, schedule, and site of the meeting or event.
- Expected total attendance and its composition.
- Description of the elements and/or activities to be included.

Domain: administration; Class: human resources; Element: volunteers; Phase: planning	
Financial	What costs will be incurred for volunteer accommodation and benefits?
Human resources	What conflicts could arise between volunteers and paid staff?
Information	What volunteer information must be considered private or proprietary?
Procurement	How will purchases made by volunteers be controlled and reimbursed?
Stakeholders	Will certain volunteer constituencies have political implications?
Systems	Which database systems should be controlled or restricted from volunteer access?
Time	What are the vulnerabilities should volunteers not show up as scheduled?
Content	Will volunteers be permitted to attend sessions, activities, or attractions?
Entertainment	What access to entertainers will volunteers be allowed to have?
Environment	Will volunteers be used to create any of the decorations?
Food/beverage	Should volunteers be restricted to specific eating schedules and facilities?
Production	What liabilities are incurred if volunteers provide any production elements?
Program	Could any activities jeopardize volunteers or be compromised by volunteers?
Theme	Are the volunteers critical or detrimental to the theme image components?
Marketing plan	Are the volunteer constituencies compatible with the target audience?
Materials	What volunteer-specific collateral materials must be developed?
Merchandise	Should volunteers be provided with distinctive T-shirts as a form of credentialing?
Promotions	Do volunteers need to be restricted from participating in any contests?
Public relations	What restrictions should be established for volunteer interaction with the media?
Sales	Do volunteers need to be bonded in order to assist with sales activities?
Sponsorship	What are the implications of using volunteers provided by sponsors?
Attendees	What restrictions should be placed on access credentials for volunteers?
Communications	Which volunteers need to have radios and what protocols will be used?
Infrastructure	Do volunteers need a specific and restricted parking area?
Logistics	Will using volunteers help or hinder the move-in/move-out process?
Participants	What are the volunteer lounge area and break requirements?
Site	What areas should volunteers be denied access to?
Technical	Are there liabilities associated with volunteers operating equipment?
Compliance	Are there any statutes or regulations applicable to using volunteers as planned?
Decisions	What mechanisms are needed to prevent unauthorized volunteer decision making?
Emergency	How will volunteer personnel be integrated into evacuation plans?
Health/safety	What training will be required to ensure volunteers perform duties safely?
Insurance	Are volunteers covered by our current insurance?
Legal	What are our legal obligations to volunteers?
Security	Will it be permissible to use volunteers as security personnel?

Figure 1.5 Sample domain-class-element assessment chart

- Organizations involved, including governing bodies (client, boards, committees, etc.), municipal and facility authorities, sponsors, and providers.
- Structure of authority, including who has the lead role as risk manager.
- When to walk away!

Goals and objectives must be specified and prioritized so that the decisions will maintain the integrity of the event purpose when alternatives are examined to provide a less risky option. The commitment to risk management must be made – in word and deed. This includes formally designating a risk manager and decriminalizing risk so that anyone who identifies a risk is not penalized for doing so (Defense Acquisition University, 2002). Sufficient resources must be allocated and risk management policies should be instituted that reflect this commitment. For example, a meetings policy that addresses risk assessment and management procedures, ethics, signature authority, etc., might be developed by a corporation or association to illustrate accepted practices and delineate decision-making guidelines.

The event's hosting organization must be made to understand the risks surrounding the event and its activities in order to make viable, effective, and acceptable decisions regarding the choices to be made. Some hosts, producers, or sponsoring organizations have different tolerance levels for risk, and for different categories of risk. Some are particularly averse to financial risks; others may be more averse to potentially damaging publicity; and some may be completely oblivious to any of the risks and, therefore, unable to even define its tolerance level.

It will likely be up to the risk manager to facilitate this understanding by illustrating the benefits of planning for and dealing with risks, and, if necessary, the disadvantages of not doing so. Scare tactics will not be as effective as the rational examination of the opportunities that proper risk management will offer. Just as there are hundreds of choices to be made about what the event will include and how it will be accomplished, there are countless ways to achieve those goals and objectives in a manner that protects the safety and well-being of the event audience and the event organization.

Summary

Risk isn't the same thing as 'risky.' Risk is merely an uncertainty, an unknown outcome. Risks can have favorable and unfavorable outcomes. Risk management is the way in which these uncertainties are properly identified, judiciously considered, and addressed so that they will have the best chance of a beneficial outcome and the least chance of a detrimental one.

The process of risk management is parallel to that of event management, which encompasses sequential and iterative systems that examine the extensive range of administrative and operational facets of the design and marketing of an event, no matter what type of event is being produced. Risk management is an integrated and integral part of the event management process for any event – any type, size, purpose, or style. Any and all events bring people together at a particular time, in a particular place, for a particular purpose. And, no matter what type of event is being produced, the systems and processes remain essentially the same.

The EMBOK Model explicitly captures, categorizes, and defines the processes, phases, core values, and functions in a framework that not only illustrates the complexity of this profession and facilitates effective competency and conformity assessments, portable knowledge transfer systems, and efficient practical applications; it serves as the strategic framework for consistent and comprehensive risk management for events.

There is no such thing as a 'risk free' event. Although the risk factors may vary from event to event, every event and every event organization is subject to risk that must be managed in order to achieve the objectives of the event and the goals of risk management – to protect assets, minimize liabilities, control potential loss, manage growth, and operate responsibly.

Key strategies

- Recognize that the meetings and events industry is a significant part of the worldwide economy offering a broad variety of opportunities – for rewards and for risks.
- Acknowledge that risk is inherent in all events but its potential rewards are often the reason the event is being held.
- Specialization in certain types of events often provides a depth of understanding that increases the ability to manage their particular risks.
- Approach risk management in a comprehensive, systematic, and iterative manner to ensure full attention is given to the scope of your responsibilities.
- Limit risk by first ensuring sufficient planning, expertise, and resources are in place.
- Infuse risk management awareness and tactics throughout the event project from inception to execution to evaluation.

Chapter review challenge

1 List the five goals of risk management and describe the benefits of achieving them and the consequences of not achieving them.
2 Using the five Ws of the needs assessment, explain how this information might affect the risks associated with an event.
3 Of the event genres listed, which types of events are you most interested in? Why?
4 Go through your local news sources (newspapers, broadcast news, magazines, Internet, etc.) and find an event example for each event genre that will take place within the next six months in your community. Plan to attend one of these events and document the risks you observe.

Practical risk management exercise

Describe an event you have attended recently, explain why you attended, and define its intent, extent, and content. Using the framework of the 35 functional areas of the

EMBOK Model, list a potential risk for each functional area that would be applicable to this event.

Key terminology

Absolute risk: A risk with no possibility of gain.

EMBOK (event management body of knowledge): A knowledge framework and descriptive summary of the scope and processes that are used in the management of events.

Event: A public or private planned gathering organized for a particular purpose.

Event management: The practice of developing, organizing, and administering a planned event.

Event marketing: The use of events or commercial participation in events as a marketing tool.

Event organizer: The individual responsible for planning and implementing an event.

Event spend: The monies spent on and in conjunction with a planned event.

Event tourism: Travel to a destination for the purpose of attending a public or private event.

Exposure: The state of being vulnerable or exposed to the possibility of loss.

MICE: The industry sector including meetings, incentives, conventions, and exhibitions.

Needs assessment: An analytical tool used to shape the development, production, and evaluation of an event.

Risk: An uncertain event or condition that, if it occurs, has a positive or negative effect on an event's objectives.

Risk factors: The event elements or processes that may contribute to bringing about any given result or occurrence.

Risk management: The purposeful recognition of and reaction to uncertainties with the explicit objective to minimize liabilities and maximize opportunities.

Risk manager: The individual responsible for the assessment, response selection, monitoring, communication, and documentation of risks and control measures for an event.

Risk resilient: Knowing the possible risks and being prepared to compensate for them.

Speculative risk: A risk with the possibility of loss and a possibility of gain.

Online resources

Association of Destination Management Executives — www.adme.org

Convention Industry Council — www.conventionindustry.org

Conworld.net (see: Associations) — www.conworld.net

Destination Marketing Association International — www.iacvb.org

International Association of Exhibition Management	www.iaem.org
International Congress and Convention Association	www.iccaworld.com
International EMBOK	www.embok.org
International Festivals and Events Association	www.ifea.com
International Festivals and Events Association Europe	www.ifeaeurope.com
International Special Events Society	www.ises.com
Meeting Professionals International	www.mpiweb.org
Meetings & Events Australia	www.meetingsevents.com.au
Meetings Industry Association	www.mia-uk.org
Society of Incentive & Travel Executives	www.site-intl.org
Southern African Association for the Conference Industry	www.saaci.co.za
WorldofEvents.net	www.worldofevents.net

Chapter 2
The risk management process, tools, and techniques

Know the risks before you take them

This chapter will examine how to:

- Develop a comprehensive and effective risk management plan for every event
- Conduct a thorough risk assessment incorporating the appropriate identification and analysis of risks
- Formulate response plans appropriate to the event's identified risks
- Establish systematic strategies for monitoring risk control actions and response plan results
- Create procedures for the comprehensive documentation of the risk management plan and outcomes

Introduction

Effective risk management requires a thorough and thoughtful procedure that examines and analyzes each possibility, then takes the necessary steps and allocates the proper resources to control the risks. It is an integrated, iterative, and on-going process throughout the life of an event, beginning at the very inception of the event and ending with the evaluation of the event, which provides valuable information and strategies to be applied to the next event.

All risks are not equal. All risks are not readily apparent. The range of possible outcomes, plus the implications and factors that contribute to those possible outcomes, must be considered so that plans may be made to ensure readiness to address the consequences should the situation or outcome occur. The event risk manager must work with the event stakeholders to determine the foreseeable risks and the levels of tolerable risk, then establish a formal record of the agreed upon roles, responsibilities, systems, and arrangements necessary to manage the identified risks.

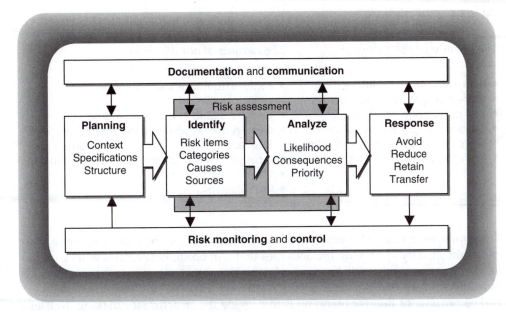

Figure 2.1   The risk management process

The risk management process

Risk management for meetings and events is a defined and deliberate process; one that must be planned and consistently applied for it to be effective. This process is sequential in nature, yet it must be iterative in practice. It is not a one-time activity that may be completed and then the job is done. Risk management must be an on-going and dynamic activity because the risks surrounding meetings and events are constantly emerging, growing, subsiding, changing, and fluctuating in terms of urgency and priority. The risk management process must also be proactive and cyclical, facilitating communication, forecasting, and forward planning. The risk management process illustrated in Figure 2.1 is based on widely accepted process models for risk management (Broder, 2000; Defense Acquisition University, 2002; Frame, 2003; Kendrick, 2003; NFPA 1250, 2000; PMI, 2000), in particular, the risk management standard for Australia and New Zealand (Standards Australia, 1999).

The event risk manager must plan for managing risk by determining the processes and procedures. The risks associated with the event must be assessed by identifying and analyzing them. Decisions about how to handle the risks must be made. The status of those risks must be monitored to ensure the risk-handling options are effective and the risks themselves are being controlled (and repeating various parts of the process if they are not). Documenting everything needs to be done in order to contribute to the risk management process for the next event. The scope of the risk management process will depend on the size and type of event being produced, but its sequential and iterative nature remains the same.

Risk planning

Risk planning is the development and maintenance of a systematic and continuous approach for identifying, evaluating, handling, tracking, documenting, and

Table 2.1 Risk planning benefits

The benefits of risk planning	The hazards of not planning
• Improved communications • More efficient use of resources • Less duplication of effort • Quicker recognition of risks • More thorough response to risks • Fewer surprises and crises	• Faulty assumptions and unrealistic expectations • Under-funding and over-spending • Gaps in risk recognition and treatment • Haphazard stakeholder participation • Inconsistent and uncontrolled decision making • Chaotic reaction and response • Increased risk

communicating risks. This organized, comprehensive, and interactive strategy must be established by specifying the activities that will occur, how efforts will be organized, the resources that will be required, and the context, conditions, or assumptions that affect the decisions to be made.

The purpose of the risk planning is to provide the structure for making decisions based on realistic assumptions and accepted methods, incorporating best practices and the lessons learned from previous endeavors to achieve maximum benefits (see Table 2.1). This requires a commitment from both the meeting or event organizer and the client or hosting organization to ensure that sufficient resources are allocated, that activities and decisions are acceptable according to the goals and objectives for the event, and that the approach is fully supported and suitable to that particular event.

The outcome of risk planning is the risk management plan, which articulates the framework for proactively dealing with uncertainties and specifies the requirements, roles, and responsibilities for implementation. This requires conscious preparation and forethought – two activities that, by their very application, serve to reduce risk.

Contents of the risk management plan

Program summary and specifications

- Type, purpose, goals, and objectives of the meeting or event.
- Dates, schedule, site, and expected attendance of the meeting or event.
- Description of the elements and/or activities included in the meeting or event program.
- Organizations involved in the meeting or event, including governing bodies (client, boards, committees, etc.), municipal and facility authorities, sponsors, and providers.
- Definitions and/or specifications unique to this meeting or event.

Organization and authority

- Requirements and objectives for the risk management for this meeting or event, including mandates from regulatory authorities and the hosting organization.
- Responsibilities and structure of authority, including who is serving in the lead role as risk manager, the functions to be performed, and how responsibilities will be delegated.
- Resources available and their sources; time, money, personnel, information, etc.

Risk assessment system

- Procedures and techniques to be used for identifying risks.
- Procedures and techniques to be used for analyzing risks.
- Procedures and metrics to be used for prioritizing risks.
- Personnel to be involved in risk assessment activities.
- Timing and schedule of risk assessment activities.
- Resources required for risk assessment activities.

Risk response system

- Procedures and protocols to be used for developing risk-handling plans.
- Procedures to be used for determining risk indicators and thresholds.
- Procedures to be used for assigning responsibility and authority for handling risks.
- Resources required for risk response activities.

Risk monitoring system

- Procedures and techniques to be used for tracking status of risks.
- Timing and schedule of risk monitoring activities.
- Personnel to be involved in risk monitoring activities.
- Procedures to be used for evaluating the performance of risk-handling plans.
- Procedures to be used for reactivating assessment and response planning functions.
- Resources required for risk monitoring activities.

Risk management information system

- Procedures to be used for documenting the risk assessment results, response plans and activities, monitoring and control functions, and evaluation conclusions.
- Reporting requirements, assigned responsibilities, and schedule integration.
- Procedures and techniques to be used for communicating activities, actions, and outcomes.
- The formats and database systems to be used for documentation and reporting.
- Resources required for risk documentation and reporting activities.

Is a formal plan such as this necessary for all events? Yes and no. For small events this is often an intellectual exercise rather than a formal document, but it is highly recommended, and sometimes mandated by law, that you prepare and document this formal plan. Doing so facilitates continuous improvement, and should something go wrong, the written plan along with other written documentation could become extremely important to show due diligence was performed. And just as writing is easier if you have done the thinking, planning is easier if you have considered the scope of responsibilities and possible tactics to achieve success, embedding the management of risk into the very design of the event.

Risk assessment

Risk assessment is the process of identifying and analyzing event elements and processes to increase the probability of success and reduce the impact of potential losses. This is a two-stage procedure that first identifies and then quantifies potential risks. Risk assessment is a critical component of risk management, frequently relied upon as evidentiary proof of compliance with best practices, and often mandated by employment law or other legislation (HSE, 1999; Ronan, 2004). Without conducting a risk assessment you have, by default, summarily decided to accept the liabilities for all risks.

The scope of the risk assessment includes the collection of all pertinent data through a variety of methods to identify as many potential hazards or vulnerabilities associated with the event as possible. This may include reviewing historical records of the event and comparable events, conducting interviews with stakeholders and the appropriate authorities, and holding meetings with staff, suppliers, and stakeholders.

This discovery process is followed by the examination and evaluation of identified risks to determine their characteristics, their likelihood of happening, the impact should they occur, and the possible responses based on the priorities and resources of the event. As there are never unlimited resources to allocate to risk management, the identified risks must be compared and ranked to establish which of the identified risks merit response and a priority for which must be handled first, second, and so forth.

It is important to involve the appropriate stakeholder constituents in the risk assessment process to achieve a comprehensive assessment, to create awareness and foster acceptance and support for risk management objectives, and to illustrate duty of care. Duty of care is the legal requirement that everything 'reasonably practical' has been done to protect safety and health.

- *Legal documentation*: The event organization should be able to provide documented evidence that a risk assessment has been conducted and that the appropriate stakeholder consultation took place.
- *Insurance companies*: Many insurance companies now require risk assessments with stakeholder consultation as a condition for issuing coverage.
- *Regulatory authorities*: The appropriate regulatory authorities must be consulted and informed of the risks and the response plans associated with the event.
- *Staff and stakeholders*: The staff and stakeholders must be made aware so that they realize the risks, consequences, and responsibilities of participating in the event project.

A stakeholder is any individual or organization that holds a functional or financial stake in the meeting or event (see Table 2.2), which will be discussed further in Chapter 8. Each stakeholder will bring a different sphere of experience, level of expertise, and point of view to the table. Each will have a different emphasis on what is important, as well as different suggestions for treatment options. Each will have different goals, objectives, motives, and requirements.

Risk response

Risk response encompasses evaluating, selecting, and implementing the techniques for handling risks, including what is to be done, when, and who will be responsible. In order to create effective risk response plans for an event, a systematic process must be employed that identifies the potential risks, analyzes their causes and effects, and evaluates the options suitable for responding to each identified risk. The response plans must specify the triggers that will instigate a response, the procedures to be followed, and the person or personnel responsible for implementing the response.

Table 2.2 Stakeholders to involve in risk assessment

Typical stakeholder involvement

- Committee heads
- Decorator
- Facility management
- Governance officials
- Key staff members
- Marketing director
- Media and sponsorship partners
- Organizer/promoter
- Outside experts (as needed)
- Participant representatives
- Public safety officials: police, fire, health department, emergency response
- Public works departments
- Regulatory authorities
- Security directors (event and facility)
- Technical director
- Transportation authority
- Vendors or contractors

Specialist involvement

- Admissions manager
- Advertising manager
- Animal handler
- Box office manager
- Catering manager
- Crowd control specialist
- Electrician
- Entertainment specialist
- Insurance broker
- IT manager
- Laser specialist
- Lighting specialist
- Parking specialist
- Public relations manager
- Pyrotechnics specialist
- Sound specialist
- Special effects specialist
- Traffic specialist

Consider this... 2.1

Building demolition turned into an event by local authorities

July 13, 1997: The Royal Canberra Hospital was demolished via implosion to make way for the National Museum of Australia. The spectacular demolition was advertised as an event so that the public could watch. Implosions around the world typically achieve international interest and over 100 000 people attended this event, making it one of Canberra's largest crowds ever. Tragically the implosion produced large pieces of shrapnel that killed a 12-year-old girl and injured nine other spectators situated more than 500 meters away. Prior to the event the engineers and relevant authorities did a risk assessment of the implosion, but this risk assessment was from the point of view of traditional civil engineering. When the implosion became an event, the risks were very different. The fact that the safety had been addressed from the civil engineering point of view obscured the fact that safety was different for the public. The risks that needed to be identified were those that were a risk to the event and its spectators. The lesson here is that risks may not be recognized, even by experts, unless they are the right experts.

Source: O'Toole (2006a), from EPMS CDROM, www.epms.net

The four typical risk treatment options include avoidance, reduction, retention, and transference. Selecting the most appropriate option or combination of actions relies on an understanding of the treatment option, its likely impact on costs, schedules and performance, and the efficacy of its usage. It also relies on the understanding of the risk itself because what can be done to deal with controllable risk and mitigate the effects of uncontrollable risk depends a great deal on its cause and impact and your resources (Kendrick, 2003).

The questions to ask when considering the risk response options:

- Will it still meet the needs of the event?
- Will it be effective?
- Is it affordable? Is it economical?
- Is there enough time to develop and implement it?
- What effect will it have on the event plan?
- What effect will it have on the other identified risks?

Not all risks merit response actions; some will be so insignificant or improbable that action is not necessary and many might be mitigated through simple adjustments or improved planning. A realistic balance of the resources required for implementing the response, its likely benefits, and the resources available must be achieved. Investing time, money, and other resources in risk treatment requires assurance that the investment is justified for the level of risk reduction or control achieved. In order to obtain approval, illustrate how difficult, costly, and time-consuming it would be to recover should the risk occur.

All personnel, departments, and other stakeholders affected by the response option(s) selected must be advised of the response to be taken and its potential impact. This may uncover secondary risks, a risk that arises as a direct result of implementing a risk response, which must be addressed. Making the risk assessment and response planning visible to stakeholders often provides additional incentive to adopt the risk management strategies recommended, and prepares people for the response actions, enabling them to respond quickly, intelligently, and without panic or indecision.

Once the risks have been identified, described, and analyzed, the risk manager creates a risk register that details all the identified risks, the results of the analyses used to evaluate them, the proposed responses to handle them, the processes and persons assigned to monitor and track them, and the effects on cost and the schedule (see Appendix B: Risk register worksheet). It should provide the definitions of risks, the integrated priorities as a basis for decisions, and the descriptions of how risks will be treated. It should be used to integrate the individual risk response plans with each other and with the overall event plans.

The response plan addresses:

- *Who*: Who will be responsible for monitoring the risk and implementing the response.
- *What*: The definition of the risk, its priority, and what corrective action is to be taken.
- *Where*: Where that risk fits into the overall plans and its effects on other risks.
- *When*: When monitoring reports are due and when a corrective action will be indicated.
- *How*: The procedures for taking the action and the resources required if implemented.
- *Why*: The consequences if the response action is not taken.

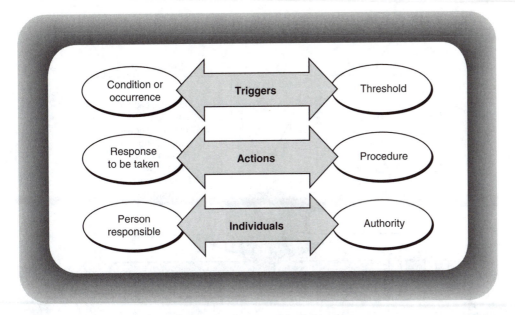

Figure 2.2 Response plan triggers, actions, and individuals

As shown in Figure 2.2, the response plan must specify the triggers or thresholds that will cause the response to be implemented. There may be sequential triggers as secondary or residual risks emerge. It must specify the corrective or response actions to be taken at each trigger, including the procedures for taking those actions. The individual responsible for implementing the response must have the decision-making authority to do so.

Risk monitoring and control

Risk monitoring is the systematic tracking of the status of risks and the performance of risk control actions and developing further risk-handling options and actions as needed. This must be a preplanned, continuous, and iterative process that proactively collects and analyzes information so progress, status, and conditions may be observed and responded to with corrective tactics in a timely manner. As illustrated in Figure 2.3, risk monitoring is conducted throughout the life of the event project, from inception through completion.

Risk monitoring might be viewed as preventative as well as predictive maintenance; seeking validation that the meeting or event and its risk management plans are on track and that variances can be addressed with the appropriate responses. Monitoring activities focus on the impacted areas if a risk occurs using a variety of targets, measurements, and thresholds, known as triggers.

Triggers, indications that a risk has occurred or is about to occur, are typically determined in the risk identification process. A trigger is activated when a specific threshold has been reached and will put a response plan into action. Thresholds are established by the levels of risk tolerance identified by the event specifications, stakeholders, and available resources, and are often expressed in boundaries, capacities, deadlines, policies, regulations, requirements, and restrictions (see Figure 2.4).

Risk control responses must be based on the actual conditions or amount of variance; one does not implement a thousand-dollar solution to a one-dollar problem.

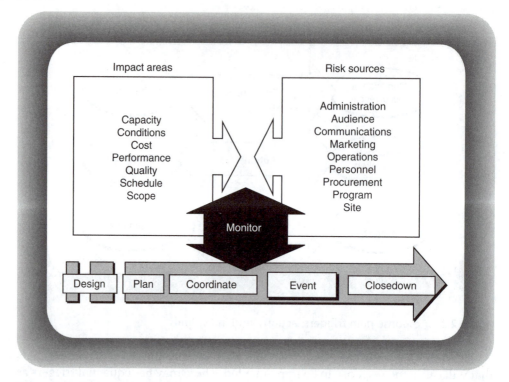

Figure 2.3 Risk monitoring

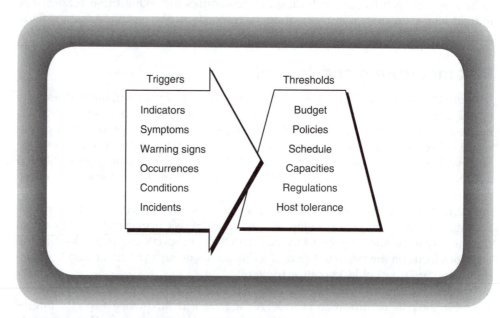

Figure 2.4 Risk response triggers and thresholds

This is where the iterative nature of the process and flexibility comes into play. It is the nature of risk that, as it represents uncertainty, it is unlikely to occur exactly as anticipated. The risk manager, or the individuals tasked with monitoring and responding to risks, must understand the nature of that risk and the extent of its influence on other risk areas in order to employ (or improvise) the proper type and level of response. This often requires reapplication of the risk analysis and response planning techniques, and always requires knowledge, experience, and common sense.

The fallacy of 'control'

It is critical to understand the singular importance of conducting a thorough risk assessment in the context of 'controlling' risk. The plain fact is that one does not 'control' what can or will happen at an event. It is often noted that event management, and consequently risk management, encompasses the initial and iterative planning and then it is all about change management. And there are ALWAYS changes or incidents occurring at an event … things NEVER go exactly as planned … and one can never eliminate ALL risks. You have NO CONTROL over changes happening, only your ability to react effectively to those changes. You must be proactive about the ability to be reactive.

Effective change management (proactive reactions) relies on information, familiarity, good judgment, and being prepared, not paralyzed. One must know how to properly identify problems, how to analyze problems, and how to solve problems. In the throes of an event the rapid cognition of our adaptive unconscious plays a significant role in our judgment and decision making, but the efficacy of these decisions is determined by the depth and breadth of our experience and knowledge (Gladwell, 2005).

Incorporate preventative measures to prevent what you can prevent, and then focus on preparedness. The more aware you are of what could go wrong, the better prepared you can be to react and respond properly and effectively to an incident or occurrence. For example, as illustrated by Hurricanes Katrina and Rita hitting the U.S. Gulf Coast in 2005, there was nothing one could do to stop the hurricanes from happening; one could only control the way in which one prepared for and reacted to the hurricane.

Risk communication

Risk communication involves both information transfer and consultation, requiring two-way capability for giving and getting messages about the entire scope of the event and its risk management activities, actions, and outcomes. Effective risk communication should facilitate this collaboration and the acquisition of proactive data that helps predict and prepare for risks, and getting risk messages before, not after, something has happened (Smith and Merritt, 2002). The decriminalization of risk should be ingrained throughout the event team (we won't shoot the messenger) so that everyone feels empowered and obligated to communicate risk messages.

Communications procedures and methods should be embedded throughout the event project, from inception through evaluation, to ensure the right information gets to and is received from the right people at the right time. In addition to written communications such as performance or status reports, change orders, and other documentation, meetings offer the unique opportunity for tapping into the collective intelligence of the event team.

When the risk manager is included in meetings early in the planning stages, it is possible to establish the relationships with the key stakeholders that will foster acceptance of risk management as an inherent and necessary initiative. It is helpful to prepare a stakeholder analysis that identifies each stakeholder's role, expectations, concerns, and influence over the decisions about the event project. Meetings are exceptionally valuable during the risk assessment phase, bringing together all those who will be involved in the event's implementation and allowing them to form into a team

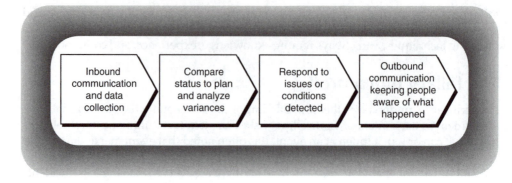

Figure 2.5 Risk communications information flow

and build on each other's experience and expertise. This teamwork becomes even more important as the event project goes into production.

A sound communications infrastructure is critical to the effectiveness of risk monitoring and control strategies, and must facilitate the proper flow of information (Kendrick, 2003) as illustrated in Figure 2.5. The information must be timely, accurate, and to the point, and once a corrective action has been taken, this must be communicated to internal and external staff, suppliers, and stakeholders. Regularly scheduled meetings will support these objectives as progress, changes, and emerging risks can be reviewed and addressed.

Risk documentation

Risk documentation includes the recording, reporting, maintaining, and archiving of assessments, analyses, response plans, monitoring and control results, and other records and documents. Creating such documentation should be formally mandated as an administrative 'deliverable' of the event project – part of the tasks specified in the event plans and work breakdown structure – and acknowledged by the event management as a due diligence responsibility. Establishing a formal documentation procedure demonstrates that a systematic and appropriate risk management process was conducted and, due to its visibility as an obligatory function, often results in a more comprehensive risk assessment.

Risk documentation should be conducted throughout the event project in order to capture important information that serves the current risk discovery, monitoring, and control activities, as well as archives such information for future use. When documentation is generated it provides valuable data and important evidence that leads to a robust risk management process. It supports retrospective analyses, mechanisms for authorization and accountability, and the 'paper trail' necessary to validate actions and verify outcomes.

Documentation adds to an event organization's knowledge base, supplying relevant data that not only promotes the identification and understanding of what could go wrong (risk management); it also provides a method for identifying what could go better (opportunity management) in order to take full advantage of the possible results. Strategies and activities may be evaluated to determine which areas or actions are efficient or deficient and effective or ineffective, as well as which program elements, policies, and procedures should be continued, revised, or deleted. Such background material is critical for new personnel or new event projects.

The decision-making process can be reconstructed and decisions reviewed to determine and understand the underlying rationale, correct or incorrect, on which those decisions were based. This identification leads to improved awareness of current and future assumptions and constraints, as well as defining and validating for stakeholders why specific actions are (or were) required or recommended, providing event management and risk management decision-makers with the strategy for acquiring approval and authority for implementation because an audit trail is clearly defined and supplied.

The evidentiary nature of documentation is two-fold. First, it provides verification of the results and outcomes realized. This information supports the current monitoring activities, retrospective and prospective analytical activities, plus audits and other assessments. Second, documentation provides official and/or legal evidence of occurrences, incidents, and the exercising of duty of care.

The tools and techniques for effective risk management

A variety of tools and techniques can be used throughout the risk management process to ensure an effective, comprehensive, and proactive approach. Determining which tool or technique to use at any given phase should be based on the type, scope, and magnitude of the meeting or event, as well as the experience, expertise, and engagement of the stakeholders involved. Each tool or technique offers a different practical method for accomplishing the task at hand, and using a combination provides the most effective results.

Risk identification

Risk identification is the examination of event elements and processes to define possible risks, triggers, and thresholds using a variety of methods. Numerous techniques can facilitate this discovery process, but it all begins with the clearly identified program or project plan defining the goals and objectives for the event, the type and extent of activities included, the people involved, and the processes to be used. The outcome of the risk identification process should be a list describing potential risks to be analyzed and prioritized for risk response actions.

Berlonghi (1990) suggests questions to ask to spark the discovery process include:

- Who is exposed to harm?
- What is exposed to loss?
- What could cause loss?
- Who would suffer loss?
- What are the consequences?

Many risk management manuals and practitioners recommend the sorting of the various areas of risk into categories to make identification (and analysis) more efficient and effective. These categories could be activities, tasks, departments, event components, specifications, needs, objectives, key performance parameters, processes, or any number of groupings. The risk manager must develop the types of categories that best suit the type, size, scope, and/or purpose of the event, and that best suits the stakeholders participating in the process. However, establishing a consistent set of categories, particularly for recurring events, facilitates the development of a knowledge management system for continuous improvement.

Risk identification tools and techniques

Brainstorming

A group technique for stimulating creative and intellectual ideas that may be used to identify risks using a group of team members, stakeholders, and/or subject matter experts wherein each participant's ideas are recorded for later analysis. It is important to remember that this is an idea or item generation exercise, during which no evaluation of value or possibility should take place. Such critique will stifle the exercise and prevent the emergence of unique or unusual risk possibilities and potential opportunities and solutions.

Documentation review

All documentation generated for the current meeting or event should be reviewed (see Table 2.3). This should reveal areas and activities of concern, interactions and integrated planning matters to be addressed, stakeholders to be interviewed or included in meetings, and gaps in the documentation appropriate for a meeting or event of this type or scope (a risk factor in itself). In addition, a retrospective analysis of lessons learned and historical data from past and comparable events will likely reveal risk factors and areas that need attention.

Gap analysis

An analytical tool used to detect gaps (i.e., disparities or missing parts) in the plans for or delivery of an event, its purpose is to determine any potential discrepancies

Table 2.3 Pertinent documents to review

• Budgets	• Performance evaluations
• Checklists	• Permit applications
• Contracts and agreements	• Policies and procedures
• Design specifications	• Previous risk reports
• Emergency plans and procedures	• Procurement documents
• Event evaluations	• Production schedules
• Event specifications	• Program of activities
• Facility regulations	• Proposals
• Guest lists/attendee profile	• Security plans
• Historical archives	• Site plan/diagram
• Inspection reports	• Site inspection survey
• Insurance policies	• Sponsorship plans and sponsors
• Job descriptions	• Staffing plans and policies
• Marketing plans	• Timeline
• Operational plans (all departments)	• Volunteer plans and reports
• Organizational flow charts	• Work breakdown structure

between expected and actual performance and system deficiencies. The gap analysis is typically applied after an event, but its results from previous events will highlight areas and activities of concern.

Hazard mapping

This technique examines the event environment (site, surroundings, structure, or systems) for areas and items of concern. This exercise is particularly useful for identifying health and safety hazards, as well as pointing out areas or activities that foster combined risk factors or root causes for risks. This exercise should include those actually working in that or those environments (e.g., staff and volunteers) to garner practical input.

Interviews

Consultation with all department heads, key stakeholders, and others involved in the event operations is an important component of risk identification. Interviewing peers and subject matter experts can also be useful. These interviews could be conducted one-on-one or within a group setting and are used to determine existing concerns, identify risk factors, and establish what is or should be done about them (and the resources available and required to deal with them). Questions should be prepared according to the area of responsibility as well as a set of questions to be asked of each person interviewed, which might uncover difficulties, inconsistencies, misconceptions, misunderstandings, and conflicting assumptions.

Risk assessment meeting

This is a very effective method for the identification of risks. All participants in a risk assessment meeting should be required to complete any necessary pre-work, such as compiling risk lists or reports, and each participant should sign in so the risk manager has a record (evidence) of who was in attendance. The number and scope of the risk assessment meetings will depend on the size, scope, and type of event being produced. To ensure full participation, the risk manager should make certain all those in attendance are called upon to contribute their ideas and perspectives. This is often achieved by holding a brainstorming session wherein all ideas are accepted without critique until the later, analytical phase of the meeting. Using the 'round robin' method, a group technique wherein the members of the group are required to participate in a sequential manner, ensures all the members of the group will contribute to the discussion and will be heard.

Scenario/tabletop exercise

This is an exercise wherein participants are given a scenario or description of an event incident or situation and are asked to discuss and examine the causes, effects, and other implications by taking the scenario to its logical or worst case conclusion. This 'What might go wrong?' or 'What's missing?' analysis often reveals omissions or undesirable conditions and encourages participants to go beyond the 'obvious' and penetrate further to identify and understand the risks, their root causes, and their potential outcomes.

SWOT analysis

This analytical tool examines the strengths, weaknesses, opportunities, and threats of past or comparable events, and identifies or predicts the advantages and deficiencies associated with the current or future event (see Figure 2.6). All identified

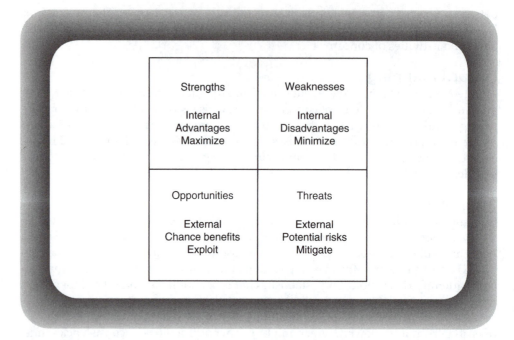

Figure 2.6   SWOT analysis

strengths and opportunities should be capitalized on, and all weaknesses and threats should be carefully analyzed, addressed, and monitored.

Work breakdown structure (WBS) review

A typical project management tool, the WBS is the list of the activities, tasks, or work packages required to accomplish the event project. This 'decomposition' of the event elements into their task components provides a realistic and comprehensive overview of the scope of the event project and the resources necessary to complete it. The WBS should be examined in conjunction with the timeline or schedule and the critical path, showing deadlines for conducting certain actions in a logical and necessary sequence, to reveal inadvertent oversights and potential conflicts.

Risk analysis

In order to develop effective risk response and treatment plans within the constraints of limited resources, the risk manager must analyze the identified risks to determine their causes, consequences, correlations, probability, and priority. Risks must be ranked to determine their order of importance or urgency so that the most critical ones will be addressed in the proper order according to legal, ethical, and risk tolerance parameters. The safety and welfare of people must always be the number one priority, with the loss of vital information second, particularly in an emergency situation. The loss of property, reputation, and finally, the financial investment in the event are usually less critical because they can likely be replaced.

The analytical tools used consist primarily of three types: root cause, decision, and influence analyses. These qualitative and quantitative methods are used to evaluate and estimate the reasons risks are present or arise; the likely occurrence and impact severity of a risk; the criticality and time sensitivity of the risk; and other or overlapping areas affected by the risk item. It is advisable to consider a combination of analytical tools so that risk drivers and residual or secondary risks are identified and a holistic and comprehensive understanding of the risks is achieved.

Jeynes (2002) suggests that typical evaluation factors include:

- The people affected.
- The extent of potential harm or damage.
- The likelihood of occurrence.
- The possible disruption of the event.
- The likely impact on owners, stakeholders, or public image.
- The urgency or immediacy of impact.
- The ability to recover.
- The cost implications.

It is important to consider both the direct and indirect exposures when analyzing risks. Direct exposures are those that have an actual and immediate effect, such as actual or threatened injury or damage to persons, loss or damage to property, or injury or damage to the environment. Indirect exposures are those that have incidental or subsidiary effects such as economic, legal, or political impacts.

Risk analysis tools and techniques

Cause/effect analysis

This is a graphical predictive or diagnostic analytical tool used to explore the root causes or factors that contribute to positive or negative effects or outcomes. The categories can include environment, budget, time, and any other resource factors pertinent to the end effect. The most typical form is the Ishikawa or fishbone diagram (see Figure 2.7), named for its developer Kaoru Ishikawa, a pioneer in quality management processes.

Constraint analysis

Constraints are the factors that limit capability or capacity and they fall into four categories – scope, quality, schedule, and resources (any may include political or regulatory constraints). Each must be recognized and analyzed to determine its flexibility, priority, and impact on the decisions to be made regarding response options and actions. The adage 'good, fast, cheap: pick two' illustrates that trade-offs will often be necessary.

Decision tree analysis

This evaluation tool describes a decision under consideration and examines the implications of selecting one risk response option over another (see Figure 2.8). Each alternative will have different costs, benefits, and secondary risks (those that arise after the response has been implemented), and must be analyzed based on their feasibility, cost, and schedule implications.

Fault tree analysis

Another form of the cause/effect analysis, this deductive tool begins with a conclusion, and then attempts to determine the specific causes of this outcome (see Figure 2.9).

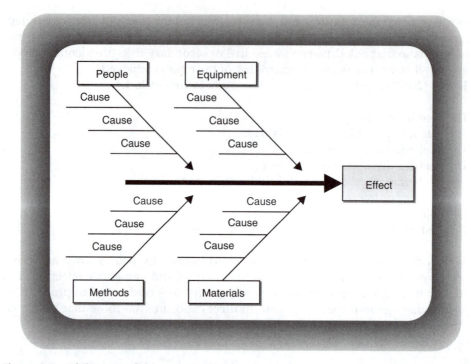

Figure 2.7   Ishikawa or fishbone diagram

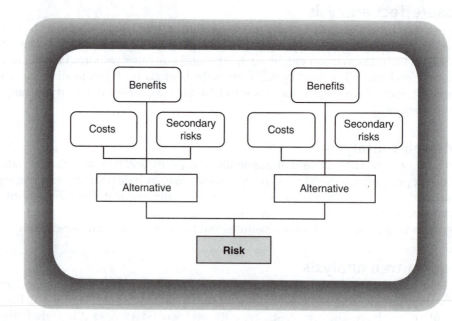

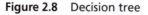

Figure 2.8   Decision tree

It provides a graphical representation of the combination of failures and/or errors and the most common causes that result in a condition or occurrence. It also helps to identify the risk drivers – those choices, causes, or conditions that have the most impact on the risk, as well as the risk drivers that affect numerous risk factors.

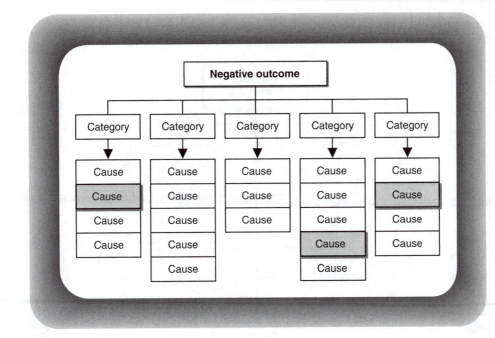

Figure 2.9 Fault tree

Influence diagram

This graphical evaluation tool is similar to mind mapping and illustrates the effects and scope of interactions any one element or change will have on other event elements, plans, and associated risks. Sometimes referred to as a relations diagram, this tool may also be used to help identify factors in a situation that are driving many of the other symptoms or factors (see Figure 2.10). The arrows start at the influencing factor and end at the factor being influenced. The factors with the most outgoing arrows will be root causes or drivers.

Probability/severity matrix

This tool is used to quantify the likelihood and impact of identified risks in order to prioritize risk response activities (see Figure 2.11). Experts advise that the probability should be evaluated first, followed by estimating the potential severity of the consequences. It helps identify the risks that are most urgent or must be avoided, those that should be transferred or reduced, and those it is reasonable to retain.

This tool is often used to quantify risk by assigning numerical values to each block and then multiplying the probability by the severity to reach a risk score. It is helpful to specify the precise meaning or range of each axis descriptor (see Table 2.4), often based on statistical information, cost estimates, and historical records, so that ratings based on expert opinions and historical data will be consistent. A rating scale can be established giving an evaluative score to each factor that prompts specific response or decision protocols. For example, if 'certain' had a rating of 0.9 and 'catastrophic' a rating of 0.9, the risk score would be 0.81. It might be predetermined that any score above 0.65 requires an alteration of the event plan or consultation with additional experts.

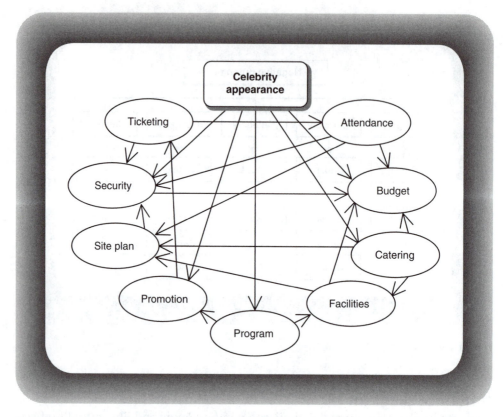

Figure 2.10   Influence or relations diagram

Probability	Severity				
	Insignificant	Minor	Moderate	Significant	Catastrophic
Certain	High	High	Extreme	Extreme	Extreme
Likely	Medium	High	High	Extreme	Extreme
Possible	Low	Medium	High	Extreme	Extreme
Unlikely	Low	Low	Medium	High	Extreme
Remote	Low	Low	Medium	High	High

Figure 2.11   Probability/severity matrix

Risk response options

For every risk identified a decision must be made about how to respond to that risk.
This decision involves a process just as with all other aspects of risk management and

Table 2.4 Sample probability/severity matrix axis definitions and scores

Probability		Severity	
Certain	Happens most of the time	Catastrophic	Death or permanent damage
0.9	>90% chance of occurring	0.9	>$100 000 in losses or liability
Likely	Happens frequently	Significant	Serious injury/major damage
0.7	75% chance of occurring	0.7	$75 000 in losses or liability
Possible	Happens occasionally	Moderate	Medium or temporary impact
0.5	50% chance of occurring	0.5	$50 000 in losses or liability
Unlikely	Seldom happens	Minor	Minor injury or damage
0.3	25% chance of occurring	0.3	$25 000 in losses or liability
Remote	Rarely ever happens	Insignificant	Little or no impact
0.1	<10% chance of occurring	0.1	<$10 000 in losses or liability

event management in general. Each decision must be a conscious decision, based on a solid cost/benefit analysis, not by default or evasion. Ignoring or deferring such decisions increases rather than decreases risk. The risk manager must identify and analyze treatment options and prepare and implement treatment measures until the risk is acceptable.

Risk avoidance
The removal of risk liabilities or hazards. This may be achieved through the modification or elimination of those elements, requirements, practices, or activities that cause or generate the risk. It is not realistic to avoid all risks; events simply would not take place. The risk manager should consider methods that remove or decrease risk sources, substitute less hazardous options, or modify the concept, specifications, and/or procedures until the risk is acceptable when contingency plans are in place. For those risks that are extreme or very high and cannot be modified, it is prudent to abandon or cancel those elements.

Risk reduction
The mitigation or lessening of the impact of a risk by reducing the probability or likelihood of its occurrence and minimizing the severity of its consequences should it occur. Loss prevention methods may be employed including various forms of protection strategies, security and supervisory personnel, and protective equipment and devices. Risk diffusion and/or separation tactics may be used in which vulnerable objects or operations are segregated or relocated. Contingency plans may be made that ensure the availability of redundant or alternative equipment or services.

Risk retention
The conscious acceptance of a risk without engaging in any special effort to control it and retaining financial liability for losses that may occur. This does not mean that these risks may now be ignored. Acceptance still requires monitoring to ensure the risk does not become unacceptable or increase in its significance. Sufficient resources to overcome a risk should it occur must be allocated, as must sufficient funds be allocated to pay for losses should they occur.

Risk transference

The reallocation or transfer of the liability for and the impact of a risk to a third party. Also known as risk deflection, this is typically achieved through contractual transfer, purchase of insurance coverage, use of waivers of indemnity, or joint venture or partnership structures. Depending on the type of transference, an additional risk may arise as the entity to which the risk has been transferred may not have sufficient resources or risk control capabilities to effectively manage the risks now under its jurisdiction.

Other response plans that should be in place include contingency plans, crisis plans, and recovery plans. Contingency plans are the strategies and arrangements made to deal with and recover from uncontrollable known risks and unforeseen risks. A crisis plan is the formal record of agreed upon emergency management roles, responsibilities, strategies, systems, and arrangements. Recovery plans define the recovery activities, typically including workaround or deactivation strategies and continuity measures, which will allow the event organization to resume its business operations.

Risk monitoring and control techniques

There should be a monitoring system, activity, or process specified for every risk identified, and these may aid in identifying and responding to risks that have not been identified (see Table 2.5). Monitoring systems should also supply data for subsequent feedback, review, and evaluation activities for the refinement of future risk management plans.

Control measures are those physical, behavioral, and procedural actions, devices, strategies, and systems employed to prevent or reduce loss (see Table 2.6). Control measures must be continuously monitored and evaluated as closely as the hazards or risks they are designed to control.

Risk documentation techniques

Documentation is the formal recording of information, and this information is an event asset – an incredibly valuable resource that must be collected and protected properly. Documentation exists in many forms including written documents, graphical representations, audio recordings, video recordings, and photographs. Typical documentation includes records, reports, evidence, and evaluations. The techniques for ensuring this documentation is generated and collected properly rely on incorporating these procedures into the event's operations and administrative functions (see Table 2.7).

Historical records comprise the information assets and institutional memory of an event. Whether this information is kept in a sophisticated computer system or on various checklists, forms, pieces of paper, or note cards, effective risk management dictates establishing policies and procedures for acquiring and protecting these assets.

- *What to get*: Information to get includes all the specifications, contact details, communications, instructions, reports, checklists, and other paperwork associated with the event.
- *What to keep*: Information to keep includes anything that is mandated by law or has an impact on or provides verification of the event operations.
- *Why keep it*: Reasons for keeping this information include planning, operational, and archival functions as well as legal, ethical, risk management, and fiduciary responsibilities.
- *How to keep it*: Records must be sorted and stored appropriately so the information in the records is accessible to those who need it – but ONLY to those who need it, in compliance with privacy and proprietary information requirements.

Table 2.5 Typical monitoring systems

Alarms	Silent, audible, or visual alarms may be used to monitor restricted areas and advise of unsafe or dangerous conditions
Budgets	Budgets should be used as a financial management tool to establish spending limits and to monitor purchasing practices and expenditures
Checklists	Checklists may be used to track and confirm the completion status of tasks or receipt of information or material
Communications	Communication plans should incorporate the acquisition of monitoring data in a timely manner
Confirmations	Written confirmations should be used to verify receipt, understanding, acceptance of, and/or agreement with instructions, changes, and other information
Deadlines	Deadlines should be set for task completion or receipt of information or material in order to maintain the schedule and its critical milestones
Inspections	Physical inspections of sites, equipment, installations, and conditions should be conducted to visually verify safe and secure operations
Issue logs	The status of issues that surface throughout the event project should be tracked and evaluated to determine if and when they require formal risk assessment and action
Meetings	Face-to-face meetings may be used to acquire and/or verify the status of plans, conditions, and other information
Observation	Observers may include security personnel and/or staff and volunteers who are tasked with watching the condition, actions, and reactions of the audience and participants during the event and must be instructed as to what is important
Reviews	Reviews may be used to examine, evaluate, and/or convey actions, activities, processes, and procedures
Security	Security personnel and equipment are used to observe conditions, protect people and property, and prevent incidents
Status reports	Reports should be used to receive and convey information on the status of risks and the effectiveness of risk-handling actions
Supervision	Supervision of personnel and activities provides protection from misuse or mishandling, guidance on proper practices, and observation and notification of unsafe conditions
Walk-throughs	A walking tour and survey of the event site prior to and during an event should be conducted to observe and correct any safety hazards
Watch lists	Similar to the risk register, this list itemizes and highlights risks requiring special monitoring and varying responses depending on their occurrence or extent

Table 2.6 Typical control measures

• Access barriers	• Directions and instructions	• Regulations
• Admittance controls	• Exclusions	• Restricted areas
• Change orders	• Inspections	• Safety equipment
• Checkpoints	• Limitations	• Schedules
• Computer access codes	• Mandates	• Training
• Constraints	• Policies and procedures	• Warning systems

Table 2.7 Typical documentation procedures

• Require minutes be generated for all meetings	• Maintain copies of permits and other compliance instruments in a safe place
• Require written status reports, even if initially delivered verbally	• Take photographs of the event site before, during, and after the event
• Require after-action and incident reports	• Take photographs of any incidents or unsafe conditions
• Require written confirmations for all change orders	• Use sign-in sheets for meetings and staffing check-in
• Include date and/or version number on all planning documents	• Use conversation diaries to track telephonic discussions
• Require department or committee heads to maintain a record of activities and occurrences	• Keep copies of all marketing and collateral materials
• Execute written contracts for all goods or services procured	• Develop and use forms for data collection
	• Back-up computer data on a daily basis

Table 2.8 Typical evidentiary documents

• Certificates of insurance	• Incident reports	• Promotional collateral
• Complaint letters/forms	• Meeting minutes	• Property damage reports
• Contact lists	• Misconduct reports	• Risk analysis reports
• Correspondence/memos	• Monitoring reports	• Risk management plan
• Duty rosters	• Permits and licenses	• Risk register
• Evaluations and analyses	• Photographs and videos	• Schedules/timelines
• Event planning checklists	• Police reports	• Vehicle accident reports
• Feedback forms	• Policies and procedures	• Witness statements

Reports are a written account or record of information gathered or actions taken. They should facilitate the timely and efficient distribution of information to those who need it. They should also be required to ensure the timely and efficient collection of information from those charged with specific duties and tasks to perform.

- Status reports should be linked to critical milestones in the planning process and the trigger points in risk response plans.
- Risk analysis reports should include conclusions and recommendations, and must be timely and convincing.
- Post-event reports should also include conclusions and recommendations, plus all the supporting documentation necessary to verify and/or confirm those conclusions and recommendations, as well as any necessary evidentiary materials.
- Ad hoc reports may be necessary from time to time in order to track risk response and control functions.

Proper evidentiary documentation will become critically important for the prompt and satisfactory resolution of commercial or legal disputes (see Table 2.8). From the boardroom to the courtroom, this documentation may facilitate independent audits, provide proof of compliance with regulatory requirements, and demonstrate that proper procedures were employed.

Table 2.9 Typical evaluation techniques

Analyses	The various analyses conducted should be re-examined to determine the efficacy of the assumptions and conclusions
Feedback	In order to get feedback you must provide the mechanisms and systems for receiving feedback (suggestion boxes, meetings, surveys, focus groups, etc.)
Interviews	Interviewers must be provided with the questions to ask that will glean the information desired or required
Performance audits	The quality, quantity, timeliness, and capability of all products, services, personnel, and providers should be assessed
Post-event meetings	Post-event meetings (debriefings) are a primary method for collecting anecdotal information, expert reviews or analyses, and important feedback
Questionnaires	A set of open-ended and closed-ended questions allow opinions, attitudes, and observations to be collected efficiently and anonymously (if desired)
Reports and reviews	Reports and reviews must be purpose-specific and properly structured in order to gather the desired intelligence
Statistics	Statistical data must be captured efficiently and effectively – in order to count you must plan to count. Incorporate the collection of data for your reports in your standard operating procedures and implement measures to capture numbers and statistics.

Evaluation is the process of critique and measurement or rating against established values. Typical evaluation methods such as questionnaires, interviews, and statistics are primarily used for a post-event evaluation, but may also be used in risk monitoring functions in combination with techniques such as status reports and observation. All evaluation techniques include the collection and analysis of information (see Table 2.9), which must be scheduled appropriately and the results distributed properly on order to be effective.

Every health or safety law or code has been the result of examining and evaluating the causes and results of disasters, and every improvement or best practice originated with trial and error. It is vital that one continually learns from the tragedies and triumphs, large or small, of each event. This can only happen if the information is recorded, analyzed, and taken forward as lessons learned.

Summary

Risk planning should be as robust as the event planning. In order to create effective risk response plans for an event, a systematic process must be employed that identifies the potential risks, analyzes their causes and effects, and evaluates the options suitable for responding to each identified risk. Response plans must specify the triggers that will instigate a response, the procedures to be followed, and the person or personnel responsible for implementing the response.

Consultation and collaboration with stakeholders increases the efficacy of risk assessments and facilitates effective communication strategies. Documentation provides the data required to verify and validate decisions and risk management activities, and significantly contributes to the ability to learn from successes and fiascos.

The risk management tactics, tools, and techniques employed to protect assets and individuals from loss, harm, death, or destruction and to protect the event from disruption, disgrace, or demise must be thoroughly and carefully considered from the inception through the production of the event. This can be an awesome and intimidating responsibility, but by systematically conducting risk identification, analysis, response planning, control, and evaluation activities, this sometimes overwhelming duty will become manageable and instinctive.

Key strategies

- Prepare a comprehensive plan for managing risks so that you and your stakeholders have a clear understanding of the resources that will be required.
- Involve and consult your key stakeholders and suppliers in the risk assessment process.
- Every risk requires a decision on how to respond; deciding not to decide is usually a bad decision.
- Link risk monitoring tactics to key decision points in the event management plan and timeline.
- Make certain all event personnel know they have permission and the obligation to report risks they observe and will not be punished for doing so.
- Information does not become usable intelligence unless it is properly captured and capable of being transmitted to others.
- Use a variety of methods for identifying and analyzing risks to increase the quality and effectiveness of your risk assessment.
- Retain only those risks whose outcomes you can afford.

Chapter review challenge

1 Outline and explain the benefits of employing a systematic and iterative risk management strategy.
2 Compare and contrast the strengths and weaknesses of the various risk identification and analysis tools and techniques.
3 What other classic management tools might be adapted to the risk identification and analysis process and how?
4 List a typical event risk factor (see Table 1.2) for each risk response option and discuss why that response action should be taken.
5 What (if any) are the common causes or risk drivers in the fault tree analysis shown in Figure 2.12?

Practical risk management exercise

Prepare a *Risk Assessment Meeting Plan* for the following event that includes:

- The participants to be included in the risk assessment meeting.
- The tools and techniques to be used to identify and analyze risks.

Negative outcome Volunteer recruitment down – insufficient number of volunteers for the event				
Administration	Design	Marketing	Operations	Risk Management
Insufficient budget to provide T-shirts as before	Too many volunteers needed in the event plan	Did not recruit from the right groups of people	Volunteers feel over-worked due to long shifts	Too little training; volunteers feel overwhelmed and unprepared
Conflicts between paid staff and volunteers	Program is specialized with a very small constituency	Insufficient announcements in constituent communities	Insufficient supervisory and coaching support	Fear of safety at event site after dark
No job descriptions so volunteers don't know what there is they could do	Volunteers not available during regular business hours	Sign-up forms not distributed	Contentious volunteers disrupt team spirit	Inadequate security at restricted access areas
No follow-up calls to enquiries by potential volunteers	Competition from another event using same constituency	Volunteers do not feel valued; lack of recognition	Parking areas overcrowded; no designated parking area	Volunteers asked to do difficult or potentially hazardous jobs
Committee chairs unwilling to use people they don't know	Dissatisfaction because not assigned to same posts as friends	Volunteers not contacted after event for next year	Volunteers resent not being allowed to leave posts to see the event	Volunteers left stranded at posts without back-up

Figure 2.12 Fault tree analysis exercise

- The memo announcement for this meeting including the meeting agenda and any instructions to the participants.

The plan should illustrate:

- How you determined who should attend and why they are to be included?
- How you determined which tools and techniques should be used?
- Appropriate advance notification and sufficient meeting duration.
- How you determined the length of the meeting or if more than one meeting would be required?
- Whether pre-work would be required and, if so, what that pre-work is to consist of?

XYZ Bank will hold its annual awards gala banquet on the first Saturday in February at the convention center in the downtown of a metropolitan city to celebrate the accomplishments of their top performers in customer service. You are serving as the risk manager for this event, working with the event organizer hired by the bank. The event concept is as follows.

After parking in the convention center's parking garage and making their way past two large exhibit halls (expected to be in use during the day), the 500 guests will arrive to a large decorated entryway at the ballroom and check in at the welcome desk staffed by bank volunteers. Upon collecting their name tags and two drink tickets each, guests will enter the pre-function area and may check their coats for the evening at a commercial coat check service. Four bars will serve drinks and wait staff will pass hors d'oeuvres during the cocktail hour while a lounge singer performs accompanied by piano.

When it's time for dinner, guests will be welcomed into the ballroom decorated like a swank and elegant nightclub to the swinging sound of a 13-piece big band orchestra. Sixty well-dressed tables highlighted with pin spotlights rigged into the ceiling will surround a large dance floor in front of the stage. The tables are to be set with crisp white linens, floral centerpieces, and pre-set salads, surrounded by seats covered in striped Spandex to disguise the standard banquet chairs.

The focal point of the ballroom will be a large three-level stage jutting out into the room on an angle, flanked with stairs for the award-winning guests to ascend to accept their richly deserved recognition. Extending out on either side of the stage will be two large rear-projection video screens to provide simultaneous video of speeches, entertainers and award winners captured by a cameraman with a hand-held video camera, and selected graphics to document the award ceremonies and entertainment attractions will be interspersed via PowerPoint® slides. The screens will be flanked with giant white floral displays on top of massive eight-foot tall white pedestals, highlighted with colored up-lighting from instruments at their base. The loudspeakers for the sound system will be arranged in stacks at the far edges of the screens against the wall.

As guests finish their main course the awards ceremonies will start. Follow spots and recorded music will escort each winner up to the stage, and the simultaneous image magnification video will provide a close-up view for everyone in the audience. To punctuate between the two types of awards to be presented, a fabulous and fun dessert parade will take place with the wait staff making a grand entrance and snaking through the tables with carts bearing flaming cherries jubilee to the sound of rousing music.

After the awards ceremony the rest of the evening will feature the orchestra playing dance music to get guests out on the dance floor to demonstrate their ballroom best under the sparkling stardust ballroom effect of a mechanized mirror ball suspended above. The grand finale will be a balloon drop of 250 brightly colored balloons to signal the end of the evening at 11:00 p.m.

The convention center will be responsible for the setup of the tables and chairs by 8:00 a.m. the day of the event, and its in-house caterer will be responsible for the food and beverage service. Everything else is contracted from outside vendors, and there is one day to get everything installed and ready to go by the 6:00 p.m. start time.

Key terminology

Brainstorming: A group technique for generating ideas that may be used to identify risks wherein each participant's ideas are recorded for later analysis.

Cause/effect analysis: An analytical tool that provides a graphical representation of the causes contributing to an effect.

Constraint analysis: An analytical tool used to determine the effects that various constraints will have on decisions to be made.

Contingency plans: The strategies and arrangements made to deal with and recover from uncontrollable known risks and unforeseen risks should they materialize.

Critical path: Conducting certain tasks in a necessary sequence based on tasks that cannot begin until a prior task has been completed.

Decision tree analysis: An evaluation tool that describes a decision under consideration and the implications of choosing one or another of available alternatives.

Duty of care: The legal requirement that everything 'reasonably practical' be done to protect the health, safety, and welfare of people.

Fault tree analysis: An analytical tool that provides a graphical representation of the combination of causes that result in an occurrence.

Gap analysis: An analytical tool used to detect voids or disparities in the plans for or delivery of an event.

Hazard mapping: A technique used to identify areas, activities, or items of concern within a site.

Influence diagram: A graphical evaluation tool that illustrates the scope of effect and interactions any one change will have on other event elements and associated risks.

Milestone: A significant point in an event plan, often the completion of a specific phase or activity that must occur before subsequent phases or activities may proceed.

Probability/severity matrix: A graphical evaluation tool that rates risk according to its likelihood of occurring and its consequences or impact should it occur.

Residual risk: A risk that remains after risk responses have been implemented.

Risk analysis: The process of examining identified risks to determine causes and relationships to other risks, define the risk in terms of probability and consequence, and prioritize the risks to be handled.

Risk assessment: The process of examination and analysis of event elements and processes in order to increase the probability of success and reduce the impact of potential losses.

Risk avoidance: The removal of risk through the modification or elimination of those elements, requirements, practices, or activities that cause the risk.

Risk categories: The organization of risks into classifications or groups to facilitate analysis.

Risk control: The prevention or reduction of losses through deliberate actions, policies, and procedures.

Risk documentation: The process of recording, maintaining, and reporting assessments, analyses, response plans, and monitoring results.

Risk identification: The process of examining event elements and processes to identify, define, and document possible risks and thresholds using a variety of methods and stakeholder consultations.

Risk monitoring: The process of systematically tracking and evaluating the performance of risk control actions throughout the event process and developing further risk-handling options and actions as appropriate.

Risk planning: The process of developing an organized, comprehensive, and interactive strategy for identifying and tracking event risks, developing risk response plans, performing continuous risk monitoring, and assigning adequate resources.

Risk reduction: The mitigation or reduction of the impact of a risk by reducing the probability of its occurrence and/or minimizing the consequences to the event should it occur.

Risk register: The document that details all the identified risks, the results of the analyses used to evaluate them, the proposed responses to handle them, and the procedures to be used to monitor and track their status.

Risk response: The process of evaluating, selecting, and implementing the options for handling risks, including specifics on what is to be done, who will be responsible, and the effects on cost and schedule.

Risk retention: The acceptance of a risk without engaging in any special efforts to control it, but identifying and allocating the resources to overcome the risk should it materialize.

Risk transference: The reallocation or shifting of the impact of and responsibility for a risk to a third party, either through contractual transfer or the purchase of insurance coverage.

Scenario/tabletop exercise: An exercise wherein participants are given a scenario or description of an event incident and are asked to discuss the causes, effects, and other implications.

Secondary risk: A risk that arises as a direct result of implementing a risk response.

Stakeholder: An individual or organization that is financially, politically, emotionally, or personally invested or interested in an event.

Stakeholder analysis: The examination of internal and external stakeholders that defines their role, needs, and expectations, and measures their influence over the event project.

SWOT analysis: An analytical tool used to determine the strengths, weaknesses, opportunities, and threats of an event project.

Walk-through: A physical tour of an event site to identify and monitor conditions.

Work breakdown structure (WBS): The decomposition of a project into its task elements and the organization of those elements to define the scope of the project.

Online resources

Nonprofit Risk Management Center	www.nonprofitrisk.org
Public Entity Risk Institute	www.riskinstitute.org
Risk Management Resource Center	www.eriskcenter.org
RiskWorld	www.riskworld.com
Skymark: Management Resources	www.skymark.com

Part Two

The scope of risk management

Know your obligations

Become an event planner! Meet celebrities, travel, enjoy yourself! Plan parties, seminars, office events, cruises, corporate events, wedding parties, conventions, and make $10 000–$20 000 a month! Travel the globe planning events in exotic locations! Imagine yourself elegantly dressed, visiting swanky hotels, and checking out the food (for free!). The job requires no formal training or education; event planners generally rely on natural talent, creativity, and determination to succeed.

These claims from companies selling guides on how to start a business organizing meetings and events make it look easy, glamorous, and very profitable. Not one of them, however, mentions the liabilities associated with the job, nor do they point out the financial and legal consequences of failing to exercise proper duty of care toward the attendees, staff, clients, and others at the event. 'I didn't know' will not excuse them in the boardroom or the courtroom.

Tens, hundreds, or thousands of people are entrusted to your care when you plan an event. Lack of attention, lack of judgment, lack of caution, and lack of wisdom can all contribute to negligent behavior by the event organizer, leaving the organizer and the organization exposed to serious penalties, even imprisonment. The four chapters in this section will introduce you to the range of responsibilities that fall upon event organizers to ensure that they have done everything within their power to protect the safety, security, and welfare of all those involved in an event project.

Chapter 3
Legal and ethical compliance

'Apologize rather than authorize' is NOT an option

This chapter will examine how to:

- Recognize the responsibilities and duty of care inherent in the organization and production of meetings and events
- Determine the legal obligations pertinent to events to manage risk by securing the appropriate legal documents
- Determine the statutory and regulatory obligations pertinent to events to manage risk by securing the appropriate compliance instruments
- Establish sound ethical policies, procedures, and practices to reduce risk exposure

Introduction

Events are part of the social fabric of our lives and part of that fabric is law and order. Countries, provinces, prefectures, states, cities, and municipalities make laws to serve the common good and protect their citizens from harm. Many of these laws will affect the way in which an event may be designed and implemented. There might be laws that govern where an event may be held, when an event may be held, what activities may take place, how the event site must be laid out, and what safeguards must be in place to ensure the health, safety, and welfare of those in attendance. It is incumbent upon the event organizer and event organization to ensure compliance with these laws, and it is best practice to embed the appropriate safeguards into the very design of the event.

It must be clearly understood that the material covered in this chapter, and throughout this book, *is not to be construed as legal advice*, and may or may not be pertinent to your event or the jurisdiction in which your event is being held. You should always consult qualified legal counsel and the appropriate authorities when considering the issues presented herein. Legal counseling is a highly specialized and often jurisdiction-specific profession. The importance of proper legal counsel increases exponentially as an event increases in scope and/or crosses borders and changes language, especially in contracts.

Legal responsibility

The legal obligations associated with event management includes the negotiation and execution of the contracts and other legal documents associated with the acquisitions and endeavors of the event project, and oversight of the lawful design and implementation of the policies, procedures, and practices of the event organization and its representatives. The organization and production of meetings and events carries with it significant responsibilities to ensure the protection of the personal and property rights of others – those involved in the event and those impacted by the event. It is critical to understand the nature of legal liability and carefully consider the duties associated with accepting and controlling event liabilities.

Liability

Liability simply means the legal responsibility for one's actions and omissions (and financial obligations), and the obligation to compensate the person harmed by those acts or omissions. In other words, if one does something or fails to do something in connection with one's implicit or explicit duties that results in injury or harmful consequences, that person or entity is open to a civil lawsuit to recover damages or may be subject to criminal prosecution. Contractual liability is the legal responsibility to meet one's financial and performance obligations included within a contract. Professional liability may result from misrepresentation or the failure to inform, provide accurate information, investigate, or deliver (Foster, 2002). Tort law is concerned with wrongful acts or non-contractual duties that allow an injured person to obtain compensation from the person or entity that caused the harm or loss. Intentional torts (wrongs) are typically not covered by liability insurance. Contract law deals with breach of contract liabilities.

It is important to properly assign the liability for those duties or activities that the event organizer does not have reasonable control over. '[E]ach party should be responsible for their own acts of negligence or willful misconduct, and each party should indemnify the other party from such acts' (Connell, 2002, p. 127). This is done through the contractual process, ensuring that those providing goods and services take responsibility for their actions and the suitability and safety of their products or offerings by including the appropriate contract clauses defining these responsibilities and expectations. For example, it is considered best practice to have contract language that specifies the hotel or caterer selling and serving alcohol at the event will be in full compliance with all applicable liquor laws or for pyrotechnics providers to be contractually required to be fully licensed, secure the proper permits, and provide specific levels of insurance coverage.

Duty and degree of care

Everyone is expected to conduct themselves in such a way that their actions do not injure others, and this applies to entities such as event organizations as well. As noted in Chapter 2, duty of care is the legal requirement that everything 'reasonably practical' has been done to protect safety and health. When the standard of care has been breached by act or omission, the resultant liability is often assessed in degrees of negligence (see Figure 3.1).

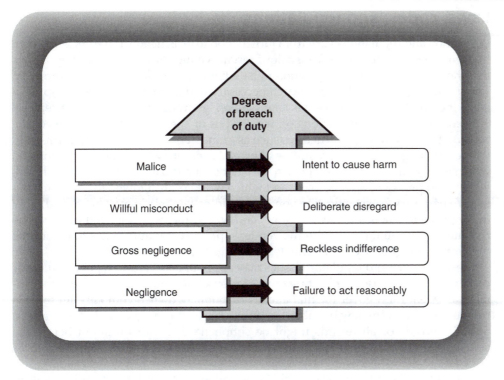

Figure 3.1 Breach of duty of care scale

Degree of care, the standard or level of caution or forethought, is based on the circumstances and evidence of the duty to act. The act of producing an event and inviting individuals to attend that event provides the evidence of the duty to act. Those who put themselves forth as professionals are often subject to a higher standard than an ordinary person because they are expected to have specialized knowledge and experience. Event organizers are expected to be able to foresee risks, assess their potential for causing injury or harm, take actions to mitigate that potential, and have a duty to warn individuals of known hazards.

Due diligence

Due diligence is the thorough and objective investigation to determine the accuracy of claims made by parties to a transaction and to evaluate the financial and organizational stability, the conditions that may cause harm, and the technical capacity and/or infrastructure necessary to deliver on those claims. Event organizers conduct these investigations to ensure they are making prudent plans and purchases. They must be able to illustrate that they have conducted them in accordance with their duty of care responsibilities in order to mitigate any claims of negligence. This is applicable to the selection of the site, service providers, equipment, materials, and even the event components or attractions. Foster (2002) advises that event organizers should have documented evidence of due diligence activities such as safety and security checklists and that safety and security matters should be discussed and included in contracts.

Laws, codes, and regulations

Legislation and regulations vary from jurisdiction to jurisdiction and from event item to event item. In addition to legislation, certain venues have rules and regulations that the event and event organization must adhere to in order to use their property. The risk manager must do the research necessary to determine what will be applicable to the event, where that event is taking place. Ignorance of the law is NO defense!

There may be legal restrictions on what types of special effects are allowed, the construction of temporary structures such as grandstands or viewing platforms, and where smoking may and may not be allowed. There may be venue restrictions on what signage may or must be posted or what sponsor banners may be displayed, which food providers may be used, and which workers are allowed to perform what tasks. There may be specifications on how loud or late music may be played, how many portable toilets must be provided, and where guests are allowed to park. The risk manager should check with the venue, suppliers, and authorities to determine the pertinent regulatory requirements (see Table 3.1).

These statutory and regulatory issues may apply to only certain types of events or certain types of sponsors or hosting organizations. For example, in the U.S., if organizing an event for a governmental agency or publicly owned company, all records surrounding an event may be subject to public disclosure, even those of the vendors. Specific records or all records might be subpoenaed in cases brought before the courts (a significant reason that proper documentation and ethical business practices are vital).

Failure to adhere to the applicable laws, codes, and regulations could result in fines or penalties, the disruption or closure of the event altogether, and even civil or

Table 3.1 Typical laws, codes, and ordinances pertinent to events

• Accessibility laws	• Insurance coverage requirements
• Antidiscrimination laws	• Intellectual property laws
• Antitrust laws (e.g., restraint of trade)	• Labor union jurisdictions
• Aviation laws (e.g., use of air space)	• Land/marine use laws
• Building and electrical codes	• Liability laws
• Business/occupational regulations	• Liquor laws
• Construction codes (e.g., temporary structures)	• Noise ordinances
• Consumer protection laws	• Occupational health/safety laws
• Electrical codes	• Privacy laws
• Electronic transaction laws	• Public assembly laws
• Emergency response requirements	• Public safety codes
• Employment laws	• Sanitation codes
• Environmental protection laws	• Security requirements
• Fire safety/occupancy codes	• Smoking ordinances
• Food service codes	• Special effects codes (e.g., lasers and pyrotechnics)
• Freedom of information laws	• Taxation laws
• Fund raising laws	• Traffic/street closure ordinances
• Gaming laws (e.g., contests and drawings)	• Transportation laws (e.g., transport of pyrotechnics)
• Immigration laws (e.g., entry visas)	• Vehicle laws (e.g., driver qualifications)
• Import/export laws	• Zoning laws

criminal prosecution. Failure to comply could jeopardize the health and welfare of the audience or attendees and the workers, volunteers, or participants, as well as jeopardize the financial well-being of the event organization.

Consider this... 3.1

The Le Race conviction

In August 2003 New Zealand event organizer Astrid Andersen was convicted of criminal nuisance and fined $10 000 in connection with the death of a participant at the March 2001 Le Race, a commercially organized 100 km cycling event from Christchurch to Akaroa. Thirty-one-year-old Vanessa Caldwell collided with an on-coming car on a blind bend while overtaking other competitors and was fatally injured. The court found that Ms. Andersen did not do enough to ensure competitors realized the road was not closed to other traffic. Although overturned on appeal in 2004, the conviction caused numerous sporting events to postpone or cancel their events for fear of liability as a result of an accident.

Sources: Grieve (2003, 2004); Lynch (2004).

Contracts and other legal documents

The risk manager must determine what contracts, agreements, and other legal documents are legally required and are standard and customary for the event operation, and then confirm that all the necessary legal documents associated with the event have been executed properly (see Table 3.2). This could include anything from engagement agreements with entertainers outlining such things as length of performance, encores, equipment needs, appropriate dress and behavior, or even specifying the appropriate material or content, to confidentiality agreements requiring employees, volunteers, and participants to protect proprietary information or prevent disclosure of design details.

Contracts

It is best practice to have a written contract for any and all goods or services procured for an event. A contract is an agreement between two parties, specifying the offer (what will be done or given), the consideration (what will be paid or given in return), and the acceptance of the terms and conditions set forth in the agreement (see Figure 3.2). It should specify what is to happen and when, what is to be provided by whom, who is to do what and when, what it will cost, and how you will come to terms should there be a disagreement about it (procedures and remedies).

Given these dimensions of a contract, the purchase of a ticket or registering for an event should be considered a contractual agreement between the attendee and the event organization, which is why the wording on such items as tickets and registration forms must be carefully considered and disclaimers regarding the limits of liability should be included in that language.

A contract or legally binding agreement should result from negotiating the offer, consideration, and terms. A written contract is not a contract until signed (accepted) by both parties; it's only an offer. Everything is theoretically negotiable, from the scope or quality of what is to be provided to the prices or rates for those goods and services offered and the accompanying terms and conditions. Make certain during negotiations that all fees and charges that might end up on the final bill are fully disclosed and are accurately reflected or limited in the final contracts, those you issue and those you sign.

A confirmation letter may be used to clarify all the negotiated terms prior to the drafting of the final contract, but if signed by both parties it can constitute a legally binding agreement, and therefore, unless this is acceptable, it should clearly state that it is not intended to be the formal contract.

Typically, the party making the offer will draft the formal contract (often a standard template used by the company), but the party accepting the offer can make changes prior to acceptance, which is in essence a counter-offer. Changes that are made after the contract has been signed by both parties should be added to the contract as an addendum or a separate letter of agreement signed by both parties. As Monroe (2006) notes, all items and costs are negotiable before the contract is signed; after it is signed, you have limited options for removing or improving any unfavorable items.

Table 3.2   Typical legal documents for events

• Change orders	• Leases
• Contracts	• Licensing agreements
• Contract riders	• Proposals
• Confidentiality agreements	• Purchase agreements
• Employment agreements	• Purchase orders
• Engagement agreements	• Sponsorship agreements
• Invoices	• Work orders

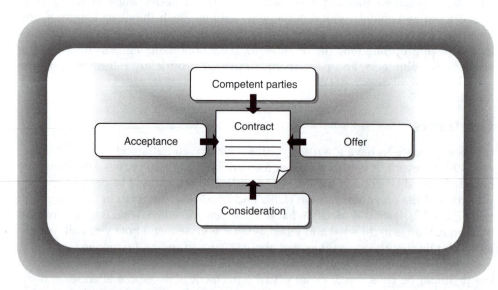

Figure 3.2   Dimensions of a contract

Contracts should contain anything that is important to both parties, and parties can agree to anything that is not illegal or against public policy (Sorin, 2003). As Hilliard (2004) notes, the contract will typically include a series of clauses that specify the precise expectations of each party and provide protections for one or both parties (see Table 3.3). It is advisable that all contracts, especially those representing a certain level of financial commitment or liability, be reviewed by competent legal counsel prior to execution.

Force majeure (French for 'superior force') is the contractual clause that allows contract cancellation or termination without liability, upon written notice, when conditions beyond the control of either party occur that make it inadvisable, illegal, or impossible to perform under the terms of the agreement. This can include acts of God (e.g., flood, drought, earthquake, lightning, etc.), war, terrorism, outbreaks of disease, epidemics, government regulations, disaster, fire, strikes, civil disorder,

Table 3.3 Important contract clauses

Indemnification	An indemnification clause may protect against liability resulting from alcohol liability, ADA violations, and intellectual property infringement.
Insurance	Specify the types and limits required of the other party. Request a copy of their certificate of insurance, but specify that failure to receive one does not waive the insurance requirement.
Permits and licenses	Specify the types of permits or licenses required of the other party. Require a copy, but specify that failure to receive it does not waive its requirement and may constitute a default or breach of contract.
Dispute resolution	Specify how contract disputes are to be resolved, which may include negotiation, mediation, binding arbitration, or litigation.
Choice of law and venue	It is expensive to litigate long distance. Specify which jurisdiction's laws will govern the contract and where disputes and/or litigation will be handled (typically where the contract is to be performed unless otherwise specified).
Agency	Contracts and agreements must be executed by only those having authority to do so (i.e., authorized signatures by authorized representatives). Specify who has authority to make changes to the contract. Ensure that there are procedures in place that prevent unauthorized persons from signing agreements.
Cancellation, attrition, and liability transfer	Pay careful attention to clauses that specify the damages and liabilities associated with conditions or restrictions (e.g., cancellation and attrition clauses that specify monetary and/or liquidated damages, cut-off dates, and other deadlines), and those that transfer liability (e.g., hold harmless clauses).
Termination	Termination clauses should be in all contracts, specifying under what conditions either party may cancel the contract without liability, including force majeure language.

curtailment of transportation facilities, or unavailability of necessary utilities. In light of current world events, the wording of traditional force majeure clauses may need to be expanded to stipulate precise parameters of force majeure language such as a disease outbreak with specific warnings by the World Health Organization, U.S. State Department, Centers for Disease Control, or the Department of Homeland Security advising against travel to the host destination (Kopecky, 2004).

Tyra W. Hilliard, Esq., CMP, an attorney, educator, and consultant on issues of law and risk related to meetings and events offers the following advice:

> *A contract only encompasses the four corners of the document – in a legal contract dispute, the court often will make a decision on the meaning of the contract purely from what is contained within the four corners of the document. Parol, or external, evidence is often not allowed, even if it would serve to clarify or explain the intention of the parties.*
>
> *There are many types of clauses and, unfortunately, headers or titles are not used consistently so what is titled 'Indemnification' in one contract may be titled 'Hold Harmless' in another. This contributes to the confusion and frustration that many people have in reading, interpreting, and modifying contracts. In writing or reviewing a contract, it is important to use common sense – review the contract for what must be there in order to memorialize in writing what may have been discussed verbally. Then consider what legal protection is needed.*
>
> *Suppose an independent event or meeting planner is drafting a contract for event management services for a client to sign. Such a contract should include, at a minimum, full contact and company information for both parties, information about the scope of services, payment terms including amount and timing. These are the business terms. Next, the event planner should consider the legal issues and make sure appropriate clauses are included to address things like payment and damages to the event planner if the client cancels the event that is the subject of the contract. The contract should also address how changes in the scope of services (greater or lesser) will be made and how they will affect payment and deposit amounts. Finally, the contract should address liability issues including indemnification and insurance.*
>
> *If an event planner is contracting with an event venue, some contract clauses will be the same. The contract should still include full contact and company information for both the event planner's organization and the venue, payment terms, and the space and services contracted for. The facility will also most likely require other terms and conditions governing the use of the venue such as what can and cannot be brought in to the building. Liability issues should still be addressed, including cancellation terms and damages, indemnification, and insurance. These are certainly not all of the terms and clauses that should be in either type of contract, but these are some examples of typical issues addressed in contracts. Legal counsel should be consulted before a contract is signed to ensure that the contract is fair and allocates risk appropriately between the parties.*

Contracts and agreements are a safeguard, protecting both the event organization and the person or other organization it is doing business with by establishing and clarifying expectations. If something is important to the success of the event, it should be in writing!

Statutory and regulatory obligations

A statute is a written law enacted by a legislative authority, rather than one established by court cases (common or case law), which typically mandates, prohibits, or defines something. Regulations are rules, criteria, or requirements established as policy by official agencies or governmental authorities that are designed to control, direct, or manage certain activities rather than prohibit them. Sanctioning is the authorization, approval, or ratification given by a governing organization, often related to sports activities.

It is important to recognize that governments enact 'tombstone legislation' based on disasters (including event disasters) and other legislation based on activities and abuses that resulted in harm. Some of this legislation may have been originally intended for some other industry or situation, yet its wording makes it applicable in the event context. Likewise, other regulations are devised based on previous instances of injury, damage, or negative outcomes. In some cases it may be possible to secure an exemption from certain regulations by demonstrating to the governing authority that the nature or activities of the event are not truly applicable or will not subvert the purpose of the law. However, one must accept the limitations or conditions required by law when selecting an event site (e.g., not being able to restrict public access to public building or providing notification of an outdoor concert to neighboring businesses and residents) or event elements (e.g., not being allowed to use open flames or providing a specific level of insurance coverage for carnival rides).

As previously shown in Table 3.1, there are numerous legal and regulatory issues to consider based on the type, size, site, and components of any specific event. It would take several volumes to cover all these issues and their relevance and implications in all locations, which is why it is incumbent upon the event organizer or risk manager to conduct the due diligence to identify those that are applicable. In addition, laws and regulations change from time to time with new legislation or rules superseding old or familiar requirements, particularly case law, which is developed via jurisprudence as lawsuits are brought before the courts. Berlonghi (1990) advises that at least one individual within the event organization be charged with the responsibility for maintaining a government affairs file that tracks the legislative and public policy matters pertinent to the event.

Accessibility

All events in the U.S. must comply with the Americans with Disabilities Act (ADA), which specifies that all public accommodations must be accessible to those with a physical or mental impairment that substantially limits one or more major life activities: walking, seeing, hearing, speaking, breathing, learning, working, caring for one's self, or performing manual tasks (see Table 3.4). In the U.K. events must comply with the Disability Discrimination Act (DDA). Most countries have adopted some form of barrier-free legislation, sometimes legislated on a jurisdictional basis.

Certain attendees, participants, staff, and suppliers may have special needs that must be provided for in order to fully participate in an event and may require special services to facilitate their involvement. The layout of the site must meet the ingress, egress, and access needs of all those attending, participating in, or servicing the meeting or event. Review physical features, equipment, and emergency procedures for the handicapped during the site inspection. Architectural accessibility will or should be the responsibility of the facility. Program accessibility is the responsibility of the sponsoring organization of the meeting or event, which may include special or preferential parking, entrances, and seating; special assistive materials, devices, or equipment; and/or space allotments for special services and service providers.

Antidiscrimination liability is not exclusive to the handicapped; it can apply to inequity based on race, color, creed, age, gender, sexual orientation, physical size, or physical deformities. It may be applicable to the policies surrounding the recruitment of employees and volunteers, the actions and reactions of event representatives, and the marketing of the event. Liability aside, sensitivity to and respect for the cultural differences within a given community or society and in other cultures can overcome

Table 3.4 Accessibility issues

Barrier-free	Special needs
• Equal access/opportunity • Architectural accessibility • Program/communications accessibility • Transportation accessibility • Visual, auditory, and ambulatory accessibility	• Mobility/dexterity limitations • Hearing impairments • Sight/visual impairments • Language and literacy limitations • Learning disabilities • Physical or religious requirements or restrictions
Architectural compliance	**Auxiliary service aids**
• Parking • Routes, pathways, and doorways • Seating and staging • Counter heights • Water fountains • Toilet facilities • Visual/auditory alarms	• Braille materials • Sign language interpreters • Assistive listening headsets • Captioning devices • Alternative materials (e.g., taped texts, large print) • TDD (telecommunications device for the deaf) • Accommodating service animals and individuals

many challenges when planning an event. These differences may be based in religion, ethnic background, historical tradition, and national, geographical, or organizational customs. The planning implications may encompass such things as:

• The scheduling and timing of the event or components of the event agenda (e.g., holidays, holy days, rituals or ceremonies, and protocol requirements).
• The foods and beverages to be served (e.g., dietary needs and restrictions).
• The setting (e.g., site restrictions, color usage, personal space requirements, and symbols or emblems).
• Behavior expectations (e.g., dress codes, gestures, interaction, and etiquette).

Failing to consider and make arrangements for those with special needs is at the very least discrimination by neglect and failure to comply with accessibility regulations can lead to fines or injunctions against the venue and/or the event organization. The constituencies to consider include the attendees, participants, hosting organization or community, and other stakeholders that are important to the success and sustainability of the event. Provide a method for individuals with special needs to identify and describe their particular requirements using neutral language that does not highlight or ignore any specific disability. Review sensitivity training provided for facility personnel and event staff regarding people with special needs.

Intellectual property

Intellectual property rights apply to the design, formation, and expression of creative or proprietary information, images, ideas, or items that have commercial value

Table 3.5 Intellectual property of concern to the meeting and event industry

- Artistic works
- Audio-visual works
- Books and manuscripts
- Cartoons
- Conference proceedings
- Corporate brands
- Databases
- Drawings and illustrations
- Event names
- Films and plays
- Illustrations
- Images of famous people
- Literary works
- Logos
- Magazine articles
- Music and lyrics
- Photographs
- Products
- Proposals
- Proprietary information
- Recordings
- Registration materials
- Services
- Software
- Speeches and speaker handouts
- Tables and graphics from published works
- Tag lines and slogans
- Technical methods
- Television programs
- Trademarked names
- Trade secrets
- Web sites

(see Table 3.5). Intellectual property consists of original creations of the human intellect that are unique, recognizable, and reproducible. Intellectual property ownership is protected by law (the tangible expression is protected, not the idea itself), and even though these images or ideas may be the source for one's own creativity, they may not be copied outright and used without permission of the owner.

Intellectual property is often identified by symbols that indicate images or words may not be used without securing permission, and perhaps paying a licensing or usage fee (see Table 3.6). This has particular implications for meetings and their exhibits and audio-visual presentations, and theme development for special events. Meeting organizers need to ensure there is contract language that places liability for infringement on the presenter or exhibitor, and special event organizers must not use trademarked and other brand images or copyrighted material in the verbal or decorative components of themed events. In addition, event logos and names should be trademarked to protect them from misuse, counterfeiting of their products, and jeopardizing their reputation. Furthermore the information assets (proprietary information) of the event organization must be protected from loss, damage, or theft.

Ray Verhelst of ConventionDisc, Inc. in Las Vegas, Nevada, offers the following advice about the digital copyrights and individual rights of those being taped when videotaping seminars:

Meeting organizers need to update their presenter waivers to include statements that place the sole responsibility for the rights to the content on the presenter. This means that any person speaking, showing a presentation, and/or handing out a document, must own the content or have verifiable rights to use that content within the scope of their presentation, including a statement that says the presenter can be recorded and distributed regardless if it is for promotional or profit purposes. This means that when they build that exciting PowerPoint® presentation that they have secured the rights to all the images, quotes, and editorial text that might have been 'borrowed' to make a point, and all facts and figures from any research need to be approved for publication and distribution. You must make sure that your presenter is fully aware of this requirement and that by signing your waiver they will be claiming all this to be true.

So often we see presenters that have taken video footage from television programs, commercials, and movies and used them within presentations to make a point. We see company logos, misuse of registered tag lines and trademarks, images captured directly from Google™, and countless passages from famous authors being thrown up on the screen with wild abandonment. When confronted with this problem in the post-recording session, they forgot they were being recorded and figured that the 50–100 people sitting in the room would never have any affiliation with these items so why worry. Not so. Large companies have entire departments that do nothing but protect the company's assets, which include logos, trademarks, and images. Movie

Table 3.6 Tyra Hilliard's overview of intellectual property

Intellectual property type	Protection	Examples
Copyright Protects original works of authorship once fixed in a tangible medium.	*Types of works:* • Literary • Musical • Dramatic • Pantomimes and choreographic • Pictorial, graphic, and sculptural • Motion pictures and other audio-visual • Sound recordings *Copyright notice:* © 2006. Jane Smith. All Rights Reserved.	• Written program • Speaker handouts • Speaker's computer-generated slides or other visual aids • Books • Articles • Music (recorded or live) • Musical score • Web site
Trademark A word, phrase, symbol or design, or a combination of words, phrases, symbols, or designs, that identifies and distinguishes the source of the goods of one party from those of others. A mark that identifies and distinguishes the source of *services* (as opposed to goods) is called a service mark.	*Trademark symbols:* • Superscript™ for unregistered trademark • Superscript^{SM} for unregistered service mark • ® for registered trademark or service mark	• Event or exhibition name • Company logo • Acronym or abbreviation of organization name • Stylized writing of organization or event name
Patent Grant of a property right for an invention.	*Three kinds of patents:* • Utility patent – process, machine, article of manufacture, composition of matter • Design patent – new, original, and ornamental design for an article of manufacture • Plant patent – invention or discovery of a new kind of plant	• Audio-visual equipment including and lighting machinery • Software • Online registration process • Staging • Chairs • Props

Sources: U.S. Copyright Office; U.S. Patent & Trademark Office

studios have extensive legal teams that do nothing but search the Internet looking for pirated content. A lawsuit could bring terrible consequences to a small association.

The second issue is for-profit presentations. When you ask someone to present at an event where attendees have paid a fee to hear others speak, you need to make sure your waiver releases you from any financial obligation to the presenter, unless you have agreed to some form of specific remuneration, and even then they must waive their rights to any additional compensation. This becomes particularly sticky when you have a presenter that earns their living by speaking on this very topic. In essence, you are asking them to provide you with free access to their livelihood.

You must get the presenter to sign off on the rights to the recorded content and that you are under no obligation to account for any revenue (tangible or intangible) to the presenter so that the content that you have gained permission to use will fall under that release. This is critical to your organization's business model. Otherwise the presenter could claim that they were unfairly compensated based on the revenue you earned from their intellectual property.

Whether you do a video and/or audio recording, you should notify all the attendees that the session is being recorded as a courtesy, allowing them time to opt out, but you are not required to obtain a release from everyone in the room. If we have the rights to record a session from the organizer and they have the rights to the content and permission to record the presenters, when an audience member is captured indirectly during a question and answer period, this is equal to journalism. But if we ask an attendee to give specific commentary directly into the camera, we then treat them as 'on-camera' talent and have them sign a basic waiver.

Music licensing

One of the most common copyright and licensing issues affecting the events industry is music licensing. Virtually all music is copyrighted and the performer, composer, and/or lyricist are to be compensated for the use of their creative property. Music licensing fees are paid to these artists through music licensing agencies or performing rights organizations (see Table 3.7). It is the host's (sponsoring organization) responsibility to pay these fees, *not* the facility or the entertainer because they are not the 'end user' that caused the music to be performed. However, a client must be apprised of this or the event organizer could be subject to vicarious liability for unauthorized use. There are very limited exceptions regarding music licensing for private use, such as private social events including only family and friends, and certain exemptions for educational or charitable purposes, but one should always check. Basically, if the event or event organization is making money while using it these fees need to be paid.

- Applies to the copyright owner's performance rights (public performance of their songs).
- Synchronization, publication, mechanical (recording) rights are different.
- Fees are based on type of performance and size of audience.
- Violations can incur damages of $50 000–$100 000 or more per song.

Privacy

There is a vast amount of personal, proprietary, and public information associated with an event, which elevates the possibility that abuses of privacy could occur, particularly given the electronic technology prevalent today. Governments around the world have adopted comprehensive information privacy protection rights such as the Australia Privacy Act, the Canadian Privacy Code, the European Union Data Protection Directive, and the proposed Asia-Pacific Privacy Charter. Rights of privacy

Table 3.7 Music licensing agencies and organizations

- AMCOS: Australasian Mechanical Copyright Owners Society
- APRA: Australasian Performing Right Association Limited
- ASCAP: American Society of Composers, Authors, and Composers
- BMI: Broadcast Music Incorporated
- CAL: Copyright Agency Limited (Australia)
- CISAC: International Confederation of Authors and Composers Societies (France)
- CMRRA: Canadian Musical Reproduction Rights Agency Ltd.
- COMPASS: Composers & Authors Society of Singapore
- ECAD: Escritório Central de Arrecadação e Distribuição (Brazil)
- GEMA: German Society for Musical Performing Rights and Mechanical Reproductions Rights
- IMRO: Irish Music Rights Organization

- ISA: International Songwriters Association (U.K.)
- JASRAC: Japanese music copyright association
- MCPS: Mechanical Copyright Protection Society (U.K.)
- PRS: Performing Right Society (U.K.)
- SABAM: Belgian Society of Authors, Composers and Publishers
- SACEM: Society of Authors, Composers, and Editeurs of Music (France)
- SAMRO: South African Music Rights Organization
- SESAC: Society of European Stage Authors and Composers
- SIAE: Society of Italian Authors and Composers
- SOCAN: Society of Composers, Authors, and Music Publishers of Canada
- TONO: Norwegian Performing Right Society

in the U.S., in contrast, are a patchwork of federal and state statutes and common law decrees that both protect and imperil the rights to control the collection and distribution of confidential information (Gindin, 1997).

Protections from invasion of privacy and for user privacy in electronic contexts are applicable to many aspects of meetings and events, including web-based registration, electronic payments, Web sites and blogs (web logs), and electronic marketing activities (Foster, 2000). Invasion of privacy torts (wrongs) include intrusion, appropriation or misappropriation of identity for commercial purposes, false light publicity, and public disclosure of private facts (Tratos, 2004).

- Intrusion of privacy torts concern direct and indirect surveillance activities (see Consider this... 3.2) typically in connection with the monitoring of employee e-mail and other online communications – activities that could create liabilities for the employer in the form of breach of confidentiality, trade secret disclosure or misappropriation, defamation, harassment, or copyright infringement. Monitoring policies that remove any employee expectation that such activities are private should be clearly specified in employee handbooks and employment contracts to prevent litigation.
- Appropriation relates to the rights of publicity accorded to celebrities, alive or dead, which is akin to intellectual property rights in that the celebrity's persona represents commercial property value. This can apply to 'look-alikes' and 'sound-alikes' as well as catchphrases used in marketing or publicity materials.
- Misappropriation occurs when an otherwise private person's likeness or name is used without consent, and 'use of likeness' waivers and cautionary language should be included in registration materials or entry signage indicating visual or audio recording for commercial purposes will take place.

- False light publicity concerns an embellishment, exaggeration, distortion, or fabricated association that places a person in an embarrassing, untruthful, and/or defamatory light, which has significant implications regarding the control of event-owned Web sites, blogs, and discussion boards. The appropriate disclaimers should be included on these sites that limit liability for third-party statements.
- Public disclosure of private facts relates not only to the disclosure of embarrassing facts. It concerns the very tenets of privacy rights – that a person should have control over the collection and distribution of their own information and a person's confidential information should be safeguarded by those who collect it. This includes the right to be informed of data collection and transfer, to limit what data is collected and how it will be used (including secondary uses), to have access to verify its accuracy and make corrections, and to have it securely maintained according to its sensitivity through the appropriate administrative, technical, and physical procedures (Awerdick, 1996; Canadian Standards Association, 1996; Foster, 2000; Gindin, 1997).

Event organizers must make certain that their data collection and protection activities in connection with attendees, employees, and volunteers are conducted so that only information relevant to the purpose is solicited, in a way that ensures confidentiality of personal information, and that this information is used only for the purpose for which it was acquired. This is extremely important regarding electronic financial transactions, which have special duties of confidentiality and require encryption and other security measures. Considering the grave concerns over identity theft and the proliferation of intrusive electronic marketing practices, it would be prudent to develop and implement a privacy policy that encompasses all aspects of an event organization's operations.

Consider this... 3.2

Smart badges and tickets: benefit or concern?

Radio frequency identification (RFID) technology provides numerous benefits but poses serious security and privacy concerns. RFID technology uses chips (tags) encoded with information that corresponds with an attendee registration file, which are embedded in name badges to track attendance, exhibit visits, and other data mining activities using tracking antennas known as readers. At the 2005 Professional Convention Management Association Annual Meeting held in Hawaii, 2600+ attendees were personally greeted on plasma screens, shown audience counts and demographic profiles at plenary sessions, and had their continuing education unit credits tracked using RFID tags in their badges (Ball, 2005). Event organizers of the Tennis Masters Cup 2005 held in Shanghai used RFID tags embedded into tickets to reduce counterfeiting and to automate and accelerate patron's entry into the Qi Zhong stadium; 100 000 ticket-holders waved their tickets past readers positioned at the stadium's 16 automated gates for admittance (O'Connor, 2005).

However, three researchers that were able to obtain official badges, which included RFID chips, for the 2003 World Summit on the Information Society in Switzerland with fraudulent identification documents (using names from an attendee list printed on the summit's Web site), expressed grave concerns over the non-disclosure of the embedded chip and the potential for illicit tracking of the movements of the prime ministers, presidents, and other high-level officials in attendance, especially considering the lax registration security (Hudson, 2003).

A U.S. congressional report noted, 'key privacy issues are notifying individuals of the existence or use of the technology; tracking an individual's movements; profiling an individual's habits, tastes, or predilections; and allowing for secondary uses of information. ... Without effective security controls, data on the tag can be read by any compliant reader; data transmitted through the air can be intercepted and read by unauthorized devices; and data stored in the databases can be accessed by unauthorized users' (GAO, 2005, p. 7, 23).

Table 3.8 Typical compliance instruments for events

• Agricultural permits	• Operator licenses
• Animal permits	• Parade/moving route permits
• Approved site or floor plans	• Parking permits
• Assembly occupancy permits	• Power generator permits
• Business licenses	• Public assembly permits
• Carnival ride permits	• Pyrotechnics permits/licenses
• Certificates of insurance	• Safety inspection certificates
• Consent forms	• Sales licenses
• Display lighting/banner permits	• Special effects permits
• Electrical installation permits	• Street closure permits
• Entertainment licenses	• Temporary fencing permits
• Food service permits	• Temporary structure permits
• Fireworks display permits	• Traffic restriction permits
• Fund raising permits	• Transient vendor's licenses
• Gaming licenses	• Waivers of indemnity from participants
• Liquor licenses	• Waterway usage permits
• Outdoor amplified sound permit	• Work permits/visas

Compliance management

Compliance management encompasses the acquisition, proper display, and retention of the necessary permissions and documents such as permits, licenses, written exemptions, and other instruments that demonstrate adherence to all accessibility mandates, property rights requirements, and other applicable statutes, codes, and regulations to signify the event project is being conducted in accordance with pertinent statutory and regulatory obligations.

Licenses, permits, and other compliance instruments

Events often require a variety of compliance instruments or permissions in order to take place (see Table 3.8). These permissions are not merely a matter of bureaucratic formality; they are control mechanisms to ensure the activities or uses for which they are issued will be in compliance with the laws and regulations governing such activity or use (Berlonghi, 1990). They warrant that those holding the event and providing goods and services to the event have the competency and authority to do so.

Many events sell merchandise associated with the event and may issue or obtain licenses that control the product quality and the images on them. Sports events often seek authorization or ratification by a sanctioning or governing sports authority. Events involving potentially hazardous activities or children's programming will often require participants to sign waivers or consent forms acknowledging the associated risks and releasing the event organization from liability. Make certain that waivers of indemnity are provided to participants early enough so that they have sufficient time to consider the risks before they invest in the activity.

Permit or licensing authorities may include health inspectors, law enforcement authorities, traffic or parking agencies, fire marshals, parks and recreation divisions, and/or other governmental departments. Check with the venue, suppliers, and authorities to determine the permits required and the process, cost, and time required to secure the necessary compliance instruments. Collect and retain all documents and documentation surrounding compliance with occupancy and regulatory issues.

Permits are typically required for:

- Public assembly (e.g., demonstrations, rallies, protests)
- Public property or space usage (e.g., parking lots, parks, public buildings)
- Encroachment on the public right of way (e.g., roadways, streets, sidewalks, medians)
- Usage of municipal or public services (e.g., police, traffic control, power, water)
- Installation of a temporary structure (e.g., staging, tenting, grandstand)
- Installation of an air supported structure (e.g., inflated 'bouncy' attractions)
- Soliciting money (e.g., fund raising activities)
- Sales of goods or services (e.g., merchandise)
- Sale or serving of alcohol
- Sale or serving of foods
- Fireworks usage (e.g., indoor pyrotechnics, outdoor or aerial displays)
- Open flame usage (e.g., bonfires, fire torches)
- Animal attractions (e.g., petting zoos, pony rides, animal entertainers).

Many municipalities have established a special events department that manages the application for and issuance of all event-related permits, and often have brochures, Web sites, or manuals that indicate policies, fees, and timelines. In various jurisdictions and for certain types of events, some applications must be submitted as much as six to eight months in advance, while others range from 30 to 120 days prior to the event. Sometimes a single meeting with all the applicable agencies may be possible and sometimes separate meetings with individual departments or authorities is required. Some jurisdictions hold these meetings on an 'as needed' basis and others might only hold them periodically.

Some permit or license applications are short and simple; others may be lengthy and complex. There may be conditions and requirements that must be met in order to secure the compliance instruments necessary for the event, such as providing proofs of financial ability, insurance coverage, site plan approvals, and/or current business or other licenses. Permits may be issued on a conditional or temporary basis, requiring certain things be done, changed, or provided before the time of the event, in which case it is important to ensure these requirements are communicated to the appropriate vendors and/or event personnel so that they will be implemented and monitored.

Certain officials might need to conduct on-site inspections to comply with the terms of the permit or license. Health inspectors may need to review the food preparation areas and waste management facilities. The fire marshal may need to confirm the actual layout matches the approved floor plan, as well as conduct flame tests on certain materials to ensure they meet safety specifications. Arrangements must be made to accommodate these inspections and ease the inspectors' access to the site and the event's records as necessary.

Develop a good working relationship with the authorities, particularly those with whom you interact regularly. This could help facilitate speedy inspections and permit issuance, plus it may provide the opportunity to educate officials about the factors unique to events that warrant exemptions and special approvals. One frustrated tent rental professional began holding seminars for local fire officials on tents and equipment typically used for events to show them the safety features and how they differ from the considerations typically covered in fire codes. These became a win-win activity for both parties because the fire fighters could receive continuing education credit for attending (Hurley, 2004). Building this relationship could also provide you with important education based on their perspectives and expertise that will improve your practices and procedures.

Securing all the appropriate licenses and permissions can be costly, particularly as governments seek to increase revenues and decrease costs by imposing various fees and taxes on events that require administrative and municipal support services such as health and fire safety inspections, traffic management, and crowd control. Large public entertainment events such as festivals and concerts are the primary targets, but private, corporate, and association events face numerous charges and fees as well depending on the level of interaction they have with permitting and licensing authorities and the impact the event has on a community and its municipal services. No matter how bothersome or costly it may be to acquire these permissions, do not be tempted to avoid or circumvent the process; the potential cost of discovery is too great.

It is very important to consider every aspect of the event plan and the event planning to ensure all decisions and activities are legally permissible, and that the appropriate contracts, licenses, and other documentation are in order. Get your permissions before you spend – make certain you are allowed to do what you want to do before too much time and money has been invested in the event, and do not promote your event until you have permission to hold the event. Create a checklist of permits and other compliance instruments each time for every event and develop bureaucratic cooperation by accommodating and educating your local authorities.

Ethical issues

Ethics encompass the judgments and choices made and the actions taken that reflect and enact beliefs of what is right versus wrong. Embedded in most codes of conduct for the event and other industries (see Table 3.9), these standards guide the decisions, negotiations, and activities in a way that promotes equitable practices and demonstrates the ethical values below:

- Truthfulness
- Integrity
- Responsibility
- Accountability

Table 3.9   Event industry codes of professional conduct and ethics

Meeting Professionals International (MPI) Principles of Professionalism

- Honestly represent and act within one's areas of professional competency and authority without exaggeration, misrepresentation or concealment.
- Avoid actions which are or could be perceived as a conflict of interest or for individual gain.
- Offer or accept only appropriate incentives, goods, and services in business transactions.
- Honor written and oral contracts, striving for clarity and mutual understanding through complete, accurate and timely communications, while respecting legal and contractual rights of others.
- Ensure rights to privacy and protect confidentiality of privileged information received verbally, in writing, or electronically.
- Refrain from misusing solicited information, proposals or concepts.
- Commit to the protection of the environment by responsible use of resources in the production of meetings.
- Actively pursue educational growth through training, sharing of knowledge, expertise and skills, to advance the meeting industry.
- Embrace and foster an inclusive business climate of respect for all peoples regardless of national origin, race, religion, sex, marital status, age, sexual orientation, physical or mental impairment.
- Adherence to these principles of professionalism signifies professionalism, competence, fair dealing and high integrity.

Source: http://www.mpiweb.org/aboutmpi/home/prin.asp

International Festivals & Events Association (IFEA) Code of Professional Responsibility

- Members shall ascribe to and promote the Mission and Ends of the IFEA, including: the Association's commitment to articulation of the value of events and celebrations to society; the recognition of festival and events management as a profession; the Association's commitment to its Members' professional knowledge and awareness of industry issues and trends; and Member compliance with professional standards and ethical conduct.
- Members shall use any and all opportunities to improve the public's understanding of the role that festivals and events play in their community and in society.
- Members shall assist in maintaining the integrity and competence of professionals in the festival and event industry.
- Members shall embrace and promote the highest standards of human resource training and management.
- Members shall practice and ensure the highest standards of safety and professionalism in the conduct of business affairs.
- Members shall not engage in any conduct that involves legal fraud, commission of a crime or violation of law.
- Members shall represent and deliver their business commitments in an honest and complete manner. Members should avoid conflicts of interest that undermine the generally accepted business practices and ethical business conduct. Members shall make every reasonable effort to resolve business disputes with clients, other members, sponsors and others in a fair and professional manner.

Source: http://www.ifea.com/about/

(continued)

Table 3.9 *(continued)*

International Special Events Society (ISES) Principles of Professional Conduct and Ethics

- Promote and encourage the highest level of ethics within the profession of the special events industry while maintaining the highest standards of professional conduct.
- Strive for excellence in all aspects of our profession by performing consistently at or above acceptable industry standards.
- Use only legal and ethical means in all industry negotiations and activities.
- Protect the public against fraud and unfair practices, and promote all practices which bring respect and credit to the profession.
- Provide truthful and accurate information with respect to the performance of duties. Use a written contract clearly stating all charges, services, products, performance expectations, and other essential information.
- Maintain industry accepted standards of safety and sanitation.
- Maintain adequate and appropriate insurance coverage for all business activities.
- Commit to increase professional growth and knowledge, to attend educational programs and to personally contribute expertise to meetings and journals.
- Strive to cooperate with colleagues, suppliers, employees, employers, and all persons supervised, in order to provide the highest quality service at every level.
- Subscribe to the ISES Principles of Professional Conduct and Ethics, and abide by the ISES Bylaws and policies.

Source: http://www.ises.com/about/principles.cfm

- Clarity
- Reliability (promise-keeping)
- Loyalty
- Self-restraint
- Fairness and decency
- Impartiality

Ethical practices

Using the word ethics as an acronym may help reinforce your understanding of the underlying tenets of ethical behavior and practices:

E   Equality – there must be equal access in all aspects of an event from procurement to participation, and there should be no discrimination or favoritism in your practices.
T   Trust – trust is established when you prove that you do what you say you will do and deliver what you said you would deliver, taking responsibility for your actions and your obligations.
H   Honesty – represent yourself honestly and appropriately, always telling the truth about your capabilities, your authority, the situation, or the costs associated with the event.
I   Integrity – avoid deception and conduct your activities with honor by asking yourself if you would want your actions disclosed to your client or published on the front page of the newspaper.
C   Clarity – set clear policies and procedures that specify what is acceptable and what is not, and ensure informed consent is accorded to all parties.

Table 3.10 Policies that guide and promote ethical practices

Behavior	• Workplace harassment and violence • Illegal drug and alcohol use • Weapons possession • Use of organization property • Electronic usage (e.g., e-mail, Internet access and usage, software usage)
Conflicts of interest	• Gifts and gratuities • Political activity • Outside employment • Family members • Disclosure of financial interests
Employee, client, and vendor information	• Maintenance of records and information • Privacy and confidentiality • Disclosure of information
Employment practices	• Equal opportunity • Diversity • Fair treatment of staff • Work-family balance • Discrimination • Proper exercise of authority
Management practices	• Accuracy of financial records and expense reports • Proper use of organizational assets • Protecting proprietary information • Perquisites
Procurement	• Negotiating contracts • Purchasing practices • Equal opportunity and access • Clarity of expectations • Transparency of process

S Sincerity – be straightforward, candid, and maintain a genuine respect for your colleagues, clients, customers, and competition.

Ethical practices are based on precedent, custom, tradition, standards, and fairness. However, what is standard and customary can vary significantly in different cultures and different locations. And what is 'right' may often be a situational challenge subject to varying justifications. This is why policies and procedures should be established that define the proper code of conduct for your event activities and operations (see Table 3.10). These policies should cover acceptable and unacceptable behavior, equal opportunity, financial requirements, procurement, and regulatory compliance, and these policies should specify how breaches will be handled.

Sound and ethical practices will reduce risk exposure and help achieve the goals of risk management. From policies on accepting gifts and gratuities to meticulous bookkeeping procedures, establishing formal policies and procedures helps one conduct the affairs and business of the event operation in the proper manner. This not only reduces risk, it helps create and enhance your reputation as an event management professional, instills public confidence, and raises the image and standards of the industry as a whole.

Consider this... 3.3

2002 Salt Lake City Winter Olympics Scandal

December 10, 1998: Scandal broke out as the head of the coordination committee overseeing the organization of the 2002 Olympic Winter Games announced that several members of the International Olympic Committee (IOC) had taken bribes. It was alleged that the Salt Lake Olympic Bid Committee doled out gifts, all-expense-paid ski trips, Super Bowl trips, health care benefits, 13 scholarships, jobs, questionable real estate deals, and thousands of dollars in cash to IOC members or their families in order to win the event. The controversy plunged the IOC and the Salt Lake Organizing Committee into embarrassing chaos for months. As a result of investigations conducted by the IOC, U.S. Olympic Committee, Salt Lake Organizing Committee, and the U.S. Department of Justice, 10 members of the IOC were expelled and another 10 were sanctioned, and a senior member of the U.S. Olympic Committee and the president and vice president of the Salt Lake Organizing Committee resigned. Although nothing strictly illegal had been done, it was felt that the acceptance of the gifts was morally dubious and stricter rules were adopted for future bids with ceilings put into place as to how much IOC members could accept from bid cities.

Summary

Operating an event and event organization legally and responsibly is a cornerstone of effective risk management, one of its primary goals. It is essential that all the legal and ethical obligations are properly identified, attended to, monitored, communicated, and documented to limit the liabilities inherent in meeting and event projects. Meetings and events may be splendid in nature, but they are serious business with serious consequences should something go wrong.

Negotiating, crafting, and executing the appropriate contracts and written agreements requires careful attention to the details included in them so that the relationships built with them are fair and beneficial to both parties. They must be approached from the perspective of a safeguard rather than an onerous task. They should clearly define the expectations and exemptions agreed to. Doing business without them is asking for trouble.

Compliance with the applicable statutory and regulatory requirements reduces risk and illustrates care and respect for those in attendance and other stakeholders. Embedding these requirements into the event plan from its inception facilitates efficient permissions and effective performance. Failure to comply could jeopardize health and safety, the financial interests of the event, and the very existence of the event itself.

Key strategies

- Respect the personal and property rights of everyone directly and indirectly involved in the meeting or event project.
- Use written contracts or other legal documentation for all event business activities and transactions.
- Ensure that the event organization has access to and uses professional legal counsel when appropriate.

- Develop positive relationships with the regulatory authorities that have jurisdiction over your event.
- Be prepared when applying for permits and other compliance instruments.
- Become educated about the issues and options associated with accommodating special needs by asking the experts and the individuals that know them best.
- Develop policies that clearly define the ethical behavior and practices expected of event employees and other personnel.

Chapter review challenge

1 How does the purchase of a ticket to an event or the registration form for a meeting constitute a contract?
2 Research the usage of RFID technology and list its potential uses and abuses in the meetings and events context.
3 Locate three examples of municipal special event permit applications on the Internet and compare and contrast their scope and requirements.
4 Find out where you would go and what you would have to do to get special event permits in your location.
5 Review the event industry codes of professional conduct (Table 3.9) and analyze their similarities and differences.

Practical risk management exercise

You are charged with preparing a report for the International Meetings and Events Association board of directors on how and why they must make their annual educational conference a barrier-free event by accommodating special needs. Include specific recommendations that encompass mobility, sight, and hearing impairments, and justify your recommendations with a minimum of three resource references.

Key terminology

Act of God: Unavoidable conditions such as natural catastrophes and unpreventable conditions over which neither party has control that would prevent and excuse performance of a contract.
Americans with Disabilities Act (ADA): The U.S. legislation requiring public facilities and programs be made accessible to individuals with disabilities.
Certificate of insurance: A document issued by an insurance company or its agent that verifies insurance coverage is in effect for a policy holder and specifies the limits of the coverage.

Clearance: Authorization for the use of restricted property or areas or to conduct certain activities.

Common law: Laws or legal principles developed through judicial case decisions.

Compliance instruments: Documents that provide evidence of being in compliance with a statutory obligation or regulation.

Contract: A binding legal agreement between two or more parties specifying the benefits and obligations of the agreed upon actions.

Contract rider: An attachment to a contract stipulating special provisions, typically special hospitality or technical requirements for a performing artist.

Disability Discrimination Act (DDA): The U.K. legislation requiring public facilities and programs be made accessible to individuals with disabilities.

Exemption: A special privilege or freedom from the requirements imposed on others.

Force majeure: (*fr.* Superior force) see act of God.

Franchise agreement: The right granted to market a product or service.

Intellectual property: Original ideas, images, information, or items that are unique, recognizable, and reproducible, which are protected by law from use without permission of the originator.

Lease agreement: A contract or agreement to rent specific property or equipment for a specified period of time, including the terms and conditions for such rental.

License: A document or certificate granting formal permission from a regulatory authority to conduct a certain activity or engage in a business, occupation, or activity that would otherwise be unlawful.

Licensing agreement: A contractual agreement in which an exclusive or non-exclusive license is granted by a manufacturer or rights holder to an individual or group to produce, distribute, or sell the trademarked product.

Liquidated damages: Negotiated financial penalties to be paid in the event of a breach of contract.

Music licensing fees: Fees collected by a licensing agency on behalf of artists for the use of copyrighted material consisting of music and musical performances.

Negligence: The failure to exercise the degree of care, by act or omission, that would be considered appropriate by a reasonable person under given circumstances.

Permit: A certificate or document granting permission for the use of certain property or conducting certain activities, secured from a regulatory or municipal agency or authority.

Regulations: Rules or requirements, established by official agencies or governmental authorities, designed to control, direct, or manage certain activities.

Regulatory official: The official or representative from a regulatory agency that issues the appropriate compliance instruments, permits, and permissions necessary to conduct certain activities.

Sanctioning: The authorization, approval, or ratification given by a governing organization, often related to sports activities.

Statutory: Pertaining to conditions or obligations specified by statute as created by law enacted by a legislative body.

Termination clause: A contract clause that specifies under what terms a contract may be terminated by either party without liability, often including an act of God or force majeure clause.

Tort: A wrong or harm other than breach of contract.

Vicarious liability: Liability imposed on third parties or on persons other than the person who performed the negligent or wrongful act.

Waiver: A written statement voluntarily relinquishing some legally enforceable right or privilege.

Online resources

Codes of Ethics Online	http://ethics.iit.edu/codes
Disability Rights Commission (U.K.)	www.drc-gb.org
FindLaw.com	www.findlaw.com
FreeAdvice.com	www.freeadvice.com
'Lectric Law Library Legal Lexicon	www.lectlaw.com/def.htm
Nolo.com	www.nolo.com
U.S. Dept. of Justice ADA Home Page	www.usdoj.gov/crt/ada/adahom1.htm

Chapter 4
Health and safety

No one should profit by putting others in jeopardy

This chapter will examine how to:

- Recognize the fire safety and life safety issues pertinent to the event and integrate them into the event plans
- Incorporate the appropriate sanitation, waste management, and other public health protection strategies into the event environment and activities
- Determine the applicable occupational health and safety requirements and implement suitable procedures throughout the event endeavors

Introduction

The event organizer and event organization is responsible for providing a safe and healthy environment for all those who have been invited to or are involved in the meeting or event. Loss of life and injuries sustained in structural fires, workplace accidents, and other disasters has been studied by experts for more than a century and has resulted in sound guidance on preventative measures. The same holds for illness caused by poor sanitary practices and exposure to unhealthy substances. This vast body of knowledge and the expertise of the public health and safety officials charged with enforcing the rules based on this research and guidance must be incorporated into the planning and production of meetings and events.

Prevention and mitigation are the first line of defense, which must be followed by proper monitoring and timely response procedures. Safety hazards are usually easy to see and typically have immediate consequences. Health hazards, however, are often harder to recognize because the effects of exposure may have delayed consequences (Rossol, 2000). It is incumbent upon the event organizer and risk manager to conduct the appropriate investigations and establish and/or enforce the appropriate policies and procedures to identify, mitigate, and respond to the health and safety hazards that may be inherent or emerge. It is also important to develop an organizational and operational culture that acknowledges safety as a priority and recognizes that safety is everyone's responsibility.

Table 4.1 Distribution network for NFPA's Life Safety Code

Argentina	France	Puerto Rico
Australia	Germany	Russia
Bahrain	Hong Kong	Singapore
Brazil	India	South Africa
Canada	Indonesia	Thailand
Chile	Israel	Turkey
China	Malaysia	United Arab Emirates
Colombia	Mexico	United Kingdom
El Salvador	Pakistan	United States

Life safety codes

The International Safety of Life at Sea (SOLAS) Convention was first devised and adopted in 1914 in response to the Titanic disaster, and the National Fire Protection Association's NFPA 101 (Life Safety Code) had its origins with its Committee on Safety to Life in 1913 in response to notable fires involving significant loss of life. The beginnings of the National Electrical Code (NFPA 70) arose in response to fires associated with the introduction and usage of Thomas Edison's light bulb in factories in 1879 in order to mitigate the hazards associated with electricity. These consensus codes have been developed based on research conducted by maritime, fire engineering, and construction associations worldwide, and have quantified and codified the strategies, life-saving devices and arrangements, and construction requirements necessary to ensure public safety.

Although every country and community throughout the world has its own fire and rescue service and governing authority (often referred to as the AHJ, Authority Having Jurisdiction) and adopts its own standards or codes, lawmakers and fire officials often rely on NFPA 101 as the foundation for public safety programs for life safety from fire and other emergencies. In addition to the U.S., NFPA codes have been adopted and adapted throughout the world including Asia-Pacific nations, Canada, European Union nations, Latin America and the Caribbean, and the Middle East (see Table 4.1). The risk manager must confirm the applicable codes with the AHJ in the location where the event is taking place.

Fire and rescue services, from volunteer fire brigades to national defense agencies, deal with more than just fire fighting. They are typically the first responders for structural collapses, hazardous material incidents, water rescues, and numerous other emergencies. They have the training and expertise to provide critical advice that will help event organizers ensure their events are in compliance with the codes developed to prevent loss of life due to fire, electrocution, or drowning.

Fire inspection, prevention, and protection

Fire safety is a primary consideration for all events, event sites, event workplaces, and event operations. It encompasses the prevention of fire as well as the safety of people and protection of property should a fire occur. Attention must be focused on the actions and equipment that will prevent a fire from occurring, as well as the ability to evacuate people and provide response access to fire fighters and their equipment.

In most jurisdictions, the mandated prevention and response requirements – the fire codes – are based on NFPA 101, which 'addresses those construction, protection, and occupancy features necessary to minimize danger to life from fire, including smoke, fumes, or panic ... Achieving an acceptable degree of life safety depends on additional safeguards to provide adequate egress time or protection for people exposed to fire' (NFPA 101, 2000, p. 23). The code addresses the following aspects of fire safety:

- Detection
- Evacuation
- Inspection
- Notification
- Response procedures
- Response services
- Site contents
- Site layout
- Site maintenance
- Suppression.

All event layouts should be evaluated by a fire marshal to ensure that the appropriate fire safety precautions and emergency plans are in place based on the type and scope of event taking place. A life safety evaluation is '[a] written review dealing with the adequacy of life safety features relative to fire, storm, collapse, crowd behavior, and other safety related considerations' (NFPA 101, 2000, p. 30). Using Table 4.2 as a guideline should help you evaluate event venues under consideration, and confirmation of proper inspections and compliance should be required from venue management.

Although life safety evaluations consider a variety of fire prevention and fire suppression capabilities, of primary concern is the means of egress and the ability of occupants to exit safely and quickly if a fire or other emergency should occur. It is important to remember that in many circumstances a fire can become lethal in less than two minutes!

Consider this... 4.1

Bradford football stadium fire

May 11, 1985: A small fire developed into a flashover event within seconds and engulfed the entire grandstand at Bradford football stadium transforming it into an inferno that claimed the lives of 53 people. When the fire broke out there was little reaction from the nearby crowd who watched it grow, apparently thinking the smoke was from a flare because smoke flares had become a typical occurrence at the football matches. The blaze took only four minutes to grip the entire stand, with the flames moving quicker than people could walk, and escape was hampered even further because more than 3500 people were packed into the main stand area and the doors at the back of the stand were locked to try to stop people coming in without paying. The only fire extinguishers were in the clubroom, put there so that they could not be used by fans as missiles. The Bradford football stadium fire resulted in the U.K. Fire Safety and Safety of Places of Sport Act 1987.

Source: *The Guardian* (1985)

Table 4.2   Components of a life safety evaluation

Nature of the event	The purpose of the event and its emotional qualities (e.g., competitiveness), the duration and time of day of the event, and the activities to be conducted will affect the calculation of safe occupancy loads.
Nature of the occupants	Factors such as gender, age, physical capabilities, sensory capabilities, purpose for attendance/participation and commitment to activities are used to predict behavior in reaction to an emergency.
Crowd density	The size and density of the crowd will affect movement ability, and this will be factored into the occupancy load allowed by the fire marshal. The occupancy load is the maximum number of persons for whom means of egress is provided (allot at least 15 square feet/1.4 square meters per person; if occupant load exceeds 6000 a life safety evaluation may be required).
Access/egress movement	Arrival and departure patterns and volumes; ticketing policies and practices; counter flow, cross-flow, congestion, and queuing situations; and the physical dimensions, complexity (e.g., wayfinding) and contents (e.g., seating) of the building affect occupancy loads and evacuation flow capacity adequacy.
Means of egress	Means of egress is a continuous and unobstructed way of exit travel from any point in a building or structure to a public way, which allows occupants to promptly exit a building or structure in the event of an emergency.
Flow capacity and control	Flow capacity is the volume of people able to go through a given space or route in a given amount of time under given circumstances and is affected by factors such as seating volume/configuration, stairs, ramps, passageways, route complexity, and the merging of flows along egress paths. The flow capacity diminishes as the crowd density increases because movement is restricted.
Communication systems	Visual and audible notification systems (e.g., fire alarms, public address systems) must be in place and have an emergency power source, their signals must be distinctive from other communication systems, and voice announcements must be capable of being effectively heard above the ambient noise level.
Fire hazards	The relative danger of contents or activities causing the start or spread of fire or the generation of smoke, gases, or explosion is evaluated based on the character of the contents, configuration, and the operations conducted.
Suppression systems	The number, functionality, and efficiency of suppression systems such as automatic sprinkler systems, fire extinguishers, and other fire-fighting equipment must be sufficient for the occupancy load and activities conducted.
Structural integrity	Permanent, temporary, and moveable structures and non-structural components (e.g., lighting) are evaluated based on static and dynamic load limits (crowds and crowd sway, precipitation, wind, etc.) and stability.

(continued)

Table 4.2 *(continued)*

Facility condition	The general condition of the facility is evaluated, including the building's features, maintenance and cleanliness, and the amenities and services offered to calculate their affect on evacuation and response capabilities.
Facility operations and personnel	The amounts, actions, attitudes, and aptitudes of personnel are considered in terms of their care of, respect for, and rapport with the attendees, as well as their training and readiness to conduct emergency response procedures.

Table 4.3 Representative decorative materials (substrates) that should be treated with fire retardant chemicals

Fabrics	Acrylic, burlap, cotton, duvetyn, felt (wool), jute, linen, metallic, muslin drops, muslin (unfinished), nylon, polyester (selected), ramie, rayon, scrim, silk, velour, velvet (natural and synthetic), wool
Wood products	Bamboo, branches, cardboard, cellulose boards, evergreens, hemp rope, lumber (raw wood), plywood, raffia
Papers	Crepe paper, confetti, maché, streamers, tissue
Foam products	Ethafoam, foamcore, polyurethane foam, polystyrene, styrofoam
Other products	Artificial flowers, hay (immersion only), leather (unfinished), pre-painted surfaces, spanish moss, paint (water-based and oil-based)
Notes	• Inherently flame retardant means that the flame retardant characteristic of the fabric was an attribute of the thread from which the fabric was woven or knitted and will not wash out. A factory-issued flame retardant certificate should be issued by the manufacturer.
	• Flame retardant means that a chemical is added or applied to a fabric to increase the resistance of that product to fire. These treatments are non-durable, meaning they can be removed by exposure to water or moisture and must be reapplied as needed, typically on an annual basis or upon washing.
	• Satisfactory fire resistance depends on proper identification of the precise content of the substrate and the proper application of the appropriate fire retardant chemical. Some fabrics and other products may not accept fire retardant treatments and therefore must be flame tested (check with the local fire authority for flame testing standards and techniques).

Source: Reprinted courtesy of Rose Brand, www.rosebrand.com

Fire prevention strategies include avoiding combustible materials such as flammable décor (see Table 4.3), keeping all areas clear of rubbish or debris, and avoiding the misuse of electrical equipment. All flammable gas containers need to be properly secured to prevent falling and protected from accidental damage or intentional tampering. Use of open flames (for lighting, cooking, etc.), pyrotechnics, spark-producing equipment, and other incendiary activities must be carefully monitored and controlled. Of particular note is the variety of products and display materials one might find in a trade show, especially cooking or equipment demonstrations and the display of vehicles, which must have their electrical system disconnected and fuel tanks sealed and/or locked. Individual exhibitors must abide by the same fire code requirements as the event organizer.

Fire detection systems include smoke and heat alarms, which should be placed throughout the event site in all hazardous, unoccupied areas without automatic sprinkler systems. This may include storage areas, backstage areas, and under stages, platforms, or grandstands. Fire officials will advise you on the need for these based on the size, location, and configuration of the event layout. Do not forget the value of an alert pair of eyes; ensure all volunteers, stewards, and security personnel are advised that they are part of the fire detection plan.

Fire suppression systems such as sprinklers and extinguishers should be confirmed at any facility used for the event. Extinguishers should be in a conspicuous and clearly visible location, unblocked and readily accessible for immediate use, located along normal paths of travel and exit, and installed on hangers, brackets, in cabinets, or secured on shelves (never standing upright on the floor because a falling cylinder could break off the valve and become a missile hazard) (Safetyinfo.com). There should be at least one fire extinguisher for every 1500 square feet of floor area (Berlonghi, 1990). Fire extinguisher types differ according to the type of combustibles causing the fire (see Figure 4.1) therefore the fire marshal should be advised of the type of materials that will be used at the event (Berlonghi, 1990).

Lighting and visibility are critical in an evacuation situation (evacuation will be discussed further in Chapter 6), particularly regarding the illumination of exit signs and egress paths. Fruin (1984) reminds us that 'line of sight becomes line of flight' in emergencies. All escape routes and exits must be clearly visible, with an independent emergency lighting power source. Never cover exit signage with décor, no matter how unaesthetically pleasing that may be. Also keep in mind that smoke (from a fire or used as a special effect) may significantly impair visibility.

Consider this... 4.2

Night club disaster

February 20, 2003: Pyrotechnics set off by the heavy metal band Great White ignited the ceiling and soundproofing near the stage of the Station Club in West Warwick, Rhode Island. The audience initially perceived the fire as part of the pyrotechnic show, but flames engulfed the building in less than three minutes and the dense smoke rendered the lighted exit signs invisible. Rhode Island Governor Don Carcieri said that 'the building went up so fast no one had a chance.' Hundreds were left dead and injured as panicked patrons fled for their lives, jamming exits as they tried to escape the heavy smoke and fire. West Warwick Fire Chief Charles Hall stated that because the wooden structure was small and built before 1976, it was not required by law to have a sprinkler system. The nightclub fire triggered an overhaul of the state's fire safety code that implemented stringent new regulations.

Source: CNN.com (2003)

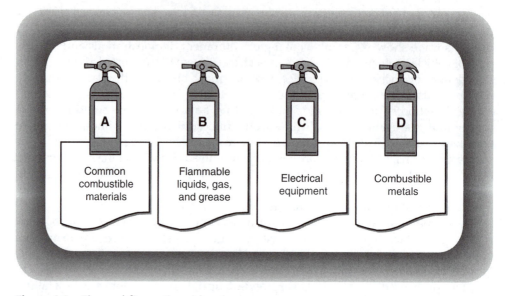

Figure 4.1 Fire and fire extinguisher types

Assembly occupancy

Any occupancy of a building or structure for a gathering of 50 or more persons is considered an assembly occupancy (NFPA 101, 2000) and subject to fire code regulations covering the type, number, and location of fire suppression systems, the types of materials that may and may not be used, the warning and communication systems, and the condition and composition of evacuation routes. According to the U.K. Occupiers Liability Act of 1957 the occupier of premises has the legal duty to 'see that the visitor will be reasonably safe using the premises for the purposes for which he/she is invited or permitted by the occupier to be there' (HSE, 1999, p. 185).

The occupancy includes all the areas used in conjunction with the event, including parking areas, staging areas, storage areas, and overnight camping areas. These codes are also applicable to open spaces and temporary or one-time event sites (including tents and marquees). The risk manager should also consider adjacent areas, even different floors in a multi-story building, and the potential for fires or incidents (e.g., transportation accidents) affecting the safety of the event site.

Considering the propensity for using unique venues as sites for events it is even more important to seek input from fire safety officials. The temporary or unusual nature of using such venues for an event may not have been considered when it was originally inspected for its primary use. These sites require an inspection as a key component of the risk assessment. The primary focus will be on the capacity, contents, and configuration of the event site. When inspecting a building or event site as an assembly occupancy, the fire official will be looking at, among other things:

- Occupant load
- Number and condition of exits
- Doors; unblocked, unlocked or with panic hardware, swing out in direction of egress
- Egress arrangement and travel distance

- Emergency lighting
- Exit marking
- Protection of hazards and openings
- Interior finish and furnishings
- Temporary structures; stages, platforms, exhibits
- Crowd managers if >1000 occupants
- Fire extinguishers; placement and usage training
- Detection systems; smoke and/or heat detectors
- Alarm systems; visual and audible alarms
- Electrical installations.

Although the probability for fire may be low in any particular purpose-built or unique venue, the potential for loss of life is extremely high. It is best practice to become familiar with the fire safety measures required in your jurisdiction and work closely with fire officials to confirm your event site and operations meet the highest possible standards. This need for cooperation also holds true for aviation, coastal, and law enforcement authorities as applicable.

Consider this... 4.3

India consumer fair inferno

April 10, 2006: Fire engulfed the three huge marquees packed with shoppers in which the five-day Brand India Fair (a popular consumer goods show) was held at Victoria Park in Meerut, India. Skepticism exists about the official toll but news reports proclaimed 52 dead and 131 injured in the blaze that was purportedly started by a short circuit in one of the haphazard wiring systems supplying electricity to the air conditioners. The steel-framed tents shaped like aircraft hangars were about 100 meters long each, interconnected in a Y shape, with no emergency exits and only one entry–exit corridor with stalls on either side. Although the organizers received authorization from city officials to operate, they did not obtain the mandatory fire safety clearances from the city's fire department. Arrest warrants on charges of homicide and criminal negligence were issued for the organizers of the fair, but they had fled after the fire.

Source: www.newkerala.com

Other safety hazards

Anything and everything included in the event agenda or attractions and everything at the event site has potential safety implications. Injuries have occurred when items thrown into the crowd by participants on parade floats have struck spectators and others that run into the street to gather these souvenirs have been struck by float vehicles. Spectators rhythmically stomping at sports events can cause vibrations that result in structural weaknesses or knock over equipment. Fans seeking a better view of the stage might climb up on just about anything.

Electrical installations with their tangled web of power cords and cables not only pose slip and trip hazards; they become a potential ignition source for fire and electrocution. Pressurized gas cylinders (including those used for carbonated drinks) can become missiles if they fall over and the nozzle breaks off, and inadequate lighting can make hazards on pathways invisible and criminal behavior anonymous (Silvers, 2004a). All temporary structures and decorative items must be properly constructed and securely anchored. All equipment must be installed and operated correctly and protected from damage or misuse. Barriers must be placed around any fall or protrusion hazards and exclusion zones, and appropriate safety warning signs must be placed as required.

Consider this... 4.4

Grandstand disaster narrowly averted

April 18, 1999: The Three Tenors Concert in Pretoria, South Africa was delayed so that approximately 4000 audience members could be moved off five grandstands and re-seated elsewhere. Although two structural engineers had approved the structures as safe, just prior to the start of the performance parts of the scaffolding system were beginning to buckle under the weight of the audience. An observant security guard heard metal groaning, cut through the side webbing of the grandstand to inspect the area, and quickly communicated the situation to the command center. Without hesitation the evacuation of the stands was ordered and within moments all available event staff started quietly asking people to exit the stands. This subdued and hushed evacuation was to ensure a panicked and rushed mass movement did not cause more damage, and was accomplished in less than 10 minutes.

Source: Ransom (2001)

Don't forget Mother Nature. Severe storms can bring down power lines, high winds can send a tent crashing into people and hurl things hundreds of meters away, heavy rains can flood waterways or render open fields a massive mud puddle, and lightning can strike poles, towers, trees, or golfers trying to get that hole in one. Carefully consider the flora and fauna at any outdoor event site. Pests, pollens, and poisonous plants are only part the hazard picture. Low branches, thorny bushes, and unwanted animals are potential problem-makers, as is the health of the vegetation – falling tree limbs have caused serious damage and injury.

Safety meetings and inspections

During the risk assessment meeting(s) the risk manager needs to elicit all possible health or safety hazards associated with the goods, services, and personnel to be used to produce the event. Specifically ask all vendors and suppliers to identify potential physical hazards and the safeguards necessary to prevent exposure to illness or injuries. Use this opportunity to communicate a commitment to safety in all aspects of the event. Reiterate this in contractual language and reinforce it on-site with safety meetings with all event personnel, even subcontractor laborers. Unequivocally state that unsafe practices or conditions are not acceptable. Let everyone know that safety is everyone's responsibility and give everyone permission and the protocols for reporting unsafe conditions.

During preliminary site inspections the risk manager should look for any event element or aspect of the event site that might have the potential for injury, scanning the environment above, below, from side to side and front to back, and from event start to finish. Use a site inspection checklist to make certain all obvious and obscure elements are examined (see Appendix C: Site inspection checklist).

All safety inspection certificates should be checked, including their expiration date. For example, all U.S. sailing vessels (including those one might use for a dinner cruise event) are inspected annually by the Coast Guard and there will be a certificate of inspection posted on board, which ensures that the vessel meets all safety regulations and that the crew is able to perform its emergency duties. Ask the venue for its current public safety inspection certificates or compliance documentation, and discuss its policies and procedures for maintaining a safe and secure facility.

Walk-through inspections should take place just prior to the event to identify safety hazards that were unanticipated or have emerged. Walk-through inspections must also be conducted periodically during the event to monitor the status of the safeguards that were put in place and to identify any emergent hazardous conditions. This is particularly important for multi-day events, and a daily safety briefing is highly recommended.

Public health issues

Public health legislation, enacted in various forms throughout the world, seeks to ensure a sanitary environment, the surveillance and control of infectious disease, and the promotion of healthy behaviors and personal hygiene. Event organizers and risk managers have a duty of care obligation to do everything in their power to identify and prevent the accidental or intentional exposure to health hazards at an event. Guidance on mass gatherings offered by Australia (Emergency Management Australia, 1999), Canada (Hanna, 1994), the U.K. (HSE, 1999), and the U.S. (FEMA, 2001) are all in agreement on the scope of health hazards at events (see Table 4.4).

Many of the public health hazards at events will be identified when evaluating the event site, the activities included in the event agenda, and the likely composition and behavior of the event audience (to be addressed further in the operational safeguards

Table 4.4 Public health hazards at events

• Alcohol usage	• Insects (e.g., ants, wasps, bees, mosquitoes)	• Swamps
• Broken glass		• UV radiation
• Chemicals	• Laser usage	• Water courses (e.g., depth of water, currents, water temperature)
• Cliffs and steep inclines	• Marshes	
	• Neighboring land use	
• Domesticated animals	• Noxious weeds	• Weather (e.g., extremes of temperature, wind)
• Drug usage	• Pollution (e.g., dust, noise)	
• Fireworks (unexploded, debris)	• Potential weapons	
	• Quarries and pits	
• Food-borne illness	• Rodents	
• Infectious disease transmission	• Snakes	
	• Spiders	

covered in Chapters 10, 11, and 12). Mitigation of most public health hazards relies on the provision of a sanitary environment and hygienic conditions to ensure that exposure to contaminants is eliminated or limited through proper planning, policies, and procedures. It must also be remembered that rain, wind, heat, humidity, and cold can affect sanitation and health exposures.

Waste management

Waste management consists of planning for the collection and disposal of all the solid and liquid waste created at the event. Sanitation and environmental regulations dictate certain aspects of this because an event site that is littered with rubbish may become a health hazard, creating the possibility of accidents, injuries, and illness. Sufficient trash receptacles, efficient clearing and cleaning, meticulous grounds keeping, and properly scheduled waste removal are necessary to mitigate potential hazards (Silvers, 2004a).

The event organizer is considered the waste producer and as such must comply with all sanitation or environmental protection codes, including the selection of suitable waste contractors and the legal disposal of all waste products (HSE, 1999). Waste management should be contracted rather than delegated to volunteers to ensure it is done properly and the event site is well maintained (Berlonghi, 1990). Toxic or hazardous waste, including some household and cleaning supplies (see Table 4.5), and other sewage and sullage must always be disposed of according to prescribed and required procedures (Silvers, 2004a).

Improper or haphazard maintenance practices can lead to infestations, fire hazards, and generally unsanitary conditions. Diligent collection throughout the event prevents rubbish build-up and facilitates efficient post-event clean-up. Storage areas should be properly positioned, monitored, and maintained to ensure packing materials, excess inventory, equipment, and supplies do not create unhealthy or unsafe conditions. Access to these areas should be strictly controlled for security reasons and as a safety precaution. Rubbish and combustible materials should not be stored near tents, structures, or fire exits.

Particular attention needs to be paid to food service areas and sanitary facilities areas. Food waste can putrefy in a very short period of time and rapidly attracts insects and vermin. The waste associated with toilet facilities, including feminine

Table 4.5 Hazardous household materials

• Automotive products (e.g., antifreeze, gasoline, waste oil, tires)	• Lawn/garden chemicals (e.g., pesticides, fertilizers, herbicides)	• Lead acid and dry cell batteries
• Cleaning products (e.g., sanitizers, polishes, drain openers, solvents, pool chemicals)	• Propane and other compressed gas cylinders, tanks, and aerosol cans	• Paint products (e.g., oil based paints*, stains, varnishes, thinners, and solvents)
• Glues		

* Latex paints are often designated as recyclable and used in municipal graffiti abatement programs.

sanitary supplies and disposable diapers/nappies, is sometimes considered a form of hazardous waste requiring special handling. In addition, clinical waste, also designated hazardous material, may be generated by first aid stations and must be disposed of accordingly.

Particularly for outdoor sites, pest control may be important, perhaps requiring clearing or cleaning out of infested areas, spraying for insects, and coverings for all waste receptacles. The risk manager should determine if vector-borne diseases are prevalent or possible and work with public health authorities to control the vector (e.g., insects, birds, dogs, rodents, or vermin). If domestic animals such as dogs are allowed at the event, owner rules must be established for their control and the clean-up of their waste.

A pre-event inspection should be conducted to determine the condition of the event site or property, then conditions must be monitored throughout the duration of the event. The site should be inspected after the event to make certain it has been cleaned and repaired to its original (or better) condition to prevent damage surcharges or cleaning fees.

Sanitation and hygiene

Cleanliness and hygienic conditions are imperative for many reasons, including health and safety from injuries or illness, but also for the comfort and welfare of the event audience, participants, and personnel. Depending on the type, scope, activities, and site of an event, providing the appropriate sanitation systems and conditions could entail special equipment and services, importing power and water, the provision of supplies and personnel, and numerous scheduling and other logistical requirements.

Water is a critical component of health and hygiene. The quantity and quality of water supplies must be assessed, particularly for outdoor events and temporary event sites, including the potential for water supply sabotage and the location and logistics of getting emergency water supplies. Free and freely accessible drinking water must be provided at all events. Potable (drinkable) water must also be provided for cleansing needs (and hot water is often a requisite for catering operations), and non-potable water may be needed for dust abatement. Ad hoc swimming or washing in contaminated water can cause gastrointestinal disease and access should be restricted with fencing and/or warning signage if water quality is unsuitable.

Sanitary facilities (toilets) must be in sufficient numbers to accommodate the expected number and types of users for the expected duration of the event. They must be positioned appropriately to serve the various event populations (facilities for staff and vendors may need to be segregated from the general public population). They must also be properly monitored and maintained to ensure they are clean and well stocked with the necessary supplies (HSE, 1999).

Standards vary according to jurisdiction (check with the local authorities), but guidance suggests a minimum of two stalls (toilet plus urinal) per 100 people should be provided for events with less than six hours duration. However, this does not take into consideration the flexibility of access timing (e.g., everyone heading to the toilets during intermissions or breaks) or the activities taking place (e.g., consumption of alcohol, coffee, or other fluids). One must also consider 'potty parity' (gender equity) when evaluating the number of toilet facilities. Studies reveal that, on average, it takes five minutes for women to go to the toilet and three minutes for men; and women take 55 to 65 percent longer in public toilets than men due to waiting for stall availability. Therefore more facilities must be provided for women and separate facilities for men and women may need to be re-designated depending on the composition of the crowd.

For undeveloped or under-developed sites, portable sanitary facilities may need to be brought to the event site. Handicapped accessible facilities may need to be provided and deluxe portable toilet trailers may be used for upscale events. Handwashing facilities should always be provided. Note that these facilities should be monitored to ensure they are not being used for illegal activities. Portable toilet units must be positioned and anchored properly to prevent accidental or intentional tipping. Toilet facilities should be well lit, well marked, and separated from food service or storage areas. Access for delivery, maintenance (pump-out and cleaning), and removal must be incorporated into the site and operational plans.

Food safety

Food and water is fundamental to life. The preparation and delivery of food and beverage service must be safe, sanitary, and sufficient, and is governed by specific governmental regulations and operational requirements. Food service regulations vary from jurisdiction to jurisdiction and may include health permits, zoning laws, specific business and occupational licenses, levels of insurance coverage (including product liability), employment laws, and other laws and codes pertaining to preparing and serving food to the public.

From the in-house catering departments of hotels and event facilities to independent off-premise caterers to take away providers such as restaurants and grocery stores, caterers and catering organizations vary widely in quality, experience, expertise, and capability. Food and beverage concessions at public festivals, stadiums, and arenas may need to be selected from authorized vendors (those with contracts with the facility or municipality). All caterers and concessionaires should be checked to ensure they hold the appropriate and necessary health permits, business licenses, and insurance coverage. Sanitary conditions from sufficient potable water and facilities for washing foods and equipment to employee hygiene to pest control must be in place and impeccable for any catering operation, on-premise or off-premise.

Food-borne illness, often referred to as food poisoning, is caused by the consumption of a contaminated food with the common symptoms of diarrhea, nausea, vomiting, abdominal cramps, headache, and/or fever. It is often the result of improper sanitation and handling or the incorrect preparation of foods with inherent contaminants (see Table 4.6). Foods with inherent contaminants (e.g., seafood, poultry, and

Table 4.6 Sources of food contamination

• Animals, rodents, insects	• Food handlers	• Pesticides
• Bacteria	• Foreign objects (e.g., hair,	• Polluted water
• Broken/worn equipment	stones, dirt, metal, glass,	• Spoilage
• Cleaning chemicals	staples, bandages, wood)	• Toxins
• Cooking utensils	• Ingredients	• Viruses
• Food contact surfaces	• Packaging materials	
• Food containers	• Parasites	

Source: McSwane et al. (2003) and National Assessment Institute (1998).

dairy products) should be identified in the risk assessment for off-premise events or events using food concessionaires. These foods require special attention because although the food itself is safe when cooked properly, hazardous substances may be left on the preparation surfaces that must be cleaned and sanitized properly to prevent cross-contamination. Gastrointestinal illness questionnaires should be filled out by anyone suffering from symptoms because numerous instances of similar illness within a short period of time can indicate a contamination problem. The Hazard Analysis Critical Control Point (HACCP) food safety assurance system highlights potential problems in food preparation, transportation, display, storage, and service (see Figure 4.2). It may be wise to confirm adoption of a food safety management system such as this with any caterer or catering operation under consideration for an event in order to identify, monitor, and control contamination risks and hazards associated with food-borne illness.

Occupational safety is also a consideration. The catering operations must guard against such hazards as burns from cooking and serving equipment, cuts from knives or broken glass, slips and trips on spilled liquids or electrical cords, falls, fire, and fumes. Those preparing and serving foods and beverages should be properly trained in food handler hygiene and food service proprietors must have an incident reporting system to identify and report any infectious diseases in the staff.

Consider this... 4.5

Hepatitis on the trade show floor

September 22, 2005: The Clark County Health District (CCHD) in Las Vegas, Nevada, was notified that a person serving free ice cream samples at the Global Gaming Expo (G2E) 2005, held September 13–15 at the Las Vegas Convention Center, was infected with hepatitis A, a viral infection of the liver. People who were served ice cream samples by the infected food handler may have been at risk for developing the illness. Although there is no treatment for hepatitis A, symptoms can be prevented in exposed persons who receive gamma globulin within 14 days of their exposure, in this case no later than the 28th of September. The G2E organizers immediately provided the CCHD with the names and contact information for everyone registered as a conference attendee and the CCHD distributed a public health notice via e-mail to all attendees on September 23, 2005 with the name of the specific booth, the dates that the infected food handler was working, and the nature of the disease so that any person who ate free samples served at the booth could contact their local health department and/or physician to determine the need for gamma globulin.

Occupational health and safety

The event risk manager is not only concerned with the health and safety of the event audience, but also with all those who have come together to create and operate the event. All job sites and workplaces should be safe and healthy places for workers and others – a legal responsibility for both the employer and the employee. This is something the event organizers must consider when planning the event site and operations.

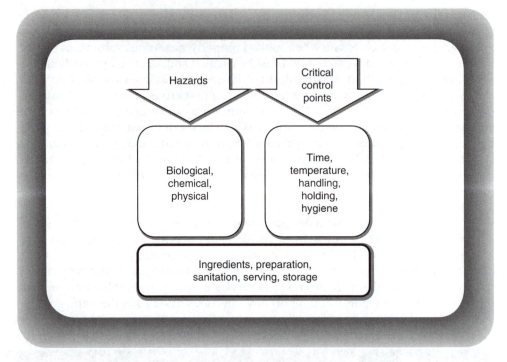

Figure 4.2 The HACCP food safety system

Occupational health and safety (OHS) is regulated in most countries via legislation and standards. There are 14 jurisdictions in Canada (federal, provincial, and territorial) each having its own OHS legislation based upon Part II of the Canada Labour Code. OHS standards in Australia are administered by the National Occupational Health and Safety Commission. The European Agency for Safety and Health at Work was set up in 1996 in the European Union to collect, analyze, and promote OSH-related information. South Africa has the Occupational Health and Safety Act of 1993 and the Health and Safety at Work Act of 1974 governs OHS standards in the U.K. In the U.S., standards are promulgated by the Occupational Safety and Health Administration and adopted and enforced by the states.

What all OHS legislation, standards, and various regulations developed for specific industries and activities have in common is the mandate to provide a work environment that is safe and employees are protected from hazards that may cause injury, damage, or disease. This is not the exclusive responsibility of employers. Employees have a duty to share in this responsibility by complying with the policies and procedures that are designed to protect health and safety, as well as report unsafe and unhealthy conditions to their employers and work together to identify dangers and develop control and precautionary measures to improve workplace safety.

OHS standards extend further than the employer and employee. 'Event organisers, concert promoters, licensees, specialist contractors and venue owners all have a statutory duty to protect the health and safety of their workers and others who may be affected by their work activity' (HSE, 1999, p. 187). In this light, providing a safe and healthy work environment encompasses volunteers, participants, and attendees as well. Whether mandated by law or not, event organizers and risk managers should strive to ensure compliance with the highest standards of workplace safety possible. The typical OHS standards address the following OHS issues:

- Behavior policies
- Duty to warn
- Electrical safety
- Equipment maintenance
- Equipment training
- Fall protection
- Fire protection
- Hazardous substance handling
- Janitorial maintenance
- Machinery usage
- Manual handling procedures
- First aid provision
- Noise exposure
- Protective clothing
- Protective equipment
- Respiratory protection
- Sufficient time and tools
- Sanitation
- Workplace violence.

Occupational hazards

Everyone, from the event organizer to the suppliers to the volunteers, must be committed to a safe working environment and safe work practices and must be active participants in the commitment to on-the-job (OTJ) safety. Everyone is responsible for identifying the health and safety hazards of any work being done, anything being produced, processed, used, stored, handled, or transported, as well as any equipment or machinery being used.

As shown in Table 4.7, OTJ hazards are often categorized by type as physical, chemical, ergonomic, infectious, or stress. Conducting a risk mapping exercise with employees and other stakeholders in order to locate and highlight the places where these hazards occur on a map or floor plan of a work or event space will allow the risk manager to prepare effective risk reduction and control strategies (Hazards Magazine, 1997).

Time, training, and precautions

The key components of OTJ safety are sufficient time, training, and precautions. Most job site accidents at events occur when people are rushing to complete a job. This is when workers forego the appropriate safety precautions in order to get the job done as quickly as possible. For example, climbing on things or standing on a chair to reach something instead of getting the ladder or appropriate lift device, or using the wrong tools for the job at hand are frequent causes of accidents. Adequate time must be allocated to accomplish the work to be done, particularly during the move-out, which is often done late at night and with personnel that are already tired.

Table 4.7   Typical occupational hazards

Chemical	Air contaminants (e.g., dusts, vapors, fumes, gases, mists, smoke) and contact contaminants (e.g., solvents, powders), and other fluid and dry substances that enter the body through skin contact, inhalation, or ingestion
Ergonomic	Repetitive motion, manual handling procedures, awkward positions, whole-body or local vibration, twisting, prolonged static postures, forceful exertions, and other stresses on the body due to work process, stations, or methods
Infectious	Viruses, blood-borne diseases, body fluids, molds, bacteria, and other communicable or contagious pathogen exposures
Physical	Noise, heat/cold, illumination, equipment, slips and trips, lack of equipment guards, fall hazards, electrical shock, ventilation, floor surface levels and condition, and other injury exposures
Stress	Insufficient training, work speed, harassment, fear, anxiety, fatigue, and other pressures that cause physical and emotional tension

Bob Estrin, event venue infrastructure consultant with b.e.creative in Orange, California, offers this perspective on the causes of event accidents:

Event accidents occur at a much greater rate to employees and staff than to attendees. These end up being classified as workplace injuries so we tend not think of them as 'event' accidents. A large number of unreported injuries occur during load out. If we want to be totally accurate we should track accidents from the time of departure en route to the venue until all staff have retuned to their point of origin. So what causes these accidents?

Time:
- *Rushed travel*
- *Inadequate load in time*
- *Not enough set up time*
- *Rushed take down*

Equipment:
- *Misuse*
- *Incorrect items*

Staffing:
- *Training*
- *Lack of event information*
- *Not supplying correct number of staff*

A more detailed analysis leads to the conclusion that the true underlying cause is economic. The cost of doing a properly staffed event with adequate venue time is not often factored into the proposals in the event industry. Profit margins are thin and time is a costly commodity. The true cost of an accident can be extreme. Most businesses can't bear the burdens that can exist beyond what insurance covers.

Consider this... 4.6

Dangerous tent handling practices result in tragedy

October 2004: Three workers in Arkansas were electrocuted when the supports in the intact tent they lifted over a fence touched power lines. Three other workers handling the tent survived. The practice of moving a tent without dismantling it is common in the event rental industry, often the result of tight deadlines and last minute changes demanded by clients. The high turnover rate of the low-wage workforce typically used by rental companies to install tents contributes to the lack of awareness of the possible dangers and safe tent handling procedures, but this should be mitigated by proper supervision, including pointing out power lines and other hazards prior to moving a tent. The tragedy was repeated nine months later (July 25, 2005) when four scout leaders were electrocuted and three others injured while pitching a dining tent under power lines at the Boy Scout Jamboree in Virginia.

Source: Special Events Magazine (2004)

Workers must be provided with the proper tools, equipment, and materials to efficiently and safely do the work required. Proper training must be provided to all personnel operating machinery, vehicles, or other equipment that could be dangerous to the worker or others in close proximity. Personal protective equipment (PPE) and proper clothing is required when handling certain materials and doing certain tasks and could include safety chains, rails, or straps, safety boots, hard hats, surgical or metal gloves, long-sleeved shirts, goggles, face guards, respiratory masks, back braces, harnesses, hearing protection, toe guards, and other gear.

In addition, proper equipment such as ladders, aerial lifts, forklifts, hand trucks, platforms, and scaffolding must be provided when installing, moving, and removing décor and production equipment. Numerous worker injuries are the result of incorrect manual handling procedures, including lifting, carrying, pushing, or pulling, causing back injuries and muscle strains. These often lead to muscular-skeletal disorders, which can cause chronic debilitating pain. These are the cause of many workers' compensation claims, which can be very costly as insurance rates rise. Many injuries are due to fall hazards, including falling off something, something falling on someone, or falling with a collapsing structure or piece of equipment. These injuries, and sometimes deaths, occur primarily during installation and/or construction, but fall hazards associated with the site terrain must also be considered. Guidance suggests that fall protection should be provided when the work surface (e.g., stage) or worker is six feet (1.8 meters) or more above the ground.

The work environment

The health and safety of work environments has been studied extensively by industrial hygienists. Unlike most workplaces, however, events are temporary in nature and often occur in unusual or unfamiliar settings or venues that are not built with the theatrical capabilities so often employed for event productions. Typically the workers, paid and volunteer, do not work regularly in a particular venue doing the same thing day after day. Add to this the pressure to get the event set up in time for 'the show to go on' and the fact that the 'show' is rarely repeated, the assurance that the work environment is safe and healthy can be problematic. Exposure to hazardous substances, excessive heat or cold, extreme noise levels, and unsatisfactory illumination so often endured by event personnel must be controlled.

Exposure to hazardous substances or conditions may be the result of using unsuitable or mishandling equipment, inadequate ventilation, improper storage practices, or not using the appropriate protective equipment and clothing. Indoor use of diesel or propane powered equipment (e.g., vehicles or vehicle mounted platforms, cooking or grilling devices, etc.) can cause significant carbon monoxide exposure. Exposure to air-borne chemicals, dust, or other toxic emissions can occur when using aerosol sprays, solvents, paints, certain adhesives, and atmospheric special effects (e.g., fog and haze effects, artificial snow, and pyrotechnic smoke).

High noise levels can cause health hazards ranging from headaches to permanent hearing loss. Noise protection must be provided for workers exposed to occupational noise levels of more than 85 decibels (dBA), which would encompass many event activities and event personnel, particularly for concert or sports events (typically having levels of 120 dBA and higher). Poor lighting can cause eye strain and obscure slip or trip hazards. Make certain sufficient illumination is provided throughout the duration of the job from set up through move-out. Good job site housekeeping is also important. Slip and trip hazards are often the result of improperly placed equipment, poorly stored materials, uneven surfaces, spilled liquids, and debris.

Duty to warn

All workers have the right to know the hazards associated with the use of various materials or equipment and conditions in the workplace. Material safety data sheets (MSDS) should be procured for all hazardous materials (e.g., chemicals) and must be made accessible to workers using these materials. MSDS include information about hazardous or toxic ingredients, physical or chemical characteristics, fire and explosion data, health hazard data, special protection information, special precautions, reactivity data, spill or leak procedures, and emergency procedures (McSwane, Rue, and Linton, 2003).

Hazard warning, prohibition, fire safety/equipment, and other mandatory, directional, and informational signs are required on job sites. Safety and warning signs should be placed at all hazardous locations (e.g., 'Caution: Wet Floor' signs) and on all hazardous equipment or supplies. At times inspectors have required warning signage in places that are not accessed or accessible during an event, such as backstage electrical installations, but the signs must be posted regardless. Warning tags or labels, which will be on original containers or packaging, should be placed on all hazardous materials and must be replicated if the contents are transferred to and stored in another container so that in the event of an accident, illness, or spill, emergency responders will know what they are dealing with (Rossol, 2000).

Proactive safety policies

Many OHS standards suggest or require companies with a certain number of employees create a safety officer position or a safety committee that has oversight responsibilities to ensure health and safety hazards are identified and addressed according to the standards. Best practice guidance suggests that event organizations do the same by establishing policies and procedures that limit undesirable behavior and conditions. Although compliance with OHS standards may or may not be a legal responsibility toward event volunteers, it is certainly a moral obligation. The development and implementation of employee and volunteer standards of conduct that address areas of activity that pose potential problems or hazards will help prevent accidents and injuries and create a culture of safety awareness. Train all employees and volunteers about safety issues in general and their specific duties in particular. Make certain they have adequate experience before undertaking hazardous operations. Periodically update information and retrain them as necessary (Reiss, 2001).

Many event professionals feel that it is up to the event manager or event risk manager to set the standards for safety on the event job site by holding a safety meeting with the suppliers and their workers prior to the installation of an event. This meeting should instill in workers (paid or volunteer) the commitment to a safe work environment and empower them to participate in and enforce that commitment. This includes workers advising supervisors when hazards are identified, including co-workers working improperly. The event organizer or risk manager should also confirm that all independent contractors have appropriate safety programs in place, paying particular attention to any bids that are significantly lower than others, which might indicate substandard equipment or untrained personnel are being used (Silvers, 2004a).

Summary

Event organizers have a legal, ethical, and financial responsibility to make certain that the event and event operations are at the highest standards of safety possible. Neglecting these public health and safety issues indicates an indifference to the probable consequences that should have been recognized by a professional and exposes the organizer and/or organization to liability for any harm that occurs.

Existing statutes and codes legislated by municipalities and jurisdictions responsible for their citizenry cover many of these issues, and are based on standards established by national and international organizations that have studied accidents, injuries, emergencies, and disasters to determine the preventable causes. The event risk manager works with representatives of the applicable regulatory agencies to ensure a safe and healthy event, event site, and job site.

Sanitary conditions are critical to the protection of the public health. Requirements are based on the health codes of a jurisdiction as well as the cultural and cosmetic standards of the event type, scope, and location. The monitoring of sanitary conditions is exponentially more important as the duration of an event expands and food service is provided. Special attention must be paid to outdoor and undeveloped event sites.

The health and safety of every audience member, provider, participant, and paid or volunteer worker is the primary responsibility of the event risk manager. Appropriate training must be delivered, precautionary measures to control hazards must be devised, and abiding by these measures must be enforced for everyone's safety. Although some may argue that compliance with occupational safety and health regulations is too burdensome for volunteer-driven events and would add too much expense to the production budget for all events, protecting the health and welfare of these people will help protect the event's assets (and its existence) by reducing the liabilities that subject the event to financial risk.

Key strategies

- Seek to make your local fire marshal your mentor and share what you learn from him or her with your clients and colleagues.
- Personally review each means of egress in an event venue from the center of the event site to the final exit discharge.
- Note the locations of all fire extinguishers on site plans or floor plans.
- Conduct walk-throughs periodically throughout the duration of the event.
- Identify or establish policies regarding the disposal of event waste and ensure that all vendors and participants comply with them before, during, and after the event.
- Make certain all food service vendors or providers have the requisite credentials.
- Incorporate sufficient time in move-in and move-out schedules to reduce the likelihood of accidents.
- Create a culture of safety awareness throughout the event organization.

Chapter review challenge

1 What is the link between fire safety and occupancy loads?
2 Imagine you have a client that has requested you provide a two meter high maze made out of bales of hay. What are the fire safety implications of this?
3 Compare and contrast the causes, audience reactions, and effects of the Bradford football stadium fire and the nightclub fire described in Consider this… 4.1 and 4.2.
4 List all the potential uses for potable water at an event site and discuss ways in which you might provide for them at a remote outdoor site without a source for running water.
5 Why are occupational safety and health issues important to an event's risk management plan?

Practical risk management exercise

You have been retained as a risk consultant by the XYZ Fun Fest, a nine-day family-oriented event that has an attendance of more than 50 000. One of your tasks is to develop criteria and policies for selecting food and beverage concessionaires at their annual outdoor festival that will avoid or mitigate food and beverage service and safety hazards. These criteria should focus on 'proofs' that their practices are such that health and safety hazards will be minimized, and may include food-borne illness, scope of menu items and ingredients, occupational safety hazards, alcohol service, and compliance issues.

Write a 10-point food and beverage concessionaire policy that the festival can use when soliciting and contracting concessionaires (e.g., Concessionaires shall provide documentation that they follow the HACCP food safety system), and justify your recommendations citing a minimum of three reference resources.

Key terminology

Assembly occupancy: An occupancy of a building or structure, or portion thereof, for a gathering of 50 or more persons for such purposes as deliberation, entertainment, dining and drinking, amusement, or awaiting transportation.

Capacity: The maximum number of people that will fit into a specific function space in a specific setting.

Decibel: (dBA) A unit for measuring the relative intensity of sound, from zero for the average least perceptible sound to about 120 dBA for the average pain level and beyond.

Ergonomics: The science of work energy and body movement in relation to working conditions.

Fire retardant: A liquid, solid, or gas that tends to inhibit combustion and/or reduce flame spread when applied on, mixed in, or combined with combustible materials.

Fire suppression system: A fixed system consisting of devices and equipment designed and installed for detecting, controlling, or extinguishing a fire or otherwise alerting occupants and/or the fire department that a fire has occurred.

Flow capacity: The volume of people able to go through a given space or route in a given amount of time under given circumstances; flow capacity diminishes as the crowd density increases because movement is restricted.

Hazardous/toxic waste: Waste material or products that can cause harm to people, wildlife or the environment, including contamination and contagious viruses, and subject to special handling, shipping, and disposal requirements.

Manual handling procedures: The procedures for correctly handling goods and materials manually, including lifting, carrying, pushing, and pulling.

Means of egress: A continuous and unobstructed path of exit travel to a public way, including the exit access, the exit, the exit discharge, doors, hardware, arrangement, capacity, marking, and illumination, allowing prompt exit from a building or structure in the event of an emergency.

Occupational safety and health: The rules and regulations surrounding the requirements of employers to provide a safe workplace by saving lives, preventing injuries, and protecting the health of the workers.

Risk mapping: The process of identifying health and safety hazards by locating and highlighting the places where these hazards occur on a map or floor plan of a work or event space.

Sewage: The wastewater that includes liquid, semi-liquid, and solid human waste; also known as black water.

Sullage: The wastewater that results from the disposal of liquids and semi-liquids from sinks, showers, and hand-washing basins; also known as grey water.

Waste management: The assessment, procurement, direction, and control of the collection and disposal of solid and liquid waste from an event site.

Online resources

Canadian Centre for Occupational Health and Safety   www.ccohs.ca

European Agency for Safety and Health at Work   http://osha.europa.eu/OSHA

F.D.A. Center for Food Safety (U.S.)	www.cfsan.fda.gov
Health and Safety Executive (U.K.)	www.hse.gov.uk
Human Resources and Skills Development Canada	www.hrsdc.gc.ca
National Occupational Health & Safety Commission (Australia)	www.nohsc.gov.au
Occupational Safety & Health Administration (U.S.)	www.osha.gov
OSHWeb.com	www.oshweb.com
South Africa Department of Labour	www.labour.gov.za
WorkSafeBC	www.worksafebc.com

Chapter 5

Loss prevention and security

Cover your assets

This chapter will examine how to:

- Select the appropriate loss prevention and loss control strategies for identified risk exposures
- Conduct forward planning by developing the appropriate contingency and continuity plans
- Evaluate the risk exposures of an event project to obtain bids and secure the proper insurance coverage
- Select the proper security personnel, equipment, deployment, and communications suitable for an event based on the type, scope, and identified risks

Introduction

There are probably as many ways to incur losses as there are ways to acquire gains (see Table 5.1). Losses can be large or small; accidental, intentional, or due to negligence; controllable or beyond one's control; due to internal and external sources; or due to conditions or incidents (e.g., natural, man-made, technological, or political). For every item on the strategic or operational planning list and for every facet of the event project, there are potential losses to be considered that could jeopardize the resources and reputation of the event organization.

Loss prevention

Loss prevention means different things to different industries. In the retail industry, it focuses on stopping or reducing loss from shoplifting and employee theft; in the

Table 5.1 The dimensions of loss

How do losses occur?		What could be lost?
Accidents	Fraud	• Capability
Arson	Injuries	• Credibility
Delays	Lawsuits	• Equipment
Damage	Liability (tortious,	• Functionality
Defects	professional, or statutory)	• Information
Deficiencies	Misplacement	• Materials/supplies
Destruction	Misuse of equipment	• Money
Disasters	Omissions	• Personnel
Disruptions	Pilferage	• Property
Embezzlement	Sabotage	• Time
Errors	Theft	
Fines and penalties	Vandalism	
Forgery	Violence	

Table 5.2 Loss prevention strategies

• Safety precautions and protocols	• Security personnel and equipment
• Risk separation and distribution	• Contingency and continuity plans
• Redundant equipment and systems	• Response training
• Communication systems	• Insurance coverage

construction industry it focuses on safety to reduce workers' compensation liability; in knowledge industries it focuses on information asset protection. Fischer and Green (1998) contend that external theft accounts for only half the loss that internal theft does, suggesting that the event organization needs to look inward as well as outward when assessing vulnerabilities. Whether using bar codes to track raw materials in the prop shop or inventory in the souvenir sales booth, restricting access to office supplies or client lists, or checking for falsified purchase orders to kickbacks from suppliers, loss prevention begins within.

Some think loss prevention is synonymous with protection services (security), while others see it as all measures used to reduce the frequency of losses. Loss prevention encompasses these perspectives and, in fact, all the topics covered in this book. It employs numerous strategies (see Table 5.2) to address or treat the identified risks in order to protect financial, physical, environmental, and human assets from loss and destruction, and to control the negative impact should it occur.

Loss prevention, as illustrated in Figure 5.1, encompasses five areas of activity that should be applied to the event purpose, product, processes, place, people, and practices. It may also be seen as a progressive strategy that, first, puts in place all the preventative countermeasures possible, which are identified in the risk response plan. These must then be monitored in order to detect if the countermeasure has been compromised or if a hazard or vulnerability has been exposed. Once an exposure has occurred, its impact must be controlled and overcome, if possible, through contingency

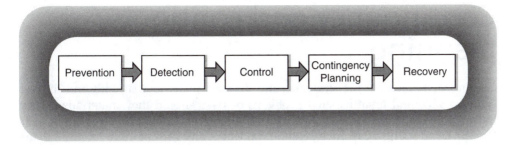

Figure 5.1 Loss prevention process

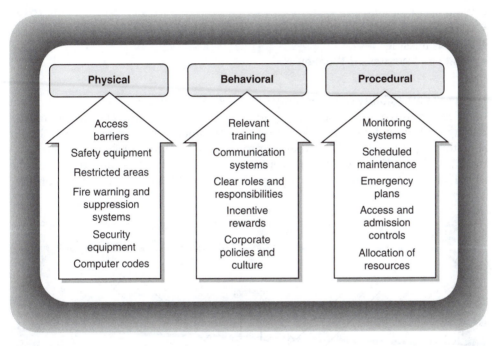

Figure 5.2 Loss prevention tactics

planning. And, finally, if a loss occurs, the organization needs to be able to recover from its impact.

To facilitate proper detection, Berlonghi (1996) suggests that safety patrol teams be developed with the lone responsibility of circulating through the event looking for safety hazards and unsafe activity and reporting such to the proper supervisory or security personnel or authorities and assisting response personnel as requested. Control measures, as noted in Chapter 2, are those physical, behavioral, and procedural actions, devices, strategies, and systems employed to prevent or reduce loss (Jeynes, 2002) and there should be control measures specified for each identified risk (see Figure 5.2). According to Jeynes (p. 62), 'There are as many ways to control or reduce the impact of a hazard as there are types of hazard.' It is also important to fully understand the critical functions of the event operations to ensure these are protected with effective control measures and timely contingency plans.

Contingency and continuity planning

Contingency plans are the strategies and detailed plans to deal with and recover from possible and unanticipated problems or risks should they materialize. They must be developed to address those risks that will be retained (often referred to as Plan B). Conducting a gap analysis should uncover any gaps or vulnerabilities in the event's planning, site, or operations. The gap analysis should examine the following.

- What is critical?
- What is vulnerable?
- What is uncertain?
- What is missing?
- What else? What else? What else?

For every vulnerability or uncertainty identified, alternative ways to overcome them must be carefully considered (see Figure 5.3). This may include alternative, redundant, or additional dates, sites, activities, equipment, and/or personnel should something go wrong, such as weather problems, equipment problems, or procurement problems. There will be different costs, logistical impacts, and triggers to be established with each contingency plan considered. It is also important to consider

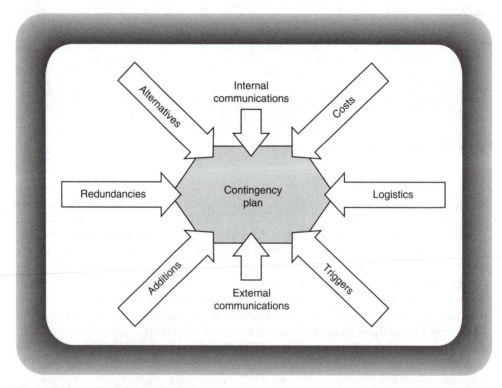

Figure 5.3 Facets of a contingency plan

the 'domino effect' (Berlonghi, 1990) wherein one failure or incident prompts or causes subsequent failures or risky conditions, which trigger further failures, which produce further breakdowns, and so on. Think about and fully integrate how a single vulnerability and the facets of its contingency plan affect other facets of the overall event plan.

If inclement weather could be a problem for an outdoor event, a tent might be secured or a substitute indoor space might be reserved. If power is critically important to the event, a back-up portable generator would be considered. If already using a portable generator for the event power, perhaps a second generator as redundant equipment will be ordered. One of the more noted speakers at a conference might be asked to move his or her presentation to the keynote slot if the keynote speaker is a no-show. Berlonghi (1996) advises securing commitments from personnel and suppliers to be prepared to provide goods and services if called upon in an emergency only if needed, which can reduce the costs associated with a contingency plan. It is also best practice to confirm and collect contingency plans from each of your suppliers so that these may be integrated into your overall contingency planning (ICCA/COPE, 2005).

Consider this... 5.1

Hurricane causes cruise conference havoc

August 1996: An association had selected a five-day cruise as the venue for its annual professional development conference. Months and months of hard work lining up and plotting out an extensive and compact schedule of educational sessions that left the time in the ports of call free had to be tossed out the port hole when Hurricane Dolly approached the Caribbean on the first night out. Cruise ships have the option to simply sail around such things as hurricanes and their contract with you (your ticket) says that they intend to go to these ports, but are free to change the itinerary. And change it they did, overnight. The planner had to completely rearrange and reschedule the conference agenda to coordinate with the ship's new itinerary. Instead of 14 hours of 'at sea' time for the conference sessions, there was now only nine and a half hours. In addition, not only was the conference planner scrambling to rearrange everything; the ship was scrambling with all their programming for the thousand other passengers as well. The planner had to coordinate and confirm all conference plans using the various public lounges with the ship's plans for those lounges. In the end, only two concurrent session options were canceled, one session was changed from a general session to a concurrent session as one of the speakers canceled because he was due to have boarded in Cozumel (no longer on the itinerary), and two general sessions were shortened.

Once the contingency plan options have been identified, the deadlines and protocols for implementing the plan must be determined, including who will do what, when, and where. These deadlines must then be incorporated into the time line and other operational plans. Certain contingency responses can be made at any time during the event time line, but some decisions must be made by a certain time prior to the event, such as ordering and installing a tent or portable generator. It is also advisable to test your ability to activate back up and contingency plans with a trial run (ICCA/COPE, 2005).

Communications are an important aspect of contingency planning because the decision to activate a contingency plan must be conveyed to those who will be involved in and impacted by its implementation. Although most contingency plans are put in place to assure a seamless operation (an invisible work around) should something go wrong, it may be necessary to impart certain information to other internal and external constituents should it become necessary to implement the contingency plan. This may include informing the client, staff, performers and participants, suppliers, authorities, attendees, and perhaps the neighboring residents or general public.

Contingency planning must incorporate the event needs with the event budget. According to Silvers (2004a, p. 57), 'You must verify and validate your contingency plans with the host organization or your client so that the resources required to implement a risk response or contingency plan are fully funded and supported.' Sometimes the client or host may decide not to invest in these safeguards, but the event risk manager is responsible for making the client aware of them. If the client does not wish to invest in them (their cost–benefit attitude may be different than yours), other recovery strategies must be devised or the client's written agreement that nothing is to be done (and that the client accepts the consequences) must be secured.

Continuity planning addresses how the event or event organization will recover from an incident or disaster. The objective of continuity planning is to be prepared and able to work around and continue normal operations with minimal or no interruption. This plan should focus on salvaging, reconstructing, and/or replacing damaged or missing equipment, hardware or software, records, workforce capacity, environmental conditions, venue capability, or other vital support in order to resume business (FEMA, 2004). Continuity plans, like contingency plans, need to consider the replacement time and costs for key personnel, equipment, and supplies (Broder, 2000), and they must be devised before an incident occurs or they will be at best expensive and at worst ineffective (Smith and Merritt, 2002).

Risk financing and insurance

Risk financing and risk management funding are not the same thing (AIRMIC, ALARM, and IRM, 2002). Risk financing is the allocation of funding for the financial consequences of risk exposure, either through the retention of the risk (self-insured) or the transfer of risk through the purchase of the proper insurance coverage for the event and event organization. Risk management funding is the allocation of sufficient resources to conduct effective risk management processes and procedures and implement risk treatment activities. Sufficient financial resources must be allocated for both.

When determining whether to retain risk and pay for it through the event organization's own financial resources or transfer the risk through the purchase of insurance coverage, NFPA 1250 (2000) offers the following guidance.

- *Low severity/low frequency*: Retain; affordable risk.
- *Low severity/high frequency*: Retain; predictable costs.
- *High severity/low frequency*: Transfer; costs too high.
- *High severity/high frequency*: Avoid; do not be in that business (transfer only if cannot avoid, but insurance likely to be costly).

Consider this... 5.2

Lighting balloon sails away

Giant lighting balloons were used to add illumination to a large outdoor company party. These patented helium-filled glowing globes are made from rip stop nylon with a lighting filament suspended inside and anchored to the ground by their power cord. Even though the weather was wonderfully calm the night of the party, late in the evening a wind gust came up and before the event staff could get all the balloons brought down to earth, one snapped loose from its power cord and sailed off over the desert in the dark. There was no way to track its trajectory to recover it, leaving the event company that leased it liable for replacement costs. Luckily, the event company had insurance coverage for such a loss; otherwise the costs could have wiped out the entire profits for the event project.

Insurance management

Insurance coverage is purchased to pay for losses that the event organization cannot afford. These losses may include the costs of litigation or event cancellation, the replacement costs due to loss or damage of property, the loss of key personnel, and the financial exposure and legal settlements that may be awarded due to negligence, injury, or death. Insurance management deals with ascertaining liability exposures and contractual insurance coverage requirements, sourcing suitable providers, and acquiring the proper insurance policies in order to maintain suitable loss prevention coverage and risk financing for the event project.

Within the menu of risk responses, insurance is the transference of financial liability from one entity to another; in this case the insurance carrier or underwriter. Some think that risk management is simply the purchasing of enough insurance to cover potential losses (perhaps a valid but assuredly expensive attitude). The insurance industry, however, may be reluctant to offer coverage to the meetings and events marketplace because it does not thoroughly understand what the exposures are. Even with those underwriters that do understand the exposures, insurance coverage may not be available for every liability or risk. And, even if it were, it would likely be too expensive in the context of most events. The hosting organization must evaluate the event exposures and secure the appropriate insurance coverage based on what is legally required and fiscally prudent.

Use a professional broker/agent

This discussion should not be construed as advice on what insurance coverage you should purchase, but instead, a guideline for what should be discussed with competent insurance consultants. There are hundreds of insurance products that might be applicable to events and event organizations (see Table 5.3). Event risk managers and event organizations must make decisions about what insurance coverage to purchase based on the particular type, purpose, scope, program of activities, components, audience, legal obligations, marketing, sponsors, merchandising, organizational structure, personnel, vendors, and location of the event.

Every event is different and every event organization is different. For example, a convention might be most concerned with event cancellation and host liquor liability

Table 5.3 Typical types of insurance for event professionals and organizations

• Accidental death and dismemberment	• Fidelity bonds
• Automobile, owned and non-owned	• Fire legal liability
• Building and personal property	• Host liquor liability
• Business interruption	• Independent contractors
• Business owners policy	• Inland marine (property) insurance
• Commercial crime (3D: dishonesty, disappearance, destruction)	• Medical payment coverage
	• Non-appearance
• Commercial general liability (public liability, spectator insurance)	• Prize indemnification
	• Product liability
• Contingent business interruption	• Promotions indemnity (e.g., coupon redemption programs)
• Directors and officers	
• Door receipts	• Travel
• Employers liability	• Valuable papers and records
• Errors and omissions	• Volunteer or participant liability
• Event cancellation, abandonment, or postponement	• Weather
	• Workers' compensation

insurance; an independent event organizer would likely purchase errors and omissions insurance; a historical battle re-enactment event would want its insurance to cover the use of archery, black powder, cavalry, or cannons; an outdoor festival might seek weather insurance; a charity hole-in-one contest might purchase a prize indemnification policy; an incentive travel program may consider travel delay protection; and staging a concert event on a sports field may require turf insurance. However, **all** public events **need** some form of commercial general liability coverage (also known as public liability or spectator insurance).

Note that these are products. You must be a savvy consumer and buy only what you need. Insurance salespeople have a knack for outlining every possible bad thing that could happen – adverse weather conditions disrupting air transport or affecting outdoor activities; the venue is damaged by fire or storm; no-show speakers or entertainers due to illness or delays; strikes or natural disasters causing disruption to scheduled services; terrorism dissuading people from traveling; outbreaks of infectious diseases leading to quarantine or restricted access; unforeseen political events such as coups or disputes with other countries causing border closure; and death of heads of state causing periods of official mourning (www.event-assured.com). Any of these things (and many more) can and have happened, but you must be realistic about what insurance coverage is mandated, essential, and sensible based on your event or event organization.

The event risk manager works with a qualified insurance agent or broker to evaluate the event liabilities by reviewing the event operations and its risk assessment. Determine the contractually required coverage, including the requirements from the venue, client, and perhaps certain suppliers. Determine the necessary and pre-existing coverage. Examine the pre-existing coverage to determine any gaps or exclusions. Finally, determine if the limits of coverage are sufficient. Note that independent agents and brokers represent a variety of insurance carriers; exclusive agents work for a single underwriter.

Full, candid, and continuous explanations of what operations and activities are included in an event and conducted by the event organization, as well as the geographical extent of those operations and activities, are critical because this will not only assist with identifying and purchasing the proper types and amounts of coverage, it is a contractual issue. An insurance policy is a contract, and as such, the information provided by the insured becomes the legal basis for payment or rejection of a claim. In addition, the purchaser (the insured) has a continuing duty of disclosure to the seller (the insurer) to communicate any changes in assets, new or unusual activities, or risk exposures that will be undertaken at an event.

Analyze the insurance coverage you are purchasing to ensure the coverage meets your expectations. For example, liability insurance covers legal defense costs as well as damages awarded up to the limits of the insurance policy, after which you must pay the remaining costs (Sorin, 2003). You must understand the policy limitations and exclusions, the perils (causes of loss) covered and how those perils are defined, the locations and property covered, the persons covered, the time periods covered, the deductibles, and your duties in the event of a loss (Berlonghi, 1990). Foster (2002) advises that a rider should be purchased for any exclusions in a liability policy as needed, with particular attention paid to contractual liability associated with indemnification and hold harmless clauses, and also advises that general liability and professional liability coverage should be procured from the same carrier to prevent separate carriers assigning a loss to the other. Considering the increase in frivolous lawsuits, the soaring costs of legal representation, and the high damages awarded by juries, Sorin (2003) recommends a minimum of five million dollars in general liability coverage for event companies.

Consider this... 5.3

Traveling product demonstrations

Traveling exhibitions are a common event for companies wishing to demonstrate their products to a variety of people. The live exhibition is presented as entertainment and is often more effective in promoting the product than television or radio advertising. At one of the periodic risk management meetings for a traveling product demonstration for a major insurance company one of the risks identified was people slipping on purpose and suing the company. This is a form of fraud. It was regarded as a 'possible' to 'high' risk because insurance companies are often predisposed to settling such claims and may have been seen as an easy target for insurance fraud. The exhibition with performance stages traveled around the country and was very popular, attracting thousands of people every day. However, in this case, the risk was not picked up at the beginning of the tour but the management of the event was 'risk aware' and soon realized their exposure.

Source: O'Toole (2006a), from EPMS CDROM, www.epms.net.

Cost-saving options should be explored with the insurance broker, such as higher deductibles, riders, umbrella policies, extensions to existing coverage, and being listed as additionally insured or co-insured on client and supplier policies. Additionally insured requirements may be reciprocal with venues and other vendors, which must

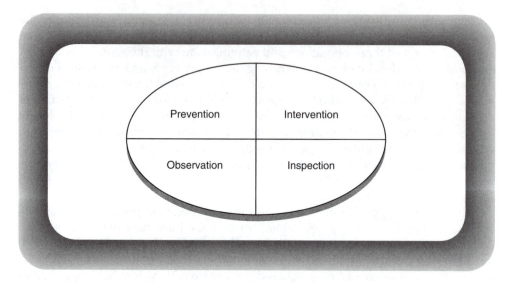

Figure 5.4 Security tactics

be confirmed with and arranged by your insurance company. This may entail a fee or increased premium, which should be passed along to the requestor if possible. Also require the insurance company of those that have listed your organization as additionally or co-insured on their policies to provide you with a notice of any policy cancellations, non-renewals, or changes in coverage (Connell, 2002; Krug, 2000).

The event risk manager should also collect certificates of insurance from all suppliers and subcontractors, and must confirm the validity of those documents as well as the viability of those underwriters with your own insurance broker. This certificate is issued by the insured's insurance company or agent and specifies the types and liability limits of coverage carried by the insured and its expiration dates. This proof of insurance coverage limits your liability exposure and ensures that sufficient financial resources are available to support indemnification in case of a loss.

Security

According to Broder (2000) security is the application of protection techniques to minimize loss opportunity. The role of security is to protect the harmony of the event and the assets of the event organization using a variety of tactics (see Figure 5.4). Security management covers the sourcing, selection, and deployment of the personnel and equipment to be used to provide protective services and support for the event project, and the implementation and supervision of the appropriate command and control systems to ensure its efficacy.

Security plans, personnel, equipment, and procedures are an integral part of risk management. They are put in place to protect people, property, image, reputations, and event assets from damage, harm, injury, loss, or worse (see Table 5.4). Security personnel may also provide important safety and welfare assistance and fill important emergency response functions. Security is required at virtually all events to protect

Table 5.4 Typical security functions

• Access control	• Emergency response	• Property protection
• Admissions control	• Enforcement	• Staff, visitor, vendor, and public
• Asset protection	• Escorting	safety
• Behavior control	• Evacuation	• Stewarding
• Crime deterrence	• Incident response	• Surveillance
• Crowd control	• Intrusion control	• VIP protection

property and attendees from criminal or dangerous acts or to assist with crowd movement and management.

Security planning

The security plan is only one facet of a risk management plan, specifying methods and devices to be used to provide the protection requirements pertinent to a particular event or organization. It is widely recommended that a security vulnerability assessment (SVA) be conducted to determine the weaknesses that could be exploited and the appropriate countermeasures and the defensive systems that will mitigate those exposures. The National Fire Protection Association's guidance on premises security practices (NFPA 730) recommends this methodical and systematic process to ensure that assets, physical features, policies, operations, obligations, internal activities, and external environments are thoroughly examined and analyzed from a protective perspective. The threat assessment in particular classifies critical assets, identifies potential targets, and investigates potential adversaries to determine what is known about them and their tactics (NFPA, 2005).

Examine the event plans and survey the event site to determine what areas, activities, items, or individuals are secure, secure only at certain times, or vulnerable (see Table 5.5). Assess the security infrastructure of the event location, including the crime prevention plans of the city, security plans of the venue, and emergency and evacuation plans for both (Tassiopoulos, 2005). Identify past or potential problems that must be addressed. Define what can and will be done, and what improvements will be necessary to provide the level of security required. Specify when and by whom these actions or improvements will be accomplished.

The security plan should address general, high-risk, and other specific security needs pertinent to your event and event site (IAEM, 2004) and specify your security-related measures and procedures, yet the plan must be flexible enough to respond to changes and unexpected events (NFPA, 2005). It should address the following elements (Berlonghi, 1990; NFPA, 2005):

- *Risk factors*: critical assets, inherent and historical risks, and dangerous situations, conditions, controversies, or rivalries.
- *Access control systems*: procedural, physical, mechanical, and electronic barriers.
- *Security personnel*: sources, procedures, command structure, deployment, and schedules.
- *Site maps*: site plan, restricted areas, assembly points, interior and exterior routes (access and escape), and surrounding vicinity as appropriate (local, district, regional, national, air fields, harbors, border crossings).

Table 5.5   Security survey checklist

• Admittance controls	• Exhaust conduits	• Service personnel
• Alarms	• Exhibits	• Sewer openings
• Air intake pipes	• Fences	• Shipping and receiving
• Barriers	• Gates	• Stairwells
• Building overhangs	• Hallways	• Storage areas
• Cashier functions	• HVAC system	• Street people presence
• Cash repositories	• Landscaping	• Surveillance devices
• Classified/confidential	• Lighting	• Trash pickup
document handling	• Loading docks	• Utility connections
• Communications network	• Lobbies	• Vehicular movement
• Computer access	• Locks and key systems	• Vendors
• Culverts and drains	• New construction	• Walls
• Doors	• Parking garages	• Windows
• Elevators	• Rooftops	• Youth gang activity
• Entrances and exits	• Safes and vaults	

Sources: Broder (2000), BOMA (2001), and Fischer and Green (1998)

- *Surveillance systems*: human and electronic.
- *Alarm systems*: detection, intrusion, response and reporting procedures.
- *Security lighting*: interior and exterior.
- *Communications*: internal and external.
- *Emergency response plans*: accidents, natural disasters, criminal or terrorist attacks.
- *Outside resources*: public safety agencies (e.g., law enforcement, fire and medical services), healthcare facilities, utility companies, transportation authorities, embassies, and cooperating agencies as applicable.

Each type of event (and each time an event is held) presents its own unique vulnerabilities. A convention, for example, might have different high-profile guests or presenters each time it is held that require specific procedures, levels of protection, and personnel ranging from confidential arrival and departure facilities and personal bodyguards to canine bomb detection sweeps and the vetting of all event personnel. If the convention includes a trade show, there may be hundreds of exhibitors displaying expensive products or proprietary equipment that must be protected from theft (actual property or industrial secrets). If the convention might attract demonstrations or confrontations due to its controversial nature or presenters, one must remember that, in the U.S., people have freedom of speech and freedom of assembly rights – as long as they don't block entrances or exits, prevent persons from entering or leaving any premises, use physical force on any person, throw any type of matter, use offensive language likely to promote violence, or commit any criminal act (Beene, 1992) – and plans must be made to accommodate yet control them.

In general, the cost of security measures should not exceed the monetary value of the assets or areas to be protected (NFPA, 2005) but in terms of protecting human safety and welfare, which should be your Number One priority, there is no established 'value' for a human life that would justify or ratify a cost/benefit analysis. However, no organization has unlimited resources to devote to security measures. One must make these decisions based on the realistic assessment of the vulnerabilities specific to the event, the available resources of the event organization, and the capabilities of the available protective measures. For example, the 2002 Winter Olympic Games had a security budget of $350 million and the security workers out-numbered the athletes by four to one at the Opening Ceremonies, which was appropriate for an event of that size and status at that time in that location. A statistical understanding of prior occurrences at the particular location or type of event production will help evaluate investment options, and the risk manager should collect this information from law enforcement officials, industry resources, and the event's historical records.

It is also important to balance the security measures from a marketing standpoint and a liability perspective. One must look at the impact security measures will have on the event experience. Will they cause undue inconvenience for the attendee or give the event a militaristic atmosphere? These objections can often be overcome with careful planning, integrating the security measures into the very design of the event and communicating their importance to the audience in the context of providing a safe and secure environment. Investing in and implementing security measures will also need to be considered as if one were defending one's decisions in a courtroom, which subjects the defendant to the 20:20 hindsight definitions of what a 'reasonable person' would have done. The courts (and juries) will look at the foreseeability of the risk, its magnitude, and the severity of harm caused measured against the expense, practical inconvenience or difficulty, and usefulness of the security measures *not* employed to determine the reasonableness of your decisions and whether or not negligence occurred (Risk and Reliability Associates, 2003). When choosing not to employ certain security measures you must weigh the significance of the risk and the effort and resources needed to reduce it, and be prepared to defend your choices.

Personnel

The term 'security' encompasses the protection of property as well as the personnel used to maintain a safe and secure event environment. Depending on the type and scope of the event, you might use volunteer event stewards, in-house or venue-supplied guards, private security company personnel, and/or uniformed police. In some cases peer or volunteer personnel in event staff shirts may be more acceptable to or appropriate for an audience than uniformed security guards or law enforcement personnel. In other contexts, the presence of highly visible security may provide a feeling of safety and prevent the outbreak of violence or vandalism. In all cases security personnel should be trained observers and enforcers.

- *Contracted*: An outside company or private firm that supplies uniformed security personnel. The company may require a Private Patrol Operator's (PPO) license to conduct business and supply security guards (IAEM, 2004) and security guards may need to be licensed as well (Van der Wagen and Carlos, 2005). Some guards may be authorized to carry weapons.
- *Law enforcement*: Officials whose primary responsibility is to maintain law and order and protect the public safety – not the event's business interests (Somerson, 2003). Officers may be restricted to outside a venue unless there is a public disturbance. Off-duty police might be used but they will likely be required to respond to outside emergencies if needed. They may be uniformed or undercover (plainclothes), should be used for ejections and arrests whenever possible, and should be the only personnel authorized to carry firearms at an event.

Table 5.6   Security firm assessment factors

Scope of work	• Schedule, locations, duties
	• Performance standards
	• Chain of command
Personnel selection procedures	• Past employment and reference checks
	• Background checks (criminal records)
	• Polygraph/psychological/aptitude testing
Training programs	• Classroom training and materials
	• On-the-job training and testing
	• Continuing and advanced training
Supervision	• Supervisor ratio
	• Response capabilities
	• Employee evaluation reports
Operating procedures	• 24-hour/365-day operations
	• Uniform provision
	• Emergency response
Administration	• Insurance coverage
	• Financial stability
	• Contracts (including terms and conditions)
	• Employment practices (wages and benefits, records)

- *Peer*: Trained security personnel of the same general age and appearance as the audience. They are typically dressed in T-shirts or event-specific logo clothing and are often supplemented with and supported by uniformed security guards and/or law enforcement.
- *Personal*: Bodyguards or special security forces that provide personal protection for individuals. The level of protection is based on threat vulnerability. Their scope of authority and actions are often non-negotiable.
- *Proprietary*: Employed or subcontracted in-house security personnel provided by a venue or company employees of the client charged with protection responsibilities. Their scope of authority and actions may be negotiable, and they may be supplemented with other types of security personnel.
- *Volunteer*: Voluntary personnel charged with observation duties and directing people to the appropriate or authorized areas. They should not be required to perform any dangerous or confrontational functions. This type of security may include the active or passive presence of psychologically persuasive persons such as ministers and mothers known as 'God Squads' (Tarlow, 2002).

The need for personnel is based on the need for response (NFPA, 2005). Event organizations should always use a detailed request for proposal (RFP) outlining specific needs when outsourcing a security force (see Appendix D: Security plan worksheet), and then thoroughly assess the policies and practices of the firms under consideration, particularly their pre-employment screening, drug testing, and training programs (NFPA, 2005). This is both a sound procurement practice and the performance of the due diligence to prevent negligent hiring liability. Assessment criteria must be established in order to evaluate potential providers (Berlonghi, 1996; Fischer and Green, 1998). Factors that should be considered when selecting a contracted security firm are shown in Table 5.6. The criteria that should be considered in the performance evaluation are shown in Table 5.7.

Table 5.7 Security personnel performance evaluation criteria

• Appearance	• Discipline/judgment	• Response tactics
• Attendance	• Flexibility/adaptability	• Teamwork/cooperation
• Communication	• Initiative	• Work knowledge and attitude
• Customer service	• Integrity/ethics	
• Dependability/reliability	• Report writing	

Table 5.8 Typical security equipment

• Barricades	• Locks and key systems
• Cameras (still and video)	• Metal detectors (hand-held and walk-through)
• Cellular phones	• Motion detectors
• Closed circuit TV	• Protective lighting
• Contraband receptacles	• Security cages or cabinets
• Equipment malfunction alarms	• Traffic barriers
• Flashlights	• Two-way radios
• Gloves (for bag inspection)	• Vehicles (e.g., golf carts, four-wheel drive
• PA systems (e.g., loudhailers and recorded announcements)	vehicles)
• Intrusion alarms	• X-ray screening conveyors

Sources: Berlonghi (1990), NFPA (2005), and Silvers (2004a)

Security personnel should always be fully briefed on the event site and expectations, including the risk factors and vulnerabilities, procedural requirements, response duties, and personal demeanor. The attitude of security personnel can affect a situation positively (pacification) or negatively (escalation) (NFPA, 2005). They must not use excessive or unreasonable force nor abuse their limits of authority. Whether security personnel are used to conduct searches for controlled substances prior to admission to an event or they are used to assist with medical or emergency evacuations, they are part of the event team and part of the event experience. They should be employed and deployed in a manner that befits the goals, objectives, and purpose of the event, and they should provide comfort rather than confrontation (Silvers, 2004a). However, Rogers (2004) advises that all event staff should be trained in 'aggressive hospitality,' the observation and polite confrontation of suspicious behavior, which allows them to assist the lost or confused individual and warn those with criminal objectives that their presence has been noted, as well as staff awareness of suspicious packages or activity.

Equipment

The security plan and personnel may employ a variety of equipment and technology to support security operations and enhance their effectiveness (see Table 5.8). Technological forms of security, such as closed circuit TV cameras and other surveillance equipment, allow specific areas or activities in the event to be monitored constantly by fewer personnel. Security personnel assigned to control items or objects prohibited within the event area may use passive and active search methods requiring special equipment.

Consider this... 5.4

Mag and Bag

At the 2002 Winter Olympics in Salt Lake City, Utah, all people entering a venue were required to pass through the 'Mag and Bag' security inspection. This included all spectators, volunteers, contractors, athletes, officials, and dignitaries. They were required to walk through magnetometers (metal detectors) and submit their bags and any containers to a physical search to prevent prohibited items from being carried into the venue. All spectator tickets included this requirement in its instructions and recorded announcements reinforced the procedure as people approached venue entrances.

'Low-tech' equipment may also be employed, including simple flashlights for investigating under grandstands or stages, and the humble whistle to gain attention. If a threat is sufficient (a bomb, illegal drugs, or other dangerous vulnerability), canine sweeps, patrols, or package inspection may be in order. Special equipment may also be necessary to allow security personnel to effectively communicate with supervisors and event organizers, as well as move to and through the event site to respond to incidents. In addition, an important part of the security plan is the documentation of incidents and conditions, which may become evidence in lawsuits and/or evaluations, and security personnel should always have the materials needed to provide this documentation (e.g., clipboards, cameras, tape recorders).

Two of the most effective preventative security devices are access credentials and proper lighting. Access credentials (to be discussed further in Chapter 12) should be a primary precaution employed at any event, and may be as simple as a badge or as sophisticated as an electronic key card. Badges may be color-coded by area or date authorization, and colors should be changed daily depending on the duration of the event, including set-up and tear-down, and security personnel must be trained to recognize the credentialing system. All event and subcontracted vendor personnel should be required to wear identification badges to prevent thefts, tampering, and other criminal activity. Security lighting should illuminate all event activities, areas, perimeters, and sensitive locations or equipment to discourage or deter intruders or criminal acts by making detection certain (NFPA, 2005).

Deployment

Deploying the appropriate security measures and personnel depends on the identification of vulnerabilities – those areas, items, and people that require protection (see Table 5.9). The number and types of security personnel and equipment will be dictated by the identified risks to persons and property, and the requirements and capabilities of the venue or event site. Deployment includes the schedules and areas, posts, or positions where security personnel are assigned, and encompasses the duties the various personnel must perform. Proper deployment should prevent duplication of effort as well as lack of effort (leaving things undone or ignored).

Security personnel should be deployed and equipment positioned in a manner that provides increasing stages of protection (NFPA, 2005), as illustrated in Figure 5.5. The use of physical or psychological devices and methods to discourage undesirable

Table 5.9   Typical security deployment

- Admission points
- Alcohol service zones
- Cash collection points
- Concealed areas
- Critical assets
- Critical operations
- Delivery areas
- Equipment installations
- Event offices
- Exhibit areas

- Exit points (property removal inspection)
- Stage areas
- Food and beverage set-ups
- HVAC systems
- Parking areas
- Perimeters
- Public areas

- Registration areas
- Restricted areas
- Roving
- Storage areas
- Utility controls
- VIP and media areas
- VIP personal protection

Sources: IAEM (2004), Shuster (2003), and Silvers (2004a)

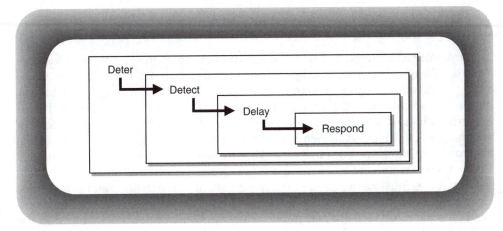

Figure 5.5   Elements of protection

action is the first level to be employed. Next, one must be able to detect if, when, and where an undesirable action or intrusion has occurred. Obstructions should be used to impede or limit the action or intrusion if it occurs. Counteractive measures are then used to interrupt or neutralize the action or occurrence. Somerson (2003) advises that defensive strategies should prevent, isolate, and then contain a situation, and the deployment of procedural and technological tactics must be sufficient for the response to be timely and effective.

   Security personnel must be provided with clear instruction regarding where they are to be, what they are supposed to be protecting, how long they are to be doing their job (beginning and ending times), and the procedures for responding to actions, occurrences, or conditions that might be encountered. It is advisable to also explain why they will be doing this, particularly for volunteer personnel. Berlonghi (1996) advises that you must clarify the areas of responsibility, actions, and rationale of the job assignment, the rules and regulations pertaining to one's conduct, and the specific actions for responding to various incidents.

These instructions may be the basis for an RFP or tender brief, which becomes the responsibility of the contracted security firm to incorporate into their job descriptions and post assignments. Event organizers should not attempt to directly manage contracted or facility security forces; they should only define their needs and expectations, including specific or emergent vulnerabilities, and leave the supervision of implementation to the security firm to limit liability and increase accountability (Silvers, 2004a).

Job descriptions should focus on the purpose and objectives rather than detailed specifics to facilitate flexibility appropriate to the situation. For example, one might specify the need for security patrols around the floor of a trade show to guard against thefts or the perimeters of a festival to guard against unauthorized entry. Such patrols should be conducted at irregular intervals so that perpetrators cannot time their activities according to a scheduled absence (NFPA, 2005), and stipulating a specific schedule could be counterproductive. In addition, increases or decreases inherent in the fluctuation of crowds might dictate more surveillance be conducted or be focused on specific areas at certain times.

Communications

Communications between and with the security personnel must be planned for carefully (see Table 5.10). Getting the right information to and from the right people will be critical, particularly in an emergency situation. The event risk manager should seek the advice and counsel of the appropriate law enforcement and other safety and security authorities to determine the appropriate types, levels, and deployment of security, and the most effective and efficient communication strategies and protocols, based on the type, purpose, scope, site (and vicinity), activities, and audience of the event.

The chain of command and control must be clearly defined and all the appropriate security forces must be included in the development of the policies and procedures. Obviously, as the intent, extent, or content of the event increases in size or threat vulnerability, the more security and public safety entities will become involved in the event protection strategy. Each agency or entity will have its own internal hierarchy that must be coordinated within the overall command structure. Protocols must be established that clearly define which agency or entity will be responsible for what, and when and how command is transferred from one to another.

Military, law enforcement, industrial security specialists, crowd management specialists, and other security experts all agree on the need for an incident command center or joint operations center (JOC) to serve as a central site that co-locates security agencies and operations and serves as the centralized hub of on-site communications (Beene, 1992; Berlonghi, 1990; BOMA, 2001; Emergency Management Australia, 1999; FEMA, 2001; Fischer and Green, 1998; Hanna, 1994; HSE, 1999; U.S. Army, 1985). Whether an on-site trailer, office, room, booth, or simple table at the

Table 5.10 Elements of the security communications plan

• Chain of command	• Media/public relations policy
• Command post	• Procedures and protocols
• Equipment	• Represented groups
• Information needs	

back of the room, this command post should be established from which the stewards, guards, or other security personnel are deployed, and through which all security-related communications take place.

On-site communications equipment may include telephones and mobile phones, multi-channel two-way radios, pagers, the public address system, and hand-held loudhailers. It will be important to establish which entity will provide what equipment and how these will be integrated into the communications plan. Radio frequency allocations and message authentication protocols may be required, equipment exchange and/or interfacing may become necessary, and visual signals such as flags or hand and arm gestures may be employed (U.S. Army, 1985). Event-specific equipment such as projection screens and variable message boards may also become part of the security and emergency communications arsenal.

External communications strategies must also be devised. This can include security and safety advice and advisories for attendees and participants disseminated prior to and during an event. Tarlow (2002) advises that security pamphlets and warning signage be developed that includes information about people and things to avoid, safety and security tactics, and emergency procedures. Public relations communications in general and procedures for crisis situations in particular must be established (to be discussed further in Chapters 8 and 9) and integrated into the security communications network.

Incident response and reporting

Although many of the situations listed below may seem outside the realm of most special events, primarily due to the typical celebratory nature of events, it is important to realize that as the stakes and stakeholders rise in value and visibility, and the audience and activities increase in scope and scale, such incidents become more possible and probable. And, in today's world, terrorism and agenda-motivated violence cannot be discounted.

- Bomb threats
- Crimes
- Defections
- Demonstrations
- Disorderly behavior
- Evacuations
- Explosions
- Fire
- Hostage/kidnapping situations
- Illness/injuries
- Man-made disasters
- Natural disasters
- Property damage
- Riots/crowd panic
- Terrorist acts
- Violence

Security personnel will most certainly be involved in responding to such incidents, as might other responders including law enforcement, medical personnel, rescue personnel, and others. Many of these incidents will be discussed further in Chapter 6, but the event's security forces (peer, private, proprietary, volunteer, or contracted) must be prepared to handle the initial response because they will most likely be the first on the scene. They must know what and what not to do, who to contact, and what their level of authority and responsibility is. Make certain the training and briefing is commensurate with the responsibilities surrounding the response to an incident or condition, and provide written instructions for specific threats (see Appendix E: Sample instructions for security personnel).

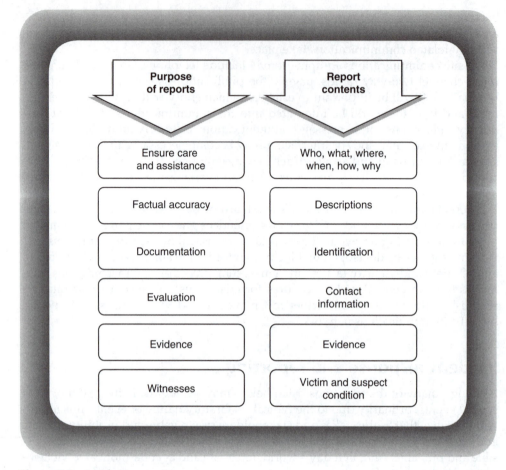

Figure 5.6 Incident reports

An incident report should be written for each and every incident or condition that occurs (see Figure 5.6). These reports not only serve as evidence for law enforcement and liability protection in lawsuits, they are critically important to the ability to anticipate and analyze future event security plans and procedures. As Berlonghi (1990) notes, incident reports must be factual, unbiased, and accurate. They must be prepared on-site, at the time of the incident, so that the individuals are interviewed correctly and the actions and/or conditions observed are recorded properly. Security personnel must be provided with the materials (incident forms, witness interview cards, pens, cameras, etc.) and the training on how to properly complete the documentation required (see Appendix K: Sample incident report form).

Incident logs should also be kept so that patterns of injuries or incidents can be identified and investigated. For example, numerous cases of gastrointestinal distress could suggest a food safety problem with one of your festival's concessionaires and recurring incidents of theft near the back of the trade show might indicate that there is an unlocked door at the rear of the hall that should be locked or guarded.

The incident reporting system should have a centralized data entry methodology to ensure information collected can be used effectively, allowing risk managers to show that decisions and strategy recommendations have been made based on data rather than instinct (Somerson, 2003). After action reports that enumerate the lessons learned and recommendations for future events should always be prepared. It is important that you be able to identify what worked well and contributed to the safety and security of the event as well as the challenges encountered that must be overcome, both of which serve as examples in future security planning.

Summary

Risk could be defined as a situation wherein losses could occur. No event is, or ever could be, risk free; there will always be exposures to risk. The role of risk management is to prevent and/or reduce the potential loss associated with such exposures, which may be achieved by implementing the proper safeguards. Knowing the risks and being prepared to compensate for and finance them will make the event organization risk resilient.

Loss prevention encompasses prevention, detection, control, contingency planning, and recovery, and must be financed with the appropriate resources, including the purchase of insurance coverage as a risk response strategy. The use of an insurance professional skilled and experienced in events will be an important contributor in securing the proper insurance coverage to transfer risk liability.

Security, a key component of loss prevention, relates to both the protection of people and property and the personnel used to maintain a safe and secure event environment. A security plan must be devised based on the risks identified and the resources required to respond. Security measures should be examined and employed throughout the event planning process, including physical and procedural deterrents and communicating event rules, regulations, and advisories to event attendees and personnel in advance. The type and level of security will have an impact on the image or marketing objectives of the event, but should always be based on the established protection priorities and the objective of avoiding opportunities for dangerous or criminal acts by anticipating and controlling access, invisibility, and indifference.

Key Strategies

- Identify and integrate no-cost or low-cost loss prevention tactics as standard operating procedures.
- Calculate the amount of the potential loss to determine the level of protection to invest in.
- Develop contingency plans that will allow you to work around the condition or incident with as little disruption to the event as possible.
- Find an insurance broker that has experience in the type of events you produce, or spend the time to educate the broker using your risk assessment.
- When procuring security services clearly specify what needs to be protected and when in an RFP that is based on a thorough risk assessment.
- Select the right type of personnel for the event context; pop concert security is different from conference security and providing personal protection is different than guarding property.
- Let attendees know what to expect regarding security issues and procedures in advance with advisories as appropriate.

Chapter review challenge

1 Compare and contrast the strengths and weaknesses of the loss prevention tactics illustrated in Figure 5.2.
2 How could epidemics such as SARS or avian flu affect attendance at your international meeting or tourism festival? What contingency plans might you devise and what insurance coverage might you procure to compensate for this?
3 How would you define the difference between safety and security? What duties would you assign to a Safety Director and what duties would you assign to a Security Director of a large event such as a public festival or a big convention?
4 Suppose you are having a controversial speaker at your convention that will surely attract demonstrators. What strategies might you use to accommodate yet control them?
5 List the components you would include in an 'aggressive hospitality' training program for your event staff.

Practical risk management exercise

You are coordinating a three-day collector car show at a major expo center that includes an auction of American and European classic cars, muscle cars, custom-built hot rods, and celebrity vehicles. Approximately 1300 hundred bidders from throughout the U.S. and 14 countries are expected as more than 400 cars will cross the auction block over the three days, and many of these buyers are planning to pay in cash (total sales at last year's event were $22 million). The ticketed gate show also includes 250 exhibitors offering related goods and services as well as souvenirs and collectibles to the estimated audience of 5000 each day, but the auction itself is only open to qualified bidders.

The exhibitor set-up schedule is from 8:00 a.m. to 6:00 p.m. on Wednesday and Thursday; the show is open to the public from 10:00 a.m. to 5:00 p.m. on Friday, Saturday, and Sunday; and the exhibitor tear-down schedule is from 5:00 p.m. Sunday through 5:00 p.m. on Monday. Twenty-five of the celebrity vehicles, scheduled to be auctioned off on Sunday, will be on display in the center of the main exhibit hall (Hall A), with the remaining vehicles garaged in an adjacent exhibit hall (Hall B) until their appearance on the auction block situated inside a third adjacent exhibit hall (Hall C). The exhibit hall used to garage the vehicles (Hall B) is open to the public for an additional fee (free to registered bidders), but the auction block hall (Hall C) is only open to registered bidders, which is where they will obtain their buyer credentials and conclude their purchases at the registration office (open from 9:00 a.m. to 6:00 p.m. on Friday, Saturday, and Sunday).

Prepare a security plan for this event that illustrates the following:

- *Who*: the number and type of security personnel and equipment to be used.
- *What*: the functions security personnel and equipment are to serve.

- *Where*: the post assignments where security personnel and equipment are to be deployed.
- *When*: the security schedule.
- *Why*: the risk factors identified in a risk analysis and why the personnel and equipment you selected will serve the security needs of the event.

Key terminology

Closed circuit TV (CCTV): Television monitors programmed from one source only and closed to all outside broadcast or cable services, often used for security surveillance with cameras focused on various areas of a building or property.

Contractual security: The use of an outside firm or private company to supply individuals for the purpose of protection and loss prevention.

Incident: A term used in liability coverage to describe any negligence, accident, or omission that may later result in a claim or lawsuit.

Incident report: Documentation that records details about an incident, accident, or occurrence.

Indemnification: Compensation for loss by the repair, replacement, or payment of the value of a loss.

Insurance broker: A professional who negotiates the buying and selling of insurance coverage between individuals or companies and various insurance providers.

Intrusion detection alarm: A device that will signal when a restricted area has been entered; may be an audible alarm or a silent alarm that sends a message to a control center.

Magnetometer: A walk-through or hand-held device that detects metal objects.

Peer security: Security personnel of the same approximate age as the audience, often in event-specific logo clothing rather than uniforms.

Personal security: Security personnel that provide private protection for individuals; also known as bodyguards.

Premium: The money paid for an insurance policy.

Proprietary security: The use of company employees charged with the responsibility of protection.

Screening: An investigation to determine suitability and discover security risks or prior criminal activity.

Security deployment: The schedules and areas, posts, or positions where security personnel are assigned.

Stewards: Personnel charged with the security function of observational guarding as well as providing audience comfort, direction, and other welfare assistance.

Vetting: The process whereby background checks are conducted to determine whether someone poses a threat, often requiring the provision of full name, address, birth date and birthplace, and passport or Social Security number.

Online resources

American Society for Industrial Security (ASIS)   www.asisonline.org
Federal Association of Security Officials (Canada)   http://faso-afrs.ca

IAAM Safety and Security Task Force	www.iaam.org/CVMS/CVMSsafety.htm
International Professional Security Association (IPSA)	www.ipsa.org.uk
National Australian Security Providers Association	www.naspa.com.au
Security Industry Authority (U.K.)	www.the-sia.org.uk
Security Management Online	www.securitymanagement.com
South African Security Industry Associations	www.security.co.za/associations.asp

Chapter 6
Emergency preparedness

Prepare when it is calm

This chapter will examine how to:
■ Determine the proper emergency response procedures and services for the event project
■ Prepare and implement an effective emergency action plan
■ Determine and secure the appropriate level of medical services for an event based on the type, scope, site, and audience
■ Identify, notify, and integrate plans with the proper authorities and emergency responders

Introduction

Emergency preparedness is a discipline and a condition. As a discipline, it is delegated to public safety professionals and often mandated by governments to ensure its citizenry is protected in situations that threaten the health and welfare of humans, damage to the environment, and threats to homeland security due to acts of God, human accident or intention, or technological failures. The condition of preparedness is the objective of governments, businesses, event organizations, and individuals to ensure emergencies can be dealt with quickly, safely, and effectively, although this is not always a certainty.

Various governments and organizations use different terminology for the discipline and the various degrees of emergency including civil protection, crisis management, disaster management, and emergency management. The event risk manager should become familiar with and use the terminology of the jurisdiction in which the event will take place. For our purposes the following terminology is suggested:

- *Crisis*: A sudden or evolving situation that results in an urgent problem that can turn into a catastrophe.
- *Disaster*: A situation or event that exceeds normal response capabilities requiring the use of assets beyond a jurisdiction's scope of resources.
- *Emergency*: A condition, situation, or occurrence that is or is believed to be endangering life or property and that requires an urgent response.

The event risk manager must consider and prepare for the possibility of small and large incidents occurring before, during, or due to the event. Emergencies or disasters can cause damage, losses, injuries, and fatalities and may be precipitated by unforeseen, unpredictable, or uncontrollable actions or conditions (or they could actually be foreseeable, predictable, and controllable as is often identified in postmortem investigations). They may occur within an event or outside the event; either way, they can have an impact on the event and its ability to operate. No event is immune.

Consider this... 6.1

Disasters, terrorism, and event incidents

1996: Atlanta Olympics bombing

1999: Texas A&M bonfire collapse; Troitsa Festival disaster in Belarus

2000: Puerto Rico Day parade in New York City; Pearl Jam concert at Roskilde Festival; dance hall fire in Luoyang, China; São Januário soccer stadium crush (Brazil)

2001: Wedding hall collapse in Jerusalem; Ellis Park soccer stadium disaster (South Africa); Taliban terrorist bombing at concert in Bangladesh; September 11th attacks on the World Trade Center and the Pentagon

2002: Bali nightclub bombing; Moscow theater siege; Ukraine air show disaster

2003: Hurricane Isabel; SARS, mad cow disease, avian flu; Rhode Island nightclub fire; northeast U.S. power grid blackout; Jakarta Marriott hotel bombing

2004: Four Florida hurricanes; train bombing in Spain; Indian Ocean earthquake and tsunami

2005: London Underground bombing; hurricanes Katrina and Rita; Christmas party crowd crush in Slovenia; Bangladesh Hindu festival stampede

2006: Hajj pilgrim disaster at Jamarat Bridge; Philippine stadium stampede for game show tickets; fire at consumer products fair in Meerut, India

Emergency management

Emergency management encompasses the identification of possible emergencies, the assessment of their potential impact on the event and event population, determining the appropriate responses and the resources available to respond, the protocols for declaring and responding to an emergency, and the event organization's and its audience's ability to react appropriately. The event risk manager must consider organizational and regulatory policies, support services, facility capabilities, training programs, evacuation plans, communication methods and messages, personnel, equipment, vehicles, and current events (the political, social, or atmospheric climate occurring during the event).

Widespread guidance identifies the scope of emergency management as a four-part approach as shown in Figure 6.1, often described as the life cycle of a disaster. The two proactive phases of activity – mitigation and preparedness – include the assessment of potential threats and the capacity to deal with them should they occur.

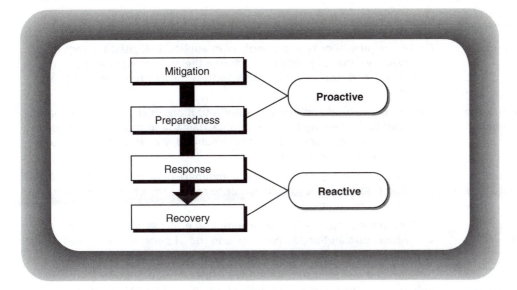

Figure 6.1 The scope of emergency management

The response and recovery phases address the activities undertaken when it becomes necessary to react to an incident or condition and its consequences once it has occurred.

Event organizers are not responsible for managing a major emergency or disaster if it occurs; this is the duty of the local authorities. However, there are two important reasons one should understand what emergency management professionals do and how they do it. First, the event organization needs to know how to react to and interact with responders to an emergency. They have a system and procedures that will go into effect once they are called in, and although you will surrender control to the responders, you will still have responsibilities to your constituents (e.g., attendees, staff, suppliers, etc.). Second, the tactics and protocols they use should be emulated in your own plans because these principles and procedures have been proven to be effective. The core elements of emergency management functions are shown in Table 6.1 and may be used to assess the emergency management capabilities of your event organization.

Mitigation

Mitigation is an important first step in the management of emergencies because it involves identifying and understanding the types of emergencies, large and small, that could occur at an event and then developing strategies that will eliminate those hazards that can be avoided and reduce the impact of the others should they occur. Awareness is fundamental to the ability to properly prepare for, respond to, and recover from the direct and indirect consequences of an emergency (Crown, the, 2005a). This is part of the duty of care owed to attendees – the due diligence that the event organizer should conduct. Organizers also have a responsibility to the hosting organization to implement appropriate loss prevention strategies to ensure its interests are effectively protected during an emergency. These two realms, the attendee

Table 6.1 Major emergency management functions

Laws and authorities	Confirm legal authority and comply with applicable legislation, regulations, and industry codes of practice that define the emergency powers, authorities, and responsibilities, and address the needs for revisions that evolve
Hazard identification and risk assessment	Identify the natural and human-caused situations or conditions that have the potential of causing injury to people, damage to property, or damage to the environment, and analyze the likelihood, vulnerability, magnitude, and consequences of incidents
Hazard mitigation	Develop and implement strategies to eliminate hazards that constitute a significant threat to the jurisdiction or to reduce the effects of hazards that cannot be eliminated
Resource management	Develop methodologies for the prompt and effective identification, acquisition, distribution, accounting, and use of personnel and major items of equipment for essential emergency functions
Planning	Develop and maintain comprehensive strategic, emergency response, mitigation, recovery, and continuity action plans that specify roles, responsibilities, and lines of authority
Direction, control, and coordination	Develop the capability to manage response and recovery operations using a suitable incident management system that complies with applicable statutes and regulations and is based on the resources available
Communications and warning	Develop and maintain a reliable and interoperable communications capability to alert public officials and emergency response personnel, warn the public, and effectively manage response to an actual or impending emergency
Operations and procedures	Develop and implement policies, plans, and procedures to support response and recovery operations that address life safety, incident stabilization, property and environmental protection, and management succession
Logistics and facilities	Establish logistical capability to manage the identification, location, acquisition, distribution, and accounting of services, personnel, materials, facilities, and other resources procured or donated, including primary and alternate facilities from which to manage operations
Training	Assess training needs and develop training programs for public officials and emergency response personnel to create awareness and enhance skills necessary to execute effective response and recovery operations
Exercises, evaluations, and corrective actions	Conduct regularly scheduled tests and exercises to evaluate elements of response and recovery plans, procedures, and capabilities and take corrective actions as needed to ameliorate deficiencies
Crisis communications, public education, and information	Develop procedures and capabilities to disseminate emergency and awareness information to and respond to requests for pre-disaster, disaster, and post-disaster information from internal and external audiences
Finance and administration	Establish fiscal and administrative procedures in accordance with appropriate authority levels to support emergency measures before, during, and after disaster events and to preserve vital records

Sources: FEMA (2001), Haddow and Bullock (2003), and NFPA (2004)

and the organization, are both served when the potential threats are identified and contingency plans are put into place to mitigate them.

Consider this... 6.2

Bees for breakfast

Errol Ninow, specialist risk consultant with the firm of Alex Gintan Associates in Johannesburg, South Africa, recounts an event he attended at a local horse racing track that demonstrated a serious lack of duty of care.

Known as 'Breeze ups' or 'Breezing,' 2-year-old juvenile horses are shown to potential buyers the day before the auction sale. The event included a champagne breakfast for the wealthy and international buyers. The setting was perfect with clear skies and sunshine on a wonderful summer's day. People milled about the beautifully decorated tented areas admiring the iced fruits and other delicious breakfast delights being served. The commentator was extolling the virtues of pedigree and conformation of the baby racehorses as each in turn galloped past the assembly of about one thousand people who had turned up to enjoy the day.

A catering truck pulled up behind one of the breakfast marquees and parked right on top of a huge African Bee's nest, which had made its home in the long grass. Within minutes the pick-up truck was virtually invisible beneath a swarm of bees. The honey, marmalade, and lush fruit on offer for breakfast were descended upon by the massive swarm of bees. The result was total chaos. People were running in every direction in a futile attempt to avoid being stung by the bees. The screams of agony and fear could be heard hundreds of meters away. Attendees were helping one another to cars and driving those badly stung to local hospitals for medical attention. Some were allergic to bee stings. Fortunately no one died, but for half a dozen people it was touch and go with their lives hanging in the balance. Here's how the event organizer was crucified at the postmortem:

1 No medical personnel were deployed
2 No ambulance was available on site
3 No local hospitals had been advised of the event
4 No competent safety officer or person in charge
5 No emergency planning was done
6 Access and egress was on foot only to the breakfast site, which was actually in the middle of the race track
7 The PA system could not be heard clearly 120 meters away from the site
8 No emergency telephone numbers were available (local hospitals, etc.)
9 A proper site inspection had not taken place

Threat assessment

The event organizer or risk manager needs to examine the potential causes or conditions that could create an emergency situation. A threat is defined as the intent or capacity to cause loss of life or create harmful consequences to human welfare, endanger the supply of essential services and supplies, cause severe damage to property or the environment, or jeopardize national or personal security. This could include natural, human-made, or technological threats, and may be related to the event location, timing, activities, or attendees. They could have a sudden or slow onset, and could occur a considerable time or shortly before an event or during it. They could occur at the event, adjacent to it, or elsewhere completely yet seriously affect access or attendance.

Everything from catastrophic natural disasters to technological failures to weather patterns should be examined (see Table 6.2). Is the event site vulnerable to a nearby industrial accident? Is the location subject to severe meteorological conditions such as hurricanes, tornados, or snow and ice storms? Is it subject to geological disasters such as earthquakes or land subsidence? How would a power outage affect the event activities or an epidemic or pandemic affect the attendance? One must also be aware of the social, economic, and political atmosphere; upheavals can cause disruptions, decline or collapse of service capability, and may be grounds for complete avoidance (cancellation).

It is incumbent upon the event risk manager to research the possibilities and contemplate what actions or strategies should be employed to reduce the negative impact should any of these disasters occur before or during the event. Conduct the necessary investigations to identify the types of historical, geographic, geopolitical, technological, and regulatory hazards that exist (Wahle and Beatty, 1993). For example, a meeting organizer might secure facility or area crime statistics from local law enforcement or a festival organizer might secure weather statistics from the weather service. All event organizers need to pay attention – not only to the internal conditions of the event and event organization, but also the world outside the insular microcosm of the event project.

Review the types of emergencies that have occurred at similar events, at that event location, and at other facilities in the area. Look at the proximity of the event site to geographic features and hazards such as seismic faults, bodies of water, major airports, or facilities that produce, use, or transport hazardous materials. Consider the results should a technological system fail (e.g., power, computers, heating/cooling systems). Carelessness, misconduct, substance abuse, lack of training, fatigue, and other factors can result in emergencies caused by human error. The location, design, construction, or layout of a facility or structure may enhance safety or pose hazards. Look at the regulatory requirements pertaining to the event audience, activities, and providers. Look at everything: the event, its surrounding area, the critical infrastructure in the community, and the situations in the world at large.

Terrorism

With every actual or threatened terrorist incident that occurs, intense concern grows as the incident or threat is covered extensively in the news media, which is precisely what the perpetrators are hoping for. The actual casualty statistics from terrorist incidents, although sensational due to their nature, are small. That is not to say that terrorism should not be a concern for event organizers because, in today's world, such acts are possible anywhere at any time and guidance suggests that planned public events may be prime targets due to the large number of people in attendance, the certain sensational and emotional impact, and the guaranteed media coverage (FEMA, 2001). Cetron, DeMicco, and Davies (2006) predict that the amount of terrorist activity is likely to increase throughout the world in the upcoming decade and advise that hotels, restaurants and clubs, transportation systems, and major sports events are particularly vulnerable.

Table 6.2 Potential threats (variable according to geographic location)

Natural

Biological	• Disease (plague, smallpox, anthrax, West Nile virus, SARS-type disease, influenza epidemic/pandemic, foot and mouth disease, rabies)
	• Infestation (animal or insect)
Geological	• Earthquake
	• Landslide, mudslide, subsidence, coastal erosion, avalanche
	• Tsunami
	• Volcano
Meteorological	• Extreme temperatures (sudden/prolonged, heat, cold)
	• Fire (forest, range, urban, urban/wild-land interface)
	• Flood (river, flash flood, seiche, tidal surge)
	• Rain or electrical storms (thunderstorm, deluge, lightning)
	• Snow storms (blizzards, ice, hail, sleet)
	• Wind storms (tropical cyclone, hurricane, typhoon, tornado, gales, water spout, dust/sand storm)

Human-caused

Accidental	• Air pollution/contamination
	• Building/structure collapse
	• Communications systems interruptions/failure
	• Energy/power/utility failure
	• Equipment failure
	• Explosion
	• Fire
	• Food contamination
	• Fuel/resource shortage
	• Hazardous material (Hazmat) spill or release (chemical, radiological, biological)
	• Mechanical failure
	• Medical trauma
	• Transportation accident (rail, aircraft, watercraft, vehicles)
	• Water control structure failure (dam, levee, reservoir)
	• Water pollution/contamination
Intentional	• Arson
	• Bombs, bomb threats
	• Civil disturbance, public unrest, mass hysteria, riot
	• Crime, criminal disorder, gang violence
	• Electromagnetic pulse
	• Military disturbance (enemy attack, war, insurrection)
	• Incursion (rivalries, protests, refugees)
	• Kidnapping, hostage taking
	• Psychological crisis (person threatening harm to self or others)
	• Sabotage
	• Strike
	• Terrorism (conventional/explosive, chemical, radiological, biological, cyber)

Sources: Crown, the (2005b), NFPA (2004)

Mitigating actions include standard safety and security precautions such as procedures for handling unattended packages or unauthorized parcel deliveries, conducting pre-event security sweeps of the site, limiting concealment areas where weapons or perpetrators may be hidden, and employing appropriate admittance controls (FEMA, 2001). It should be noted that although responding to terrorist (and other intentional) incidents may be the same as any other emergency in terms of life safety and property protection, such incidents will fall under the control of law enforcement and special tactics may be required to preserve important evidence (Crown, the, 2005a).

Mitigation through contingency planning

Determine the critical operations and assets of the event (e.g., key people, revenue sources, information, infrastructure, etc.) and focus your efforts on protecting them with contingency plans. As discussed in Chapter 5, contingency plans should be developed to mitigate the consequences of the identified threats by addressing the disruptions that will occur. Define the potential impact of the incident on human welfare, property, and the business of the event. Determine what internal and external preventions and protections exist; decide if you are willing to live with that. Then decide how you will respond should a threat manifest itself and support that decision with the appropriate funding, physical and human resources, and planning.

- What will you need to do if severe weather requires event postponement or cancellation?
- What will you need to do if there is an interruption or loss of power, telecommunications, or other utility services?
- What will you need to do if local transportation service is interrupted due to damage or a strike?
- What will you need to do if all your computer systems go down?
- What will you need to do if the facility you were to use has been destroyed by a fire or flood?

Contingency planning is necessary for both the small scale interruptions to the ability of the event to continue as planned and being able to withstand the consequences of a large scale emergency or incident. If the threat or its consequences are too great, or the resources available to mitigate the consequences are too meager, the decision to avoid must be seriously considered.

Preparedness

Preparedness includes all the plans made and actions taken to ensure the capability to respond to an emergency. Event organizers and/or risk managers should conduct an assessment of the external and internal resources, capabilities, and capacity for responding to an emergency with the objective to coordinate and integrate response activities (see Figure 6.2). Identify the existing plans, programs, policies, and response resources of the jurisdiction's public safety authorities, review those of the event organization, and determine what gaps or resource conflicts need special attention (Wahle and Beatty, 1993). Berlonghi (1996) advises that meetings with these authorities can be very beneficial to the event organization because, in addition to providing a

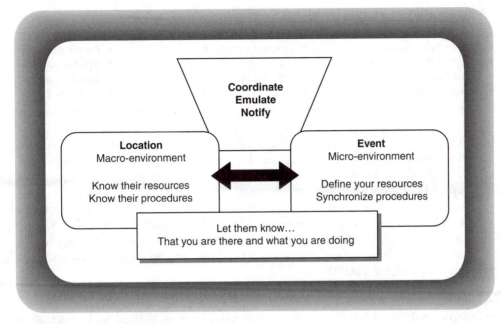

Figure 6.2 Capability assessment and integration

clear picture of what will happen should an emergency occur, they will also give the event organization insights into how it can synchronize plans and procedures in its emergency action plan. At the very least, such meetings will be an opportunity to let the local authorities know what to expect regarding the nature and activities of the event and to ensure those authorities include the event in its response activities should an emergency occur.

Identify the type, quantity, response time, limitations, capacity, and costs of the resources that will be used to respond to an emergency, which can include personnel, equipment, supplies, energy sources, communications systems, medical services, food and water, and shelter (NFPA, 2004). Also determine if or how those resources might be restricted or appropriated in a community-wide disaster. For example, is the facility you are using designated as a shelter or the last resort refuge in the event of a severe weather incident? If so your event space, supplies, and equipment might be appropriated for use in response activities. Are any of your vendors designated and contracted as suppliers in the community's response plans? If so they may become unavailable or unable to respond to your needs (e.g., busses or power generators) because the government's resource needs are going to take precedence.

Emergency action plan

Emergencies must be planned for by preparing detailed plans (see Table 6.3). This could include how to quickly and effectively transfer authority from the event organizers to the lead emergency response agency, the designation of assembly areas for evacuees, the use of public address (PA) systems to cellular telephones for communications, or the need for a first aid kit to a fully equipped on-site mobile hospital. The level of response to be provided by the event organization will depend on its legal responsibilities, the event context, and the services available.

Table 6.3 Emergency response planning considerations

• Authority transfer	• Evacuation plans	• Personnel
• Communication plan	• Lighting	• Sheltered areas
• Equipment	• Media plan	• Special needs
• Escape routes	• Medical response	• Vehicles

In order to protect life and limb within a crisis or disaster situation, there must be a specific, reasonable, and agreed-to plan of response that can be implemented efficiently and calmly. Every event project should have a formal, written emergency action plan (EAP) that addresses the arrangements for emergencies not requiring outside help and for those that do. It should clearly describe what will be done by whom, when, where, and how (Emergency Management Australia, 1999; FEMA, 2001; Hannah, 1994; HSE, 1999). Such plans must be clear, unambiguous, and easy to use, include robust notification and activation procedures, and be supported by adequate resources (Crown, the, 2005b).

- Identification of the emergencies the organization is prepared to handle.
- Clearly established internal and external roles, responsibilities, and structure of authority.
- Decision protocols for declaring an emergency and when, by whom, where, and how warnings will be issued.
- Monitoring systems, personnel, and protocols (early warning significantly improves outcomes).
- Notification of the type and location of the emergency situation to and from a central point.
- Activation of fire/evacuation alarms or other warning or audience notification systems.
- Evacuation of the premises by everybody who does not have specific duties to perform.
- Shutdown of machines, appliances, or equipment, securing records and cash, and safe storage of chemicals or materials in use.

Virtually all assembly occupancy facilities in the U.S. are required to have an EAP, which should be incorporated into the event's emergency planning – when and if the facility provides you with a copy. Some facilities are hesitant to release their EAP for security reasons, but if so, you should have them provide you with the salient points necessary for you to coordinate and cooperate with them. At the very least have the facility provide a staff tour through the facility to familiarize them with the layout of the facility, emergency exits, and the procedures for contacting in-house security or emergency personnel. The contents of a site-specific EAP, according to U.S. Occupational Safety and Health Administration (OSHA, 2002, 2005), are shown in Table 6.4.

Event-specific plans should include individual action plans for the most likely emergencies according to the event location and activities (see Appendix F: Emergency plan worksheet). For example, an event held in a tornado-prone area might have specific instructions regarding warning alarms and shelter locations, and an event including controversial topics or presenters might include instructions on what to do if a bomb threat is received. These instructions may be printed on separate sheets or cards for distribution to the appropriate staff.

Table 6.4   Emergency action plan elements

Range of emergencies	• Common and facility-specific sources of emergencies • Impact such emergencies would have on operations • Devised response strategies
Reporting procedures	• Preferred methods and instructions for reporting emergencies • Reporting to external responders • Internal reporting protocol according to type of emergency
Notification and warning systems	• Alerting personnel (including disabled) of actions to be taken according to type of emergency • Distinctive alarms for different alerts • Independent power source
Evacuation policy and procedures	• Conditions and authorization protocol for declaring an evacuation and issuing an all clear • Escape route assignments for different areas of the facility • Exits and routes clearly marked and sufficiently posted
Emergency shutdown procedures	• Utilities (gas/electric) shutdown locations and instructions • Critical systems and/or equipment shutdown procedures • Shutdown responsibility assignments
Shelter-in-place procedures	• Conditions requiring a shelter-in-place (e.g., storm or biohazard) • Shelter location, equipment, and supplies • Personnel responsibilities, including personalized supply kits
Accounting procedures	• Designation of assembly areas where evacuees are to gather • Method for ensuring everyone is accurately accounted for • Protocol for identifying and reporting last known locations
Rescue and medical responsibilities	• Location and use of common emergency equipment • Names and duties assigned to qualified personnel • First aid equipment and procedures
Personnel training	• Orientation and training on roles, responsibilities, and procedures • Schedule of practice drills • Specialized training and retraining requirements
Key contact lists	• Names and numbers for personnel assigned duties (including alternates) • Names and numbers for personnel that can clarify plan aspects • Names and numbers of key personnel to be contacted during off-hours emergencies

Training

Two of the most common problems with emergency response plans include personnel not knowing what actions to take in an emergency and the lack of training and practice for those who have been assigned duties. All event staff, volunteers, and other personnel expected to play a role within an emergency action plan must be provided with the proper training and sufficient opportunity to test the equipment and protocols they will be asked to employ in the event of an emergency. They must know how to summon help, how they will receive instructions, what their duties and responsibilities are, and the limits of their authority. Training activities provide desensitization to the crisis, allowing individuals to proceed with their assigned responsibilities – doing what they need to do to get through the emergency.

Conducting training exercises are also important from an evaluation perspective because they can help identify planning weaknesses and resource inadequacies, and test the efficacy of the command and communications structures (Berlonghi, 1996). Debriefings should always be included after any exercise, drill, or simulation to allow the personnel involved to articulate their concerns about skill levels, expectations, and shortcomings as well as potential emotional effects.

Response

Emergency services personnel are the best trained and equipped to handle emergencies, and you should recognize and include them when planning your internal response plans. Emergency responders include variety of public and/or private safety agencies designated to respond to emergencies of various types as established by a jurisdiction's emergency response plan. The primary emergency response services to be considered include fire, police, and medical response, but other response services may be included based on the event's location and activities or the scope of the incident (see Table 6.5). The event risk manager should have full contact information for all applicable responders.

Depending on the size and type of event being held and the activities to be conducted at the event, emergency response services may be required on site during the event or may simply need to be accommodated efficiently if response is necessary. For example, although having firefighters and firefighting equipment on site is not typically necessary (other than the requisite fire extinguishers), if the program included pyrotechnics then personnel and equipment would likely be mandated. High-risk events such as powerboat or automobile races and air shows will require significant on-site emergency services for participants and spectators.

If on-site emergency personnel and equipment are not required, the response time for firefighters, police, and ambulances to come to the rescue must be determined. The access routes for emergency services to the event site must be open and direct, and these routes might need to be dedicated exclusively to this purpose. For large

Table 6.5 Possible responders to an emergency

• Aeromedical (e.g., Medivac)	• Maritime/coastguard agencies
• Coroner (if deaths occur)	• Military organizations
• Emergency management officials	• Political officials
• Emergency medical services	• Port authorities
• Environmental control agencies	• Private emergency organizations (e.g., Red
• Event officials	Cross/Red Crescent)
• Facility contractors	• Public information officers
• Facility owners/operators	• Risk managers
• Fire departments/brigades	• Search and rescue teams
• Hazardous materials teams	• Security personnel
• Health and safety personnel	• Ski patrols
• Insurance inspectors	• Technical experts
• Law enforcement	• Transportation authority
• Lifeguards/divers	• Utility department officials

events or expansive event sites, the event organizers should provide all emergency response services with a grid overview map of the event site so response to the right place within the event site will be quicker. If emergency services personnel are on site during the event, they should be provided with full access to all areas of the venue, including performer and other restricted areas, and must be provided with the appropriate access credentials to ensure such access is not given to imposters.

Crisis communications

One of the key elements in a crisis or emergency action plan is the collection, protection, and dissemination of vital information. An emergency communications system needs to address and enable the notification of emergency responders regarding the existence and nature of the emergency, and inform the affected publics (attendees, staff, participants, and providers) about the actions that need to be taken. One of the hazards of a poorly crafted communications plan is that dangerous vulnerabilities may be created due to people being uninformed or unconvinced about conditions or consequences. Haddow and Bullock (2003) advise that a communication plan must have the following attributes:

- Be responsive and informative and manage expectations.
- Provide information and combat misinformation.
- Be timely, accurate, consistent, and easy to understand.
- Prevent confusion and maintain credibility.

Communication plans must also include the strategies and protocols for informing the internal and external publics regarding the status of the emergency through a designated spokesperson and a specific media plan. When dealing with the media, your objective is to tell your story before someone else tells it for you (Regester and Larkin, 2002). Designate an area where the media may work, provide an interview area that will accommodate cameras, provide escorts to other areas of interest, and have a one-page handout for the media on the background history and nature of the event (Hodge, 2005). Additional guidance on media plans and spokespersons will be covered in Chapter 9.

The event organizer should develop an event-specific communications plan that includes such strategies as creating and distributing an emergency contact list to staff and volunteers; collecting emergency contact information from attendees and designating someone to call the emergency contact should an attendee become ill, injured, or die; designating someone to follow up with attendees who were treated and released; and arranging for emergency message boards, Web sites, and call-in centers. This plan should be integrated with a facility's plan, specifying the duties and responsibilities the event staff will assume on behalf of the event organization.

A specific who-to-contact protocol should be established that identifies the hierarchy for notification and the individuals (and their alternates) charged with notifying emergency response personnel. Guidance may also be included on the use of cellular phones, which may or may not be reliable in certain circumstances, and the most effective emergency numbers. For example, cellular phone calls to the universal emergency telephone number (e.g., 911 in the U.S. and Canada, 112 or 999 in the U.K., 112 in the E.U., 000 in Australia, 120 in the mainland of the Peoples' Republic of China) may require the provision of information such as exact location and caller identity for the proper dispatch of services, and calls to the in-house emergency number may be more appropriate or effective when in a hotel or convention center.

Recovery

Being prepared for an emergency includes being able to live through and carry on after an emergency. All emergency management or disaster plans should include post-incident recovery components. These recovery strategies may encompass anything from the recovery from the psychological and emotional trauma by the personnel and participants involved in the emergency to the administrative, financial, promotional, and operational recovery of the event organization.

Examining the recovery responsibilities and tactics employed for a major disaster illustrates the most extreme consequences, which can then be scaled down for the event organization according to the severity of the incident. The recovery functions the authorities will be undertaking are shown in Table 6.6 and may serve as a guideline for the actions the event organization may also need to conduct.

A disaster takes the scope of an emergency into a mass casualty situation with a broader impact than simply the event itself. It should be noted that a casualty is a person that has been either injured or killed and a victim is a casualty or a person directly impacted by the incident. The first priority is the protection of people and getting them safely out of danger should a crisis or catastrophe occur. Then the emphasis is on consequence management and the continuation of services.

Consequence management encompasses the actions necessary to prevent the escalation of an emergency's impact by protecting public health and safety, restoring essential government services, and providing relief to governments, businesses, and individuals affected by a disaster. In the U.S., for example, the Federal Emergency Management Agency (FEMA) has existing arrangements with 26 federal agencies and the American Red Cross that may be involved in response and recovery operations including the emergency support functions of transportation, communications, public works and engineering, firefighting, information and planning, mass care, resource support, health and medical services, urban search and rescue, hazardous materials, food, and energy (Haddow and Bullock, 2003).

For the event organization, particular attention should be focused on the care and treatment of its affected publics including the attendees, participants, and personnel, including the injured, uninjured survivors, the deceased, and the family and friends of casualties (Crown, the, 2005a). Medical treatment for the injured, from on-site first aid to transportation to a medical facility, will be an immediate need. Short-term shelter and first aid will likely be needed for uninjured survivors who could be suffering shock, anxiety, or grief, or may simply need assistance with contacting friends and relatives or finding alternate transportation or temporary accommodations. They will also be important witnesses in any incident investigations and interviews will likely need to be conducted. Fatalities will fall under the jurisdiction of law enforcement and the coroner's office, yet it may fall upon the event organizers to assist with identification and family notification.

Family and friends will be deeply and urgently concerned about the status of the incident and the condition of their loved ones, sometimes resulting in overloaded communication systems. Call centers may be set up by response agencies or the event organization to accommodate incoming inquiries. Care must be taken to authenticate the relationship of the inquirer to the casualty to ensure confidential information is not released, and one should never release the name of a victim until the next of kin is notified. Sheltered locations may also need to be set up for survivors and relatives

Table 6.6 Disaster recovery activities

Containment	• Account for personnel • Provide medical aid and preserve life safety • Activate or establish triage, treatment, marshalling, and shelter areas • Isolate incident scene and maintain security to protect undamaged property and potential evidence
Command and control	• Initiate incident stabilization procedures to reduce suffering and loss • Establish recovery organization structure and staffing • Ensure continuity of management with succession plans • Coordinate and collaborate with response organizations • Develop action plans
Care and assistance	• Provide victim and survivor shelter and assistance • Provide emotional support and deal with psychological trauma • Respect victim dignity and privacy • Promote self-help and empowerment
Assessment	• Assess range and scope of property damage and begin debris clearance and salvage operations • Conduct situation assessment to identify infrastructure outages and status of critical facilities and services capabilities • Conduct on-going risk assessments • Conduct incident investigations with appropriate government agencies • Conduct needs assessment to estimate resources required for victim assistance and to restore critical services
Communications	• Activate notification procedures for victims and survivors • Maintain contact with response organizations, authorities, vendors, insurance carriers, and other stakeholders • Initiate public information procedures to prevent rumor, misinformation, and speculation • Coordinate and conduct public relations and media activities
Finance and administration	• Activate contracting and purchasing authority and procedures for necessary expenditures • Maintain accounting records and damage-related cost estimates • Submit insurance claims and requests for loans, grants, and government assistance • Plan for transition to normal operations
Resource management	• Establish priorities for restoration and acquire alternate facilities and equipment as necessary • Identify organizations and government agencies that can supply support • Coordinate support from internal and external sources including donations of funds, goods, and services
Documentation	• Maintain comprehensive records of all events, injuries, decisions, and follow-up actions • Collect photographic and videotaped evidence of the incident scene • Preserve vital records, incident records, and recovery records • Prepare after action reports and capture lessons learned

Sources: Berlonghi (1996), BCPEP (2005), Crown, the (2005a), Haddow and Bullock (2003), OCIPEP (2006), Tarlow (2002), and Wahle and Beatty (1993)

waiting information about missing family and friends to provide welfare and protect them from the more aggressive and less reputable media.

Consideration must also be given to the effects an emergency could have on the event operations if the emergency occurs before the event is scheduled to take place. If a disaster occurred at a destination you had selected for an upcoming event, you will want to know its recovery capability and prognosis. In addition to the condition of the facility and event-specific services you had contracted, you must assess the condition of the other attributes and attractions that contributed to the selection of the site, as well as the location's infrastructure in general. For example, although a premium destination prior to hurricane Katrina in late August 2005, projections indicate that it will be at least 2008 before a high percentage of meeting planners will schedule their conventions in New Orleans again (Cain, 2006). A planned event could not realistically be postponed for three years, therefore alternate arrangements would need to be made, and quickly, in order to proceed within a reasonable time period.

Evacuations

Events typically involve large numbers of people gathered in a limited space. Therefore it is important to understand the characteristics of and techniques for effective evacuations of an event site or premises. The need to evacuate an event site could occur for any number of reasons including natural, accidental, or intentional emergency incidents, with severe weather the most probable for outdoor events and fire for indoor events. Berlonghi (1996) notes that there are three intentional reasons for evacuation including remedial – in response to something that has taken place; precautionary – in anticipation or for the prevention of a dangerous situation; and tactical – in response to a specific warning and targeted area, often related to geological or meteorological threats and hostage or terrorist situations.

Consider this... 6.3

NCAA game delay

March 16, 2006: The Cox Arena at San Diego State University was evacuated when a hot dog cart attracted the attention of two bomb-sniffing dogs during a security sweep about two hours prior to the first-round game in the National Collegiate Athletic Association tournament, an immensely popular national college basketball championship. The start of the game was delayed by about 70 minutes as the concession cart was investigated and another full security sweep was conducted. The teams and fans had not yet entered, but some personnel and vendors were inside the 12 000-seat arena and were evacuated, and all were kept at a safe distance until it was determined there was no danger to the public. In an effort to get back on schedule for the nationally televised series of four games that day, pre-game warm-ups for the teams in the second contest were moved to a nearby gymnasium and the transition time allotted to clear and refill the arena between the first and second sessions was reduced, which resulted in many fans missing the starting portion of the second-round game.

An evacuation plan delineates the decision-making procedures, audience communication methods, and exit route configuration and condition. As noted in Table 4.2, the evaluation of the efficacy of an evacuation plan will include the nature of the event, nature of the occupants, crowd density, access/egress movement, means of egress, flow capacity, communications systems, and personnel preparedness.

Most public assembly facilities have detailed emergency and evacuation plans in place, but the event risk manager should not take this for granted. Unusual or undeveloped sites will require the creation of an emergency response plan including evacuation procedures, protocols, and means of egress. This should be prepared in consultation with the applicable emergency response services and public safety agencies. Typically it is a facility's legal responsibility to declare and instigate an evacuation in an emergency, and the event organizer has the obligation to comply and coordinate efforts with those in authority. Once official emergency responders arrive (e.g., police, fire department, etc.), they have authority over all other private entities.

The event organization should integrate its resources into the evacuation plan as appropriate. For example, security personnel and event staff may be used to help direct people at critical points along the evacuation route, and pre-determined gathering points away from the building or event space may be established where attendees and personnel may be accounted for. Any evacuation plan should also include specifics for assisting those with special needs such as those with mobility, hearing, or sight impairments and those who speak a different language, including any additional requirements or characteristics specific to the event production and audience.

Audience preparation is a key component of preparedness and successful emergency response (NFPA 101, 2000). Audience preparation for properly responding to an emergency begins before an emergency occurs by ensuring they are in a state of awareness. This may include pre-event communications and on-site signage, materials, and announcements.

Consider this... 6.4

The Special Event adopts author's recommendations

In 2005 The Special Event, the annual convention produced by *Special Events Magazine*, adopted my recommendation to request all presenters make fire safety announcements at the beginning of each session, and included the following instructions and script I wrote for them in their Speaker Information Packets:

- Please take a moment to review that attached guide to emergencies. As the person 'in front,' you WILL be the ones counted upon to interpret announcements, sirens, or alarm bells and to instigate a quick and calm evacuation of the space you are in.
- In all sessions please announce: 'In accordance with The Special Event's commitment to safety at ALL events, please note in case of emergency, leave by the nearest exit, which may not be the way you came in. Please look around now and locate the nearest exit to you.'

A Guide to Emergencies brochure provided by the Miami Beach Convention Center was also included in the Speaker Information Packet, which outlined their emergency capabilities and procedures for evacuation, fire, hurricane, and bomb threat, and included all the appropriate contact numbers.

Table 6.7 Factors of human behavior in fire

Occupant characteristics	Population size and distributed or concentrated density; alone or with others; familiarity with venue; location; age; physical and cognitive ability; focus on activity
Response to cues	Types of cues (visual, audible, verbal, olfactory, tactile); number and repetition of cues; familiarity with cues; credibility and clarity of cues; interpretation/perception of cues (peril/urgency)
Decision making	Amount, accuracy, and ambiguity of information; timing of information; number of alternatives; movement toward familiar options
Movement capability	Exit route quality, familiarity, clarity; flow capacity and merging of flows; speed; congestion; density; lighting; wayfinding; weather

Human behavior and movement factors

Safe and effective evacuation is not reliant exclusively on physical factors such as clear and unobstructed exit routes and signage. It must also incorporate the psychological behavior of the people involved in the evacuation situation. The Society of Fire Protection Engineers highlights the factors that contribute to the ways in which people respond to an emergency situation – a fire (SFPE, 2002). These factors are also applicable to movement behavior in practically any crowded or crowd situation. People's movement is based on the cues received, the pre-movement and trans-movement decisions they make about those cues, and the physical conditions facilitating or impeding that movement, as shown in Table 6.7.

Au, Ryan, Carey, and Whalley (1993) identify the response behavior process as to sense, interpret, plan/decide, and act; they identify the following factors that affect individual ability to perform these functions:

- *Ability to sense*: conditions in the environment; availability and clarity of information.
- *Ability to interpret*: content of information; information source; knowledge, experience, and expectations.
- *Ability to plan/decide*: knowledge and experience; goal and objective; alternatives and choices; consequences; mental condition and emotion.
- *Ability to act*: physical condition of the individual; physical characteristics of the venue; physical conditions at the venue.

Fruin (1984, 1993) identifies the four interacting elements in a crowd situation as time, space, information, and energy or crowd force, which significantly impact an evacuation egress. These can converge to create potentially fatal crowd densities due to bottlenecks caused by architectural configuration and inaccurate perceptions of conditions and urgency. Still (2001) characterizes the factors in emergency egress dynamics as objective (escape from danger), motility (individual movement speed), constraint (density and environment interactions), and assimilation (reaction time), and compares this model to Jonathan Sime's 13 egress assessment parameters including communication, mobility, social affinity, alertness, role, position, commitment, focal points, familiarity, visual access, crowd density, enclosure, and complexity. Mileti and Sorensen (1990) describe these as warning receiver attributes:

- *Environmental attributes*: physical and social cues (others reacting) and proximity in distance or time.
- *Social attributes*: network (family, community), resources (physical, social, economic), role (age, gender, responsibility, status), culture (ethnicity, language), and activity (working, resting, engaged in recreation).
- *Psychological attributes*: knowledge (of hazards, protective actions, plans), cognitions (stress, risk perception, locus of control), and experience (type and recency).
- *Physiological attributes*: disabilities.

What should be noted is that one of the common factors is experience or familiarity – familiarity with the hazard, the venue, the cues, the options, and the exit routes. Research shows time and again that, in an emergency, most people will try to leave the same way they came in, which is why it is important to familiarize attendees with their other options before an emergency occurs, and may indicate the need to employ stewarding personnel to redirect individuals to the closest or most appropriate exit.

The other common factor is information – the accuracy and authority of the information the individual is given that shapes their reaction and decision to start to move. Mileti and Sorensen (1990) contend that a warning system must incorporate the warning response process of hearing, understanding, believing, personalizing, deciding to respond, and confirming in order to take appropriate protective actions. The nature and the content of the warning will also have an impact on whether or not it is effective, including the warning source (officialness, credibility, and familiarity), channel (types and number of mediums used), frequency (number and pattern), and message attributes that make them convincing and reasonable (Mileti and Sorensen, 1990), shown in Table 6.8.

Fruin (1984) advises that people in a crowd situation cannot see the whole picture and are highly susceptible to rumor unless clear and complete communications take place, and stresses that a PA system must be connected to the emergency lighting circuit or other standby power source in case of a power failure. Still (2001) advises that people rely on authority figures in times of crisis and suggests that clear chains of command are almost equally as important as clear routes of exit.

Mileti and Sorensen (1990) suggest that frequent and official warnings help people focus on accurate information rather than rumor and inaccurate or non-official data. They also expose several myths about emergency warnings such as public hysteria, keeping information simple, the 'cry wolf' syndrome, the first warning instigates action, and people follow instructions blindly. People do not panic except when in a confined space and there is an immediate and clear threat of death or injury. People are information hungry in a warning situation and repetition is important. People will trust a new warning if the explanation is given regarding why the information in the previous alarm was false. Most people seek more information and validation of a warning message before taking action, often because they do not recognize what various signals (e.g., alarms or sirens) mean. People will not automatically follow instructions without the reason for them and that reason must make sense.

Berlonghi (1990, 1996) recommends the preparation of carefully worded scripts for emergency announcements that a well-trained announcer can deliver in a calm and authoritative manner. All such announcements should begin with a polite request for attention, end with a thank you, and be repeated a minimum of two times. Some

Table 6.8 Warning message attributes

Content attributes

Hazard	Described in sufficient detail so its characteristics are understood
Guidance	Direction regarding the protective actions people should undertake
Location	Identification of the locations at risk and the locations NOT at risk
Time	When they are to respond and how much time they have to respond
Source	Warnings need to come from credible sources that have authority

Style attributes

Specificity	Regarding hazard, guidance, location, and time
Consistency	Regarding the content factors and explaining changes if/as they occur
Certainty	Stated with confidence in a tone that projects calm and belief
Clarity	Use simple, declarative language
Accuracy	Must contain timely, accurate, and complete information

announcements may need to be coded fictitious welfare announcements, such as 'Will Mr. Able please meet your party at the event office' as an instruction to security personnel that a specific type of incident has occurred. Evacuation information and instructions may also be printed in event programs and posted on on-site signage for non-controversial circumstances such as severe weather or earthquakes.

Medical emergencies

The most likely emergency that will occur at an event is a medical emergency wherein someone has been injured or suffers from an illness that must be attended to immediately. It is estimated that one percent to two percent of an event audience will typically require medical attention during the course of an event; approximately 99 percent of these casualties representing mild to moderate injuries or illnesses that may often be handled on-site. Good sense and duty of care demands that the provision of emergency medical services (EMS) to respond to this must be carefully considered.

In order to assess the likelihood and potential severity of a medical emergency, the event risk manager should consult with the venue and local emergency medical responders such as ambulance services or other health authorities regarding the type and scope of the event, audience demographics and expected behaviors, and the size, location, and layout of the event site. Outdoor or undeveloped sites in particular need special consideration regarding geographic conditions and the anticipated weather. Special attention must also be given to audiences including the very young and the elderly, events of long duration, those including alcohol service, and events with a history of crowd disturbances (e.g., concerts or sports events). It is also important to include the pre- and post-event operations and personnel when planning EMS.

It is highly recommended that a medical services provider be appointed to oversee this assessment and develop, as well as deliver, the emergency medical response system for larger, more complex public events (Berlonghi, 1996; HSE, 1999). At the very least the event risk manager must determine the existing capabilities of the event venue and local community, and then develop the response plan accordingly. The capability assessment should consider the services available at the event venue, including the first aid facilities and equipment such as portable automated external defibrillators (AEDs), and identifying which staff members have been certified in first aid procedures such as cardiopulmonary resuscitation (CPR) and the Heimlich maneuver. Private and public ambulance systems and response times should be identified, and the location of and route(s) to the designated receiving hospital or the closest medical facility or emergency room to the event site should be determined.

Consider this... 6.5

Helicopters for medical evacuation

In the lead up to a community festival, a representative from the local hospital mentioned that there must be a space for helicopter to land in case there was an emergency. The festival takes place near the coast and the emergency helicopter is used for sea rescues, transporting victims of any accident at sea to the hospital. The festival committee's response to this problem was to 'rope' off a helicopter landing area. This was to make sure that the public would not be in danger and that the helicopter could land. On the surface this solution seems logical and one that most festival organizers would use to exclude crowds from an area. During the festival, however, the helicopter needed to land. When it came to the landing area the blades of the helicopter caused such an updraft that the rope was in danger of being sucked into the blades. The result was that the helicopter could not land in that space. The life experience of all the committee members did not include helicopter landings, therefore could not foresee such a problem. Had they discussed the plan with the aeromedical provider directly, and appropriate perimeter control strategy could have been devised.

Source: O'Toole (2006a), from EPMS CDROM, www.epms.net

Scope and level of on-site medical services

Guidance varies widely on what scope and level of medical service is sufficient at an event, primarily because every event is different. Berlonghi (1990) suggests that a registered nurse with a physician on call should be the minimum requirement for a small event. NFPA (2005) specifies that EMS personnel should be on site for events with crowds over 10 000, and the telephone number for calling them should be readily available at all events. Mass gathering manuals for Australia and the U.S. advise that events with fewer than 500 patrons and located in close proximity to ambulance or hospital services generally do not require on-site EMS personnel; at least one on-site first aid post with two trained personnel are required for any event with more than 500 patrons; two on-site posts and 12 personnel for events with 10 000 patrons; and that every event venue should have at least one designated climate-controlled first aid room with power and running water (Emergency Management Australia, 1999; FEMA, 2001). The Health and Safety Executive (HSE, 1999) in the U.K. suggests a formula that specifies, at a minimum, two first aid personnel per 1000 for the first 3000 in attendance at small events where no special risks are considered likely, and that no event should have less than two first aiders. Tarlow (2002) recommends a baseline of one EMS staff person per 1000–1500 participants and four paramedics per every 10 000 participants. Although there are no international standards there may be specific requirements in individual jurisdictions, therefore the event risk manager should always check with local authorities.

EMS can range from having an ambulance stationed on site, a first aid tent or room, or an on-site infirmary or hospital, and personnel can range from first aiders certified in basic first aid to emergency medical technicians (EMTs), paramedics, and registered nurses and physicians on site or on call. The factors to be considered will include the number of people expected (including personnel and providers), the environment, the activities, the audience demographics, and the access routes and response times for responders.

It is best practice for event organizations to ensure all their staff is trained in basic first aid. Such courses are affordable and widely available from such charity-based international organizations as the Red Cross or Red Crescent Societies and St. John Ambulance. Many of these societies and other community organizations often have experience in and are prepared for providing EMS to events at a reasonable cost (possibly partially deductible as a charitable donation), and a local hospital or health service organization might be willing to coordinate and provide this service as a sponsor at a large public event. Ensure that all volunteer or contracted EMS providers and personnel have the proper credentials and malpractice insurance (Berlonghi, 1996).

Site considerations for on-site medical services

In medical emergencies, quick response can mean the difference between life and death. The site considerations for positioning on-site medical services include the scope and layout of the area, how help will be summoned, how help will reach the injured person, and casualty extraction and transportation to the first aid station and evacuation to the hospital. All event staff and security should know the location and route to the first aid area or areas, and these positions should be on highly visible on-site navigational signage, identified in PA announcements, and printed in collateral materials.

Communication modes and methods must be established between event personnel and on-site medical personnel. All medical response personnel must have communications capability with off-site medical services. All on-site first aid personnel should be uniformed distinctively (e.g., T-shirts, tabards, or jackets) so that attendees will be able to locate the correct assistance in a crowd. These uniforms should be uniquely color-coded and words such as 'Medical' or 'First Aid Team' printed on them (Berlonghi, 1990). Of note, a red cross, as designed by and registered to the International Red Cross and its National Societies, should not be used unless officially sanctioned by them. A white cross on a green or dark background with the words 'First Aid' is often used instead.

Crowd density conditions may indicate the need for roving first aiders or medical teams on foot, bicycle, or golf carts. Injured person extraction might include hand-carried stretchers or golf carts equipped with litters for large event grounds, and evacuation could include ambulances, four-wheel drive vehicles for difficult terrain, or even a helicopter pad or landing strip for aeromedical response. It is not recommended that private vehicles be used for transport unless absolutely necessary.

On-site first aid facilities for patient evaluation and attention should be positioned to ensure rapid access from all areas of the event site and provide patient privacy (Silvers, 2004a) and it may also be important to consider religious, cultural, or ethnic requirements that may relate to medical treatment and gender proximity issues (Crown, the, 2005a). These facilities must be clearly visible and provide rapid and unobstructed access for the entrance and exit of ambulance service. If more than one first aid post is provided, one must be designated as the primary facility (HSE, 1999) and should be located near the event entrance or the location with the best ambulance ingress and egress capacity.

Medical incident procedures

Untrained personnel responding to a medical incident should immediately call for medical help, should not do more than they are trained to do, and should not attempt to move a victim unless it is necessary in order to remove them from imminent danger. Consent should be obtained from the victim, or the parent or guardian if the victim is a minor, before providing care (consent is implied if the victim is unconscious). The immediate vicinity should be cordoned off to protect the privacy of the victim and prevent further injury or interference with medical treatment by curious or concerned by-standers. An injury or illness incident report should be filled out for every medical contact made with event staff or medical personnel, even if minor, and especially if care or treatment was refused.

Incident reports, treatment logs, and refusal of treatment records must be documented and maintained for potential liability claims, public health and medical insurance requirements, and event history and statistical purposes. Medico-legal issues such as access to records, record and data retention, and consent forms must be considered when planning this documentation (Emergency Management Australia, 1999) and strict control must be exercised over the confidentiality of this medical information (Berlonghi, 1990) including medical condition and contact information collected prior to the event. For example, many convention and meeting organizers ask for emergency contact information (e.g., name and day/evening/cell phone numbers) as well as the name of the attendee's hotel in the registration process, which is then stored in a different database and discarded after the conference. Sport events often require medical information from participating athletes, also disposed off after the event.

Summary

Emergency preparedness is just that – being prepared to respond to and manage an emergency. Key components of managing an emergency or crisis efficiently are early warning, the unambiguous delegation of duties, and avoiding panic. In many event contexts and sites, emergency response plans are created and governed by local public safety agencies. This, however, does not excuse an event organizer from seeking out these plans and providers. It requires the event risk manager to confirm their existence and merge them into the event's operational plans, or in their absence create, organize, and implement them. The proper methods for monitoring the potential causes of an emergency situation, including precautionary measures and trained observers, must be incorporated into the overall event plan and operations.

The event manager or event risk manager should emulate and coordinate efforts with emergency responders, including access requirements, evacuation and the treatment of victims, and the protocols for multi-agency response or mutual aid agreements. Should an emergency occur, the appropriate response must be implemented, which could range anywhere from assisting or ejecting specific individuals to evacuating the entire event site. And in an emergency, attendees must be clearly informed of the situation and the appropriate behavior. They must be given credible and forceful information regarding the severity of the situation and practical instructions for the actions to be taken.

Being prepared is legally, morally, and professionally the right thing to do. Medical, fire, and weather emergencies occur all the time. Some are small, some large, and some catastrophic. It is far more likely that it will be the smaller emergency that you will need to deal with, but if a natural disaster such as hurricane Katrina can virtually destroy one of the most popular tourist and convention destinations in the U.S., it could happen where you are planning to hold your next event. It is your duty to be prepared.

Key strategies

- Liaison with applicable emergency response services and public safety authorities to become familiar with their procedures for emergency response and to ensure they are aware of your event and activities.
- Confirm that the event location and the facility have formal emergency action plans in place and that these are regularly tested with the appropriate drills.
- Create an internal, event-specific emergency action plan for every event.
- Create a contact list for all key emergency response services.
- Ensure there is a succession plan for people assigned key responsibilities or decision-making authority.
- Conduct audience preparation activities such as pre-event advisories and on-site signage and announcements.
- Determine the distance and directions from the event site to area hospitals and/or trauma center and the response times to the event site for ambulances.
- Ensure all volunteer, employed, or contracted event personnel know how to recognize emergency and medical incidents and how to summon the proper help.
- Ensure key event staff are certified in basic first aid, CPR, and the Heimlich maneuver.

Chapter review challenge

1 Identify the natural disaster threats in your geographical location (e.g., earthquake, tornado, etc.) and outline the ways in which you can be prepared to survive them. Assemble a disaster preparedness kit for your home (see Appendix G: Disaster preparedness supply kits).
2 When evaluating a potential event venue, what items would you include in your site inspection checklist regarding emergency preparedness?

3 **Create a chart of the various human behavior and movement factors identified by Au, et al., Fruin, Mileti and Sorensen, Sime, the Society of Fire Protection Engineers, and Still and discuss how these may be incorporated into evacuation planning.**

4 **Write evacuation announcements for a variety of causes (e.g., fire, severe weather, etc.) using the message attributes identified in this chapter, keeping in mind that a bomb threat should never be identified as such.**

5 **Contact your local EMS providers to determine the availability of first aid and CPR certification programs in your area. Become CPR certified.**

Practical risk management exercise

As the risk manager for the Main Street [your town] Arts Festival, you are charged with preparing the emergency action plan for this two-day outdoor event held over a three block area along the main city street in your downtown area. The event attracts 20 000 people each day and includes arts and craft vendors, food and beverage concessions (including beer and wine), children's activities, and highly popular concerts each afternoon and evening.

Using the emergency management functions shown in Table 6.1 and the EAP elements shown in Table 6.4 as a guide, prepare an emergency action plan that addresses the following range of emergencies:

- Weather
- Fire
- Security (criminal activity or civil disturbance)
- Explosion
- Medical emergency
- Bomb threat.

Key terminology

Advanced life support: Emergency medical care provided by trained paramedics including patient assessment, airway management, and early management of severe trauma prior to transportation to a hospital.

Automated external defibrillator (AED): A portable, computerized electronic device that provides on-going voice prompts to its operator to treat cardiac arrest by delivering an electric shock to re-establish an effective heart rhythm.

Basic first aid: Emergency medical care including airway management, bleeding control, and fracture or spinal immobilization.

Basic life support: Emergency medical care including airway management, resuscitation, artificial ventilation, intravenous therapy, spinal immobilization, and infection exposure management.

Cardiopulmonary resuscitation (CPR): A first aid maneuver used to restart a person's breathing and/or heartbeat.

Emergency action plan (EAP): A formal record of agreed emergency management roles, responsibilities, strategies, systems, and arrangements.

Drill: A training exercise wherein the participants walk through and/or perform the processes and procedures to be conducted under a real situation, often followed by an evaluation of the systems and problem areas.

Emergency management: The process and procedures used to assess, prevent, prepare for, respond to, and recover from emergencies.

Emergency medical technician (EMT): An individual trained to administer emergency medical care including airway management, AED, bleeding control, CPR, oxygen administration, spinal immobilization, and traction splinting.

Emergency responders: A variety of public and/or private safety agencies designated to respond to emergencies of various types as established by a jurisdiction's emergency response plan.

Emergency response plan: A plan developed by an agency, with cooperation of all the participating agencies, that details specific actions to be performed by all personnel who are expected to respond during an emergency.

Evacuation plan: A formal record of agreed procedures and routes for an emergency exodus from a building or site.

First aider: A person trained to administer basic first aid.

Heimlich maneuver: The application of thrusting pressure on the diaphragm to help expel a foreign body blocking the airway of a choking person.

Paramedic: An individual who has received extensive training in advanced life support including defibrillation, intubation, intravenous therapy, ventilator and IV pump management, and pre-hospital Trauma Life Support.

Receiving hospital: Any hospital designated by health authorities to receive casualties in the event of an emergency.

Response capability: Capacity or ability to respond to and recover from a particular threat or hazard.

Search and rescue (SAR): Operations for locating and retrieving persons in distress, providing for their immediate needs, and delivering them to a place of safety.

Shelter-in-place: Taking refuge inside an interior room with no or few windows, in your home or office or present location, in the event of the release of chemical, biological, or radiological contaminants.

Simulation: A training exercise wherein an actual situation is simulated as closely as possible and participants are expected to perform at the level they would if an actual situation.

Threat: The intent and capacity to cause loss of life or create adverse consequences to human welfare, the environment, or security.

Trauma center: A medical facility with specialized equipment and training for dealing with severe medical emergencies.

Online resources

Emergency Management Australia — www.ema.gov.au

Emergency Response and Research Institute — www.emergency.com

Federal Emergency Management Agency (U.S.)	www.fema.gov
International Federation of Red Cross and Red Crescent Societies	www.ifrc.org
National Center for Disaster Preparedness	www.ncdp.mailman.columbia.edu
Public Safety and Emergency Preparedness Canada	www.psepc-sppcc.gc.ca
St. John Ambulance (Australia)	www.stjohn.org.au
St. John Ambulance (Canada)	www.stjohnambulance.com
St. John Ambulance (New Zealand)	www.stjohn.org.nz
St. John Ambulance (South Africa)	www.stjohn.org.za
St. John Ambulance (U.K.)	www.sja.org.uk
U.K. Resilience	www.ukresilience.info
United Nations International Strategy for Disaster Reduction	www.unisdr.org

Part Three
Organizational safeguards

Every event is a complex business

Our festival is 30 years old and it's always been a success. Just have my administrative assistant organize the meeting. We've always done things this way and have never had a problem. Let's put on an event; it will be so much fun. What's the big deal … this isn't rocket science.

These common assertions reflect the misunderstanding of the serious business of events and the scope of activities required to produce one. A badly organized or poorly managed event is a very risky situation. And the fact that an event went well does not guarantee that it was well managed – it may have been just lucky! (Even for 30 years.) Luck has no place in the events industry, and luck certainly has no place in sound risk management practices. Good luck, or to put it more accurately the *illusion* of good luck, requires hard work – to paraphrase Thomas Jefferson, 'the harder I work, the luckier I get.'

There are countless parts to an event that must be linked together to create an effective business plan that achieves the purposes for having the event. And events must be approached as a business, complete with a robust organizational foundation and excellent business practices. The three chapters in this section will familiarize you with the interconnected and interdependent complexities of the business of events, including administration, communications and marketing, because the quality of the event's business practices will have a direct correlation to the type and scope of risks associated with that event.

Chapter 7
Administrative safeguards

Decisions made upstream affect results downstream

This chapter will examine how to:

- Allocate and direct the resources of the event in order to maximize the effectiveness of risk management
- Determine, control, and protect the tangible, intangible, and human assets of the event
- Analyze the extent and comprehensiveness of event preparations in order to manage the scope of risks
- Integrate the risk management plan throughout the organizational and decision-making systems of the event

Introduction

An event is a project, and the administrative functions such as time management, financial management, human resources management, and procurement management, and the systems used to implement and integrate them are typically included within the discipline of project management. The tools, techniques, terminology, processes, and procedures used by project managers in many other industries serve the event organization equally well, particularly in the pursuit of effective administrative practices and risk management.

Project integration, in particular, is critical in order to coordinate, synchronize, and merge the variety and multitude of interactions, dependencies, and interconnected elements and resources included in an event project. This is to ensure that decisions made incorporate all the factors influencing and influenced by those choices. The integration of risk management throughout the organizational structure and project planning helps manage of the scope of an event and its exposures to risk.

Scope management, one of the key tools the project manager uses to manage a project's resources, is comprised of scope definition and scope control. Scope definition is the specification of the sum total and the limits of the responsibilities and elements included in an event project, which are established within the design of the event program (the intent, extent, and content). The statement of work (SOW) and the work breakdown structure (WBS) define the responsibilities, elements, and tasks required to create the event (PMI, 2000). The definition of success, which comes from the host or key stakeholders, helps to identify those items and elements that must be included, should be included, and could be included. Establishing a sound organizational structure, business plan, and timeline will help define the resource allocation and logistical requirements as well as contain the scope by defining the sources of potential scope creep (changes to the scope) and the responsibilities and tactics for its control.

Time management

Time management is the establishment and verification of the timelines, production schedules, and schedule controls that will facilitate the activity architecture necessary to accomplish the tasks associated with the event project. As discussed in Chapter 1, every event project has a limited time dimension into which all the tasks required to produce the event must be scheduled. Being a limited and finite resource, time restrictions will determine the tempo of the event management processes, as well as define certain critical milestones and areas of risk. Kendrick (2003) advises that the sources of schedule risk fall into the three categories of delays, dependencies, and duration estimates.

Schedules will typically include the overall timeline that encompasses the entire scope of the project and a production schedule that will cover the event from move-in to move-out, both of which are created using the techniques shown in Figure 7.1.

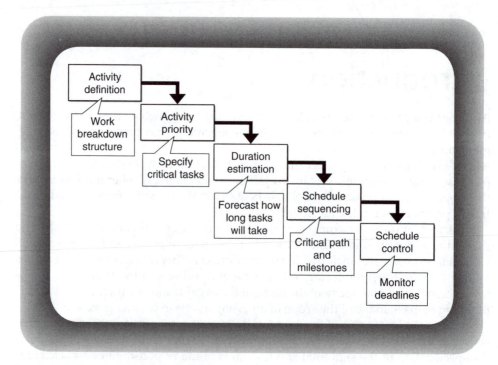

Figure 7.1 Development of a schedule

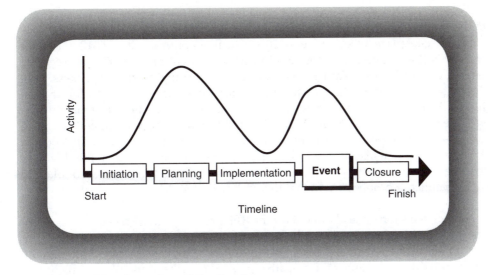

Figure 7.2 Activity dimension of the timeline

These schedules may be seen as time maps showing the scope and intensity of activity required in order to achieve objectives throughout the life-cycle of the event project, as illustrated in Figure 7.2.

Activity definition

The scope and deliverables of the event project must be clearly defined in the SOW, including the dates and times of the event and its components. Incomplete scope definition will lead to inaccuracy throughout the development of the timeline and will increase vulnerabilities throughout the event project. The SOW is then used to create the WBS, which may be approached from the top down – decomposing or carving the project into pieces, or from the bottom up – brainstorming the required activities and organizing them into clusters.

It is often useful to organize the WBS into the hierarchical categories (e.g., departments and committees) to be used for the organizational structure and the budget to facilitate integration and efficient tracking. Identify the various tasks and determine those whose responsibility it will be to accomplish them, and seek input from these individuals to uncover additional task requirements and potential constraints that could affect the efficacy of the schedule.

Consider this... 7.1

Peace conference causes controversy

After attending a peace conference in India in 2005 as an invited speaker, a state senator returned home in the U.S. with a vision to conduct a similar endeavor in his state. The senator introduced legislation during the 2005 and 2006 sessions and got approval for two consecutive budget appropriation requests for the conference, totaling $420 000. Both appropriations were transferred to the state's tourism department, which would be in charge of planning the conference, scheduled to take place in September of 2006. The first appropriation of $120 000, allocated on July 1, 2005 (the beginning of the fiscal year), was spent on forming an executive committee, issuing press releases, creating a web site, and contacting potential speakers.

The controversy started to brew when the tourism department put out a request for proposals (RFP) in June of 2006 to subcontract a new coordinator because the employee organizing the conference was due to retire on June 30, 2006. The RFP, published on the department's web site on June 20, 2006, required proposals be submitted no later than 4:00 p.m. on June 30, 2006. On July 1, 2006 it was reported that insufficient proposals had been submitted, and on July 17 it was announced that the tourism department was withdrawing its RFP, had hired an event planner (whom had not submitted a proposal), and that the conference would be postponed until May of 2007.

This postponement, the short-time allotment for the RFP process, and the revelation that only one speaker had been lined up just three months before the scheduled event all conspired to give the impression of poor management and misappropriation of taxpayers' money. Although the tourism department tried to counteract this negative press, the mishandling of the scheduling, especially in light of the known retirement date of the key staffer, brought a great deal of controversy to what was intended to be a public relations success. Had the tourism department released documentation that illustrated comprehensive project plans were in place, including a timeline with status reports, the tempest might have been averted, but no such documents were available, which fueled the claims of mismanagement of an ill-conceived venture.

Activity architecture: critical path analysis and sequencing

Activity architecture may be viewed as the structure of work incorporating the task dependencies, interactions, and priorities that will influence the sequencing of activity. This is often accomplished using the critical path analysis. In traditional project management, critical path analysis uses forward planning to identify the projected completion date, but in events management where the completion date (or time) is pre-determined (and typically immoveable), the critical path analysis is used as a backward planning tool (Getz, 1997; Silvers, 2004a; Tum, Norton, and Wright, 2006).

Dependencies, those tasks dependent upon prior completion of another task, must be clearly identified and given the proper precedence within the schedule. They must be closely monitored because delays here will affect the remainder of the schedule. Milestones (key deliverables) and deadlines should be established and dependencies that pose delay risks, the weakest links, should be highlighted (Kendrick, 2003). These milestones and deadlines often become the triggers and thresholds (see Chapter 2) for risk response actions. Development and use of a graphical tool (e.g., bar charts, flowcharts) to devise and communicate the critical path is widely recommended. Smith and Merritt (2002) recommend showing task connectors in bar charts to illustrate the critical path, and Thomsett (1990) urges the inclusion of decision and verification points in flowcharts so that critical choices and repetitive or alternate procedures are correctly applied.

Estimating the time it will take to complete tasks can be a significant challenge. Kendrick (2003) suggests that this is often due to optimism, over-confidence, lack of information, and scope creep. Yates (2003) calls this the 'planning fallacy' wherein the belief that we will accomplish tasks in less time than is actually required and the neglect of obstacles (i.e., best-case-scenario assumptions) when forecasting time needs leads to poor judgment. PMI (2000) recommends expert judgment and analogous estimating are effective tools, including the review of prior events to determine previous or chronic schedule variances.

Activity attributes and duration requirements must be identified and analyzed in the context of time restrictions and resource management. Time is linear and irreplaceable; the only way to expand time is to compensate by adding other resources, in other words, do more, be more productive within the time given. However, as Lewis (1997) points out, effective resource allocation is contingent upon the skill levels, capabilities, capacities, and outputs of the particular people and suppliers (i.e., a chain is only as strong as its weakest link).

Sequence and synchronize tasks in a chronological arrangement. Identify those tasks that must be conducted consecutively, those that may be performed simultaneously, and those that have flexibility (Lewis, 1997). Identify the tasks and their resources that could be diverted to critical path activities (Weiss and Wysocki, 1992), and provide redundant paths for accomplishing critical path activities whenever and wherever possible (Smith and Merritt, 2002).

Schedule development and control

Create a calendar-linked master schedule, including the agendas from all suppliers, that reflects the aggregate planning of the entire event project through all its phases. Identify areas where resource leveling and duration compression may be applied (PMI, 2000), and seek ways to minimize idle time for personnel and equipment, which can be expensive and often leads to subsequent time pressures that can create vulnerabilities and hazards as tasks are rushed and workers become frustrated and/or harried (Monks, 1996; Van der Wagen and Carlos, 2005). Make certain external or cultural restrictions such as holidays and holy days, seasonal implications (e.g., vacations or weather vulnerabilities), and working conditions (e.g., days of the week or limits on the number of hours per day) are factored in.

Develop a timeline that reflects the critical path and integration of the tasks to be accomplished (e.g., executing a venue contract will include the legal department, the site selection committee, the operations manager, various suppliers, and numerous other areas of responsibility) and distribute it to department heads. Verify the accuracy and efficacy of the proposed schedule with these key stakeholders. Make any necessary adjustments and then prepare and circulate individual schedules in the required detail based on the consensus schedule. These might include or be supplemented by timelines, Gantt or milestone charts, deliverable deadlines lists, production schedules, program agendas, or at-a-glance calendars.

Schedule control encompasses the monitoring of deadlines, tracking of performance, analysis of schedule variances, and usage of change control mechanisms. Smith and Merritt (2002) identify three primary reasons why it is important to be proactive about schedule monitoring and control:

- Late attention to problems leading to expensive workaround tactics.
- Late detection of problems precluding solutions available earlier.
- Late surprises limiting the time to develop adequate resolutions.

Create and implement performance measurement methodology that will signal schedule variances, indicate its magnitude, and guide corrective actions. As noted above, the earlier the problem is diagnosed, the more response and reaction time there is and options there are to overcome it. Develop and utilize change control mechanisms that will indicate a change is required, authorize that change, and integrate that change into the project scope and schedule. Make certain schedule updates are communicated throughout the event organization when any changes have been made, because no change is a small change (Augustine, 1997).

Financial management

The risk manager must have a good understanding of financial management in order to mitigate the financial risks associated with an event operation. Financial management is the development and use of budgets, proper costing and pricing strategies, standard accounting practices, and asset and cash flow management to achieve the financial goals of the event enterprise. Money, or its equivalent (e.g., goods or services), is necessary for any event to take place. There must be sufficient funding allocated to every aspect of the event organization and operation, including risk management, for the event to be realistically feasible.

The typical financial risks associated with events are shown in Table 7.1, many of which are preventable or controllable if the proper policies and procedures for accounting and budgeting are developed and consistently implemented. Legal compliance (operating legally) is the first line of defense against financial losses and the use of written contracts and change orders will control the scope of financial obligations and liability. Then, effective budgeting, sound bid procurement and evaluation practices, and sensible cash management procedures will enable one to anticipate income and expenses correctly, allocate financial resources properly, plus maintain the appropriate financial records.

Policies and procedures for operating legally

Every event and event organization should have a reliable accounting system that accurately records how, when, where, why, and by/from whom monies are expended and received, as well as the measurement of assets (e.g., money, accounts receivable), liabilities (e.g., accounts payable), and earnings. This system, and the bookkeeping functions associated with it, is best devised by or in collaboration with financial professionals such as certified or chartered public accountants. The financial data that is categorized, summarized, interpreted, and communicated through this system helps the event organization make good financial decisions (Silvers and Nelson, 2005).

Table 7.1 Typical financial risks for meetings and events

• Currency exchange fluctuations	• Lack of procurement policies
• Failure to track budget performance	• Theft, fraud, or fines
• Improper bookkeeping practices	• Uncontrolled spending
• Inaccurate revenue and expense projections	• Unexpected revenue reductions
• Inadequate cash flow	• Unforeseen or increased costs
• Insufficient or uncertain funding sources	• Vulnerable cash handling practices

The financial records and the policies and procedures used to document and control spending are essential to illustrate compliance with many of the legal requirements for doing business – and an event should be run as a business. One must be able to show shareholders, stakeholders, or auditors that there are sufficient and effective internal controls that safeguard assets and justify expenditures, and that these are implemented in a consistent and comprehensive manner. These controls might include, but are not limited to, the following:

- Bookkeeping procedures (e.g., transaction posting, coding underlying documents, etc.)
- Budget approval procedures (e.g., committees, client, governing board, etc.)
- Contract approval procedure (e.g., review by counsel, signing authority, etc.)
- Credit policies and procedures (e.g., extending credit, payables and receivables, etc.)
- Expenditure approval process (e.g., requisition forms, change orders, etc.)
- Procurement policies and procedures (e.g., RFPs, purchase orders, etc.)
- Refund policies and procedures (e.g., cancellation deadlines, prorated amounts, etc.)
- Reimbursement policies (e.g., per diems, expense reports, etc.).

Budget development and control

The budget is one of the primary planning documents used when organizing an event, and according to Bowdin, Allen, O'Toole, Harris, and McDonnell (2006) it is an effective control mechanism used to impose financial discipline and track the status of the event plan performance. When developing the budget, profit objectives must be determined (which influences pricing decisions), costs and revenues must be forecast, and financial resources must be defined and then allocated according to priorities. Then the budget performance must be closely monitored with budget-to-actual reports to identify and correct deviations in a timely and cost-effective manner.

Budgets are created in a progressive manner beginning with a draft budget based on conceptual estimates from historical records or comparable events (Bowdin et al., 2006; Goldblatt, 2002). This will likely be refined and validated by various event departments or committees and then approved by the client or governing entity. Although Berlonghi (1990) suggests that budget preparation should occur prior to operational planning, the final pro forma (projected) expense budget, which is based on quotes from and contracts with suppliers, is typically not completed until late in the planning process (Nadler and Nadler, 1987) because cost (and income) estimates are more accurate as the event nears (O'Toole and Mikolaitis, 2002).

Bowdin et al. (2006), Nadler and Nadler (1987), O'Toole and Mikolaitis (2002), and Van der Wagen and Carlos (2005) all emphasize that the budget is a plan, not a definitive document, and as such must remain flexible and responsive to changes that may be needed due to additional line item costs, revised priorities or opportunities, or if expected revenues (e.g., sponsorship money or ticket sales) under perform. Budgets reflect the decisions made about the event and communicate the income and expense estimates, which is not the same as authorizing expenditures (Nadler and Nadler, 1987). They should be used to show various departments or committees the projected spending limits (Bowdin et al., 2006), but it must be made clear how and by whom financial commitments may be made.

Consider this... 7.2

Host committee busts the budget

An international association typically held its annual educational conference in a city that had a local host chapter, with the host chapter expected to provide assistance in locating appropriate local vendors and content presenters and to cover the costs that exceeded the per person budget allocation of the opening night reception. The host committee was provided with the entire pro forma budget showing all categories and projections, and was relied upon to find local sponsors for increasing the quality of the reception and to forward all other supplier recommendations to the conference planner at headquarters.

Not understanding their limits, the host committee proceeded to enter into contracts and make purchases for all areas of the expense budget without approval from international headquarters, which ultimately put the final costs for the conference at nearly 30 percent higher than projected and resulted in a net loss rather than the profit that was expected for this important portion of the association's annual revenues. Immediately following this financial fiasco the association put together a policy manual that defined the procedures for authorizing expenditures and circulated it to all future host chapters, yet it still took several years before host chapter attitudes and spending could be completely reined in.

The structure and scope of a budget will vary according to the type, size, and governance of the event, but it should identify all sources of revenue and expenses in sufficient detail so that variations can be identified and corrected easily. This also facilitates the ability to make changes based on priorities rather than panic. When forecasting income and cost estimates, revenue projections should be conservative and expense projections should be generous. Examples of typical revenue and expense budget categories may be found in numerous meeting and event management texts (see, e.g., Bowdin et al., 2006; Connell, 2002; Goldblatt, 2002; Krug, 2000; Van der Wagen and Carlos, 2005).

The budget should also be integrated into the project timeline with cash flow and decision milestones carefully noted because changes typically increase in cost the closer one gets to the event (Bowdin et al., 2006) and last-minute changes can be expensive because there is little time or supplier impetus for price negotiation. Nadler and Nadler (1987) recommend a budget allocation of 3–10 percent to cover inflation and changes between budget approval and the time of the event, and Van der Wagen and Carlos (2005) suggest this contingency category be funded at 5 percent if there is confidence that costs are controllable and 10 percent if there are numerous variables or cost uncertainties.

Budgets should have pre-determined cost-cutting strategies integrated into the expense side linked with decision deadlines in the timeline in order to make changes that are guided by the prioritized goals and objectives of the event. Budget performance must be monitored closely to ensure these decisions minimize financial risk, maximize opportunities, and maintain the integrity of the event. Silvers and Nelson (2005) offer the following observations and suggestions:

- Link payables and receivables within the cash flow schedule.
- Develop creative cost-saving and cost-avoidance opportunities.

- Standardize budget categories for easy comparison.
- Prevent fraudulent activities with clear policies and procedures.

It is important to recognize that the expenditures allocated to risk management activities are often viewed as an expense that can be reduced when budgets must be cut because they seemingly do not directly contribute to the event content, environment, or experience. This faulty perception must be overcome with forceful justifications that defend these expenditures, reiterating the advantages of such investment and the liabilities for its avoidance. Spending money up front prevents having to spend even more money at the back end.

Costing and pricing

Costing and pricing are closely linked together because the cost of the event will determine the price of admittance to the event, or the feasibility of the event if admittance fees such as tickets or registration fees are not a factor. The purchase price ceiling (the maximum the buyer is willing to pay) for attending or hosting an event will affect what types and levels of goods and services can be included in the budget.

Profit requirements must be determined. Is this event meant to make a profit (and how much), break even, or to be hosted? If the event is expected to generate revenues over expenses or to break even, then a break-even analysis (also known as a cost-volume analysis) must be conducted that identifies at what point (number of attendees or per person admittance fee) the revenues will equal the expenses, and consequently at what point profits are generated. If the event is hosted, with the only revenue source being the host, a bottom-up analysis should be conducted, which calculates the sum total of all the costs and the 'price' the host will have to pay to fund the endeavor.

Accurate cost estimates require a very detailed list of line items that encompass all the direct and indirect costs, fixed and variable costs, time and opportunity costs (e.g., personnel numbers/skill levels, in-house/outsourcing, extending credit), cost of goods and services, selling costs, and countless 'hidden' costs (see Table 7.2). Make certain all bids and subsequent contracts specify all charges and potential charges

Table 7.2 Typical hidden or unanticipated costs

• Cleaning fees	• On-site technicians
• Commissions	• Overtime labor costs
• Comps and perquisites	• Parking fees and tolls
• Connection charges	• Resort fees
• Delivery charges	• Room set-up charges
• Import or export duty	• Service charges
• Gratuities	• Shipping and handling fees
• Installation charges	• Shuttle transfers
• Last-minute changes	• Sponsorship benefits
• Late charges and other penalties	• Taxes
• Maintenance fees	• Unexpected site preparation costs
• Meals for personnel	• Unforeseen equipment rentals
• Mileage reimbursements	• Usage surcharges (facility or utility)

Reprinted courtesy of Silvers and Nelson (2005)

(e.g., attrition or per person price increases if number decreases) to control unanticipated expenditures.

Cash flow and cash handling

Cash flow represents the financial 'life blood' and its circulation through the financial system of the event project. Without sufficient infusions of revenue at the right times, even the best-laid event plans will soon fail. In addition, because revenues typically do not start coming in before expenses must start being paid out for a high percentage of events (Silvers and Nelson, 2005; Van der Wagen and Carlos, 2005), funds in the form of capital must be identified and secured in order to safely operate during this deficit period. For annual events such as festivals or conventions, this capital most often comes from the profits from the previous event. One-off or first-time events must seek this capital elsewhere, often relying on sponsorship sales, government grants, credit, or deposits from the host or hosting organization.

Manage cash flow with a time-phased budget that indicates when revenues and expenses are expected in order to negotiate and schedule income and disbursements to your best advantage. This may include time-phased pricing strategies, providing or exploiting incentives for prompt payment or seasonal discounts, and establishing timetables for contractual deposits and other payables and receivables.

Cash, checks, and credit card transactions constitute the primary ways that revenue comes into the event and secure money handling procedures must be established to mitigate exposures to theft, fraud, and errors. From cash payments from petty cash to cash income from such things as ticket sales, registration payments, donations, or concessions at the event, these procedures must encompass all the ways that cash flows into and out of the event enterprise throughout the life-cycle of the event project.

Good office procedures are important for pre-event cash handling. For example, Berlonghi (1990) advises that pre-numbered cash receipts and petty cash vouchers be used and carefully monitored, and 'For Deposit Only' with the account name and number should be stamped on all checks immediately upon receipt. On-site cash management will entail preparing point of sale reports, preparing cash reports, reconciling cash, and processing debit and credit card transactions. Collections and monitoring cash handling at an event must also be supervised carefully so losses do not occur. Silvers and Nelson (2005) suggest the following on-site cash handling procedures:

- Set up a secure office or area with a lockable safe to serve as an on-site bank or treasury.
- Establish the issuance and closeout protocols for cash drawers.
- Make certain anyone that handles money on-site is bonded.
- Keep the numbers of personnel handling cash funds to a minimum.
- Schedule the periodic cash collection and cash drawer culling from cash collection points based on the volume of cash expected.
- Establish the counting procedure to ensure the amounts are recorded by location.
- Establish internal and external auditing procedures for ticket sales and souvenir sales (e.g., sales records, unsold tickets, and cash deposit receipts).

Financial reporting and record keeping

Accurate financial data drives quality decision making, authenticates successes, and illustrates weaknesses in the financial plan. Therefore, this data must be captured, interpreted properly, and communicated within an appropriate reporting and record keeping system that provides clear, accurate, and complete reports for stakeholders, staff, management entities, and governmental authorities. Tum et al. (2006) stress that this system must be capable of providing fast and accurate financial data in order to ensure the financial agility and stability of the event enterprise, which highlights the importance of meticulous bookkeeping procedures and the benefits of using technology such as financial management software.

Reports must be prepared at such times and in such a way that the financial data is presented in a manner that communicates the necessary information (in the appropriate context) to those receiving them. Financial statements must be prepared according to regulatory requirements and are generated at a variety of times and for a variety of purposes such as at tax time or when seeking loans or sponsorships. Financial records, including underlying documentation, must be retained as legally required and in such a manner that facilitates access in order to analyze and take advantage of the valuable information they contain. And because this information has value and is often proprietary, access to it must be protected and the release of it must be prudent.

Human resources management

It is widely recognized that people are one of the most valuable resources for an event, and guidance on strategies for managing the paid and volunteer human resources for events is available in numerous books on events management (see, e.g., Bowdin et al., 2006; Getz, 1997; Goldblatt, 2002; Silvers, 2004a; Tum et al., 2006) plus countless additional sources on human resources management in other contexts (see Online resources at the end of this chapter). Human resources management encompasses the formulation of the appropriate organizational structure, policies, and procedures for the recruitment, orientation, motivation, training, compensation, supervision, and discipline of employees, contracted workers, and volunteers according to applicable employment and labor legalities to provide a suitable and diverse workforce to meet the needs of the event project. The typical risks associated with human resources for meetings and events are shown in Table 7.3.

Table 7.3 Typical human resource risks in the events industry

• Abandonment of or at post	• Lack of job descriptions
• Abuse or neglect of employment laws	• Lack of policies
• Ambiguous reporting relationships	• Lack of recognition
• Criminal behavior or motives	• Lack of supervision
• Idle or bored workers	• Loss of key personnel
• Inadequate labor pool	• Overworked staff
• Inappropriate conduct	• Toxic personalities
• Incorrect scheduling and deployment	• Uncertain task/authority boundaries
• Inexperience	• Unclear or inappropriate expectations
• Insufficient number of personnel	• Unreliability
• Insufficient or ineffective training	• Unsafe working environment
• Labor union restrictions/disputes	• Unsanctioned decision making
• Lack or improper use of expertise	• Unsuitable attitude or aptitude

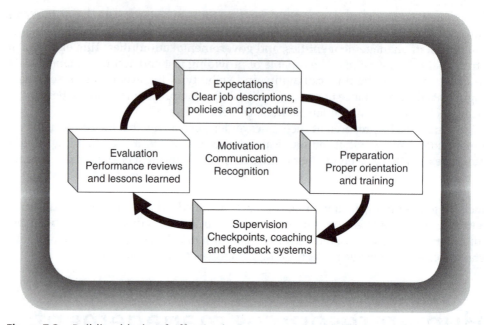

Figure 7.3   Building blocks of effective human resources management

Successful personnel management is dependant upon establishing and employing the basic building blocks shown in Figure 7.3. It must be noted that this represents a cyclical and integrated system that relies on building the organizational structure and culture that serves the needs of both the event enterprise and the people within it. Workforce planning must be conducted, roles and responsibilities must be determined, the hierarchy of authority and responsibility must be established, and job descriptions and selection criteria for personnel must be developed. Then staff and volunteers must be recruited, inducted, oriented, trained, assigned, guided, and rewarded in a suitable manner so that these valuable human assets are able to be productive and may be retained for continued success.

Building the organizational structure and culture

It takes lots of people to produce a successful event, even the smallest event. All their personalities, preferences, experience, functions, and levels of expertise will help shape the success of the event. Making certain all these people come together and perform efficiently and effectively is like putting together a puzzle. The organizational chart, sometimes called an organogram, is a graphical representation of the structure of authority (i.e., the right to determine and direct the actions of others) and responsibility (i.e., accountability for assigned duties) for the event operations or the event organization and will be the picture revealed when the puzzle is complete.

This chart should include all the necessary departments, committees, subcommittees, and/or event elements. It should illustrate the lines of authority – who is in charge of which elements, who is responsible for what, who can and will make decisions, and how they all relate to each other. It must take into consideration those stakeholders or influencers within the event organization and those outside the event organization in order to establish the appropriate chain of command and channels of communication.

The scope and arrangement of the organizational chart for an event will depend on the scope of the event and its elements, plus the various departments required to conduct the business of the event organization. According to Getz (1997) the organizational chart outlines the functions in a compartmentalized manner along with the inclusion and a clear definition of the governance structure of the enterprise. These charts should be comprehensive and descriptive yet, as Van der Wagen and Carlos (2005) advise, simple and streamlined enough to illustrate reporting relationships at a glance, particularly for emergency situations, which may indicate the need for macro- and micro-versions for different recipients.

Whereas the organizational structure defines the hierarchies, reporting relationships, and the way that work flows through the event enterprise, the organizational culture is shaped by what the organization does, its mission and values, its leadership style, in short – its personality. Many event organizations reflect a less bureaucratic system than other businesses might due to their very purpose (typically to create and produce a jovial gathering), but this makes it even more important to ensure that the span of control, limits of authority, and channels of communication are clearly defined and specified within the organizational chart.

Getz (1997, p. 136) warns that although a less formal or team-oriented structure may facilitate a certain level of camaraderie and efficiency, it 'can subvert policy and control processes' and Silvers (2004a, p. 387) cautions against allowing committees or functional teams to become 'fiefdoms' with uncontrolled power. Given these caveats, Frame (2003, pp. 251–252) advises creating an 'environment of competence … where people will not cause problems through their actions and inactions and where they are capable of solving problems effectively when they arise.'

When assessing the risks associated with an organization's structure and culture, the risk manager should first look for well-crafted and coherent mission and vision statements that are supported with written policies and guidelines that facilitate empowerment to make decisions that conform to legal and ethical requirements (see Table 7.4). Policies or procedures often reflect statutory compliance issues governing employment as well as the organization's guiding principles, and they need to be communicated and implemented consistently throughout the event organization and the event operations. The number and type will vary based on the size, scope, and location (jurisdiction) of the event organization, but it is prudent to consider and address a broad range of these issues early in the organization's development because they often represent common improprieties and previous legal disputes. This is also why legal counsel should be consulted regarding all written policies to ensure compliance with pertinent employment laws and regulations.

Staff acquisition and preparation

Finding enough people, and the right people, to bring an event to life is far more complicated than simply putting out a Help Wanted sign. It requires workforce planning including a job analysis, job summary, job descriptions, job specifications, and selection and evaluation criteria (Bowdin et al., 2006) before recruitment ever begins. The extent of this planning will vary depending on the size, type, and jurisdiction of the event, but without at least minimal planning the event workforce, paid or volunteer, may become a liability instead of an asset. Typical risks include personnel that do not perform as expected because they do not understand their duties, they do not have the skills or experience to do the jobs assigned, or the real reason they are there is to watch or 'be at' the event rather than work the event.

Table 7.4 Typical policies and procedures for event organizations

• Anti-discrimination policies	• Equipment usage policies
• Anti-substance abuse policies	• Gifts and gratuities policies
• Attendance and leave policies	• Health and safety rules and procedures
• Behavior expectations and restrictions	• Hiring procedures (e.g., background checks)
• Bylaws and governance policies	
• Compensation and benefits policies	• Performance appraisal procedures
• Confidentiality policies	• Personnel records policies
• Conflict of interest policies	• Procurement procedures
• Data access and handling policies	• Reimbursement policies
• Dispute and grievance procedures	• Restricted and prohibited items/actions
• Discipline and termination procedures	• Promotion and succession procedures
• Diversity policies (e.g., affirmative action)	• Public and media relations procedures
• Dress code and/or apparel restrictions	• Sexual harassment policies
• Employment categories	• Technology usage policies (e.g., e-mail, Internet, software)
• Employment eligibility policies	
• Employment of relatives policies	

A needs assessment should be conducted that identifies the number of personnel (with which skills) necessary to accomplish the tasks required. This is often accomplished using the WBS, reviewing previous staffing plans, and polling committee or department heads. The various jobs need to be analyzed to determine the major functions and performance elements associated with each job, often called a functional analysis, and a job summary should be created that outlines the purpose and responsibilities of the position. One should also factor succession planning into the needs assessment to mitigate the loss of key personnel through resignation, incapacitation, or large or small disasters (or unreliability – that volunteer just didn't show up).

The job analysis and summary are then incorporated into a job description that should clearly identify the principal duties and expectations of the person filling that position, including the time commitment (Bowdin et al., 2006). It may also be advisable, especially for volunteer positions, to specify why the task/job is important and the consequences if not performed properly, and it may be necessary (i.e., duty to warn) to specify any potential exposure to contaminants, weather, ergonomic dangers, or other hazardous working conditions.

Some positions require specific qualifications – competencies necessary to perform the job at the level of performance required. The job analysis should include the definition of the specific physical or technical skills, training, credentials, or licenses required for the position, plus the personal characteristics or attributes someone performing that job should possess (e.g., attention to detail, dependability, etc.), which is included in the job specifications. Berlonghi (1990), for example, advises that minimum age requirements (e.g., 21 years of age) be set for volunteers. One must be careful, however, not to delimit abilities or discriminate against disabilities when establishing these specifications.

The job description and specifications will form the basis for the selection criteria, which should be clear for both the event and the applicant in order for expectations to be met, and must comply with legally approved criteria to prevent liability. The selection criteria should be mirrored in the evaluation criteria for performance appraisals, and the evaluation criteria should reflect and feed back into the job summary and job specifications. Again, these must fall within legal parameters in order to prevent liability for unlawful or unfair dismissals.

Recruitment activities should be designed to ensure all expectations and opportunities are transparent. They should be conducted at such times and places and with various methods so they are accessible and the event will be able to attract a competent, committed, and diverse workforce. This may entail traditional as well as innovative recruitment strategies, particularly for volunteer corps as discretionary time dwindles. The first place to look is within the event's constituency (e.g., supporters, fans, etc.), but care must be exercised because it is precisely these people who will be most interested in 'attending rather than working' while on the job.

Gloria Nelson, CSEP, president of Gloria Nelson Event Design, LLC in Wisconsin, engages student volunteers in 'learn' or 'learn and earn' opportunities whenever they arise. She advises that you must 'make sure you provide the student volunteer(s) with a comprehensive packet of overview, policies and procedures, job descriptions, production schedule, logistical mapping, signed waiver of liability and emergency/safety/radio protocol. Depending on the number of volunteers and the length of project and/or service, ensure provision of things such as a Green Room for their comfort and security of their personal belongings, appropriate meal and beverage availability, and reimbursing them for mileage or public transportation if possible.'

Hiring and induction activities may include conducting background, criminal, credit, and/or reference checks for certain positions, particularly those dealing with money handling or contact with children. The event organization needs to know who it is hiring or accepting as a volunteer because it could be held liable for recommending incompetence (Foster, 2002) or jeopardizing safety and security (Moody, 2005). This reinforces Berlonghi's advice that 'walk-up and last-minute volunteers should not be allowed' (1990, p. 57). A personnel record should be created for every employee and volunteer staff member that includes, at a minimum, all contact information (e.g., name, address, telephone numbers) and an in case of emergency (ICE) contact name and number. The scope and content of employee records will be dictated by the employment laws within your jurisdiction. All personnel records must be prepared, stored, and protected as confidential information.

Following the administrative induction, all personnel should be provided with a formal orientation wherein the individual is introduced to the event, its mission and history, its culture and leadership, and its location and the staff. This is when key policies and procedures, typically included in an employee manual or volunteer handbook, should be reinforced, and should be delivered in both written and oral formats due to different learning styles and literacy limitations. Although such orientations for events are often designed to build enthusiasm and boost social interaction, it is important to communicate the risk messages that will protect the safety and welfare of the personnel as well as the attendees. These include guidelines regarding handling incidents, reporting hazardous conditions or activities (decriminalizing risk), and permission to avoid danger. Safety is everyone's job.

From the event organizer to the casual volunteer, inexperience is often cited as one of the biggest risks in events management. This can usually be overcome through training, mentoring, and, to put it bluntly, experience. The job analysis identifies the tasks and the level of performance required, which will be used to evaluate the training needs of the personnel available and acquired. Show individuals how and allow them to practice the procedures and operation of equipment they will be asked to use during their job. Van der Wagen and Carlos (2005) emphasize the fundamental responsibility of customer service for all personnel and point out that anyone wearing a uniform or staff badge, regardless of their role, will be expected by attendees to be able to answer questions. Therefore, all staff should be provided with the answers to the most frequently asked questions and know where assistance can be provided (e.g., first aid, welfare services, etc.).

Performance motivation and monitoring

Motivation is a personal state based on an individual's motives. It is incumbent upon the event organization to identify the reasons their paid and volunteer personnel take on a job and craft the compensation, recognition, and stimulation strategies that will fulfill these needs and desires and thereby motivate high-quality performance. It is advisable to ask why an individual is applying for the paid or volunteer position, either on the application form or when conducting a job interview. This may identify strategies that will enhance their effectiveness and reliability, such as placement within a team comprised of or scheduled with their friends or free admission to allow access to an event component upon completion of duties (a typical reason for volunteering). It can also expose potential problems such as the desire to be near certain celebrities or participants, which could be mitigated with increased supervision or, in the case of volunteers, declining their offer of service for this particular job. Care must be exercised, however, to ensure this is not done in a prejudicial manner.

Supervision, particularly of inexperienced personnel, is crucial to ensure the performance of one's duties meets the needs of the event organization. This is not a policing activity; it is a mentoring and coaching activity – being accessible to answer questions and providing guidance. Supervision, and performance appraisal, is a two-way activity; there must be feedback systems integrated into this process and questions and recommendations from staff should be vigorously encouraged. It is advisable to develop checkpoints within the timeline and during the event production that allow for corrective actions to be taken in a manner that protects the event operations and takes advantage of learning opportunities for the worker. Never leave a worker 'stranded' – without access to the physical, informational, and emotional support needed to accomplish his or her duties.

Conduct performance reviews at the close of the event for all personnel and on a periodic basis throughout the duration of employment for employees. This, again, is not an adversarial or faultfinding activity. Look for ways to enhance individual performance and professional growth. Look for weaknesses in the recruitment, orientation, training, monitoring, and recognition strategies so that the lessons learned may be integrated into future endeavors.

Workforce relations

The workforce for an event becomes a small, often insular community, and within any community there are sure to be conflicts, personal or procedural, and times when discipline and even dismissal becomes necessary. Conflict and dispute resolution procedures should be established that provide the mechanism for grievances to be heard and addressed in a timely and impartial manner, and without disrupting the event operations (e.g., take it outside, take it up with this manager, take it up after the event). If and when discipline becomes necessary, it is important to use corrective rather than punitive disciplinary measures because 'errors are rarely due to malice' (Silvers, 2004a, p. 390), however it should be made perfectly clear what behavior or actions will not be tolerated under any circumstances (e.g., violence, theft, intoxication, etc.). Discipline, and termination if it becomes necessary, should always be conducted in private and in such a way that protects the individual's dignity and he or she is accorded proper respect.

Many events are held in places and facilities that fall under the jurisdiction of certain labor unions, which will dictate specific (or specific numbers of) personnel and working conditions such as hours and pay rates. There are several distinctive risks that should be considered when dealing with unionized labor. First, contracts for workers acquired from a labor union should be carefully scrutinized to ensure you have a complete understanding of the work rules and restrictions you will need to abide by, as well as the rates you will be charged (e.g., straight time, overtime, double time), which, according to Sorin (2003), can also include employee benefits such as health insurance, vacation, and retirement contributions, as well as payroll administration. Second, the event organizer should investigate the status of union contracts at a selected facility or locale to determine the potential for labor disputes that may lead to labor strikes, picket lines, or other disruptions. Also, in some cases there are several different unions representing different areas of work (e.g., electricians and craftsmen) that must be dealt with, and occasionally there are jurisdictional disputes between unions regarding their authority claims to the work to be done.

When securing temporary staffing or contract workers from personnel agencies or casual labor services you should also scrutinize the contract to make certain you have a complete understanding of your financial and working condition obligations. In addition, you must recognize and adhere to the supervisory protocol specified within the contract so that any liabilities rest with the appropriate entity; if direction and control authority and responsibilities are subverted, you may find liability shifts over to you. It is also a wise strategy to require all contracts with vendors or independent contractors specify that their workers shall not be considered your employees.

Procurement management

Procurement management is the sourcing, selection, and contracting of the suppliers and vendors from whom goods and services will be procured using accurate solicitation materials and quality criterion, suitable documentation, change controls, and cost avoidance to ensure purchases will deliver cost value. Good procurement management practices facilitate risk management by determining the risks associated with the individual vendors or suppliers and the business interactions with them, including but limited to those shown in Table 7.5.

As illustrated in Figure 7.4, procurement is a sequential and integrated process consisting of procurement planning, solicitation planning, solicitation, source selection, receipt/consumption and review, and contract administration and closeout (PMI, 2000; Silvers, 2004a; Tum et al., 2006). Monks (1996) clarifies this by stipulating the responsibilities associated with procurement include delineation of needs, identification of supply sources, supplier selection and contracting, and performance monitoring, and suggests that purchasing should be done in collaboration with individuals with specialized product knowledge to prepare the specifications, as well as with those receiving and using the goods or services and those administering the contracts and payment functions. Tricker (2001, pp. 97–98) advises that ISO 9001:2000, international standards

Table 7.5 Typical procurement risks for meetings and events

• Ambiguous or incomplete specifications	• Lack of change controls
• Failure to monitor contract fulfillment	• Lack of procurement policies
• Inadequate contract management	• Lack of purchasing procedures
• Inadequate supplier communication	• Lack of supplier integration
• Improper bid/proposal review procedures	• Poor supplier relations
• Incompetent suppliers	• Sole-source suppliers
• Incomplete bids/proposals	• Unclear selection criteria
• Ineffective quality control	• Unethical solicitation practices
• Insufficient supplier sources	• Unfair selection practices

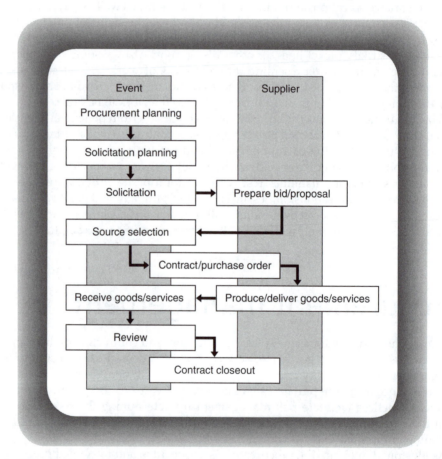

Figure 7.4 The procurement process

for quality assurance, specifies that an organization must have documented procedures and 'a process to ensure appropriate selection, evaluation and control of all purchased products [or services].' This encompasses the procedures for identifying requirements, the evaluation and selection of suppliers, usage of solicitation and purchasing documents, verifying the product or service meets specified requirements, and the administration of contracts and purchase documentation.

Procurement policies and practices

Procurement is a sales process, often subject to highly variable quantitative and qualitative criterion, numerous alternatives, and significant pressure on buyers from sellers. It is important to establish procurement policies in accordance with legal requirements and ethical guidelines that provide a framework for procurement decision making. The need for a formal framework increases as the scope and complexity of the purchasing to be done increases, with large events requiring significant collaboration across numerous departments (MPI, 2005). For example, sponsorship agreements generated through the marketing department may restrict the use of direct competitors as suppliers for the event, and the purchase of products or services from those suppliers could jeopardize sponsorship negotiations or result in a breach of contract with the sponsor.

In addition, increasing regulatory attention is focused on the procurement practices of public or publicly held entities, including events and event hosts (e.g., corporations), that seeks to limit or prohibit questionable activities that may influence purchase decisions (e.g., gift giving, amenities, complimentary travel, etc.) (MPI, 2005). It is advisable to develop procurement policies that address the ethical issues identified in Table 3.10 in Chapter 3 so that all procurement activities are transparent and principled.

It is also important to develop decision-making systems that include the accurate delineation of product or service specifications; the application of pertinent criteria, rules and restraints to the decision process; the facilitation of suitable deliberation and collaboration; and ensuring the proper authority and empowerment are granted. This may include defining the bid and/or proposal review process, including appropriate consultation, and standardizing contract language (MPI, 2005) in order to facilitate negotiation within specific parameters. Decision systems should identify the applicable decision mode or modes (i.e., who or what will make the decision) (Yates, 2003). This might include, for example, consensus decision making, a single decision maker, majority vote, scoring system, or threshold criteria (e.g., every purchase over a certain amount requires three bids).

Most event organizations will establish specific purchasing practices, such as tracking and payment systems for payables and receivables (e.g., purchase orders, invoices, etc.) and authorization procedures to ensure only those with authority are able to spend the money. As illustrated in Consider this… 7.2, without clear purchasing policies and procedures, unsanctioned spending encumbrances may be made that undermine effective 'supply chain management,' which strives to create efficiencies that reduce costs (MPI, 2005; Tum et al., 2006).

Procurement planning and solicitation

The first step in procurement planning and solicitation is to determine the need for and scope of contracted goods and services. Consider what you need, when you need it, and whether this is best procured from inside or outside the organization. Monks (1996) suggests conducting a value analysis in which the function and cost of a potential purchase is examined, including whether the need is actually valid and the features are truly necessary, and if there are lower-cost options that will perform the same functions. One must know which products or services are critical to the event to ensure quality control and that contingency plans are in place.

The next challenge is to stipulate the specifications for contracted goods and services and identify the supplier sources that are suitable, capable, and qualified to provide

Table 7.6 Types of solicitation briefing documents

• Invitation for bids (IFB)	• Request for offer (RFO)
• Request for bids (RFB)	• Request for quote (RFQ)
• Request for information (RFI)	• Specification brief
• Request for proposal (RFP)	• Tender brief

them. It is important to remember that there could be liability for recommending incompetence based on supplier or subcontractor performance or carelessness (Foster, 2002). It is also prudent to identify alternatives to sole-source suppliers. Monks (1996) recommends that a database of potential suppliers be developed and continuously maintained. Large organizations will often create a list of approved or preferred vendors that have been previously assessed based on capabilities, capacity, and compliance, have agreed upon pre-set payment processes, and have been incorporated into the procurement system. One may also encounter suppliers (e.g., hotels, convention centers, etc.) that have preferred or exclusive vendors, which may limit an organizer's choices (or increase costs) regarding the full scope of the procurement needs and must be identified and analyzed when evaluating bids or proposals.

Develop complete and accurate solicitation briefing documents, which may be called by various names and for various purposes as shown in Table 7.6.

In order to choose providers based on an equitable selection process, selection criteria must be determined and should be clearly specified. This criteria may be subjective or objective, tangible or intangible, and can include, among other things, quantity, quality, service, cost, delivery, understanding of need, creative approach, reliability, technical capability or support, and terms of purchase (Monks, 1996; PMI, 2000), plus any restrictions or preferences imposed on either the products and services sought or the selection process itself (Silvers, 2004a). It is widely recommended that selection criteria be assigned numerical importance ratings that will result in a quantitative score that eliminates (or at least lessens) personal influence or preference in decision making, which facilitates equity and accountability when interpreting and evaluating bids and proposals. This is often accomplished using a decision matrix technique, an exercise based on the multi-attribute utility theory (MAUT) and sometimes referred to as an analytical hierarchy process (Yates, 2003), as shown in Figure 7.5. It is also wise to remember that there is a 'difference between cost and value and between simple commodity and complex services' (MPI, 2005, p. 14).

Contract and contractor management

Once potential suppliers have been selected (and references checked), negotiations begin to arrive at agreed upon prices, deliverables, and other expectations, and then contracts are executed (see Chapter 3). Suppliers bidding on an event should include ALL the costs in their bid, but this cannot be taken for granted and must be confirmed during the negotiation and contracting process. Finalize contracts as early as possible to facilitate budget control (Van der Wagen and Carlos, 2005) and integrate these 'partners' into the event's administrative and logistical operations. The event organizer might be viewed as a general contractor – managing the integration and organization of all the subcontractors (suppliers) and securing the appropriate purchase documentation. These suppliers all have their own administrative practices,

Criteria	Supplier			
	Hotel A	Hotel B	Hotel C	Hotel D
Location/vicinity Weight: 1	5	5	1	2
Function space Weight: 10	2	2	5	1
Room rates Weight: 8	3	3	4	5
Catering Weight: 7	4	4	3	5
Property amenities Weight: 2	5	4	2	5
Security Weight: 9	1	2	5	3
Emergency plans Weight: 4	2	3	4	5
Total score Score × Weight	104	115	169	144
Score = rating: 1 (poor) to 5 (excellent) Weight = importance: 1 (not important) to 10 (very important)				
Note: Even though Hotel D had more of the highest individual scores, when the weight of each criterion was factored in Hotel C received a higher total score.				

Figure 7.5 Example of a MAUT decision matrix

varying deposit and payment stipulations, and varying lead time and logistical requirements. This has significant implications regarding schedule development, communications, budget management, and change management.

Contracts must be tracked to ensure decisions are made and obligations are met in accordance with the contractual terms and conditions. Compliance instruments must be acquired or issued as necessary, applicable policies and circumstances must be communicated, and an effective change control system must be implemented. Formal, written change orders requiring signed authorization should always be used (see Appendix H: Sample change order form), and this is even more important for any changes on-site at an event because these changes are often costly in money, quality, and potential risk.

Quality control procedures should be developed and implemented that verifies the products and services delivered satisfy the agreed upon specifications. Performance evaluations should be conducted using evaluation criteria that reflect the selection criteria and the objectives of the event in order to provide business intelligence for future events. Contract closeout and final payments should be completed in compliance with established contractual requirements and purchasing or payment policies

Table 7.7 Typical systems used in events management

• Attendee management systems	• Governance systems
• Bookkeeping systems	• Inventory systems
• Change control systems	• Project management systems
• Communication systems	• Purchasing systems
• Database systems	• Quality management systems
• Decision-making systems	• Reservation/booking systems
• Document generation and routing systems	• Scheduling systems

and procedures. It is important to remember that donated goods and services, either from volunteers or in an in-kind sponsorship context, must meet the same regulatory standards and compliance requirements as those purchased in order to limit the event's exposure to liability.

Systems management

Systems management covers the implementation and coordination of the various accountability, database, knowledge management, and knowledge transfer systems using suitable technology applications and equipment to integrate the needs of the event project and enterprise (see Table 7.7). A system, simply put, is the interrelated activities or parts that work together to form a whole or process to perform a task. The development and usage of physical and conceptual systems that automate recurring and monotonous tasks, delineate methodologies, and standardize procedures has the advantage of promoting consistency and reducing errors and costs, thereby contributing to the 'effectiveness and efficiency of the organization' (Tricker, 2001, p. 37).

Identifying and understanding systems

Identify the types, scope, and complexity of the organizational and technological systems employed by the event organization and, where possible, recommend the development or acquisition of systems that will increase productivity and promote risk management objectives. A system can be as simple as checking off items on a checklist or as extensive as elaborate project management software. It is not the financial investment that counts; it's the ability of the system to provide an orderly and comprehensive process that accomplishes the function required.

Determine whether or not the people using the systems recognize the impact of their actions (or inaction) on those systems. Weaknesses in the implementation of a system are a risk and steps must be taken to either improve the training in the use of the system or improve the system itself (e.g., revision, simplification, replacement). Weaknesses in the integration of systems, a problem when systems are devised (conceptual) or purchased (technological) by different people or departments at different times, may be overcome by viewing (and reviewing) all of the systems together *as a* system itself.

As discussed throughout this chapter, establishment of policies, procedures, rules, and structures facilitates effective risk management by providing guidance based on best practice and the lessons learned from trial and error. An organization that embraces systems thinking – understanding the linkages, interactions, and processes of systems and system elements – is capable of continuous improvement that will lead to increased safety, security, and sustainability.

Decision making

One of the critical areas in which development of a system will facilitate effective risk management is decision making. This is closely linked to the hierarchies of governance, accountability, and responsibility established when devising the organizational chart in order to prevent unsanctioned decision making. The purpose of a decision-making system is not to make people have to ask permission to make a decision; rather, it is to give them the tools for making good decisions. You want people to take on responsibility and to be able to contribute their experience and expertise, but you don't want over-confident or over-emotional vigilantes taking things upon themselves without the proper authority, especially in high-risk or crisis situations, which may be subject to a strict hierarchy as described in Chapters 5 and 6. Nor do you want to over-burden individuals with the sole responsibility for making a decision when collaborative deliberation is advisable.

An effective decision-making system has standardized and sequential processes with feedback loops that reveal the choices for and consequences of the decisions to be made and includes many of the tools and techniques described in Chapter 2. Yates (2003) contends that decision making has a structure and delineates the facets of decision making as need, mode, investment, options, possibilities, judgment, value, trade-offs, acceptability, and implementation. Although intuition should not be discounted (Gladwell, 2005), with all the elements included in and decisions surrounding an event, developing and using a structured decision-making system can help ensure the scope and impact of those decisions are well reasoned and justify those decisions to clients and constituencies. It can also help one discern and address the difference between the 'urgent' and the 'important' (a condition extremely prevalent in the high-stress atmosphere of meeting and event management).

Managing the technology

Many conceptual systems (e.g., policies and procedures) are captured in handbooks, checklists, or manuals, but are also supported by and implemented through technology (e.g., databases, networks, communication technologies, and web technology). The procurement, operations, maintenance, and upgrading of this technology must be managed, including the security and integrity of these technological systems. The equipment, materials, machinery, suppliers, accessibility, compatibility, capability, and reliability should be examined, and any inherent hazards should be analyzed and mitigated.

Office equipment breaks, computers crash, networks go down, and web-based tools can be compromised. Exclusive reliance on any single technology leaves administrative operations vulnerable. Redundancy and back-ups of all data within systems is a must. Equipment must be maintained properly. Computer usage must be governed by policies that control access and activities that put the organization and its equipment at risk (e.g., Internet surfing and downloads). Wireless and networking technology must be judiciously studied to ensure business intelligence is secure and private information is protected. This should all be incorporated into a security system that includes the physical, behavioral, and procedural loss prevention tactics discussed in Chapter 5.

Summary

Risk management will entail the investment of time, money, and human resources. Without sufficient investment, risk management will not be effective. The amount of resources budgeted will vary greatly depending on the size, type, and purpose of the event, as well as the host or hosting organization's objectives and perception of the importance of risk management. Meticulous identification of the resources available for the event project will determine the allocation of those resources (or re-allocation if necessary) and the practicality of the project, as well as specify any obstacles and the strategies to overcome them. There must be sufficient resources to ensure feasibility and there must be a balance of resources to mitigate risk.

Time is a resource that cannot be increased unless the date of the event is flexible. Its allotment and arrangement must be efficient and effective, which needs to be reflected in and communicated via comprehensive agendas, calendars, and/or time maps. From the task definition through the proper sequencing and scheduling of those tasks, risk planning and control tactics must be integrated throughout the timeline and the production schedule.

The financial resources of an event must be budgeted carefully. The more limited the budget, the more focused one must be on the event goals, but a quality event does not depend on a large budget. Budgets must be allocated appropriately based on the priorities identified by the needs assessment, and they must be monitored to make certain the revenues and expenses are within their projected amounts and cash flow is sufficient to cover the expenses in a timely manner.

Sufficient human resources (full- or part-time staff, volunteers, or contracted labor) must be recruited. They must be provided with the proper orientation, training, and motivation for the jobs they are to accomplish. Their use must be evaluated to ensure you have enough of the right people in the right places at the right times doing the right jobs. Well-trained, experienced personnel may cost more, but they are often more efficient, effective, and risk aware.

Every element included in the event will have a cost, and practically every event element will have options at varying levels of quality and price offered by potential suppliers. From planning for procurement through completing and closing out the contractual relationships with suppliers after the event, the objective is to select the best products and services available to meet the event's needs within the budget allowed. All supplier agreements should be in writing and all changes should be acknowledged by all parties in writing on a change order. Finally, all suppliers and contractors should be evaluated on their performance so the lessons learned may be incorporated into the next event.

Managing quality, productivity, and proficiency is facilitated by the development of systems that reduce errors and produce improvements. Such systems also help identify, mitigate, and control risk. Conceptual and technological systems should be devised or acquired to make good decision making possible and lessen the possibility of mistakes that can jeopardize the procedures and outcomes of the event.

Key safeguards

- Use the timeline and budget as your primary administrative tracking tools.
- Pay close attention to the delays, dependencies, and deadlines that can wreak havoc on a schedule.
- Maximize limited time by looking for tasks that can be done concurrently and tasks that can be done by staff during times when they might be idle or under-utilized.
- Incorporate go/no-go decisions into the income projections of the budget.
- Ensure procurement restrictions and approval requirements are specified.
- Create and consistently use change control instruments.
- Key suppliers should be included in pre-con, post-con, and other briefings.
- Identify and implement systems to organize tasks, schedules, and resources and that facilitate the efficiency of internal and external procedures.

Chapter review challenge

1 In what ways does changing the scope of an event affect the risks of the event?
2 How would you use the cause/effect analysis to help you determine the critical points in a planning timeline?
3 What procurement procedures would you include in the policy manual for an event organization?
4 Why would it be inadvisable to accept walk-in volunteers on the day of an event?
5 What are the strengths and weaknesses of employing technological systems?

Practical risk management exercise

As the risk manager for the international association discussed in Consider this… 7.2, you have been asked to help develop the policy manual for host chapters. Prepare a list of policies and procedures that incorporates clear guidance regarding the administrative systems of time management, financial management, organizational hierarchy and authority, and procurement management for the annual educational conference. Be sure to frame these in the context of what should be done and why, rather than what should NOT be done, and make sure they are explicit.

Key terminology

Accounting: The design and maintenance of the system for the recording and counting of sums of money, those paid and those received and the value of property, and the records and reports associated with these sums.

Analogous estimating: The use of comparable projects to determine the likely amount of time or effort required for a first-time project.

Attendee management system: A term often used to describe web-based registration systems or software.

Attrition: Monetary penalties or loss of amenities when numbers do not meet contractually guaranteed performance projections.

Bookkeeping: The process of recording transactions (revenues and expenditures) in the accounting system, including the preparation and collection of the underlying documents.

Bottom-up analysis: The totaling of estimated costs to determine required revenues.

Break-even analysis: Determining the point at which revenues will equal expenses.

Budget: A financial statement outlining and itemizing the estimated total revenues and expenses associated with an event or event organization.

Cash flow: The transfer of monies into and out of an enterprise.

Change order: A form used by a facility or event organization to confirm, authorize, and communicate any changes to original contracted items and orders.

Chart of accounts: A numbering system used to identify individual line items that make up the revenue and expense categories in a budget so income and expenses are posted to the correct accounts.

Flowchart: A chart or diagram of the sequence and progress of a series of operations for a specific project.

Guidelines: A set of procedures and/or directions for accomplishing a task that allow some interpretation or flexibility by the user.

Instructions: A set of procedures and/or directions for accomplishing a task that do not allow for interpretation by the user.

Invoice: An itemized bill, including prices, of goods and services sold or shipped.

Multi-attribute utility theory (MAUT): A structured methodology for comparing alternatives using a numerical value for measures of interest that reflect the decision makers' preferences or multiple objectives.

Organizational chart: A graphical representation of the structure of authority for an event or organization.

Policy: A course of action or formal rules adopted by an organization specifying actions that are desired, required, permissible or forbidden; usually developed to address common occurrences or anticipated procedures.

Post-con: A post-event debriefing meeting between the event organizer, facility staff, and suppliers to review and evaluate the implementation and outcomes of the event; derived from 'post-convention'.

Pre-con: A pre-event briefing meeting between the event organizer, facility staff, and suppliers to review the details and expectations for the event; derived from 'pre-convention'.

Procedure: A particular method, process, or course of action based on qualified measures of efficiency and/or effectiveness; see also guidelines and instructions.

Procurement management: The processes required to acquire the necessary products and services from outside the event organization.

Production schedule: A detailed chronological outline of all activities and tasks required to implement an event for the time period from directly before move-in through move-out.

Pro forma: Financial forms (budgets, profit and loss statements, balance sheets, etc.) based on future expectations.

Project management: The science and profession of managing projects by applying knowledge, skills, tools, and techniques to project activities to meet the project requirements.

Request for proposal (RFP): A written solicitation used to convey to potential suppliers the requirements and specifications for goods or services that the buyer intends to purchase.

Scope creep: The subtle expansion of the scope of the project, often in small and insidious increments.

Statement of work (SOW): A description of the scope of products and/or services to be supplied or performed.

Timeline: A detailed chronological outline of all activities and tasks required to implement an event that encompasses the schedule surrounding the entire event management process from inception to completion.

Underlying documents: The documentation (e.g., receipts, invoices, etc.) used to substantiate income and expense sources and authorizations.

Union Jurisdiction: The jobs that may be performed by a specific labor union.

Volunteers: Individuals who donate their time and talents to fill the various jobs required to produce the event that are not filled by paid staff or other providers without formal employment or financial compensation.

Online resources

Corbin Ball's Meetings Technology Tool Chest	www.corbinball.com/tipstools/
Free Management Library	www.managementhelp.org
HR-Guide.com	www.hr-guide.com
JobAnalysis.net	www.job-analysis.net
PCMA Program Planning Timeline	www.pcma.org/pdf/613.pdf
Society for Human Resources Management	www.shrm.org

Chapter 8
Communications

Understanding is not automatic

This chapter will examine how to:

■ Develop suitable internal and external communications systems and strategies for an event and its scope of operations
■ Select the appropriate communication methods and messages based on the event type, scope, site, and audience
■ Establish and implement the proper procedures for the collection, distribution, and protection of information to meet the communication and operational needs of the event project
■ Determine and address the communication issues and risks applicable to the stakeholders and various constituencies of the event project

Introduction

Communication is a vital component of the risk management process and system, which includes timely information acquisition and distribution plus the appropriate consultation in decision making. It is the critical link between the information surrounding the event project and the stakeholders involved in the event project. It is used to warn, inform, connect with, and advise the various publics (stakeholders and audiences) of the existence and conditions of the event project and to collect, convey, confirm, and publicize information that will guide and influence behavior according to the needs of the event and its risk management objectives.

Communication is a vast yet simple concept wherein there is a transmission of a shared understanding between people using a variety of tools and techniques and commonly understood language, symbols, and signals. In order to communicate there must be a sender, a message, a channel (i.e., transmission method), and a receiver, and the words and symbols must be recognized and comprehended by both the sender and the receiver. In other words, communication is composed of the message, mode, and medium, as illustrated in Figure 8.1. It is also important to understand that communication is a two-way process. Feedback and confirmation systems should always be incorporated into the system to ensure the information provided or instructions

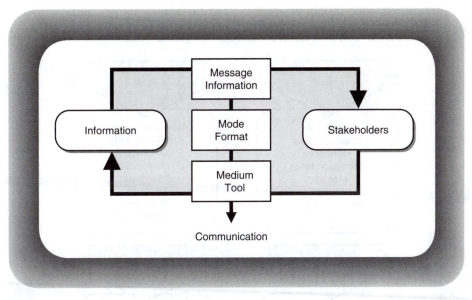

Figure 8.1 The dimensions of communication

given are understood. A flaw or breakdown in any part of this chain can result in miscommunication or missed communications.

Communications may be written, verbal, audible, or visual and the message delivery efficiency and efficacy associated with these communication channels (i.e., formats) should be considered carefully when deciding which will best serve the event project's information acquisition and distribution needs:

- *Written word*: memos, reports, manuals, notes, contracts, signs, etc.
- *Spoken word*: conversations, telephone calls, meetings, announcements, etc.
- *Gestures*: expressions, voice tone, actions, etc.
- *Multimedia*: a combination of methods, often involving technology.
- *Visual images*: illustrations, photographs, charts, etc.
- *Symbols*: icons, characters, figures, visual and audible signals, logos, uniforms, insignias, etc.

Many communication experts advise that using several channels of communication to deliver a message will enhance interest, retention, and comprehension of that message. Using the written word, the spoken word, and visual aids or images throughout the event communications plan should ensure important messages are received and properly understood.

Communication channels must be open, effective, and inclusive, and communication blocks must be reduced or eliminated. According to Heller (1998) communication problems are often due to timing, method, environment (noise, interruptions, etc.), or emotion (personality conflicts, hurt feelings, etc.). Haddow and Bullock (2003) propose that the blocks to communicating risk include competing demands for attention, complacency, denial, conflicts with existing beliefs, and message and messenger credibility. FEMA (2005) suggests that the communication variables that may become barriers include the difference between sender and receiver (e.g., attitude, information levels, and social systems), differences in communication styles, differences in previous

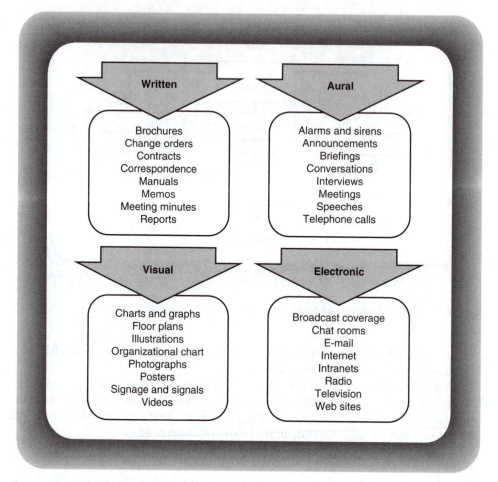

Figure 8.2 Communication tools

experiences, cultural differences, mismatched message and body language, and, of particular pertinence to event production staff, stress, change in routine, and lack of sleep. These vulnerabilities must be considered when devising the communication plan and procedures.

The typical communication tools used at and for events are shown in Figure 8.2. Each tool has multi-functional capabilities within an overall event communications plan, from operational purposes (project management) to marketing purposes to risk management purposes. In addition, each method of communication will have different applications and implications within both the normal functioning of an event and a crisis or emergency situation. Some of these issues are shown in Table 8.1.

Communication is the skill that supports the entire event management process and a comprehensive and carefully crafted communications plan is critical to the entire risk management process from assessment to control to evaluation. Communication skills include the ability to listen to, comprehend, interpret, write, and verbally present information in an effective and efficient manner. These skills are used to negotiate, persuade, report, explain, identify relevance and urgency of information, and make logical and compelling arguments, as well as recognizing and overcoming 'wishful listening' and other sender and receiver miscommunications.

Table 8.1 Communication tool issues

Written	• Written documentation is necessary in any evidentiary situation (if it isn't written down, you can't prove something did or did not happen) • Brochures may be considered a type of contract (what is promised must be delivered) • Reports and meeting minutes are an effective way to monitor project activity in a timely manner • Manuals are created to facilitate the communication of standard operating procedures and obligations to staff and volunteers • Urgency and delivery medium (e.g., fax or e-mail) does not negate the need for good writing, spelling, and grammar
Aural	• Verbal messages are quick and interactive but may be forgotten or misinterpreted (Heller, 1998) • Anything from a conversation that may have a financial, legal, or operational affect on the event or event organization should always be followed up with a written memorandum outlining the items discussed • A PA system should have its own primary and back-up power source and must be audible (adequate volume and clarity) throughout the event site including inside and outside the building, in dressing rooms, toilet facilities, and elevators, and in all auxiliary areas such as parking lots and staging areas (Wertheimer, 1980) • Audible announcements must be simple, enunciated clearly, and repeated often enough to reach the entire audience as it changes and/or moves through the event site (FEMA, 2005) • New fire codes are expected to require audible announcements advising patrons of emergency exits at all public assemblies of 50 or more persons
Visual	• Variable message signs may be used to provide both marketing information and safety announcements or warnings • Photographs or other illustrative graphics can provide important instructions such as egress direction or the way to operate an emergency shutdown mechanism • Projection devices used within an event program may be used to display emergency instructions and reinforce emergency announcements
Electronic	• Broadcast networks, both radio and television, may be used to publicize event-related conditions, and will be critical in a disaster situation; radio and television are best for creating awareness and urgency, but print media is best for providing detailed information • The Internet may be used to host event-related Web sites, create chat rooms where event stakeholders may hold synchronous or asynchronous discussions, and should be used to research external threats and vulnerabilities • All electronic communications should be presumed to be public • E-mail can be altered and forwarded to unintended audiences without your permission • Cellular telephone calls and two-way radio transmissions should not be presumed to be private • Any e-commerce activities must be conducted through a secure server that protects buyer and seller information, particularly credit card information

Senders have the responsibility for ensuring messages are clear, concise, and complete, including selecting the most appropriate message, mode, and medium for transmission, and confirming that the message has been understood; receivers are responsible for ensuring the messages received are complete and properly understood

(PMI, 2000). FEMA (2005) asserts that in order to make messages clear, they should be presented in sequence (e.g., the reason for the message, supporting information, and the conclusions, recommendations, or action required), use precise wording, and omit unnecessary details. In addition, one must know the multi-lingual, multi-cultural, multi-modal, and multi-media needs of the intended audience.

One must also recognize the nonverbal interpersonal communication skills and cultural implications related to body language (kinesics), eye contact and behavior (occulesics), personal space (proxemics), touching (haptics), vocal intonation (vocalics), time usage (chronemics), and appearance (physique, attire, etc.). Nonverbal cues take on much more importance during in-person human interaction, sometimes comprising up to 90 percent of the communication taking place, and will supersede verbal messages if not in sync. Use these nonverbal cues to send cohesive messages and interpret the receiver's reaction and understanding.

Communications management

Communications management encompasses the acquisition of the necessary equipment and development and implementation of the modes and protocols for on-site briefing and debriefing activities and information exchange with internal and external constituents of the event project, including the preparation and incorporation of applicable documentation and contact information into a comprehensive and readily accessible format. Communication strategies must be developed that ensure the people involved in the event have the information they need to accomplish their jobs, duties, goals, and objectives, and that problems due to miscommunication are minimized. The typical communication risks are shown in Table 8.2.

As noted in Chapter 2, the overall risk management plan includes development of the procedures and techniques to be used for communicating activities, actions, and outcomes. A communications plan must be devised that incorporates the flow of adequate and accurate information through the operational structure of the event's internal and external organization throughout the life of the event project. The scope and need for rigorous and formalized plans increases as the scale and complexity of the organization and/or event increases or compliance requirements are imposed.

Table 8.2 Typical communication risks

• Ambiguous messages	• Lack of multi-modal/media methods
• Ambiguous or unknown terminology	• Lack of technology redundancy
• Conflicting messages	• Misinformation (malicious or mistaken)
• Confusing instructions	• Missed messages
• Delayed transmission of messages	• Misunderstood messages
• Equipment damage or failure	• Overloaded communication system
• Inability to properly operate equipment	• Reliance on a single technology
• Inconsistent communications	• Unclear lines of communication
• Insufficient or ineffective equipment	• Uncontrolled rumor and speculation
• Interoperability problems	• Unreliable information
• Lack of centralized control	• Unsanctioned spokespersons
• Lack of communication protocols	• Wishful listening

Pre-event communications will be focused on the project management aspects of the event operations. A great deal of information must be collected from vendors, suppliers, regulatory authorities, and other important stakeholders and influencers in order to create effective event management and event risk management plans for an event production, as well as collecting and distributing information to monitor the progress and performance of task assignments. With all key communications, written confirmations of receipt and understanding should be required, particularly when related to changes in timing, cost, or quality.

On-site during the event, the communications plan will be focused on the immediate transfer of critical information to and from those charged with monitoring functions, as well as the transmission of information necessary to the health, safety, welfare, and participation of those in attendance at the event. When responding to an emergency, the channels of communication used for information exchange during normal operations will be used and expanded to include the appropriate emergency response agencies and authorities (Silvers, 2004a).

Post-event communications will include debriefings and reports that capture the outcomes and lessons learned from the event project, as well as the administrative closure of the event operations and obligations. These communications may extend to a year-round strategy with certain constituencies, such as maintaining a volunteer base for a festival or extending the educational programming for conference attendees, not to mention the marketing and customer relations strategies associated with retaining sponsors and clients.

Consider this... 8.1

Air travel changed overnight

August 10, 2006: Television news reports announced that a terrorist plan to blow up 10 planes headed to the U.S. out of Heathrow airport in the U.K. was thwarted. The plan was for suicide bombers as passengers to combine specific liquids while on board to create the explosive devices. New security restrictions were instituted immediately throughout the U.S. by the Transportation Security Administration (TSA) that prohibited virtually all liquids and gels from carry-on luggage and other hand-carried items.

Beth Cooper-Zobott, Director of Conference Services of Equity Residential in Chicago, Illinois, was in Sunny Isles, Florida, managing a conference of approximately 75 people that was to end that day. As is her habit when traveling, she turned on the news at 6:15 a.m. to check on potential travel delays for her group and heard of the events. The first thing she did was go to the TSA Web site to get all of the latest information. She made an announcement at the first scheduled gathering of the day about the situation and read what the TSA Web site had to say to the group. Because most of the group's departures from the hotel to the airport didn't begin until 2:00 p.m., her guests had plenty of time to pack newly prohibited items in their checked luggage. Additionally, she was able to obtain 'live' information from one of her executives who had had a 6:45 a.m. pick-up and was at the airport by 7:30 a.m. and called her with an update on the security procedures being enforced. She moved up the departure times that the ground transportation company had given her by one hour to ensure early arrival for security delays.

Despite all this, rumormongering was rampant almost from the start. One woman told Beth that she needed to tell the group that they would have to throw away their metal sunglass cases because they were no longer allowed. Beth asked her where she learned this and the woman said 'Good Morning America' (a popular television program). Beth told her that the information was unconfirmed and that she wouldn't make announcements unless information was officially posted on the TSA Web site. Another woman said that her husband read that the TSA was confiscating automatic car door openers/remotes. Again, Beth told her that this information was unconfirmed.

Beth was able to respond to changing events as they happened because she had a communications plan in place that allowed her to get information on external conditions (turning on the news every morning), acquire accurate information (going to the TSA Web site), and add 'man on the scene' information to what she told her group (the call with her colleague already at the airport). She was also able to counteract rumors and speculation by refusing to report unconfirmed and unofficial information, as well as make arrangements to accommodate the likely time delays caused by the new restrictions.

Developing a system for internal and external communications

A communications system incorporates the communications requirements (i.e., the type and format needed by whom, when, and where) and the communications technology to be used based on those requirements (PMI, 2000). Alexander (2002, p. 168) contends that a communications system must address the four components of the communication process.

- *Technology*: the hardware used for the composition and transfer of messages.
- *Procedures*: the formats and methods used with the technology.
- *Human factors*: perceptions and the capability to operate the technology.
- *Organizational context*: the framework of rules, cultures, targets, and priorities.

This quartet is similar to NFPA's Standard 1221 (2002, p. 36), which identifies the four basic elements of a communications system as equipment, operating procedures, personnel training, and the message types, quantity (system capacity), content, and timing, and goes on to identify 'common terminology,' the 'use of clear text or plain language and established standard terms and phrases,' as a communications concept necessary for good system performance. Glaesser (2006) advises that the agility of the communications system is dependent upon preparation for the scope, modes, and mediums necessary.

It is vital that the communications system be devised as a whole using systems thinking as discussed in Chapter 7: understanding the linkages, interactions, elements, and processes of the system. Just as our own circulatory system regulates the flow of blood throughout our bodies, so, too, must the communications system ensure that the flow of information encompasses all those who have or need information to do their jobs properly, efficiently, and effectively. This includes all the internal and external constituencies of the event project, as shown in Figure 8.3, and different modes of communication will often be necessary for these stakeholders and stakeholder groups throughout the event project, particularly during the run of an event.

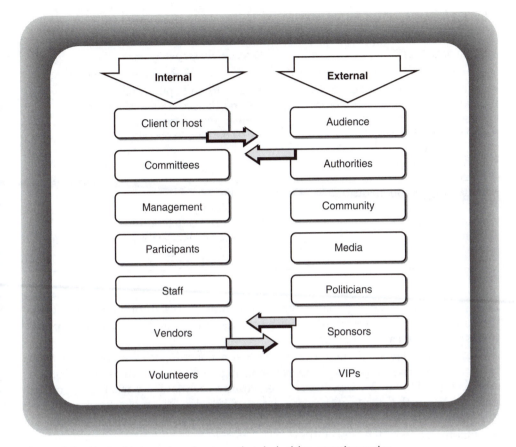

Figure 8.3 Typical internal and external stakeholder constituencies

Internal stakeholders may include a broad variety of personnel, participants, providers, and people with important political influence on the way in which the event will be operated. External stakeholders may encompass many of the same types of people as internal stakeholders, yet may not need to be included in many operational communications (and sometimes should not be included for security reasons).

For example, depending on the type and scope of an event, the client may wish to or need to be considered an external stakeholder, such as the mother of the bride for a wedding; she doesn't need to be included in all your communications with the suppliers before the event, but will need to be included in any communications regarding changes to the event or emergencies. A corporate sponsor of a large festival, however, may need to be included in the entire event planning and risk assessment process to ensure its investment in the event will be effective from a marketing and liability standpoint (and may be able to provide valuable perspectives and resources to the risk management process). Certain authorities may need to be included as internal stakeholders during pre-event and on-site communications for compliance reasons, and some vendors will only need to be advised of changes or cancellation after the initial procurement communication has taken place.

The typical internal and external messages (types of information to be collected and disseminated) are listed in Table 8.3. Internal messages will likely concentrate on operational and monitoring information. External messages will likely be more

Table 8.3 Typical messages for internal and external constituencies

Internal messages	External messages
• Chain of command and control • Conditions, changes, cancellation • Emergency notification • Goals and objectives • Job descriptions • Performance expectations • Policies and procedures • Regulatory requirements • Safety mandates • Status reports • Training	• Benefits and opportunities • Conditions, changes, cancellation • Emergency notification • Establishing expectations • Financial and community support • Mission, purpose, nature of event • Promotional (creating awareness, interest, desire, and action) • Regulatory compliance • Rules and regulations • Safety and welfare initiatives and announcements

promotional or marketing related, yet will include sufficient operational information and instructions to establish the correct expectations and encourage the proper or desired actions and behavior.

External messages may be targeted at specific constituencies within an external group, which may be political, operational, regulatory, or promotional in nature. According to Hoyle (2002, p. 104), 'Research into each target market is essential in understanding the needs and major areas of interest inherent among them.' As Berlonghi (1990) notes, target markets and marketing messages will be important in the identification of the expectations and expected behaviors of those who are targeted as potential attendees for the event as well as those that might be attracted for the purposes of disrupting the event.

Of particular importance will be communicating safety, security, and transportation information to event audiences and affected community neighbors, such as advising of traffic conditions or closures due to the event's operations or advising event goers regarding prohibited items before they reach the entrance (so they will not bring contraband in the first place). Wertheimer (1980) advises that special notices and prohibitions for an event should be publicized well in advance of an event.

On-site connectivity, command, and control

The on-site communications plan takes on a more dynamic character as the pace typically quickens and the need for efficient informant/decision maker/responder connections heightens (HSE, 1999). Communications between the organizers, staff, volunteers, security and stewarding personnel, performers and participants, suppliers, attendees, authorities, and the media needs a comprehensive and effective network that provides information that is timely, accurate, and to the point. Action, activities, and conditions are continuously monitored, and, as noted in Chapter 2, once a corrective action has been decided upon and taken, this must be communicated to internal and external staff, suppliers, and stakeholders.

The risk manager should ensure that this network covers all aspects and all areas of the event. Procedures must be established for who will transmit information, to whom it will be transmitted and how, and in what order and format it will be transmitted.

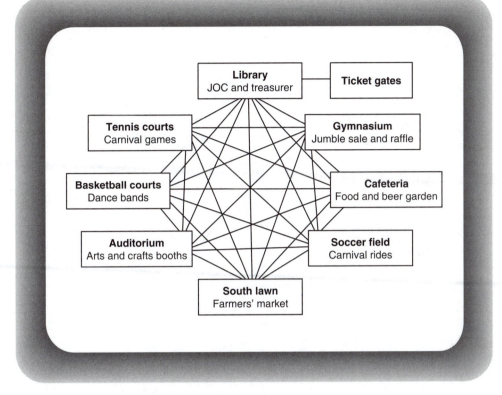

Figure 8.4   Decentralized communications network

The chain of command and control must be specified, and it is widely recommended that a centralized command post be established for communications, security, and emergency response efficiency. As illustrated in Figures 8.4 and 8.5, based on a one-day fundraising carnival held throughout the grounds of a boarding school, there should be communications capability to and from all areas and the joint operations center (JOC), which is accomplished with numerous radio frequencies or messengers (runners) to notify each other and the JOC. However, this becomes much more efficient if all messages come in to the JOC and are then broadcast from the JOC after the appropriate analysis and decision making has taken place.

Designating official spokespersons is also important in order to limit the number of individuals transmitting 'official' information about an event, particularly in an emergency situation. The media and other stakeholders should be given one point of contact during an emergency, and all communications should be funneled through that contact. Creating a joint information center (JIC), typically within or adjacent to the JOC, provides the central point for all information and communication activities to coordinate acquisition and release of accurate and consistent information (Haddow and Bullock, 2003).

Communication networks should also incorporate alerting strategies for internal and external stakeholders, particularly for crisis situations. Establish a flowchart that specifies the communication responsibilities according to the audiences or constituencies affected and the modes and mediums to be used. For example, establishing phone trees can facilitate the quick dissemination of information through delegation.

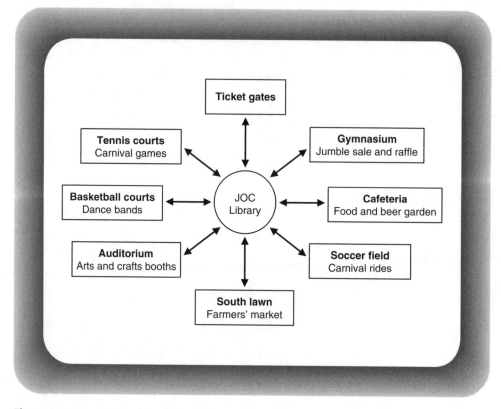

Figure 8.5 Centralized communications network

It may also be advisable to designate an off-site control center location and personnel so that external advisories (incoming and outgoing) are not dependent upon on-site capabilities that might become damaged or overwhelmed in an emergency. A security assessment of all the on-site communication systems and equipment should be done because, as Berlonghi (1990) points out, these will likely be a prime target for those wishing to disrupt the event.

Communications equipment

A variety of communications equipment is available to meet the on-site communication needs of an event, the most common of which is two-way radios (walkie-talkies) for internal communications and the public address (PA) system for public communications. All communications equipment should be tested to ensure it is in good working order and capable of covering the entire event site. All primary communications equipment should have its own power supply and a back-up system (e.g., loud hailers for PA announcements) and/or redundancy.

The use of common telecommunications equipment such as mobile phones and pagers may be a simple way to enhance communication capabilities amongst staff and other personnel. When working in a distant locale, pre-paid telephone cards may be used to facilitate access to pay telephones or long distance service (and perhaps even control costs). It might be advisable to purchase two cellular phones with

Figure 8.6   Illustration of an actual exit sign documented by Dr. G. Keith Still

a 'fresh' number and post this number around the venue for attendees to call if they have or see an emergency or incident (the second phone serves as the back-up). It is also advised that the event organizer, risk manager, and key staff members program emergency contact numbers into their cellular phone address books, and then delete them after the event.

There are many additional types of equipment used for the production of the event program that may also be integrated into the communications planning from a risk management perspective, including scoreboards, lighting, sound systems, and projection equipment. It is also important to consider the visual and nonverbal forms of communications equipment such as uniforms and signage and even hand signals. Distinctive uniforms (e.g., vests, jackets, or T-shirts) not only indicate authority (and access to event information) to audience members, it allows these personnel to be quickly identified within a crowd by organizers and responders (HSE, 1999). The staff of one event company, for example, always wore bright, neon pink event jackets that were visible in a field with more than 10 000 spectators. Pre-determined hand signals or gestures can visually communicate specific conditions or messages. For example, Berlonghi (1990) reports that ushers removing their hat is a common way to signal the need for security at their location.

Signage is an important component of the communications plan as well as site management, which will be discussed further in Chapter 11. Informational and warning messages should be posted on signage at critical points throughout the event site, particularly at entrances when there are restrictions on who or what may be brought into the event. Signage is especially important in emergency evacuation plans, and must be highly visible and unambiguous (see Figure 8.6). Dr. G. Keith Still of Crowd Dynamics Limited in the U.K. offers the following perspective on signage and communicating with the audience:

'One of the main failings of the many sites we've reviewed is information and communication systems. Poor signage not only confuses and frustrates people but, in the event of an emergency, can cause frustration that

leads to crowd violence. When dealing with an uncontrollable circumstance (such as the weather), you do control one thing: how you communicate with the crowd. 'We are sorry but there is no further information at this time' is an announcement that keeps the management in contact with the crowd. No announcement can increase frustration so consider talking to the crowd, keeping people informed of the situation even if there is no change in the circumstances.'

Communications protocols

Communications protocols include the assignment of radio frequencies or channels to be used for various personnel, the types of messages, and the procedures necessary for maintaining radio discipline. These protocols should also include the decision making and accountability hierarchies and the language to be used for internal radio messages and external announcements.

Radios often become a mode for carrying on idle conversations between personnel unless specific procedures and codes of behavior are established and enforced. Too many people using the same frequency can confuse the system, therefore specific and different channels should be assigned to operations and emergency communications, and for different departmental teams. Assign response team members with specific communication responsibilities, such as one to communicate with authorities, another to attendee questions and concerns, and another to liaison with facility management and other vendors (Doyle, 2005).

Limits should be placed on nonevent communications and extraneous or emergency information, particularly when such transmissions could be heard by the general public or specific stakeholders that should not hear what is being said until the message has been acted upon. If certain radio conversations need to be restricted to only certain personnel, it may be necessary to change channels to a frequency restricted to only those personnel, typically accessible only to senior staff.

The decision-making hierarchy must be clearly established so that unauthorized decisions are not acted upon nor are improper instructions given. Specific codes may need to be established that authenticate certain messages. Make certain those with radios and communication responsibilities understand the chain of command and exact notification procedures for different types of incidents.

Cultural, linguistic, educational, and work background diversity often leads to radically different vocabularies, jargon, and perspectives (Kendrick, 2003). This is why it is important to establish a common lexicon for radio communications, particularly when public safety authorities are included in the on-site communications plan and protocol. Each public safety agency (e.g., fire department, police department, etc.) has its own norms, guidelines, and internal culture (Latoski, Dunn, Wagenblast, Randall, and Walker, 2003), which is why the 'ten-codes' (e.g., '10-4' to indicate message received, '10-20' to request one's location) are prohibited in an official incident command system because their meanings vary from agency to agency.

Voice procedures for good radio discipline should be devised and all radio users should receive training to ensure these instructions are properly carried out (see Table 8.4). Talk groups (frequency channels), call signs (an individual's personal radio identification name or title), radio call process (how to make, receive, and end a call), and terminology (words or codes to be used) should be clearly specified and adhered to (see Appendix I: Radio protocol).

Table 8.4   Common voice procedures for two-way radio usage

Call signs	• Each person with a radio should have a unique identification designation that is descriptive of the position/location/station or specific talk group • Use of personal names is not advised for large networks • Call signs typically have a word and a number or letter designation (e.g., 'Exhibit Hall Delta') • Letter designations for call signs and for spelling out words should conform to the International Phonetic Alphabet (Appendix I: Radio protocol) • Pronunciations should be distinctly different ('Base' and 'Gate' or 'Race' would be incompatible call signs)
Making and receiving calls	• All transmissions should be identified with call signs or caller and intended receiver identification • All calls should be punctuated with 'Over' to indicate end of a transmission and 'Out' to indicate end of a conversation and the channel is free for others to use • Specify the order in which the caller and receiver should be identified, e.g., caller first, followed by receiver: 'This is [sender's call sign] to [target receiver's call sign]. Over' • If there is no response, let others know the channel is clear for the next user, e.g., 'Nothing heard; [sender call sign] Out' • Receiver should acknowledge a call and the caller, e.g., 'This is [receiver's call sign]. Go ahead [sender's call sign]. Over'
Message content	• Terminology and standards should be established for transmitting different kinds of information • Messages should be brief, simple, and direct using clear language • Code numbers or words may be necessary for quick and/or protected communications (e.g., '10-13' or 'Code Blue' for an emergency, '10-25' or 'Relocate' to indicate the need to move out of hearing range of others) • Have a specific code that will activate immediate response by security personnel • Ten-codes should only be developed for event-specific users and abandoned if public safety responders become involved • Procedures should be established for verifying that messages have been received, understood, and acted upon • Personal messages or chatter should be prohibited • Profanity and indecent or obscene language must be prohibited
Channel usage	• Most two-way radios have numerous frequency channels • Channels should be designated according to talk groups and/or message types (e.g., even channels for patrols, odd channels for emergency communications) • Establish protocol for channel switching (i.e., under what circumstances and a pre-designated pattern) • Vendors using their own radios should be advised of available frequency allocations that will not conflict with the event channels • Radio coverage must be checked to ensure frequency channels are operable throughout the event site • Perform an all-radio check-in at the beginning of each shift done in a pre-designated order (e.g., alphabetically)

Consider this... 8.2

Radio protocols

During the 2002 Olympic Winter Games in Salt Lake City there were more than 6000 radio users on the communications network, which required specific radio protocol and procedures in order to manage this large number of users. Each talk group was assigned a channel for those users with whom a member needed direct contact in order to perform his or her job. Each user was assigned a call sign that was descriptive of the person's position within that group, and users were instructed not to use personal names when initiating radio calls. Users were also advised that many people would be listening to their conversations, including users located near the public or the press, so they needed to be sensitive about the information they were discussing.

Source: SLOC (2000)

The PA system, particularly at large spectator events such as sports events and outdoor events such as festivals, will likely be used for general event information and welfare announcements throughout the duration of the event. There must be a distinct difference between these regular announcements and emergency announcements delivered over the PA system. Certain emergency messages should be delivered via a code word or phrase so as not to cause undue audience stress or panic, yet allow staff to prepare for response activities. (Review the crisis communications section in Chapter 6 and the warning message attributes in Table 6.12.)

Smaller events that have a sound system for the entertainment often plan to use that sound system for emergency announcements, and most public assembly venues have a house sound system that serves as a PA system. It is important to ensure that the entertainers are fully informed and willing to cooperate regarding use of their sound system, and there must be a way to override that sound system with the house (or other) PA system if the entertainers are unable or unwilling to cooperate, and if the house PA system is the primary emergency notification system.

Support documents and documentation

Numerous documents acquired throughout the planning process may need to be available on-site in order to facilitate decision making and communications. Most event organizers create a production book (also called a specifications guide or operations manual) that includes contracts, plans, meeting minutes, correspondence, and copies of permits, licenses, or approvals that may become necessary to confirm authority and/or instructions.

Maps, site plans, technical diagrams, flowcharts, and other visual aids should be developed or acquired to enhance communications, and these should be available on-site. As discussed with radio protocols, agreed-to naming conventions (i.e., unique reference labels) should be established to eliminate confusion regarding locations, positions, and levels of urgency, which should be consistent on all documents and in all communication procedures (HSE, 1999).

Creation and distribution of a standard operations contact list and an emergency contact list should be standard operating procedure (see Appendix J: Sample contact list). The event organizer should have all pertinent contact names and numbers of all key staff, stakeholders, and vendors in the production book, and a specific list of emergency response contact information should be included as a separate document that is quickly accessible at all points of communication such as information booths and registration areas. All key personnel with emergency response duties should have a copy, and all personnel issued communications equipment such as radios should have a list of external contact numbers and internal call signs on a small portable card.

For some events, such as meetings or expositions, the delegate, exhibitor, or participants may be asked to provide an 'in case of emergency' (ICE) contact name and number on their registration form, and these numbers will be maintained in the event's registration database and perhaps even printed on the back of the individual's badge or credential. Note, however, that in some jurisdictions, Germany for example, it is illegal to require such information due to privacy laws, but it certainly may be a voluntary practice. These numbers should be properly removed from all event records after the event.

All on-site briefings and debriefings, monitoring and response activities, and communications should be documented. This may be accomplished using a variety of tools and techniques including, among other things, agendas, incident report forms, incident registers, activity logs, message logs, status boards, and videotape from closed circuit televisions. This documentation should include and illustrate the sequential aspects of these activities, conditions, and decisions so that this intelligence may be incorporated into future planning and risk assessments (as well as evidentiary material).

Information management

Information management encompasses the acquisition, distribution, control, and retention of information through the implementation of customary reporting, record keeping, and protection procedures for privacy and proprietary information in order to ensure the necessary business intelligence and institutional memory is captured and preserved. Information management facilitates knowledge management; data does not become knowledge until it is captured, comprehended, and capable of being transmitted.

There are vast quantities of information involved in a single event project and for the event organization's general operations, ranging from all the planning documentation to the attendee and personnel databases to the communications throughout the project and more. All this data must be managed or it will slip away (one individual simply cannot remember everything), be lost by mistake or malfunction, or be compromised due to intent or error. Table 8.5 lists some of the typical risks associated with managing the information assets of an event organization.

Kennedy (2006) reminds us that confidentiality, integrity, and availability are the foundation for effective and secure data systems. Strategies, policies, and procedures should be developed for acquiring and organizing information, and training must be provided to ensure that those with data management responsibilities are able to properly collect, organize, store, and protect that information in a comprehensive and efficient manner. Whether the event is massive and complex or small with only a few people involved in its planning and production, one must remember the Big Truck Theory… what happens if you get run over by a big truck (metaphorically speaking)? What data will vanish with you (or your laptop)? How long would it take to reconstruct all the lost information? Will the event project even be able to proceed?

Table 8.5 Typical information management risks

• Access control	• Lack of security level classification
• Confusing filing system	• Lax backup practices and procedures
• Equipment malfunctions	• Loss of key personnel
• Equipment misuse	• Malicious software (viruses)
• Inattention to compliance requirements	• Mobile computing and teleworking
• Insufficient business continuity measures	• Response to system breaches
• Insufficient user training	• Sabotage or vandalism
• Lack of cryptographic controls	• Sloppy maintenance practices
• Lack of documentation procedures	• Theft of equipment
• Lack of privacy policies	• Uncoordinated data storage

Table 8.6 Typical types of event data and documents

• Activity logs	• E-mails	• Meeting reports
• Advisories	• Employee records	• Memorandums
• Assessments	• Evaluations	• Press releases
• Attendance counts	• Financial records	• Registrations
• Bids and proposals	• Incident reports	• Rosters
• Change orders	• Inquiries	• Schedules
• Charts and maps	• Instructions	• Scores
• Checklists	• Inventories	• Scripts
• Confirmations	• Mailing lists	• Sign-in sheets
• Contact lists	• Manifests	• Status reports
• Contracts	• Manuals	• Telephone logs
• Correspondence	• Marketing materials	• Verifications

Information acquisition, distribution, monitoring, and reporting

Getting and giving information (the loop of communication) requires recognition of the ways in which one captures, assembles, and otherwise obtains pertinent data and information from various internal and external sources. Data, documents, and other documentation comes into the event project through a broad spectrum of portals and throughout the entire planning and production process. Some of these are listed in Table 8.6 (also review Tables 2.3, 2.8, 3.2, and 3.8).

Research is conducted and historical records are reviewed in the initial planning phases, particularly during the risk assessment, as well as when changes occur in the plans or conditions surrounding the event project. Monitoring activities also generate important data, which must be processed in the appropriate written and/or computerized formats, and should be supported with established data reporting and monitoring systems that are integrated into the communications plan. Intelligence gathering activities, such as monitoring external conditions, or the tracking of attendance, lead retrieval systems, or continuing education units must be captured and incorporated into an agreed-upon data management architecture.

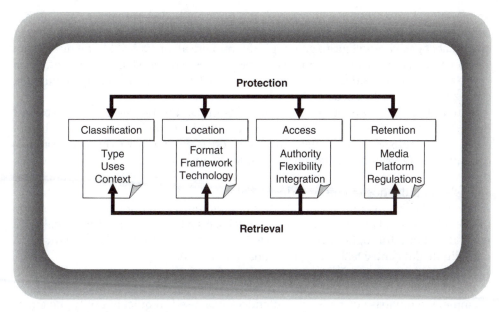

Figure 8.7   The facets of information systems

Once captured, all information and data must be analyzed, interpreted, and evaluated for relevance and accuracy. These information-handling activities include, among other things, summarizing, prioritizing, collating, validating, and logging (Crown, the, 2005a). Information distribution policies and procedures, as well as the structure and system, should be developed that directs and delivers the information to the right people in the appropriate oral, written, and other methods, as well as generates the documentation that provides the evidentiary and historical records. O'Toole and Mikolaitis (2002) emphasize that this architecture and process must be simple, scalable, and, if possible, automatically integrated throughout the project management system.

Data organization system

The information management architecture must be able to receive, arrange, and preserve data in a manner that allows that data to be retrieved and protected as needed. Here again, systems thinking is required – linkages, interactions, elements, and processes – as illustrated in Figure 8.7. Although many event organizations have some procedures in place and utilize some form of computer software for these functions, it is wise to review the system as a whole to identify gaps and vulnerabilities, as well as opportunities for improvements.

Developing an appropriate structure for organizing information relies on being able to categorize that information into meaningful clusters that recognizes and illustrates the relationship between the part and the whole (Kwasnik, 1999) and identifies the proper place to put it. These classifications should acknowledge the type of data, its uses, and its context. For example, Kennedy (2006) suggests that, for the purposes of security, data classification levels of sensitive, personal, and mission critical should be used. However, this does not completely reflect the functional requirements of who, what, where, when, why, and how information is used throughout the scope of the event project, which might suggest that contextual categories based on the administrative or operational organizational structure (e.g., committees, departments, tasks, components, etc.) would be an effective strategy. Filing systems and databases may be based on alphabetical, chronological, geographical, numerical, or topical hierarchies. Essex (2006) contends, however, that the workflow process should shape the system. The key to an effective classification system, as Kwasnik (1999) asserts, is easily identifiable criteria that reflects the needs of its users.

Standardized documentation, document design, and record keeping policies and procedures (e.g., date stamping, naming conventions, and database sort fields) should be established and implemented in a consistent manner to ensure economical and effective filing and retrieval. Standardization increases efficiency, reduces errors, and reduces training needs. It may be worthwhile to conduct a functional analysis of all the documents and documentation used in the event organization to determine the extent of integration (e.g., cross referencing) appropriate for the scope of documentation. For example, various database systems offer the functionality to generate reports throughout the life cycle of an event project, as well as reduce and consolidate data entry tasks (e.g., relational databases).

It is also advisable to explore the alternative uses for various types of information in the risk management context. As illustrated in the hepatitis story in Chapter 4, for example, the database of registered attendees was used to quickly notify the entire attendee population of the potential health threat. The preparation of manifests or use of sign-in sheets may facilitate the location of personnel deployed at an event site or account for missing persons in the event of a disaster. A high volume of pre-event or on-site inquiries might indicate the need for additional signage or informational announcements. Accurate attendance counts can prevent over-charging by the catering department or exceeding room occupancy capacity in conference sessions.

Information protection and control

The broad range of information management technology and systems available to the event organization, from the humble filing cabinet to fully integrated web-based databases and intranets, offers countless opportunities for efficient and flexible information acquisition, distribution, and retention. However, they also present countless vulnerabilities that must be overcome. Policies and procedures must be established that maintain the information system security and integrity. Berlonghi (1996) advocates the creation of a confidential information policy and plan that includes the clear definition of what shall be considered confidential information, a nomenclature to be placed on all documents, access and distribution criteria, restricted and secure storage locations, third party confidentiality agreements, and enforcement measures.

Unauthorized access can expose sensitive or 'mission critical' information to theft or tampering. Access control methods should be devised that restrict access using permission-granting procedures and special access codes, which should be changed periodically and protected. Special care must be taken when wireless technology is used as well. It is advisable to create (and periodically review) an inventory of information that is critical to the event operations and/or proprietary in nature, and prohibit its storage on any portable device (Kennedy, 2006).

As discussed in Chapter 3, identity theft and privacy invasion has become a primary concern, and nearly all countries have established privacy and data protection legislation that reflects the Principles for Computerized Data Files adopted by the United Nations General Assembly on December 14, 1990. These principles include, among other things, that personal data should be

- obtained fairly and lawfully (e.g., informed consent);
- used only for the purpose specified;
- adequate, relevant, and not excessive to the purpose specified;
- not kept longer than is necessary for the purpose specified;
- destroyed after its purpose is completed; and
- protected from unauthorized access and fraudulent misuse, modification, or disclosure.

In addition, because this legislation varies in its scope and enforcement mechanisms throughout the world, many countries include conditions regarding transborder data flows, which often include restrictions according to comparable and reciprocal safeguards (Privacy International, 1998). This might have a significant impact on meetings and events held in or attracting attendees from international locations.

Considering the volume and potential abuses of personal data residing in member, employee, attendee, and electronic commerce databases, event organizations that collect and/or retain personal information should establish and institute explicit policies and procedures on how personal information shall be managed (i.e., type of information, purpose, collection method, storage method, uses, access, disclosure, and disposal). The policies should be made available to interested or affected persons, and the procedures should be closely monitored. Again, it is important to make certain those who have access permission and data entry responsibilities receive the proper training.

Data handling procedures for sensitive data (e.g., health or financial information) and confidential information (e.g., VIP arrival manifests) are particularly important. These procedures might include encryption requirements for collecting and transmitting payment transactions, registrations, or rooming lists with credit card authorizations; collection methods and access to data on medical conditions or health-related accommodation needs; and strict limitations on where such data may and may not be stored (e.g., not on laptop computers). Disposal procedures for data and documents should also be considered, including how and when data will be removed from electronic databases and how waste materials containing confidential information will be removed and/or destroyed (e.g., shredding). These procedures should be conformed to by all vendors or suppliers with access to this information (ICCA/COPE, 2005).

Information retention and preservation

The information management system serves as a knowledge repository. As such it must ensure that the data used to conduct the business of the event project and event organization is preserved through proper record keeping, backup procedures, and archiving, and employing the appropriate data and media storage technology. Record keeping may be governed by internal policies and governmental regulations that dictate how long and in what format information must be retained. These might include financial records, membership records, legal documents, employee records, and numerous other written and computerized records. An inventory should be conducted to identify the scope and requirements for all documentation.

Records preservation should be considered from a business continuity as well as the compliance perspective. Vital records, which could contain sensitive or classified information, must be protected in the event of an emergency or disaster to ensure the event business and the business of the event can continue uninterrupted, or at least recover. Vital records include 'Rights and Interest' records that are needed to protect an organization's essential legal and financial functions and activities, and the legal and financial rights of individuals directly affected by the organization. These include:

- Banking and investment information (account numbers, types of accounts, contact names)
- Contracts, agreements, and other contractual obligations
- Employment records (payroll, leave, social security, retirement)
- Financial records (accounts receivable and accounts payable records, tax records)
- Insurance records (policies, equipment inventories, appraisals)
- Proofs of ownership (leases, titles, deeds).

The location of data and records must also be identified. Data may be spread across desktop computers, laptops, electronic devices, and removable media (e.g., thumb drives, CDs, PDAs, etc.) and unless replicated in a centralized location (e.g., a network server) the loss, theft, or damage of that particular piece of technology means that data is gone. Routine and comprehensive backups of all electronic data should be employed as a standard preventative maintenance practice, including and particularly for portable devices used by teleworkers. Numerous web-based backup services are available as well as devices that may be used in-house. Copies of all electronic records (backups) and critical documents should be made and stored in a secure off-site location.

Stakeholder management

A stakeholder is an individual or organization that is financially, politically, emotionally, contractually, or personally invested in an event. Stakeholders include those actively involved in the event project, those who exert influence over it, and those whose interests may be affected by it (PMI, 2000). Typical event stakeholders are shown in Table 8.7. These constituents and constituencies, or target publics (Masterman and Wood, 2006), may be internal or external, active or dormant, supportive or adversarial, demanding or docile, champions or challengers, but they will all and always have specific interests, expectations, and requirements. It is incumbent upon the event organizer and organization to identify, analyze, classify, and manage the relationships with these varied stakeholder constituencies through engagement and communications to develop a mutual vision of and commitment to the requirements and desired outcomes for the event project.

Stakeholder management should seek to recognize and communicate with the various explicit, implicit, voluntary, and nonvoluntary constituencies of the event project to achieve advantageous and ethical outcomes, as exemplified in the Clarkson Principles of Stakeholder Management, which were devised through the Redefining the Corporation Project as a guide to corporate social responsibility in a global context (Clarkson Centre for Business Ethics, 1999).

- Acknowledge and actively monitor the concerns of all legitimate stakeholders.
- Listen to and openly communicate with stakeholders about their respective concerns and contributions.
- Adopt processes and behavior that are sensitive to the concerns and capabilities of each stakeholder constituency.

Table 8.7 Typical event stakeholders and stakeholder groups

• Activist groups	• Neighborhoods
• Attendees/consumers	• Participants
• Board members	• Philanthropic beneficiaries
• Civic groups	• Public officials
• Client/host/bride	• Regulatory agencies
• Committees	• Sanctioning bodies
• Community leaders	• Shareholders
• Employees	• Sponsors
• Investors	• Suppliers
• Media	• Volunteers

- Recognize the interdependence of efforts and rewards among stakeholders.
- Work cooperatively with public and private entities to ensure that risks are minimized.
- Avoid altogether activities that might jeopardize human rights or would be patently unacceptable to relevant stakeholders.
- Acknowledge potential conflicts and address such conflicts through open communication.

Stakeholder analysis

Conducting a thorough stakeholder analysis provides event organizers with a clear picture of the role and scope of stakeholders in an event project and the strategies for effective communications with them. This analysis should accomplish the following:

- Identify and categorize stakeholders and stakeholder groups.
- Identify key stakeholders and critical stakeholder groups.
- Determine stakeholder roles and desired support and the resultant obligations.
- Measure the stakeholder's influence.
- Prioritize stakeholders according to power, influence, and interest.
- Identify linkages between stakeholder groups.

The stakeholder analysis examines many different aspects of the nature of the stakeholders including their potential for cooperation or opposition, their span of influence, the issues they care about, whether or not their cooperation or involvement is required, whether preemptive or defensive strategies should be taken with them, and what communication methods and messages should be employed (see Appendix L: Stakeholder analysis worksheet).

Identify internal and external stakeholders and constituencies by examining all those individuals, entities, and organizations that have a role in or potential impact on the event project. This may take some probing and brainstorming to define the possible impacts of and on various stakeholders and the 'stakes' (i.e., financial, political or emotional interest, ownership share, or legal or moral rights) each stakeholder or constituency has. Some stakeholders may not view themselves as such until some aspect of the event has a negative impact on them, such as residents in a neighborhood adjacent to the event site that has become inaccessible due to the high volume of traffic. Some stakeholder groups may not become apparent until attention is focused on the political aspects of an event element, such as activists protesting against a controversial topic or speaker at a conference or the use of animals as entertainment at a fair.

Consider this... 8.3

Fair goers' parking disrupts neighborhood life

The New Mexico State Fair is held each September and attracts hundreds of thousands of people every day of its 17-day run of entertainment, concerts, competitions, rodeos, carnival rides, games, farm animals, horses, and agricultural and art exhibits. It is held on a 236-acre fairground that was on the outskirts of town when built but is now in the center of the city surrounded by residential neighborhoods and businesses. This raised numerous quality-of-life issues for the fairgrounds' neighbors. In addition to the frustrations of trying to get home through the gridlocked traffic during the fair, neighborhood residents also found their streets, driveways, and even lawns crammed with parked cars because fair goers tried to find a cheaper (and quicker) alternative to the jam-packed parking lots on the fairgrounds.

The residents formed a neighborhood association and forced the city to prohibit fair parking on residential side streets, and to enforce that ordinance with constant police patrols that would have any unauthorized vehicle towed to their impound lot, which would cost the offender US$100 to retrieve his or her vehicle. Residents are provided with vehicle stickers that indicate authorization to park in the neighborhood throughout the duration of the fair, including sufficient stickers for the vehicles of their visitors and personal guests. The neighborhood association and the fairgrounds now work together to identify any events held at the venue (e.g., concerts, sporting events, and other fairs and festivals) that would impact the residents and to develop restrictions and procedures to mitigate negative effects each event might have on the neighborhood.

Stakeholders should be categorized according to whose support and involvement or lack thereof might have an effect on the success of the event project or the event organization's ability to produce the event. Primary (or key) stakeholders are those with a direct stake in the event, are often immediate internal and external communities of interest, and those that are both influential (degree of power or control) and important (extent of impact). Secondary stakeholders are those with a public or special interest stake in the project, those with either influence or importance, and often intermediaries that become involved if the project passes a certain threshold of significance.

A threat assessment should be conducted to determine the validity, power, and urgency of each stakeholder or stakeholder group and the opportunities and challenges each presents. Identify their level of financial or emotional interest in the event project (validity); their capacity for influencing the event and its outcomes in positive or negative ways (power); and their issues, priorities, potential for cooperation or opposition, and the immediacy of these (urgency). A threat requires three things: the motivation to act, the opportunity to act, and the resources to act. Eliminating any one of these three factors neutralizes the threat. Conversely, an opportunity requires the same three factors, which, when enabled, may facilitate the ability to take advantage of that potential benefit. Level of engagement and commitment should also be considered. The level of

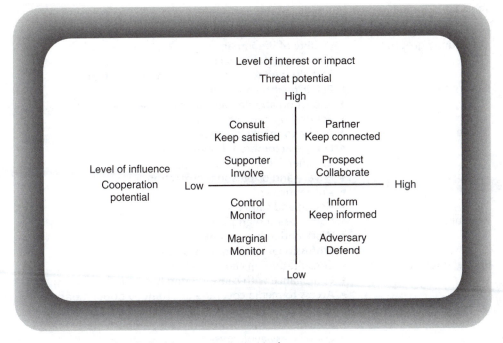

Figure 8.8   Typical stakeholder assessment matrix

engagement is based on the stakeholder's level of understanding, and the level of commitment is based on the strength of the stakeholder's opposition or support.

The role of communication in relationship management

Communication plays a big part in overcoming these risk factors through acknowledging and informing constituencies, as well as forming, changing, and reinforcing attitudes using proactive public relations tactics aimed at altering negative perceptions and improving understanding (Masterman and Wood, 2006). A communications strategy should be developed that recognizes and integrates the varied interests and goals of stakeholders, acknowledges and monitors their concerns and capabilities, and engages and actively involves stakeholders in the success of the event project.

A strategy for obtaining or enhancing support and neutralizing opposition should be developed by defining the information each constituency needs and its recommended level of involvement (MSH and UNICEF, 1998). Typical assessment matrix tools are often used to prioritize and indicate communication strategies for varying stakeholder levels and attitudes, as illustrated in Figure 8.8. In addition, O'Toole (2006a) advises creating an action matrix that indicates when communications should take place during the phases of the event project (i.e., initiation, planning, implementation, the event, and closure).

O'Toole (2006a) also recommends creating an overview chart that itemizes the stakeholders and the event elements to show the areas of concern for each stakeholder (typical issues are shown in Table 8.8). This overview can be very helpful in recognizing relationships between stakeholders that may indicate conflicts of interest or enable coalitions for cooperation or opposition to be formed. It is imperative that stakeholder analyses be redone whenever a significant change takes place because

Table 8.8 Some typical stakeholder issues

Community groups	• Quality of life impact • Environmental impact • Participation (e.g., equal access to public funding)
Government	• Public health and safety • Impact on and demand for public services • Political damage/community goodwill
Media	• Access to timely information • On-site accommodation for broadcasting • Commercial promotional opportunities
Participants	• Privacy and/or personal protection • Authenticity of credit for participation • Health and safety safeguards
Personnel	• Compensation and benefits • Workload management • Professional development opportunities
Special interest groups	• Consultation on cause-related implications • Compliance with cause-related legislation • Access to media coverage or attendee populations
Sponsors	• Return on investment (e.g., audience counts, benefits, etc.) • Brand exclusivity protection (e.g., ambush marketing) • Controversy avoidance

new stakeholders or stakeholder groups may have been added, which may mean there are new threats (or opportunities) regarding concerns, causes, clashes, and coalitions.

No event takes place in a vacuum; there are always people interested in what, how, and why the event is being held for personal, political, and professional reasons. Whether their interest becomes an asset or an impediment depends upon your recognition of and interactions with them. Strive to see things from their point of view and use good communication skills and strategies to build understanding and cooperation, and, where necessary, to minimize threats.

Summary

Effective communication is the foundation of all event management and event risk management functions. Getting the right information from and to the right people at the right time and place is paramount to the successful operation and management of an event, and particularly critical in any emergency or crisis situation. A communications plan should be crafted that includes the entire spectrum of event planning and operations, from the initial development stages through the close-out and evaluation phase, with special attention focused on the dynamic communication needs during the actual run of the event when the acquisition and distribution of information will be crucial to effective risk monitoring and controlling functions.

Communications encompasses information acquisition and distribution, and 'intention' is at the core of all communication. From internal communications within the event organization to external communications with clients, sponsors, municipal officials and others, the key is clarity of intention regarding the desired responses and understanding from the receivers. In order to avoid miscommunication, a variety of written, verbal, and visual communication techniques must be used, delivered in a timely manner, in a location where there are the fewest distractions, and in an atmosphere of trust.

The success of an event often depends on the timely and proper management of the volumes of information surrounding the event. From proposals to contracts to status reports to the production book or operations manual (often referred to as the 'event bible'), the acquisition and distribution of information must be carefully planned. Information is an asset, provides visibility, promotes cooperation, allows you to track and control risk, and it must be protected from abuse or misuse. Data protection is both an obligation and a sound business practice.

It is vital to remember that stakeholder management deals with the engagement of and interactions with the varied stakeholder constituencies of the event, including clients, committees, officials, authorities, sponsors, participants, providers, and others to develop a mutual vision of and commitment to the requirements and desired outcomes for the event project. These varied constituencies often have different perspectives and priorities, and their differing needs must be integrated into the communications plan to ensure these do not conflict with, but instead support the risk management plans devised for the event project.

Key safeguards

- Assess the communication skills of those with communication roles and responsibilities (including your own) and seek systems and training to improve potential gaps.
- Identify and implement a mix of high-tech and low-tech mediums as appropriate for the message content, context, and intended recipients.
- Ensure interoperability and redundancy for communications systems and equipment.
- Create an information management system that facilitates retrieval yet protects data.
- Make certain the backup system encompasses all important data in all locations that it is kept.
- Listen to and build rapport with stakeholders and constituencies.
- Develop plans for acquiring strategic economic and political alliances.

Chapter review challenge

1 Research the cultural implications of nonverbal communications and list two examples of cultural differences related to body language, eye contact, personal space, touching, vocal intonation, and time usage. Discuss how these differences might negatively affect communications with event stakeholders.

2 What are the differences between an overall event communications plan and an on-site event communications plan?

3 Review Figures 8.4 and 8.5 and describe the benefits and constraints of a decentralized and a centralized on-site communications network.

4 Using the date and time of an event as a piece of information, create a flowchart that traces the scope of its acquisition, distribution, monitoring, reporting, control, protection, and retention throughout the event project.

5 Besides the traffic and parking issues identified in Consider this... 8.3, what other potential impact might events held on the fairgrounds have on the neighboring residents and businesses?

Practical risk management exercise

The Association for Big Bucks Corporations (ABBC) holds two international conferences per year for its membership of 4000 corporate executives and other interested attendees, with a typical attendance of 700 at each conference. The ABBC is seeking a risk management consultant to review, analyze vulnerabilities, and make recommendations on its information management system and data protection practices in conjunction with these two conferences. Prepare a scope of work for this project that will be used to estimate your project costs and be included as the terms of reference in your contract with the association. Be sure to show what activities you would undertake and include all the likely components of the information management system you would examine.

Key terminology

Call sign: A designation used in two-way radio protocols to identify the person to whom the radio has been assigned.

Communication block: An impediment to effective communication.

Communication channel: The format and/or medium used as a two-way information pathway for sending and receiving messages.

Constituency: A group of individuals with shared characteristics, interests, goals, and/or expectations.

Cryptographic controls: The use of encryption to make transmitted information unintelligible to those without the key for decoding the transmission.

E-commerce: Conducting buying or selling transactions via the Internet.

Encryption: The encoding or scrambling of data using a cipher system.

International Phonetic Alphabet: The set of phonetically distinct words designated to represent the letters of the alphabet.

Interoperability: The ability of variable systems and communications equipment to work together and exchange information.

Intranet: An electronic communication system similar to the Internet but linked only within a single company or organization.

Manifest: A list of passengers, attendees, personnel, or cargo.

Manual: A set of guidelines, instructions, or information compiled into a booklet form, such as an employee handbook or procedures manual.

Naming conventions: A set of rules for selecting consistent and unambiguous identifier names for people, places, documents, or things.

Notice: A sign, poster, or memorandum conveying critical information or warnings used to attract special attention to the information.

Official spokesperson: The person(s) designated to speak to the media or the public on behalf of an individual or organization.

Phone tree: A pre-determined list of contact persons to call with subsequent lists of calls to be made by each contact.

Production book: The notebook containing schedules, contact lists, and other documentation used on-site during an event.

Relational database: A database system that organizes and accesses data according to shared attributes.

Ten-codes: A set of code numbers using 10 as the first of a two-number set devised to represent descriptions or instructions.

Variable message sign: A static or portable electronic sign, often used on highways, that can change the message displayed.

Wishful listening: Hearing only what one wants to hear or reinterpreting a verbal message to conform to one's preferences.

Online resources

BRINT Network	www.brint.com
MindTools.com	www.mindtools.com
Privacy links and blogs	www.privacyrights.org/links.htm
Project Management, Tasmanian Government	www.projectmanagement.tas.gov.au
Vocational Information Center	www.khake.com/page66.html

Chapter 9
Marketing issues

Know your customers

This chapter will examine how to:

■ Recognize the role and functions of marketing and their use in risk assessment activities
■ Develop strategies for employing marketing communications in proactive and reactive situations
■ Identify and manage the threats and opportunities associated with sales and sponsorship initiatives
■ Integrate marketing activities to facilitate synergy and reduce risk exposures

Introduction

Marketing is an important facet of overall meeting and event management because the event will not be successful or sustainable unless there are attendees. Many events have a distinct marketplace character (e.g., trade shows, arts and crafts fairs). Sponsorship of existing events and specially created events is becoming a key element in marketing campaigns for large corporations and small businesses around the world in an effort to take advantage of their exciting and experiential nature. Although this chapter goes into some depth on marketing theory and techniques, it does not claim to replace other texts that cover how to market an event or use events as a marketing tool. Its aim is to examine the vulnerabilities associated with marketing activities that the risk manager should be aware of, some of which are shown in Table 9.1, and how to work in conjunction with those performing the marketing functions to reduce risk.

Marketing should be, and often is, referred to as 'sales and marketing' because there is more to marketing than simply promoting a product to induce a sales transaction between buyer and seller. Marketing encompasses the range of functions that facilitate business development, cultivate economic and political support, and shape the image and value of the event project, and the placement of this chapter following the chapter on communications is deliberate because all these functions are communication functions. Masterman and Wood (2006) recognized this, asserting that organizational image has an effect on the products offered and the ability to sell those products, and contend that one must use an integrated marketing communications strategy that puts the traditional promotional mix (the four Ps: product, price, place, and promotion)

Table 9.1   Some typical marketing risks for meetings and events

- Ambush marketing or suitcasing
- Attracting unwanted attendees
- Brand management
- Campaign timing
- Competition – date, audience, event type
- Craze marketing
- Deceptive/offensive advertising
- Inappropriate/incompatible sponsorships
- Ineffective advertising
- Insufficient promotion

- Lack of an integrated marketing strategy
- Lack of sponsorship revenue
- Loss of sponsors
- Market saturation
- Media coverage – inclusion of
- Media coverage – lack of
- Merchandise licensing
- Publicity stunts
- Under-leveraged sponsorships
- Unsolicited email campaigns

into a broader and synergistic context, thereby increasing the achievement of short- and long-term objectives.

Kotler, Bowen, and Makens (1996, p. 12) define marketing as 'human activity directed at satisfying needs and wants through exchange processes.' Middleton with Clarke (2001, p. 19) define it as 'the process of achieving voluntary exchanges between two parties' (the buyer and the seller) and the decision processes that lead to this transaction. Getz (1997, p. 250) defines it as 'the process of employing the marketing mix to attain organizational goals through creating value for clients and customer.' Briggs (2001, p. 42) asserts that marketing is 'a process, rather than a series of scattered and isolated activities.'

Marketing, therefore, must be viewed and approached as an interrelated, dynamic, and continual process – one that is broader than the sales transaction itself. It must recognize the relationship between the buyer, the seller, the product, and the continuous interactions and decisions that must take place in order for the transaction to occur, as reflected in Figure 9.1. Risk is inherent throughout this continuum unless clarity is achieved in defining the customer, his or her needs and desires, the product that will satisfy those needs and desires, and the ways in which to reach that customer so that the sales objectives of the event organization are achieved. The very feasibility of the event is contingent upon this comprehensive and holistic understanding, and the success or failure of the event will depend upon using the appropriate tools, techniques, and tactics to meet the needs and objectives of both the buyer and the seller.

In addition, the nature of the event as an 'experience' necessitates a thorough understanding of the unique buyer-seller relationship associated with what is, in reality, an intangible product. Masterman and Wood (2006) note that, with events, the buyer as an attendee becomes part of and adds value to the product (i.e., the experience), which adds further impetus to define and analyze the attitudes, perceptions, and decision making processes of customers and event producers to ensure that the interactive communications are taking place at the right time and in the right ways.

Marketing plan

The marketing plan is the formal expression of the integrated process system illustrated in Figure 9.1, and from a risk manager's perspective it becomes an important

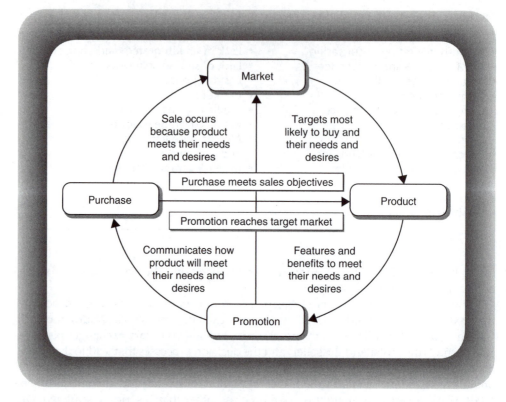

Figure 9.1   An overview of the marketing process

tool in the risk assessment process. A marketing plan encompasses the overall marketing strategy and tactics to be employed, including target customer definition, acquisition and retention, the internal and external messages and mediums, and the maintenance of positive customer or guest relations to achieve the marketing aspirations for the event project and its hosting organization. The process system includes market research, strategy development, campaign planning, communication activity definition, and evaluation, monitoring, and corrective actions as appropriate (Middleton with Clarke, 2001).

A written plan is essential to illustrate the nature of the customer (i.e., the attendees), their expectations and expected behaviors, and the status of overall organizational readiness to address and deliver on these expectations (Berlonghi, 1990). A non-existent, incomplete, or fragmented plan is not only difficult to monitor and measure, it will reduce the ability to take advantage of opportunities and respond to emerging market conditions or threats (Masterman and Wood, 2006).

Ulrich Wünsch, Lecturer for Event Management at the International University of Applied Science, Bad Honnef-Bonn, Germany, offers the following advice on how to reduce risk in marketing plans:

- Spend enough time on assessing goals and objectives and take at least two rounds in assessing them – there is often a goal behind a goal.
- Get all stakeholders involved and look into satisfying their different needs.
- Take communication seriously; communication is about understanding, not about saying something and assuming the other would know what you meant.

- Monitoring along the process according to the project plan is essential and fine-tuning your marketing accordingly as well.
- Find the right story and tell that story in clear words through all your marketing material to create a concise image.
- Look out for the sponsoring fit so that your marketing and the marketing of sponsors coincide time-wise and message-wise.
- Plan and reassess and plan and check and produce and get feedback and do and reflect – even under the typical time pressure and stress of events.
- Financial expectations are as serious as non-financial expectations; they need to be met along clearly set lines so that all parties involved can rely on an objective and agreed assessment.
- Do not trust your own belly, instinct, intuition (or whatever) solely and do not trust any other belly solely; finding the right magic takes research and verification to identify the crucial issues – creativity and artistry is 90 percent solid craftsmanship.

The development of the marketing plan consists of the situation analysis, target market definition, message and branding development, marketing medium selection, and marketing strategy integration. The situation analysis, described by Getz (1997, p. 255) as the 'factors affecting demand and the organization,' is the starting point of determining feasibility in which the environmental, competitive, and opportunity aspects of the marketplace are scanned and an appraisal of the proposed or existing product or service (the event) is conducted. Are there sufficient hotel rooms adjacent to the convention center to accommodate a convention of this size? Is the market over-saturated with fund raising galas competing for the same patrons? Could this community arts festival increase tourism during this traditionally slow season? If we decide to proceed, what are our unique selling points, what objectives should we set, and what measurements will we use to indicate success?

Target market definition and segmentation

Linked closely with the situation analysis is target market definition wherein the scope of the internal and external markets are identified and segmented; the characteristics of primary, secondary, and tertiary market segments are analyzed; the target market needs, wants, and expectations are defined; and effective customer relations strategies and tactics are determined. Kotler et al. (1996, p. 20) defines a market as 'a set of actual and potential buyers who might transact with a seller' and this definition should be compared to that of a stakeholder in order to recognize the scope and nature of internal and external 'customers.'

Segmentation helps identify, qualify, and prioritize target markets (Hoyle, 2002) and facilitates the development of the appropriate product features and benefits that will meet needs and desires, as well as the selecting messages and mediums for reaching the various segments. Segmentation creates a customer profile using different variables, as shown in Table 9.2, and this market intelligence may reveal market, product, or promotion strategy weaknesses as well as new market opportunities. The characteristics associated with these variables will also help identify consumer expectations and expected behaviors when conducting risk assessment activities (e.g., identifying adversaries that need to be monitored). Geographic density (i.e., urban, suburban, rural), for example, may suggest that attendees from rural areas coming to a conference held in an urban location might require more preparatory communications regarding travel and safety precautions.

Table 9.2 Market segmentation variables

Demographic	Geographic	Psychographic	Behaviors
• Age/lifecycle	• City size	• Aspirations	• Benefits sought
• Education level	• Climate	• Attitudes	• Buying behavior
• Ethnicity	• Country	• Beliefs	• Loyalty status
• Family status	• Density	• Lifestyle	• Perceptions
• Gender	• Region	• Personality	• Purchase history
• Income	• Zip/postal code	• Social class	• Readiness
• Occupation		• Values	• Seasonality
• Marital status			• Usage rate and patterns
• Religion			

Sources: Getz (1997), Hoyle (2002), Kotler et al. (1996), Masterman and Wood (2006), and Middleton with Clarke (2001)

A target market will include varying combinations of these segmentation variables, which could indicate affinity markets and niche markets to be approached as well as features that may appeal to these segments. A festival or sport event attracting a significant percentage of international visitors might wish to create advertising translated into these languages and may need to include translations on the on-site event signage. Socio-economic and consumer loyalty indicators may suggest preferential features such as special parking areas, entrances, or attractions, which will likely require additional or special security tactics. The risk manager needs to know as much about the potential customer as the marketer does.

Marketing messages and mediums

Effective marketing messages are developed by defining the event's unique value proposition for the attendee, determining what needs to be communicated to each target market, creating brand identity using distinctive and compelling verbal and visual imagery, and ensuring consistency in positioning, message, and branding. Brand and image management is particularly important for recurring events and should be carefully considered for first-time or one-off events. Recurring events will have a brand (i.e., image and reputation) and that brand needs to be protected, which may include everything from logo or event title trademarks to venue contracts controlling juxtaposition of incompatible groups (e.g., a hotel booking concurrent meetings of direct competitors or conflicting behaviors). First-time or one-off events need to establish a branding strategy and tactics to increase the probability of success.

Selecting the appropriate mediums for conveying marketing messages requires an understanding of the various mediums available and their relative strengths and weaknesses. As with communication in general, there are countless tools and technologies available to the marketer to transmit a message:

- Broadcast mediums (e.g., television, radio)
- Print mediums (e.g., cards, brochures, posters, publications, billboards)
- Online and digital mediums (e.g., Internet websites, email, blogs, podcasting, text messaging)
- Verbal mediums (e.g., telemarketing, word-of-mouth marketing, presentations).

The choices should be made according to target market preference and penetration, and according to the market life cycle. For example, younger markets will likely prefer digital mediums but older markets will likely prefer broadcast and print mediums. Festival or leisure events targeting a local market in a high-density urban area might select outdoor and mass transit advertising, and industry-specific conventions typically employ sequential direct mail tactics including brochures and blast emails. The tactics selected must comply with consumer regulations such as 'truth in advertising' laws (e.g., avoiding exaggeration or unsubstantiated claims of expected benefits, such as promising career advancement by attending the conference) and 'anti-spam' legislation (e.g., the 'CAN-SPAM' Act of 2003 in the U.S. that regulates commercial electronic mail messages).

Integrated marketing strategy

It is widely recommended that an integrated marketing strategy be developed to ensure objectives are achieved. This includes selecting marketing activities in accordance with target market characteristics, developing a marketing mix that builds on and reinforces each activity's strength and objectives, establishing a schedule of marketing activities to achieve awareness, interest, desire, and action (known by its acronym AIDA), and integrating all marketing activities to ensure consistency and timeliness. Typical meeting and event marketing tools are shown in Table 9.3, which should be examined by the event marketer to identify opportunities and by the event risk manager to determine vulnerabilities. Hoyle (2002) cautions that the marketing strategy must include the mechanisms for monitoring external conditions at

Table 9.3 Typical marketing tools for meetings and events

Advertising
- Broadcast
- Digital
- Direct mail
- Displays
- Print
- Indoor/outdoor

Electronic
- Blogs
- Email
- Newsgroups
- Websites

Publications
- Directories
- Magazines
- Newsletters
- Newspapers

Sales promotions
- Contests
- Demonstrations
- Giveaways
- Stunts
- Sweepstakes

Direct sales
- Merchandise
- Telemarketing
- Ticket sales
- Trade show participation

Hospitality events
- FAM tours
- Loyalty programs
- Networking
- Receptions

Publicity
- Guest appearances
- Lectures
- Media conferences
- Presentations

Strategic alliances
- Cross promotions
- Donors and patrons
- Grants and gifts
- Sponsorship

all times (e.g., terrorism alerts, competitive events, economic downturns, etc.) in order to integrate this information and/or the changes instigated by them throughout all the marketing activities, and recommends that response plans be developed concurrently with the marketing plans.

Promotions

Promotion encompasses the procurement, orchestration, and organization of advertising campaigns, promotional events, cross promotion alliances, and contest or giveaway activities conducted to generate attention, interest, and demand for the event project. It is how the message reaches the buyer using an integrated variety of marketing tools that are chosen based on how and where the target markets get their information and make their buying decisions. The primary methods used include advertising, sales promotions, promotional events, and cross promotions. Each of these methods use a variety of mediums to communicate messages and influence buyer behavior, and each has certain risks that must be recognized and addressed. Again, it is important to fully integrate all the promotional activities and reinforce all activities with consistent messages and branding in alternate mediums, as well as public relations activities. As Kennedy (1991) asserts, image congruency is vital.

Advertising

Advertising is the purchase of space in various mediums to deliver messages to promote the event project. As such, it is a procurement activity subject to the contractual issues identified in Chapters 3 and 7. The strengths and weaknesses of available media outlets and techniques must be assessed, suitable media outlets need to be identified according to target markets and marketing objectives, media buys have to be negotiated and executed, and the delivery of media buys and activities must verified and their performance evaluated. The aims of advertising include creating awareness, informing, persuading, or reminding (Kotler et al., 1996; Middleton with Clarke, 2001) and each medium offers different capabilities and limitations. The following cautions should be considered by the event marketer and risk manager.

- *Mass media*: (i.e., television, radio, and newspapers) lack of or limited target market selectivity means that everyone will know about the event, even undesirable attendees or disruptive constituencies.
- *Print*: long lead times for magazines, brochures, and other publications may limit ability to change message content; direct mail may have a junk mail image; poster, sign, flyer, or leaflet distribution or posting may be regulated and may be considered or become litter; invitations may have missing information, misspelled names, or use improper etiquette.
- *Indoor/outdoor advertising*: lack of target selectivity (see mass media) and potential for vandalism (corruption of message/image) to posters and billboards.
- *Electronic media*: email regulations may require permission marketing; website integrity may be compromised and target market access selectivity likely uncontrollable; e-commerce websites require transaction security and may be subject to disabled-access laws; online commentary (e.g., blogs, listserv groups) may be subject to defamation liability.
- *Telemarketing*: often intrusive and may be regulated (permission marketing).

- *Things change*: do not guarantee appearances or attractions (include 'subject to change' language as appropriate); make certain there is a mechanism for providing updates, refunds, and/or alternate date (e.g., rain date) as appropriate.

An advertising campaign must be carefully planned to ensure the investment provides value and the messages reach the intended target audiences at the right times. A haphazard plan or one that is based on personal preference rather than sound metrics (e.g., precise viewer/reader/listener numbers and demographics) will be expensive and ineffective. Given the cost of ad space/time and the limited characteristics of viewer/listener impression comprehension, most advertising messages should focus on simple content and attention-getting imagery that capitalizes on cognitive (information), affective (emotion), and conative (action inspiring) communication strategies (Masterman and Wood, 2006). This should be supplemented with in-depth information delivered in highly targeted event collateral and public relations activities.

Media buys will be based on cost, reach (target audience), frequency (repetition requirements), efficiency, scheduling, and impact (Getz, 1997; Kaatz, 1989; Kotler et al., 1996). Media buys are often negotiated as a sponsorship consisting of discounted or matching ad space (Getz, 1997) and must take other sponsorships and strategic alliances into account. For example, a small local festival acquired a beverage sponsor with the agreement that the beverage company would receive logo inclusion in the event's billboard advertising. However, the media buy, which included a matching donation of ad space, was not with the outdoor advertising company that the beverage sponsor had an exclusivity agreement with and therefore the beverage company could not allow their logo on the billboards, which prompted the cancellation of the sponsorship. The loss of the beverage sponsor's financial and product contribution to the event far outweighed the value of the matched media buy.

Promotional events, sales promotions, and cross promotions

Promotional events are special events and activities conducted by event marketers to increase awareness of and interest in the event project and sales promotions are activities conducted to increase ticket sales and attendance by creating demand and purchase urgency, thereby stimulating action by event customers. Glaesser (2006) notes that they can also be effective in overcoming the after effects of a crisis by communicating readiness to continue 'business as usual' or the fact that the event will take place as scheduled despite external conditions. The range of activities is virtually endless, ranging from publicity stunts to 'early bird' specials to discount coupons to giveaways. Clear and measurable objectives must be set for each activity undertaken, and each activity needs thorough planning, including its own risk assessment. Of prime importance is compatibility with the purpose and nature of the main event and its target audience.

Consider this... 9.1

Anti-Disco night causes mayhem

July 12, 1979: An ill-conceived special promotion conducted at the Major League Baseball doubleheader between the Chicago White Sox and the Detroit Tigers in Comiskey Park in Chicago turned into mayhem when spectators turned unruly and flooded onto the field after local radio disc jockey Steve Dahl exploded a box and then a metal dumpster filled with records as a mock demolition of disco music centerfield during the intermission between the two games. The discount admission scheme (98 cents and a disco record) and was devised by Dahl and White Sox owner Bill Veeck's son Mike in hopes that lagging attendance would be increased by 5000. Instead, 50 000 turned out, most of whom were not baseball fans – more like rock concert goers – who attended specifically for the demolition. In addition to the damage to the field by the intended explosion and the unintended vandalism that occurred in the pandemonium that followed, the excess records that were not collected at admission gates were thrown from the stands towards the field like Frisbees throughout the first game and during the promotional stunt causing numerous injuries to spectators as the discs hit and sliced into them. The second game was cancelled and the White Sox forfeited both games due to the damage and mayhem.

Using an event as a promotional tool in marketing campaigns for other products or services must also be carefully considered. Any event requires the same attention to the administrative, design, and logistical responsibilities associated with events management, including a proper risk assessment. Marketing professionals are not necessarily events management professionals and may lack the experience or understanding of the issues associated with bringing large groups of people together in a particular time and space. This becomes particularly evident when craze marketing strategies (i.e., a competitive rush to acquire a valued object) are employed.

Consider this... 9.2

Hazardous store openings

September 2, 2004: Swedish furniture and home goods giant IKEA's new showroom opening in Jeddah, Saudi Arabia, turned deadly when 20 000 instead of the expected 3000 to 5000 shoppers showed up to get the cash vouchers offered to the first 250 through the door. Three people were killed and 16 injured in the crowd crush caused by so many people trying to get in, which was exacerbated when the store opened an hour early due to the crowd size and those at the rear started pushing their way towards the front.

February 10, 2005: The IKEA store opening in Edmonton, north of London, offered large discounts for a limited period upon opening at midnight. Crowd management problems occurred again as up to 7000 bargain-hunters showed up when only 2000 were expected. One man was stabbed, five had to be hospitalized, and store security guards and shoppers were assaulted as the crowd tried to force their way into the store, and, once inside, were fighting over deeply discounted furniture. Although the store had planned to be open for 24 hours during this promotion, it had to close 30 minutes after it opened due to the chaos and police were called in to disperse the crowd.

Sources: Crowd Dynamics (2005) and Biz/ed (2005)

Publicity stunts must be carefully considered from a risk management perspective because they are all too often potentially hazardous and sometimes downright dangerous, with the danger being the guarantee for media coverage. Hoyle (2002) contends that the proliferation of outrageous television programming may have instigated the increase in bizarre or dangerous stunts just to break through the clutter to capture attention, but cautions that these may alienate the audience and cause negative rather than positive publicity. Celebrity appearances, often arranged within sponsorship agreements, can be very effective at creating awareness and interest through increased media coverage, as well as boost affinity and credibility through the implied endorsement, but they often require special security personnel and precautions as well as contingency plans and/or insurance coverage for non-appearance (and any scandal surrounding the celebrity will have an impact on the event).

Sales promotions such as contests, discount coupons, proof-of-purchase or donation discounts, and frequency or volume discounts are often used to increase purchases at specific times or to penetrate new or underperforming target markets. Contests, raffles, and sweepstakes require special attention due to the gaming character of such activities, especially as the value of the prize increases (Silvers, 2004a). The appropriateness and legalities of conducting these activities must be confirmed before they are undertaken, and they must be conducted in a manner that is absolutely above reproach; there must be no 'actual or perceived conflict of interest' and must be completely 'nondiscriminatory in terms of entry qualifications and access' (Silvers, 2004a, p. 333). The use of coupons, proof-of-purchase schemes, and other discount systems requires a fully integrated infrastructure to ensure the transaction procedures can accommodate them. For example, if giving a discount for bringing a canned food item for a homeless shelter, sufficient containers and transport for the collected canned goods must be arranged. Measures to prevent counterfeiting should be considered for any controlled coupon or proof-of-purchase discount system or contest.

Many promotional activities are coordinated with sponsors, charity beneficiaries, suppliers, and compatible organizations to increase market penetration and decrease the investment costs of each participant. These must be considered as partnerships and, as such, require considerable cooperation and clear communications. The roles and responsibilities of each partner must be precisely delineated, goals and objectives must be clearly specified, reciprocal logo and brand usage must be explicitly defined, and media tie-ins must be carefully negotiated. Logo usage, placement, and context restrictions should be of particular importance. For example, a civic festival arranged to have its logo included on the letterhead for all city communications, which, unfortunately, also included the solid waste department. One day this department issued a toxic waste notice that was faxed out to every city employee that included a huge skull and crossbones right under the festival logo; not the promotional link the festival was anticipating when they made the agreement.

The synergy created by cross promotions can deliver considerable cost-saving and image-enhancing benefits, but it must be remembered that an affiliation will be established in the public's perception and the activities conducted by each partner (positive or negative) will reflect on the other partner(s). The event organization must protect the integrity of its image and message as well as respect that of its partners. This is also why meeting and event organizers must take steps to control ad hoc or ancillary activities conducted by others in conjunction with their event; the same perceived affiliation will occur (Berlonghi, 1990).

Promotional collateral materials and services

A broad variety of marketing materials will be required to support promotional events and activities. These can range from displays for in-store demonstrations and trade show participation to program books for meeting delegates and festival goers to imprinted giveaways for theme parties and product launches. Content must be acquired from internal and external stakeholders and contributors, logo usage and brand or theme imagery must be monitored, and the appropriate language, style, organization, and format must be used according to the subject matter, time sensitivity, and intended audience.

Numerous opportunities and vulnerabilities occur from a risk management perspective. The opportunities include such things as providing health and safety tips in marketing brochures for festivals and meeting registration materials, including emergency contact numbers on delegate badges or site map handouts, and the inclusion of ingredients on menu cards at banquets or responsible alcohol consumption messages on table tents at receptions. Any and all special conditions and particularly restrictions should be clearly communicated via advertising and promotional materials whenever possible (FEMA, 2001). The vulnerabilities include, among other things, inaccurate, incomplete, or outdated content, improper logo usage (e.g., color, placement, or unauthorized use), counterfeited coupons or credentials, intellectual property infringement, lack of continuity (i.e., mixed messages), and lack of good old fashioned proof reading.

Public relations

Public relations is a marketing tool used to gain publicity coverage for an event project and/or the event organization using communication to build relationships with its various publics in an effort to increase awareness, credibility, and enthusiasm, as well as reduce overall promotion costs (Kotler et al., 1999). It encompasses the cultivation and conservation of beneficial relationships with the media, as well as preparing for the enhancement and control of the impressions, image, and issues surrounding the event project and enterprise, particularly in times of crisis or controversy.

Unlike advertising, coverage generated through public relations activities is not purchased, which creates a third party endorsement (e.g., what someone else says about your event), is perceived as unbiased (Skinner and Rukavina, 2003), and has greater opportunities to provide more in-depth and background information capable of influencing attitudes of the target publics. Kotler et al. refer to this as 'share of mind' (1999, p. 571). Kennedy contends that recipients of marketing messages are 'stubbornly reluctant to believe them' (1991, p. 48) and suggests that these messages must be substantiated with testimonials, statistics, research results, and other proofs in order to be perceived as credible, and Masterman and Wood assert that 'earned media' such as consumer reports, reviews, peer recommendations, and published articles are more 'believable' (2006, p. 89); all of which can be achieved through public relations activities.

Public relations strategy

Developing a public relations strategy involves identification of the scope and nature of the various internal and external publics, definition of the needs and objectives for public relations activities, development of well-articulated and credible messages that can be communicated to the various applicable publics, and the identification of the mediums and methods capable of effectively and efficiently reaching those publics. Public relations activities should be considered for all internal and

Table 9.4 Typical public relations activities

- Articles submitted to publications
- Awards program submissions
- Audio new releases
- Calendar of events listings
- Community organization endorsements
- Charitable affiliation
- Contests
- Demonstrations
- FAM tours
- Hospitality events
- Interviews
- Media conferences
- Media kits
- Newsletters (print and electronic)
- Official proclamations
- Official ambassadors or mascots
- Press releases
- Preview events
- Publicity stunts
- Public service activities
- Public service announcements (PSAs)
- School programs and activities
- Special appearances
- Speeches and presentations
- Talk show expert
- Video news releases

external stakeholder constituencies as well as the consumer target markets in proactive and reactive contexts and from both a political and a promotional standpoint, and certainly within a crisis management perspective.

There are numerous tactics that may be employed within a public relations strategy (see Table 9.4), and in large organizations these activities are typically organized through marketing, publicity, or business communications departments and performed by individuals known as public relations specialists, media specialists, communications specialists, publicists, public affairs specialists, or information officers. These responsibilities may be outsourced or assigned to a single marketing director or a committee in smaller event organizations. The risk manager should team up with the public relations person or department to ensure that the activities to be conducted are included in the event's risk assessment and to confirm their readiness to actively participate in crisis management situations.

Public relations should be viewed as a year-round activity for recurring and first-time events, and for one-off events activities should be considered before, during, as well as after the event; post-event coverage can set the stage for (or inspire) future endeavors. It is advisable to establish archival procedures that collect and retain copies of all public relations materials and coverage for evaluation purposes and future strategy development. It is also widely recommended that media kits and other background materials be developed that will enhance current public relations efforts and these will become particularly helpful when responding to a crisis or emergency situation. Materials to consider are shown in Table 9.5.

Image, issues, and crisis management

Public relations activities often focus on image and issue management objectives in addition to general promotional or publicity coverage. In this context it is important to develop governmental, community, and public affairs programs to determine issues and trends that may impact the event objectives or production as a facet of constituency or stakeholder management (see Chapter 8). Public relations personnel 'must understand the attitudes and concerns of community, consumer, employee, and public interest groups and establish and maintain cooperative relationships with them and with representatives from print and broadcast journalism' (Bureau of Labor Statistics, 2006).

Table 9.5 Typical public relations collateral

• Contact names and numbers	• Philanthropic and professional affiliations
• Copies of speeches and published articles	
• Fact sheets	• Photographs (digital, color, black and white)
• Frequently asked question (FAQ) sheets	
• History and structure of the organization	• Policy statements on pertinent issues
• History of the event	• Safety record and initiatives
• Key participant profiles	• Schedules
• Media accreditation and access instructions	• Site plans and diagrams
• Media (press) releases	• Sponsor list
• Names and profiles of key executives	• Sponsor profiles
• Newsletters, brochures, flyers	• Statistical data
• Participant rosters	• Videotapes, audiotapes, DVDs, CDs

Sources: Getz (1997), Hoyle (2002), and Regester and Larkin (2002)

Image management seeks to create name recognition and generate an affinity for an event project and event organization through the establishment of influential education and information activities to help shape positive public opinions. Equally, it seeks to protect the image of the event and event organization from degradation due to misinformation, misalignment, or malice. This protective function will be closely linked with issues management and will require close attention to activities and media coverage generated by outside sources. As discussed with stakeholder management, methods for interaction and accommodation between the event organization and its publics, allied and opposing, must be identified and cultivated.

Regester and Larkin (2002) define an issue as a point of conflict or a gap between an organization and its publics, typically due to external political, regulatory, economic, social, or technological change, as well as internal administrative or operational change. An issue can transition from a potential issue to an emerging issue to a crisis situation unless it is recognized, its potential impact is analyzed, and it is monitored closely in order to intervene in a timely manner. The emerging stage is when increasing external awareness of the issue occurs and early detection increases the organization's ability to influence reaction through public relations activities. Warning signals for identifying crisis-bound issues include public resistance, official health or safety warnings, persistent customer complaints, lax compliance standards, and pleas from employees (Harvard Business Essentials, 2004). The risk manager and public relations director should maintain an issues log that anticipates, tracks status, and prompts action in a preemptive manner.

Should an issue reach the crisis stage, an aggressive public relations approach is required. Regester and Larkin (2002) contend that the three C's of crisis management are concern, control, and commitment, and provide the following observations and suggestions for communications in a public relations context and for the communicators in a crisis:

• Act as a facilitator to explain what has happened and to ensure appropriate action is being/has been taken.
• Tell your story; information voids will be filled with rumor, misinformation, and misrepresentation so the organization must be prepared to fill it with credible information.

- Tell your story fast; the media may begin as neutral or even sympathetic, but if they believe the organization is too slow at providing information, they may become hostile.
- When appearing on television, jump on untruths, innuendo, or misleading remarks immediately, interrupting the interviewer if necessary.
- Understand, harness, and manage public emotion; communicate in language that relates to and alleviates anxiety.
- Conveying grave concern and decisive action is essential in any situation involving injury or loss of life.
- Never speculate about the cause; if wrong it will can seen as an attempt to cover up or hide the truth (and could nullify insurance coverage).
- Never admit liability; an official investigation will establish that.
- Never point the finger of blame; an official investigation will establish that.

The risk manager should confirm that there is a method for ensuring incidents or controversies are promptly identified internally, the protocols for communicating with and including emergency response agencies in public relations response activities are in place and effective, the media spokespersons for the event organization are designated and trained properly, and that information can be communicated quickly to prevent speculation and misrepresentation.

Media relations

Public relations professionals must cultivate mutually beneficial relationships with the media (i.e., newspapers, radio, television, Internet journalists, and publication editors) in order to achieve the objectives for publicity coverage. These relationships are critically important during a crisis, controversy, or emergency to ensure reporting is properly framed (Harvard Business Essentials, 2004). This relationship starts with the development of a media list that specifies contact information for individual media representatives (e.g., editors, journalists, reporters, etc.) and contact protocols for each media outlet. The relationship is then built by preparing media releases and requests that are timely and newsworthy, respecting and accommodating the media's needs and restrictions, providing the media with appropriate access and facilities, and always providing accurate and credible information. However, if an emergency, controversy, or crisis should occur, the media will likely descend on the event in aggressive droves. As Henderson (2007, p. 164) notes, '... crises attract intense media interest and modern communications technology assists in the collection and distribution of information about occurrences and their aftermath, including images recorded by victims.'

Consider this... 9.3

Media partner attracts unanticipated vandalism

A charity football game between two local law enforcement agencies was organized as a public relations event to increase positive feelings towards the officers and their important function within the community. This admirable cause drew considerable support for the all-volunteer event, including the donation of money to purchase uniforms and equipment, use of a high school stadium, and the commitment from a local television station to broadcast the game live, which was widely advertised by the television station. Upon arriving at the stadium early in the morning of game day, organizers found highly offensive graffiti aimed at law enforcement painted on the field and throughout the grandstands, which would have been visible on camera during the broadcast and jeopardized the television coverage. Such vandalism had not even been considered by the law enforcement personnel organizing the event. Nevertheless, even though the game was scheduled to start in four hours, they were able to get a work crew of prisoners from the county jail brought over to completely repaint the grandstands and steam clean the Astroturf field in time for the stadium to open for spectators and the game was broadcast as planned. The lesson was learned and the following year overnight security was provided by off-duty police officers prior to game day.

Official spokespersons

The public relations representatives deliver the good news and the bad news. In addition to creating a figurehead or focal point of authority for media appearances in a publicity context, designating and training an official spokesperson (or persons) is a key component of a risk management plan, and the first element of a crisis management plan (Kotler et al., 1999). The possibility of strong demand or loss of personnel suggests that several spokespersons be designated and Regester and Larkin (2002) recommend two or three official spokespeople be regularly available to the media. Glaesser (2006) advises that spokespersons should have a forceful personality and come from the upper echelon of the organization to enhance credibility. It is also advisable to designate the official spokespersons for all lead agencies and authorities involved, and the protocols to be followed when responding to the media and others.

Training spokespersons is necessary. The event wants to make certain the person speaking on behalf of the organization delivers the correct information and proper messages in a professional manner. In a crisis situation, reporters will likely be shouting out difficult and controversial questions in a rapid and aggressive manner. This is very intimidating and requires a cool head and calm demeanor – a skill that requires practice. The Federal Emergency Management Agency offers the following pointers for spokespersons (Haddon and Bullock, 2003, p. 162):

- Repeat information to reinforce key message points.
- Correct inaccuracies, otherwise they will be accepted as fact.
- Pair use of statistics with stories or case studies that bring them to life.
- Stay out of other people's business; let other emergency agencies answer their own questions.
- Always be honest. If you don't know an answer to a question, say so and offer to find the answer or refer the reporter to someone who can.

It is important to understand that during a crisis or emergency situation everything said by anyone in the event organization is 'on the record' – it could be quoted or referenced in the reporting done by the media. All media and other inquiries should be referred to the designated spokesperson or officials and it must be explained to event personnel why this is imperative: that in a crisis everything must be factual and they may not have all the facts, and that speculation and rumor often leads to the reporting of false information. However, internal stakeholders and personnel should be communicated with and advised of facts as soon as possible to prevent speculation and rumor.

Sponsorship management

Sponsorship management encompasses the identification, solicitation, securing, servicing, and retention of sponsors, donors, and philanthropic patrons through the proper valuation and delivery of suitable tangible and intangible benefits to provide financial and cost avoidance support for the event project. The terminology for these benefactor initiatives may vary in different event sectors, such as donor cultivation in the non-profit sector or strategic alliances in the association or corporate sectors, but the bottom line objective of fiscal support remains the same. The risks often remain the same as well, which include, among other things:

- Over confidence in or over dependence on sponsorship revenue.
- Overwhelming or overshadowing the event with sponsor imagery and activities.
- Unsuitable or conflicting sponsors.
- Lack of due diligence in evaluating sponsors or sponsorship packages.
- Non-fulfillment of contractual obligations.
- Non-compliance with legal and regulatory restrictions or requirements.
- Ambush marketing and other unauthorized non-sponsor and predatory activities.

First and foremost is the determination of the suitability of commercial sponsorship and non-commercial support for the event. Not all events are appropriate for sponsorship and for those that are, careful attention must be paid to structuring the sponsorship program and its revenue and cost-avoidance objectives to ensure the purpose and brand of the event is not diluted. Potential sponsors or donors must be solicited and selected based on their appropriateness and target market match to the event audience and its attitudes or characteristics. Will the sponsor attract controversy? Will controversy at an event impact the sponsor? Will the exit of a sponsor or the failure to attract the number or type of sponsors projected jeopardize the financial viability of the event? Answers to these questions will help shape contingency plans.

It is particularly important to specify conflict of interest criteria and limits on what can/will and can not/will not be allowed within the sponsorship agreement and on site at the event. Sponsor exclusivity categories must specify the scope of that exclusivity; a sports event, for example, may control the event but not the teams participating in the event, which may mean that a direct competitor of an event sponsor might have their name and logo on all the athletes' uniforms (IEG, 1996). Sponsor and donor on-site recognition and activities must be specified and incorporated into the event's operational plans. Signage and banners must be incorporated into the décor, and promotional displays (e.g., inflatables, vehicles, structures, etc.) must be positioned safely within the site plan (HSE, 1999).

It is also imperative that one understands the legalities of sponsorship agreements and the acceptance of donations. There may be advertising restrictions, antitrust repercussions, tax implications, and a broad variety of reporting requirements. For example, there are restrictions in many jurisdictions on the types of media exposure and signage allowed for alcoholic beverage sponsors (Berlonghi, 1990), as well as whether or not they are allowed to provide product as an in-kind donation to an event. And, although most events must actively pursue sponsors, some events may have sponsors and donors seeking them out because of the status, size, or target market affinity the event offers; in which case equal opportunity must be offered within the confines of fairly and uniformly enforced criteria in order to prevent potential violations of antitrust laws (Foster, 2002). For example, many trade shows require that all sponsors must be exhibitors. Tax implications (e.g., the unrelated business income tax (UBIT) laws in the U.S.) may center on what portion(s) of the benefits provided by the event are taxable as advertising income or non-taxable because only recognition is provided (Skinner and Rukavina, 2003).

Consider this... 9.4

Goodies in award show gift bags seen as taxable income

Gift bags given to presenters and nominees at the Primetime Emmy Awards and the Academy Awards are seen as taxable income according to the U.S. Internal Revenue Service (IRS). This is due to the advertising cost tax deductions given to the companies donating the items included in the gift bags because the products are contributed in anticipation of publicity, not given as gifts. The products included in the gift bags can consist of designer clothing, jewelry, cosmetics, gourmet edibles, sports club memberships, luggage, and vacations. The 2006 Emmy Awards gift bags had an estimated value of between $27 000 and $33 000, and the 2006 Academy Award gift bags were valued at $100 000. The Academy of Television Arts and Sciences, organizers of the Emmy Awards, notified presenters by mail of the taxable status of the gift bags, and included a waiver to sign acknowledging receipt of the letter in order to remove liability for the organizers, and recipients were required to fill out IRS forms upon receipt of the luxurious gift package.

Sources: Finn (2006) and Wiener (2006)

Selling and servicing commercial sponsorships

Of particular interest to many large public events (e.g., festivals and sports events) is the selling of commercial sponsorships to provide much needed revenues for an event's operations and to ensure prestige and growth. Commercial sponsorship, as defined by the International Events Group, is the payment of a cash or in-kind fee in return for access to the exploitable commercial potential associated with an event property (IEG, 1996). Sponsorship, also known as event marketing, is big business involving considerable sums of money and serious responsibilities. Since a commercial sponsorship is a contractual relationship between the event organization and the sponsor, careful attention must be paid to the crafting of this relationship. The event must be able to service the contractual obligations, including the delivery of all promised benefits, under whatever circumstances may occur.

Sponsorship contracts often include the following sponsor benefits: the category or exclusivity status based on level of investment, signage at the event (type, size, and number), advertising credits, merchandising rights, and access benefits such as tickets, passes, special areas, hospitality opportunities, etc. (Skinner and Rukavina, 2003). The contract will also address obligations for both parties, such as the fees to be paid, the exclusivity to be maintained, logo and trademark usage policies, and restrictions placed on either party regarding ancillary activities. Great specificity should be included in such contracts to ensure that each party to the contract (the event and the sponsor) knows their responsibilities and the limits of their benefits, authority, and acceptable activities. Many sponsorship contracts offer first right of refusal for renewal that must be honored, which should include decision deadlines that allow sufficient time for recruiting a replacement. The event should always prepare a post-event fulfillment report that documents the delivery of benefits and the media exposure received.

Commercial sponsors will be diligent about controlling their legal liability and potential negative exposure in connection with their purchase. They will also strive to increase the positive exposure associated with the alliance with an event. The event organization, and the event risk manager, should liaise with the corporate sponsor's own legal and risk management departments to coordinate assessment activities and take advantage of its expertise and resources.

Ambush marketing

Of particular interest to commercial sponsors (and trade show exhibitors) is the control of ambush marketing tactics employed to take advantage of the event's target market without payment of fees for the access to the commercial potential of the event. Such activities dilute the value of the investment in the sponsorship. The event that does not monitor and control this runs the risk of losing sponsorship revenues. Tactics such as extensive media buys by direct competitors of major sponsors using language that implies an affiliation with the event or erecting promotional displays adjacent to the event site (also known as outboarding) create a perceived relationship with the event. The event organization should be diligent about trademarking and protecting the event's brand and logo imagery and should make every effort to control adjacent activities if possible. Getz (1997) reported that some major events have taken an aggressive counteractive approach by issuing public statements confronting the ambush marketers.

Other aspects of unauthorized marketing activity that should be monitored include suitcasing at trade shows, unsanctioned hospitality receptions at conventions, and unauthorized product sampling at public events. Suitcasing refers to non-exhibitors conducting selling activities on or in close proximity to the trade show floor, which should be addressed by show floor managers, security personnel, and within facility contracts. Major conventions often have numerous sponsored hospitality receptions and hospitality suites, and non-sponsors often seek to host similar attendee-attracting activities without paying for the privilege. This should be addressed contractually with the venue (e.g., prohibiting hospitality suite bookings that are not sanctioned by the event organization) and promotionally with the attendees (e.g., including the policy in registration materials and publishing a list of official suites and receptions).

Public events such as festivals often allow sponsors to conduct on-site sampling and couponing activities wherein attendees are given small product samples or discount or voucher coupons for their products. Non-sponsors may try to conduct similar activities, particularly if the event has a large attendance and little or no entrance fee. This must be strictly controlled because not only does it devalue the sponsor's benefit, the sponsor will have provided the event organization with proofs of product liability coverage and the trespasser will not. In addition, the event may not want certain products distributed to its audience (e.g., tobacco products). Large crowds also often attract those who wish to distribute pamphlets or flyers for a particular campaign or cause. One may not be able to restrict the freedom of speech of an individual that has paid the requisite admission fee, but any distribution of material should be able to be prohibited and disruptive behavior should result in ejection for cause. The rights of the event organization to do this should be confirmed with the venue and local authorities.

Sales activities

It is hoped that all this marketing activity leads to the sales transaction – the purchase of the admission ticket or registration package, the sale of a sponsorship, the buying of a treasured souvenir or special treatment. The management of these sales activities includes the establishment and supervision of procedures, platforms, and transaction processes for all the on-site, remote, and electronic sales activities connected with the event project in order to achieve profit expectations. These sales activities include such revenue streams as registration and ticketing operations, food and merchandise concession sales, and other retail endeavors. The environment in which these activities take place must be considered from the logistical as well as an image or branding perspective.

The risk manager should confirm that a solid business plan is in place that has determined the income requirements and sales objectives for all products, event tickets, and other revenue streams, and has established product lines and pricing structures according to capacity control needs and desirability or proximity demand. Incentives used to encourage desired consumer behavior and cash flow (e.g., discounted 'early bird' registration fees or 'last chance' event souvenir bargains) should employ inventory management tactics to maximize revenues according to supply and demand conditions.

In addition, the exchange of money for goods or services typically requires the authority to do so, which may necessitate the possession of a business or merchant license and the registration with the appropriate local, state or provincial, or national taxation and revenue authorities. Failure to address these business basics can jeopardize the event (resulting in closure) and the event organization (resulting in fines or penalties). Compliance by all those who conduct selling activities on site at or on behalf of the event should also be confirmed.

Sales platforms and procedures

Event access, products, and services can be sold through many different portals, ranging from online to off-site locations to on site at the event, and purchases may be made in person, by mail, over the telephone, or through the Internet. E-commerce technology should be identified and employed as appropriate, the parameters for sales activities by authorized external sales outlets must be established, and the equipment, materials, and staff responsibilities for in-office and on-site sales activities must be determined and coordinated. Tickets, coupons, and vouchers must be considered as cash value assets and protected from loss, theft, or counterfeiting by establishing methods for accounting for and auditing unsold tickets or vouchers. All authorized on-site or remote sales activities must be closely monitored and unauthorized activities (e.g., ticket scalping or touting) must be controlled.

Transaction procedures must be established that ensure high customer service levels and protect the revenues generated from sales activities (bad customer service can result in, at best, negative word of mouth publicity and, at worst, confrontation or retaliation incidents). The appropriate equipment necessary for processing transactions must be obtained (e.g., credit card equipment, cash drawers, etc.); effective cash handling procedures must be developed and implemented (see Chapter 7); and sufficient training must be provided for personnel handling those transactions, including the procedures for processing all inducements, discounts, coupon redemptions, and refunds. The risk manager should confirm that all sales platforms and transaction procedures are thoroughly integrated and are assessed to uncover any vulnerability within the system.

Merchandise

Many events sell souvenirs that not only extend the legacy of the event experience; they also provide important revenue streams to the event organization. In addition, many events, particularly festivals and public spectator events, will sell concessionaires the rights to sell food, beverages, and retail merchandise at the event. These endeavors require a thorough understanding of retailing in order to be successful, which is why many event organizations will subcontract the event's souvenir merchandising to professionals in the retail field, and establish policies for concessionaires that clearly state the limits and requirements for authorized selling activities conducted at the event. Before embarking on such endeavors the event organization must determine the liabilities and legalities associated with merchandising, licensing, and concession agreements, some of which are shown in Table 9.6. Getz (1997) advises that, similar to sponsorship contracts, licensing agreements should be handled by legal counsel to ensure that proper expectations and limitations are contractually specified and brand integrity is protected. The same holds true for distributor agreements to make certain brand integrity is maintained through quality control and customer service, as well as revenue protection through payment policies and procedures.

Selling concessionaire rights and space at an event has profit, procurement, and product line implications. The event may be selling the concession based on a flat fee or a percentage of sales. If employing the percentage arrangement a method must be devised for monitoring total sales in order to calculate the amount due. Concessionaires

Table 9.6 Typical risk considerations for merchandising and licensing

• Concession fee calculation and collection	• On-site placement and safety of stalls
• Copyright/trademark infringement	• Order fulfillment
• Counterfeit merchandise	• Product liability insurance
• Distributor agreements	• Product line selection
• Import/export requirements	• Storage of excess on-site stock
• Inventory management	• Surplus inventory liquidation
• Lack of quality control	• Unauthorized logo usage
• Licensing agreements	• Unauthorized sales activities
• Market life cycle	• Unsafe products or services

should be selected based upon providing an effective product mix (e.g., not too many vendors offering the same merchandise) and their ability to provide proofs of compliance with all applicable regulations (e.g., business license, insurance coverage, health and safety permits, etc.). Establishing these parameters in a written policy will help prevent claims of restraint of trade or discrimination, and enforcing these policies will help illustrate due diligence by the event organization.

Concessionaire contracts should specify the rules and regulations for the set-up, operation, and dismantling of their booth, stall, stand, vehicle, display, or tent (HSE, 1999). These regulations should encompass space allotment, location, structural safety, storage location and safety, inventory replenishment (e.g., on-site vehicle movement), equipment safety, hours of operation, and selling activities (e.g., confinement to within space allotment or booth). Those conducting unauthorized selling activities (see ambush marketing) should be removed from the event site and the event organization should work with local authorities to determine methods for deterring such activities adjacent to the event site (HSE, 1999).

Summary

Everything about meetings and events is about marketing, just as it is all about administration, design, operations, and risk management. All these functions are inextricably connected and must be thoroughly integrated. Marketing is applicable on a broad range of levels, from the logistic to the strategic, and clarity must be achieved when defining the target markets, their needs and expectations, and the short- and long-term goals of the organization, including the objectives and requirements for their various internal or external stakeholder constituencies. A balance must be achieved between marketing objectives and risk management responsibilities. The goals of the event's risk management plans should be completely consistent with an event's marketing goals. Any promotional activity or event must be integrated into the overall event plans, and the risks must be assessed.

Event marketing materials and messages must be carefully crafted to ensure they are targeting the appropriate constituencies (attracting the 'right' audiences) and are providing correct and credible information (making the right promises). The information and instructions included in them must be scanned to make certain they are consistent with the operational plans and logistical constraints of the event. They must be scheduled properly so as not to strain the capabilities of the delivery mechanisms (such as ticket sales outlets or functional start times and deadlines).

Marketing activities need to be carefully considered to ensure they do not pose safety hazards or the potential for negative publicity, and public relations efforts should be widely used to educate consumers and constituencies as well as manage the event's image through the good times and bad. Sales activities and strategic alliances are meant to enhance the fiscal capabilities of the event organization and the value and dimensions of the event experience, which requires forethought and a good match between the event organization, its partners, and its audience.

Key safeguards

- Ensure the marketing plan has been thoroughly integrated into the administrative and operational plans.

- Create and analyze customer profiles of all internal and external target markets.
- Develop mutually beneficial relationships with the media.
- Prepare crisis communications plans in conjunction with the development of the public relations campaign.
- Designate and train spokespeople to communicate on behalf of the event organization.
- Establish criteria to ensure there is a 'good fit' between sponsors and the event.
- Ensure there are contingency plans for the loss or lack of sponsorship revenue.
- Make certain that cash value tickets and/or vouchers have counterfeit protection features.
- Confirm that the event and all its concessionaires have the appropriate licenses and other documents necessary to conduct business transactions.

Chapter review challenge

1 Review the demographic variables in Table 9.2 and suggest a possible meeting or event risk associated with each.
2 Prepare a SWOT analysis of electronic or digital marketing tactics and suggest ways to address the weaknesses and threats.
3 How can archives of public relations and advertising documentation for an event be used to assist in promotional and evidentiary endeavors?
4 Using the list of demographic variables, suggest a commercial sponsor for a festival that would be 'unsuitable' for each variable and explain why.
5 List five ambush marketing tactics and suggest strategies for preventing each.

Practical risk management exercise

The organizers of the Whole Globe Youth Soccer Championship have asked you to coordinate with its sponsorship sales team to help identify suitable commercial sponsors for its seven-day event that features teams of boys and girls between the ages of 8 and 16 from all over the world. Prepare a list of selection criteria that the sales team may use for evaluating potential sponsors, including justifications that explain why certain sponsors would be unsuitable and illustrates the possible consequences.

Key terminology

AIDA: The acronym typically used to describe the marketing process of awareness, interest, demand, and action.

Ambush marketing: A predatory activity used by a non-sponsor or unsanctioned vendor to take advantage of the commercial potential of and create an affiliation with an event.

Antitrust: Protection from restrictions on fair trade, price fixing, and inhibiting business competition.

Blog: (short for web log) A frequently updated online journal, newsletter, diary, or commentary.

Bounce back coupon: A coupon that is returned to the issuer in order to acquire the product, service, or discount offered.

Brand: An image and reputation for a specific level of quality and consistency for a product or service.

Commercial sponsor: A company, individual, or organization that pays a fee for the affiliation with an event in order to exploit its commercial potential.

Concessionaire: A vendor that has purchased the right to sell goods or services at an event.

Craze marketing: The tactic for creating a competitive or urgent rush to acquire a desirable or valuable object (or individual).

Cross promotion: The collaboration between two or more entities to create a mutually beneficial promotion.

Early bird: A discount given to consumers that register or purchase a ticket prior to a certain date, often offered to stimulate cash flow.

In-kind: Products or services given in lieu of money.

Loyalty program: Discounts and other special offers extended to frequent customers.

Media kit: A collection of background materials that may be used by media representatives when generating coverage on an event.

Outboarding: The erection or placement of a promotional display outside the exhibit hall or event site, often done to create a perceived affiliation with an event and gain access to its attendees.

Penetration: The level of market share achieved by reaching consumers and increasing the number of sales within a new or existing target market.

Permission marketing: The requirement or policy that marketers gain permission from prospective customers (i.e., 'opt-in') before sending advertisements.

Proof of purchase: An item or label included on a product that is exchanged for a discount or amenity.

Publicity stunt: A planned, often unusual event or action designed to attract public attention.

Public relations: The activities associated with arranging opportunities for exposure in the media capable of influencing public opinion.

Public service announcement (PSA): An announcement of public interest that is broadcast free of charge as a service to the public, often requiring non-profit status of the producer.

Sampling: The distribution of samples or small-quantity portions of a product in order to introduce or induce use.

Segmentation: The dividing of potential customer populations into groups with common attributes.

Spam: Unsolicited e-mail.

Suitcasing: Selling activities conducted by non-exhibitors within or adjacent to a trade show.

Target market: A potential customer population.

Telemarketing: Marketing research and sales activities conducted over the telephone.

Unrelated business income tax (UBIT): The tax assessed on the income received by tax-exempt organizations that is not substantially related to its exempt purpose.

Online resources

Canadian Public Relations Society	www.cprs.ca
Chartered Institute of Public Relations (U.K.)	www.ipr.org.uk
Event Marketer Magazine	www.eventmarketermag.com
Global Alliance for Public Relations and Communication Management	www.globalpr.org
IEG, Inc.	www.sponsorship.com
International Association of Business Communicators	www.iabc.com
Public Relations Society of America	www.prsa.org
The Sponsorship Report (Canada)	www.sponsorship.ca
U.K. Sponsorship Database Media and Sponsorship Glossary	www.uksponsorship.com/glosr.htm
Wikipedia article on Marketing	http://en.wikipedia.org/wiki/Marketing

Part Four

Operational safeguards

An event is the marriage of creativity and responsibility

WOW Factor... something so impressive, surprising, fantastic, sensational, powerful, amazing, unexpected, spectacular, stunning, breathtaking, astonishing, incredible, exceptional, dramatic, outstanding, dazzling, or extravagant that it elicits a 'WOW!' from people.

Meeting and event organizers, designers, and producers are constantly in search of ways to bring the WOW Factor into their event experiences. They seek the latest and cutting edge environments, activities, and technologies to make the event more exciting and memorable. Unfortunately, this rush towards exhilarating originality often leads to 'OW!' instead of 'WOW!' in terms of safety and outcomes because they haven't considered the effects these elements will have on the underlying logistics and physical requirements for bringing people together at a certain time, in a particular space, for a specific purpose.

The quest for novelty and innovation is necessary for events to remain competitive and successful, but it must always be tempered with caution so that the experience delivered will be enjoyed rather than endured and the audience will be enthralled rather than endangered. The three chapters in this section will examine the issues surrounding program design, site management, and attendee management in order to ensure the event experience is designed in such a way that it will meet the needs of the people, the place, and the pursuit whilst balancing the WOW opportunities with the operational obligations.

Chapter 10
Program design

Something to do
Something to see
Something to eat and drink
Somewhere to pee

This chapter will examine how to:

- Determine the risks associated with the attractions and activities included in an event that must be incorporated into the risk management plan
- Create a safe event environment that serves the event audience while controlling potential negative impacts
- Assess and control the risk factors inherent in the serving of food, beverages, and alcohol at an event
- Analyze the hazards and vulnerabilities associated with technical equipment, production elements, and special effects included in an event

Introduction

Design is a creative process that results in an esthetic outcome. Program design focuses on the artistic interpretation and expression of the goals and objectives of the event project and its experiential dimensions. Designing a meeting or event is creating an experience rather than simply an activity or a setting. Bowdin, Allen, O'Toole, Harris, and McDonnell (2006) describe program design as the flow of the various event elements over the duration of the event experience, and cites the need to integrate the audience expectations, venue constraints, and staging with the sequential and logistical requirements. Goldblatt (2002) highlights the extensive nature of the range of opportunities when designing a program, describing the process as web-like or kaleidoscopic rather than linear as one brings together all the aspects of the event experience together. O'Toole (2006b) emphasizes that event design must be a combination of the esthetic with the practical, which coincides with Lawrence's assertion (2006) that design is 'applied' art, 'applied to solve a particular problem.' In other words, designs must be usable.

Effective program design requires strategic, esthetic, technical, and logistical skills in order to deliver the experience that will provide economic and emotional value to

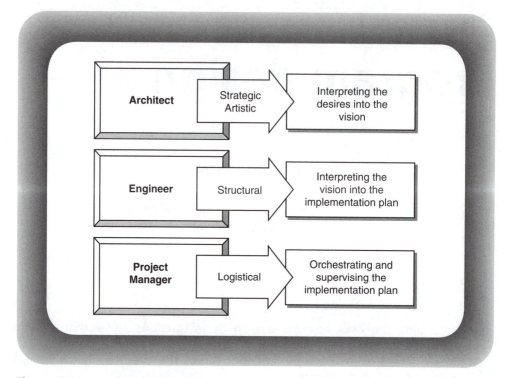

Figure 10.1 Functional aspects of event design

the event consumer, and relies on a thorough understanding of the who, what, where, when, and why. As illustrated in Figure 10.1, one must be an event architect, interpreting the client's desires and objectives to design the concept or vision for the event, but this design process must have a strong foundation in the practicalities of event production. One must be an experiential engineer, interpreting that vision and shaping that design into a structural plan capable of being implemented through the selection and sequencing of the proper program components and elements that will deliver the experience desired according to the resources available. And one must be an event project manager, ensuring the goods, services, and personnel are procured and the logistics of implementing the plan are devised and supervised.

Design relies on creativity, which is often sparked by such techniques as shown in Table 10.1, but must always start with the intent of the event and the goals and objectives to be achieved. Inspiration and ingenuity will fill the gap between the challenge and the solution, forming the plan for the content, which, in turn, establishes the extent. The creative concept that is developed must then be evaluated from a marketing, operational, and financial perspective (Bowdin et al., 2006), and accepted by the client or hosting organization. Trying innovative or unusual ideas is important but care must be exercised when pushing design into the 'new' or the 'WOW' in order to minimize the potential for failure due to the inexperience or lack of ability of those implementing the event or the misunderstanding or rejection by the audience.

Each element, each component, each activity, each feature of an event that brings the design into reality will have inherent or potential risks associated with its installation, equipment, and operation, which must all be carefully managed to control risk. The event risk manager must have sufficient knowledge about the logistics and mechanics of each individual product or service brought into the event site and made

Table 10.1 Creativity techniques

Brainstorming	A group technique for eliciting lots of ideas that are not initially assessed for value or practicality
Browsing	Researching topics in various sources to gain an overview of imagery and applications as stimulus
Free association	Using a word or phrase as a starting point and allowing connections to flow without a predetermined direction
Idea mapping	Using a problem or objective as a starting point and creating a visual map of linkages with ideas, elements, features, and solutions
Idea matrix	Creating a matrix with attributes or elements as the column headers and filling in the corresponding boxes with aspects or possibilities
Storyboarding	Putting event elements, activities, or attributes on cards and arranging and rearranging them in sequences or connected groups
Variation thinking	Using an object or outcome as a starting point and considering how one might modify, substitute, rearrange, adapt, or change its use

Sources: Monroe (2006), O'Toole (2006b), and Wujec (1995).

available to the event audience in order to be able to analyze the likely risks it may pose to the audience, personnel, participants, providers, or the event organization.

Designing the experience

Pine and Gilmore (1999) describe the nature of an experience as the personal engagement of the consumer in an enjoyable, theatrical, entertaining, and memorable encounter. The agenda of activities, elements, exhibits, and amenities that shape the composition of the event experience is driven not only by the goals and objectives of the event project. It is also driven by the attendee's demand for individual immersion in the sensations of the event as well as the benefits to be derived from attending. The risks associated with designing the event experience vary according to the type of event and the choices made by the event organizers, but it must be remembered that everything at an event has potential risks (see Table 10.2).

The scope of the elements included in an event will depend on the purpose, size, location, budget, and image of the event, the needs of the audience, and the logistical and operational requirements associated with those elements. As illustrated in Figure 10.2, anything and everything that is scheduled to happen at the event will have specific equipment needs, materials that are used, personnel to implement or operate it, and site-specific requirements. These must all be analyzed from a risk management perspective and incorporated into the overall event plan. This is precisely why the event risk manager should be involved in the entire event management process – the design, planning, and operations of the event.

Table 10.2 Typical event program risks

- Alcohol service
- Competitive rivalry or exuberance
- Complex agendas
- Controversial topics or presenters
- Expansive sites
- Extensive productions
- Food selection and safety
- High attendee population density

- Inappropriate pace or tempo
- Inapt or inept performers or participants
- Incompatible scheduling
- Insufficient sound and lighting
- Live animals as entertainment or décor
- Long duration
- Special effects safety
- Unsafe activities or attractions

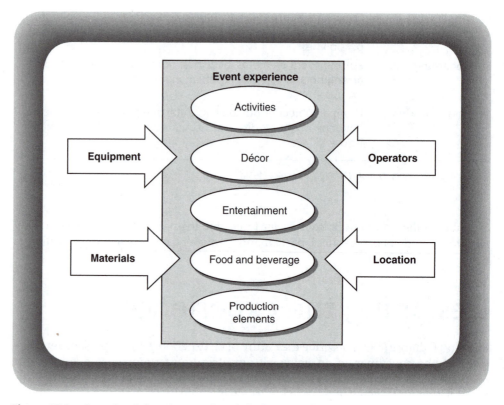

Figure 10.2 Experiential and operational dimension of an event

Activity and content selection

Whether the event is a convention where various meetings, educational sessions, and social activities are planned; a festival where numerous entertainment attractions, exhibits, and spectacular fireworks are featured; or a modest or lavish awards banquet with dining, dancing, and presentations, there will always be *Something to do* at an event. Selecting the right activities and content (i.e., subject matter) to be communicated within these activities is based upon a clear understanding of the needs and desires of the audience and the objectives and obligations of the event.

As illustrated in Figure 10.3, the possible event activities (e.g., sessions, components, features, and/or attractions) include a broad range of options, and they may have different characteristics in terms of purpose, nature, and expected outcomes.

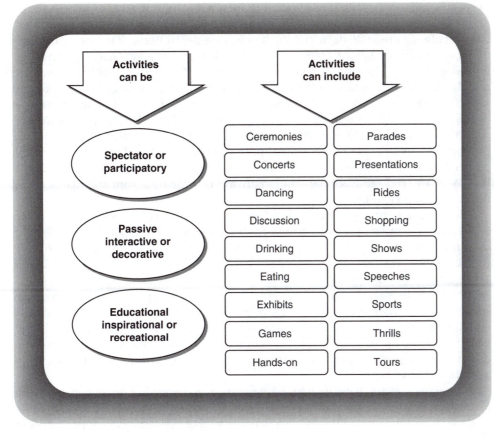

Figure 10.3 Potential meeting and event activities

The event may be spectator or participatory in nature. Activities, entertainment, and attractions may be passive, interactive, or purely 'decorative' – providing or enhancing the atmosphere or theme of an event. The content may be selected to meet educational, inspirational, or recreational objectives. For example, conferences often offer educational sessions designed to meet certification program requirements, exhibitions regularly offer educational sessions on industry issues in order to increase attendance, cause-related events typically incorporate elements designed to inspire support, and employee appreciation events frequently include recreational activities that are both entertaining and promote teamwork.

Developing the content for educational activities includes the selection of the appropriate topics, formats, and presenters to achieve the communication objectives and educational obligations of the event project. Such activities must be devised in such a way that recognizes various learning styles, techniques, and strategies, and incorporates the principles and dynamics of adult learning. The content should be designed to meet the educational needs and the experience levels of the intended audience (Connell, 2002; Krug, 2000). The speakers, presenters, and other content delivery personnel should be selected according to the content scope and topic requirements, as well as the program format or delivery systems chosen. Explicit speaker solicitation and delivery guidelines should be established that facilitate quality programming.

Some activities may be components of an event or events in their own right. Ceremonies, for example, can cause numerous potential problems if protocol requirements or specific religious or ritual requirements are not met, or if the appropriate ceremonial equipment or personnel to conduct the ceremonial activities is not procured. Parades often include floats, marching bands, groups/troupes, or troops, equestrian units, giant helium balloon characters, and vehicles, which requires sufficient staging areas for line-up and dissolution, unobstructed and traversable routes, and parade marshals to escort each unit included in the parade (Lagauskas). Animal attractions used as décor or entertainment pose hazards for the audience as well as the animal, particularly if the animal is large, undomesticated, untrained, or in poor condition. Usage considerations include attacks due to contact, discomfort, or provocation (even experienced animal performers are first and foremost animals), audience allergies and phobias, infections or infestations, sanitation, and the animal's welfare, and these animals should always be procured from and managed by reputable handlers (HSE, 1996).

Inflatable amusement devices such as 'bouncy' cages or castles, rock-climbing walls, or Velcro walls must only be acquired from reputable rental dealers and operators that enforce strict safety standards for setup, maintenance, and operation to minimize the possibility of accidents, and have sufficient liability insurance (Martinez, 2005). The hazards associated with these devices include wind instability, deflation, suffocation, and injuries due to falls, overcrowding, failure to separate larger users from smaller ones, and entrapment (HSE, 2001). Amusement or 'carnival' rides are typically regulated to ensure they are designed and built to explicit safety specifications; their installation undergoes a thorough inspection and receives daily inspections for condition and deterioration; and they are operated by properly trained operators and attendants (HSE, 1998).

Some activities are 'risky' by their very nature, some activities or elements are simply inappropriate, and there may be some dangers inherent in an activity that would suggest its prohibition, yet this is not always known or heeded by event producers or

Consider this... 10.1

Reception theme causes controversy

August 7, 1999: The welcome reception for an international association's annual conference held in Washington D.C. began with hors d'oeuvre and wine at one of the city's museums, after which attendees were loaded onto motor coaches for what was advertised as an opportunity to see the sights of the nation's capital. Once on board, attendees were told that not everything they saw that evening would be as it appeared to be. After driving past a couple of national monuments the motor coaches seemed to be taking a detour due to construction, finally turning onto a dark street with police cars at the entrance. As the coaches stopped in front of a darkened warehouse lateral fireworks exploded, shooting sparks and loud bangs like gunfire, and several people dressed in camouflage clothing and masks barged onto the bus brandishing machine guns (actually water pistols) and claiming they were taking the passengers hostage. Although this arrival was meant to enhance the 'urban extreme' theme the party designers had developed and most attendees quickly realized this was part of the entertainment, quite a few were traumatized by the incident and had to be transported back to the hotel immediately. In their enthusiasm to create a 'cutting edge' experience the event organizers had forgotten to make certain the experience was clearly identifiable as 'theater' and not reality. They were forced to make a public apology for their choices at the opening session of the conference the next morning.

planners. For example, the popular Sumo Wrestler game, wherein the participants don a padded suit and wrestle each other, has caused serious spinal injuries and death and has been the subject of lawsuits, with multi-million dollar settlements awarded to victims of such injuries. Yet, this attraction is still offered by numerous interactive game providers and ordered by many event organizers because it is not legally banned. The event risk manager must continually scan the event industry for such hazards and dangers. One cannot rely solely on a provider's assurances of safety.

Structure and sequencing

Once the menu of activities or event components has been selected, these must be structured and sequenced in such a way that a balanced, logical, and progressive experience is delivered. The location and duration requirements for each activity must be determined, the positioning of contiguous and concurrent event elements must be established, and the sequence of event elements must be arranged in an agenda, running order, schedule, or itinerary that has continuity and reflects the appropriate pace and tempo.

The program agenda or structure should be arranged so that the attendee will move through the experience in the proper order or flow (as designed) and is able to take full advantage of the individual elements as the attendee so chooses. Flow planning is important from an experiential as well as risk management perspective. For example, groups of 1000 or more require a minimum of 30 minutes to move from one room to another, such as from a plenary session to individual breakout sessions at a convention or from a reception into dinner at a banquet, and sufficient time must be allotted to ensure crowd movement problems do not emerge. Special attention must be paid to those activities or elements that will be in high demand to ensure these are not scheduled or positioned in such a way that the attendee will be forced to make an unwelcome choice or that capacity or crowd density restrictions are compromised. The risk manager should scan the program structure and sequencing to ascertain any conflicts that could cause problems. In addition, various vendors and suppliers will be contracted to provide the event activities and services. Each will have a set of needs and expectations that must be assessed in order to identify and control any associated risks. These requirements may include, but are not limited to, those shown in Table 10.3.

Effective design and delivery of the event experience relies on a threshold-to-threshold vision from the attendee's, participant's, and provider's perspective. The activities included must be scrutinized to ensure they enhance the purpose of the event. The event dates and schedule must accommodate the logistical needs and preferences of all those involved. An experience is the sum total of the features and facets

Table 10.3 Typical activity provider requirements

• Crew or personnel	• Power, water, and/or gas
• Dressing and/or green rooms	• Rehearsals
• Equipment requirements	• Security requirements
• Food and beverage requirements	• Spatial requirements
• Housing accommodations	• Staging requirements
• Installation requirements	• Storage requirements
• Load-in/load-out time and space	• Technical production requirements
• Parking	• Temporary structures

included; it is an integrated package. Failure to recognize this holistic nature could cause exposures to potential hazards, vulnerabilities, and disappointment.

Designing the environment

The setting in which the meeting or event occurs must meet the needs of its occupants as well as facilitate the achievement of the purpose for the event (e.g., learning, marketing, ceremonial, hospitality, entertainment, etc.). The selection and arrangement of décor items, props, furnishings, decorative embellishments, and wayfinding systems should enhance the attractiveness and functionality of the event environment. The designer must recognize and understand the effects of the environmental stimuli on the responses and behavior of the occupants, and seek to achieve a synergy between the physical, perceptual, and social aspects of the setting (Gifford, 2002). The factors that influence the occupant's reactions to the environment are shown in Table 10.4, which should be considered by the event designer from the esthetic, kinetic, behavioral, comfort, and safety perspective. The risk manager should consider these as well, but must look deeper into the proposed layout, construction, and installation of the environment's elements in order to reveal potential hazards, some of which are shown in Table 10.5.

Use of an event site will have an impact on that site, particularly sites or venues that are not purpose built. Careful attention must be paid to make certain the negative impacts of site usage are minimized as much as possible. Controlling damage, pollution, and waste will not only protect the environment; it will reduce the risks, financial and physical, associated with using a site or venue. As noted in Chapter 3, the event may be required to adhere to specific environmental protection regulations or codes, particularly with regard to public-owned lands or waterways and event activities or elements that might have a negative impact on them.

Table 10.4 Factors influencing the perception and effectiveness of an environment

• Activity	• Crowd density	• Novelty
• Architecture	• Esthetics	• Organization
• Arrangement	• Familiarity	• Personal space
• Cleanliness	• Legibility	• Safety
• Coherence	• Lighting	• Temperature
• Complexity	• Noise	• Utility

Table 10.5 Typical hazards associated with event settings

• Temporary structures and staging	• Obscured safety signage
• Confusing layouts	• Obstructed safety exits
• Defective equipment	• Obstructed sight lines
• Expansive or multiple locations	• Outdoor or remote locations
• Improper installation	• Overcrowding
• Inadequate lighting	• Restricted or unsafe décor materials
• Limited visibility	• Water elements

Configuration and decoration

The physical configuration and decoration of the event setting will be based upon the audience in attendance and the activities to be conducted. These environments should be designed in such a way that they enhance performance and encourage desired behavior. The layout and use of space should be established in such a way that it meets social and physical requirements within the confines of the setting conditions and restrictions. The risk manager should evaluate the décor and site or layout plan to ensure the following audience needs are carefully considered in terms of creating the appropriate functional environment and the hazards or vulnerabilities associated with them.

- *Access*: roads and parking, disability accessibility, entrances, passageways.
- *Atmosphere*: heating, cooling, ventilation, weather, noise, lighting.
- *Escape*: emergency exits, emergency response, communications.
- *Services*: information, welfare, food and beverage, sanitary facilities.
- *Signage*: information, instructions, navigation, orientation, restrictions, safety, identification, branding.
- *Staging*: décor, seating, risers, barricades, dance floors, partitions, production equipment, steps/ramps.
- *Structures*: tents, canopies, grandstands, stages, AV stands/towers, viewing platforms, archways, attractions.

Consider this... 10.2

Potentially hazardous party design

A large high-tech company hired an event designer from New Orleans to produce a Mardi Gras-themed employee appreciation party for 3000 staged in the main exhibit hall of the convention center. The exhibit hall was a vast rectangular space with a diagonal bank of doors at one corner. The designer decided to section the hall into four theme areas (Bayou, Riverboat, Plantation, and Mardi Gras) with a winding pathway (through the French Quarter) from the entrance to an intersection to the four areas, all of which was created using false walls of draping, backdrops, massive props, and facades. Low intensity lighting was used to make the height of the cavernous hall disappear, selective spot lighting was used to highlight the theme props, buffet displays, and entertainment stages, and smoke effects covered the ugly cement floors with a 'swamp' fog. The effect was stunning. Guests would immediately enter an altered reality as they snaked their way through the streets of the French Quarter and wandered through the four areas enjoying a variety of theme environments and big-name entertainment. It was also a disaster waiting to happen.

The designer had covered virtually all the fire exits with draping and stages, including putting a main entertainment stage in front of the diagonal bank of doors, which, because these led directly outside, were the main means of egress for the exhibit hall. Although the convention center had a policy of requiring a floor plan for fire marshal approval four weeks prior to the event, the event designer 'conveniently' forgot to submit one and the convention center staff never followed up. When the six trucks of props and décor from New Orleans arrived, loaded in, and were installed, the fire marshal deemed the layout unacceptable. The convention center staff pleaded with the fire marshal for a way to proceed with this very expensive (and lucrative) event.

The center received a violation citation from the fire marshal, paper 'Exit' signs had to be attached to the décor throughout the space, and a small army of firefighters had be paid for to be on-site to direct human traffic should anything go wrong. But had a fire broken out, panic would have rendered those firefighters next to useless. The reality would have been 3000 panicked people trying to push and shove their way out of a very crowded, smoky, dimly lit, completely confusing layout, with virtually no way of distinguishing where 'Out' was. Fortunately, no such disaster occurred. It is doubtful that the host company had any idea of the serious jeopardy their guests (their employees) were put in because this is something they would have never allowed at their place of business.

The goals of effective layout, according to Tum, Norton, and Wright (2006), consist of optimizing movement, reducing congestion, and maximizing the use of space. Bowdin et al. (2006) note the relationship of the event's schedule with flow planning, citing peak flow periods in the agenda of activities as a movement-capability safety factor. Facilitating safe crowd movement, minimizing actual and perceived congestion, and choreographing the flow through the space can be enhanced or impeded by the placement of activity, décor, and staging elements. Space usage for logistical activities must also be considered, including any maintenance, replenishment, and storage requirements, all of which may also be facilitated with proper spatial planning. The development of an accurate floor plan or site plan should be of particular interest to the risk manager so that functional (and regulatory) accessibility is assured and crowd density is controlled.

Gifford (2002) points out, however, that crowding and density are distinct; crowding is subjective (a perception) and density is objective (a physical actuality). These relate to personal space preferences, which vary according to cultural and environmental factors, as well as the social context of the event. In addition, density can intensify the positive or negative magnitude of whatever is occurring (e.g., increasing either pleasure or dissatisfaction), which suggests that, with all safety implications considered, establishing high density situations may be preferable for certain event activities.

Décor, furnishings, and staging

Numerous challenges and opportunities may be approached through décor strategies. Movement can be choreographed, interaction can be encouraged, visibility can be enhanced, and hazards can be obstructed. For example, a corporation held a company party with a nautical theme at a water park but did not want guests to go swimming in the wave pool due to liability and 'proper' dress concerns, so the designer cordoned off the perimeter of the pool using wharf pylons with life savers and rope lines as theme décor. Many events will use color-coded decorations or different themes to identify different activities and activity zones. Stages, platforms, and other equipment are often used to enhance visibility and focus attention on specific activities or features. Scenery and draping offers numerous ways to conceal anything from storage areas to undesirable architectural features to potentially hazardous apparatus.

The event designer has unlimited possibilities regarding methods and materials for decorating an event space, and choices are often made according to creative inspiration, theme, cost, and equipment availability. Countless decorators gather inspiration anywhere from theatrical productions to hardware stores, and will see and use materials in atypical and unique ways. This often provides extraordinary and exciting environments in which the event activities take place, but also poses numerous risk issues unless the designer has made certain that the characteristics, construction, and installation of these decorations have been fully assessed for safety and can be achieved in the specific event context.

Appropriate tables, seating, and other furnishings must be acquired and positioned according to the activities to be conducted, and must ensure suitable sight lines are maintained for both the focus of attention and the means of egress. Here, again, there are countless creative options for equipment types, materials, and configuration, which must be constructed, positioned, and assigned with safety in mind. For example, using atypical materials for tables or chairs may make them unstable or they may have unsafe edges or surfaces, and seating assignments would be important from a risk management perspective for competitive sports events due to rivalries or ceremonial events due to protocol or security requirements.

Most event elements or components require the availability or importation of specialized equipment. This may include aerial apparatus or audiovisual devices, special seating or shelters, props or production equipment, tents or toilets, stages or stoves, grandstands or garment racks, packing cases or platforms, lighting instruments or installation lifts. The risk manager must know what equipment is to be used, where it is coming from (in-house or imported), where it is going, who will be operating it, and any inherent safety hazards associated with it. This includes all the equipment needed to support the activity, perform the activity, install the activity, protect the activity, and remove the activity or attraction. What should be apparent is that the risk manager needs to know enough about every aspect of an event to be able to at least know which questions to ask to uncover potential risks. This is why it is critically important to include providers for every component of an event in the risk assessment process.

Wayfinding systems

Wayfinding, the science of personal navigation through a space, is pertinent not only to the comfort and enjoyment of the guest or attendee; it is critical to their safety and welfare, particularly in an emergency situation. It is important to provide environmental cues that facilitate navigation and spatial cognition and to develop signage systems that provide information, identification, orientation, and directions, and that enhance desired and/or required traffic flow. These cues and systems may be achieved with décor elements, furnishings, sensory cues, sensible layouts, and signage.

Gifford (2002) cites the spatial cognition work of Kevin Lynch (1960), the originator of the term wayfinding, referring to the legibility of an environment as reliant on clear paths, distinct edges, characteristic districts, and distinctive landmarks, and suggests that environmental cues such as signage, numbering, or color-coding systems facilitate the comprehension and navigation of complex layouts. Foltz (1998) asserts that navigability, the ability to move from a current location to a destination even if the location of the destination is not precisely known, is enhanced by providing unique location identities, orientation cues, well-structured paths, signage at decision points, and inviting sight lines to the attractions ahead.

The signage needed to make navigating to and through the event site as easy as possible must be carefully considered. Signs can and should be integrated into the event environment and coordinated with the overall décor and theme of the event, which offers an excellent opportunity for sponsor recognition and event branding. Directional and informational signs are placed to facilitate the event attendee's

Table 10.6 Typical signage locations and labeling functions

• Aisle designations	• Police or security stations
• Attractions	• Queue advisories
• Box office and ticket-taking points	• Restricted or designated areas
• Danger spots	• Schedules
• Decision points	• Seating assignment systems
• Entrance and exit points	• Services and service areas
• Equipment usage instructions	• Session rooms and topics
• Fire exits	• Smoking/non-smoking areas
• First aid facilities	• Sponsor recognition
• Food service areas	• Starting and finishing lines
• Information centers	• Telephones
• Lost and found centers	• Temporary caution signs
• Meeting or gathering points	• Toilet facilities
• Lost children centers	• Waste collection and recycling points
• Parking areas	• 'You Are Here' maps

Sources: Bowdin et al. (2006), Getz (1997), New Zealand MCDEM (2003), Silvers (2004a), and Tum et al. (2006)

comfort, minimize confusion, and manage behavior. In addition, as noted in Chapter 8, advisory or warning signs are used to communicate important safety messages, restrictions, and instructions. Signs must be easy to read and understand, which may require symbols or pictographic icons as well as alternate formats for varying abilities and disabilities, and they must be positioned wherever they will help the guest navigate and enjoy the event (see Table 10.6).

Food and beverage service

Food and beverages are often a key component of events ranging from the simplest water station at a meeting, to the concessions at a festival or stadium event, to a lavish banquet for heads of state, incentive event, or a wedding dinner. Managing food service and beverage service encompasses the determination of suitable catering operations and the selection of the menus, quantities, and service styles to meet the food and beverage needs of the event, including the specific requirements associated with the serving of alcohol. As discussed in Chapter 4, safe food service is a primary concern for the risk manager, including the prevention of illness and injuries. The issues surrounding food service are shown in Figure 10.4 and the typical risks associated with food and beverage service are shown in Table 10.7.

Food and beverage service is often procured from an on-premise caterer, off-premise caterer, or concession operation, and the capabilities and constraints will determine the most suitable provider for the event project. On-premise and off-premise catering operations have very different requirements and logistics. A fully equipped kitchen facility will likely be available at an on-premise location, but will need to be imported (or foods must be transported) for an off-premise location. Temporary kitchens must be properly situated, constructed, and staffed.

Contracting and communications with a catering organization must be rigorously supervised. Catering or food service contracts should specify the date, time, and

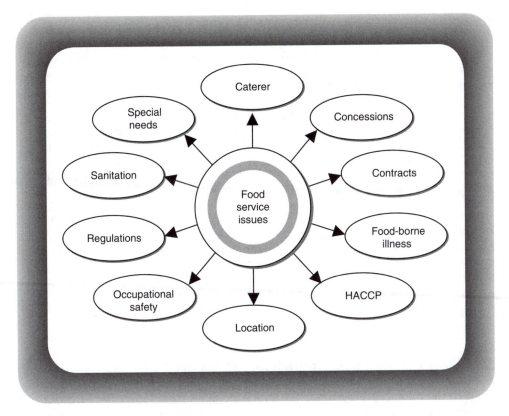

Figure 10.4 Food service risk issues

Table 10.7 Typical food and beverage service risks

• Alcohol control	• Menu or ingredient restrictions
• Food contamination	• Off-premise catering
• Inadequate kitchen facilities	• Poor food handler training
• Insufficient quantities	• Positioning of bars and food stations
• Insufficient staffing	• Spilled food or beverages
• Inappropriate/scarce tables and seating	• Unsanitary conditions

duration of food and/or beverage service, the menu items to be provided, the number of guests to be served, the staffing levels, and a complete list of all applicable charges (e.g., taxes, gratuities, service charges, equipment and setup charges, room rental rates, commissions, staffing rates, etc.), and policies such as deposits, cancellation, alcohol service, and leftover or brought-in food. All catering organizations and concessionaires should be checked to ensure compliance with all applicable regulatory requirements.

Menu selection and service planning

In order to select a suitable and sufficient menu for an event project the requirements for meal, refreshment, and beverage services must be determined and quantities must be calculated. Various attendee, participant, staff, and other stakeholder groups may

Table 10.8 Warning indicators for potential catering hazards

• Bulk condiments (i.e., not single serve)	• Outdoor grilling (e.g., charcoal, propane)
• Carbonated drink cylinder storage	• Poor personal grooming and hygiene
• Chafing dishes and steam tables	• Raw foods or ingredients
• Chipped or broken glasses or plates	• Same ice used for cooling and
• Dimly lit catering areas and pathways	consumption
• Excessive jewelry worn by personnel	• Servers or clearers touching glass rims
• Exhibition cooking	• Smoking or gum chewing by personnel
• Flambé dishes, drinks, or desserts	• Unenclosed food preparation areas
• High density intermission demand	• Unprotected access to warmers and
• Hot beverage setups	cookers
• Hot serving containers and utensils	• Unrestrained hair of food handlers
• Harried or running personnel	• Unsecured carts and tray stands
• Improper disposal of food waste	• Unsecured drop cords for electricity
• Litter and spilled liquids	• Use of propane, butane, or Sterno
• Long lines at buffets or concessions	• Untidy or unclean buffet tables
• Open-flame candles	

Sources: Hansen (1995), HSE (1999), National Assessment Institute (1998), and Shock and Stefanelli (2001)

have different nutritional requirements as well as menu preferences that need to be incorporated into the menu planning, which becomes more complex if the meeting or event runs over several days. In addition, one must consider special needs such as dietary restrictions and perhaps political issues. Religious dietary laws (Kosher, Halal, caste-specific Hindu diets, etc.), physical conditions (allergies, gluten intolerance, etc.), and philosophical convictions (vegetarians, animal rights activists, environmentalists, etc.) may require specific food items, ingredients, or preparation methods be included or excluded.

Service planning consists of specifying the serving style and timing, determining the appropriate room setup, identifying the necessary staffing and equipment, and integrating this into the site plans and scheduling. Off-premise and temporary catering sites typically have more service planning considerations, but all sites and service providers have vulnerabilities and potential hazards that the risk manager should be on the lookout for, some of which are shown in Table 10.8.

Alcohol management

Studies have indicated that the number one risk management concern is the serving of alcohol at events. However, this is only relative to certain types of events and event audiences. Serving cocktails and wine at a conservative or formal occasion is completely different than selling alcohol at a large sporting competition with rowdy fans. Nevertheless, the risk manager must always remember that alcohol can change the nature of the audience. Alcohol consumption can cause reasonable and well-behaved individuals to abandon their typical social mores and controls, resulting in an audience or crowd that is more dangerous or difficult to control.

Effective management of alcohol service requires the identification and compliance with alcohol service policies and laws, determining and addressing liabilities and insurance requirements, and incorporating responsible consumption programs.

Most communities and governments strictly control the serving of alcoholic beverages through a regulatory entity (e.g., Alcohol Beverage Commissions (ABC) in the U.S.) that is responsible for licensing and regulating the sale of alcohol. Regulations often cover such things as prohibiting the sale of liquor to persons under a certain age or to intoxicated persons, the hours of operation, the licenses and insurance required, liquor pricing, and the amounts or types of liquor that may be served. In addition, alcohol service will be governed by the same health codes applicable to all other food and beverage service.

Many jurisdictions also require specific training be provided to all those selling and serving alcohol, particularly as laws such as the dram shop and social-host laws in the U.S. impose liability on both the individual consuming the alcohol and the one serving it. Even if not mandated, server training is a sound risk management tactic. Alcohol server training typically covers signs of intoxication, dealing with intoxicated guests, dealing with minors, the effects of alcohol on the body, and local liquor codes. Responsible drinking initiatives, promotions, and policies are often adopted by event organizations (and may be required in certain jurisdictions), which may include designated driver programs, subsidized taxi or shuttle service, and on-site advisory or educational signage at the event.

Consider this... 10.3

Two receptions cause over consumption

An hour and a half opening reception for an association meeting held at the meeting hotel included a cash bar for which attendees were given a limited number of drink coupons to exchange for the beverages of their choice, and all went well. On the same night, however, a major hotel-sponsored event was held in the hotel's lobby for the hotel guests and community, including the hotel's corporate executives and the city's top elected officials. This four-hour reception included terrific food stations, music, and hotel staff delivering specialty martinis, champagne, and other drinks to anyone who wanted them and the entire bar was open and complimentary (hosted). Many of the association's attendees went down to the hotel reception after the association's reception instead of going out to dinner.

An attendee and two colleagues from the same office were among the meeting participants in the hotel lobby. One of these attendees proceeded to get extremely drunk at the hotel's event. (It was not known how much they had drunk at the association's reception prior to joining the hotel's festivities, but they did not 'appear' to be drunk when they left that function.) Hotel security attempted to cut off service to this participant who proceeded to become enraged. The police were called in and the participant (from outside the U.S., the host country) was eventually arrested and arraigned on multiple counts of felonious assault. The arrested person and colleagues wanted assistance from the association in terms of bail, contacting lawyers, etc., but the association refused to provide this. The association is now considering development of some sort of 'attendee code of conduct' to prevent such incidents at future events, including changes to their bylaws to give them the ability to impose disciplinary action toward a member in this kind of situation.

Access to alcohol should be controlled through the segregation of service and/or consumption areas (e.g., alcohol-free seating sections), limits on serving times (e.g., closing the bar prior to the end of the event), use and enforcement of identification credentials (e.g., wrist bands), use of portion controls (e.g., serving size limits), prohibition of bring-your-own or self-service operations (e.g., unattended beer kegs), and sufficient deployment of security personnel. Non-alcoholic beverage options should always be included when serving alcohol and food should also be available, even if it is only hors d'oeuvre or snacks (avoiding salty items because they increase thirst). Free drinking water must be provided at any event. Bottom line: give the guest plenty of options NOT to drink to intoxication.

Entertainment

The event organizer or designer in charge of entertainment oversees the sourcing, selection, and control of suitable entertainment, ancillary programs, and recreational activities for the event project and the coordination of the support requirements for the entertainers and activities in a manner that delivers the desired entertainment experience and that benefits the audience and organization. Everything from acrobats to Zydeco bands has been included as entertainment for events. Event audiences have enjoyed attractions from magic shows to extreme sports. Event attendees have participated in activities ranging from bungee jumping to war games and everything in between. And new entertainment acts and attractions are developed everyday.

Some acts and activities are inherently or potentially more risky than others, but the risk manager does not encourage or discourage any particular entertainment attraction or performer. He or she assesses the risk and makes recommendations that will help avoid, reduce, or transfer those risks if the entertainment choices have been made. However, the risk manager can and should identify and clearly communicate potential hazards and vulnerabilities (see Table 10.9) so that organizers are able to incorporate the appropriate safeguards (and perhaps reconsider the choices if possible), and unsafe entertainment attractions should be forcefully opposed.

Selecting entertainers, attractions, and elements

In order to select effective and appropriate entertainment elements for a meeting or event one must determine the purpose and objectives of including entertainment and attractions in the event program; the type and style of and suitable options for entertainment products, performers, and services must be identified; and the scope, schedule, and location of entertainment activities and attractions must be established.

Table 10.9 Typical risk areas for entertainment

• Amateur entertainment groups	• Intricate staging and/or equipment
• Celebrity performers	• Lack of rehearsal
• Close proximity performers	• Live animal attractions
• Contract rider fulfillment	• Music licensing and recording rights
• Excessive demand for an attraction	• Non-appearance or cancellation
• Expansive productions	• Performer behavior
• Inappropriate entertainment	• Performer's entourage

The organizer must then identify the agents, promoters, and other sources for entertainment and attractions, and book the entertainers using clear and comprehensive contracts or engagement agreements.

The risk manager should always check for and assess the selection criteria to be used in order to reveal potential problems. Reliance on assumptions, personal preferences, or one group's definition of good taste may lead to unsatisfactory or unsavory choices. For example, an organizing committee member's engagement of seven strippers for a 45-minute burlesque routine (which was stopped after about 10 minutes) as 'light-hearted' dinner entertainment for a government-sponsored conference in Canberra, Australia, outraged attendees, prompted withdrawal of conference sponsorship funding, and triggered calls for a government investigation (Murray, 2006).

Budget and availability of options will often dictate some choices; site capabilities and logistical operations will prescribe others. The host or organizers may wish to include celebrity or headliner entertainment, but the costs for the entertainer's fee plus the costs and logistics associated with the travel, hospitality, security, and staging requirements included in the entertainer's contract rider may exceed the financial and operational resources of the event. 'Big-name' entertainment may increase attendance and attract commercial sponsors, but often entails big production obligations that inexperienced organizers are unaware of and unprepared to implement, and increases the importance of non-appearance or cancellation coverage. Amateur or semi-professional entertainment is often a viable choice because these performers are typically no less talented than professional entertainers, but are sometimes less aware of expected behavior, especially in regard to entourages of family and friends.

Careful attention must be paid to the probable demand on specific performers or attractions such as close proximity performers (e.g., strolling magicians or musicians) and amenity attractions (e.g., caricaturists or photo stations) to ensure queues are manageable and the entertainers are not put in jeopardy. Environmental entertainers (e.g., costumed characters) need to be positioned properly within the site plan and schedule, must be given clear instructions regarding their role and scope of interaction with the audience (any costumed characters meant to interact with children must be properly screened with background checks), and the costume should not infringe

Consider this... 10.4

National anthems: politically powerful music

Event organizers have caused embarrassment, suspicion, outrage, confrontations, diplomatic protests, and ill will by playing the wrong national anthem at ceremonies at rival-intense events such as a 1999 goodwill rugby match in Japan and a Rugby Union match in Italy in 2001, the Mountainbike World Cup in 2002, a judo championship held in Vietnam in 2003 and the 2005 Taekwondo World Cup Championships in Madrid, the 2003 Davis Cup Final in Australia and the 2004 World Hockey Championships in the Czech Republic, the 2004 African Cup of Nations soccer championships in Tunisia, and the FIFA soccer World Cup held in Germany in 2006. Offended participants and national delegations have demanded official and public apologies, departed the field in protest, insisted that new ceremonies be conducted, and withdrawn financial support for future events. These music mistakes have disgraced event organizers and their countries, not to mention the aggravation of fierce national rivalries and the potential for crowd endangerment such incidents engender.

on any trademarked imagery or protected likeness restrictions (e.g., celebrity look-alikes). Live and recorded music is employed for many events for many reasons and both live and recorded music usage must comply with music licensing regulations.

Performer and performance requirements

Once the entertainment has been selected and contracted, the event organizer needs to make certain the entertainers are able to give the best performance possible by meeting their needs. This includes the determination and integration of production and logistical requirements into the site and operational plans (including technical and performer rehearsals), arranging accommodations (e.g., housing and on-site facilities) as necessary, and ensuring contractual fulfillment of hospitality and technical rider requirements. The scope of this responsibility is directly related to the scale of the entertainment program. Ambitious entertainment programs often require the services of a production coordinator or stage manager, and should probably not be undertaken without engaging such professionals.

As Bowdin et al. (2006), Silvers (2004a), and Sonder (2004) note, performers may come from widely divergent cultural and contextual backgrounds with varying levels of performing experience, which often results in misunderstandings concerning expectations on the part of both parties – the entertainer and the event organizer. The risk manager should work closely with the organizer to ensure that explicit expectations of entertainers and entertainment personnel are specified and closely monitored. Limitations and prohibitions (or requested inclusions) regarding performer behavior, content, interaction, and/or amenities (e.g., buffet or bar access, lounge areas, etc.) must be clearly communicated and included in contracts as appropriate. These, however, must be acceptable within the context of union or other regulatory requirements (e.g., minimum hours, minimum number of musicians, etc.), and accepted via informed consent by the performer (e.g., do not wait to tell the band that their entourage is not welcome after they have all arrived on site).

Ancillary and recreational activities

Many events, meetings and conventions in particular, include a selection of ancillary programs and recreational activities such as companion programs, children's programs and services, pre- and post-event and side tours, contests and competitions, sports tournaments, and other athletic activities that are held in conjunction with the main event program. The risk manager should pay particular attention to children's programs and sports activities. Children's programs must adhere to the strict controls typically imposed on childcare endeavors, which may require specific licenses or credentialing in certain jurisdictions. Certain athletic activities are inherently or potentially perilous, often the very reason they are attractive to the adventurous, and vigorous or strenuous sports can result in injuries and other medical complications for those less experienced or physically fit.

These programs require special attention to liability issues and insurance requirements, including provision of on-site medical services as appropriate and securing waivers of indemnity signed by participants. It is advisable, however, not to include dangerous activities in the formal event program so that there is no connection between the provider/partaker and the event organization. Any and all ancillary programs and services should be procured only from appropriate and qualified providers, and should be incorporated into the insurance policies for the event and event organization.

Production elements

Production elements, including lighting, sound, projection, and special effects, are added to many (if not most) events to enhance the event environment, the event experience, and the event's effectiveness. Whilst the incorporation, sourcing, selection, and positioning of these theatrical elements and services are considered by event organizers from a decorative or dramatic perspective, they must be assessed by risk managers from a safety and audience welfare perspective (see Table 10.10) as well as from a risk reduction perspective since many of them can and should be used to support the risk response plan. For example, lighting can highlight paths of egress, sound systems will be used for emergency announcements, and projection screens can be used to transmit variable safety messages.

Audio, visual, and multimedia technology

As with any aspect of the event or program design, there are countless audio and visual options for the event organizer to choose from to create the event experience. Some are selected for purely functional reasons; others for adding the theatrical dimension that enhances the impact. Both the event organizer and risk manager must understand the scope, capabilities, and limitations of the technology in order to select the equipment, services, and service providers that will meet the requirements for the activities to be conducted and assess the potential risks and risk management possibilities associated with each element (see Figure 10.5).

Lighting is used to illuminate a space, in both a decorative fashion and to provide the illumination needed to create a safe environment. The placement and intensity of the lighting can attract or distract attention. The absence of lighting or sufficient illumination can cause problems with crowd or individual mobility as well as lessening social control – in the dark you can be anonymous. The requirements for positioning lighting fixtures and equipment must be determined in order to achieve the effects desired, provide the illumination necessary for the tasks or activities to be conducted, and ensure that the equipment does not pose any safety hazards (e.g., falling fixtures, tripping over equipment legs, etc.).

Sound augmentation allows the audience to hear the sounds at an event, including the presentation, the entertainment, soundscaping opportunities, and especially any important announcements. The decibel level of the sound can be a hazard, both physically to the individual (i.e., damage to hearing) and to the event if subject to noise ordinances that prohibit the disturbance of surrounding neighbors or areas. If recording elements for future broadcast or products (e.g., webcasts, conference CDs, etc.), special attention must be paid to ensuring the recording equipment and levels

Table 10.10   Typical risks associated with production elements

• Exposed or unsecured cables and wires	• Special effects consequences
• Inadequate load-in/load-out scheduling	• Technology breakdowns
• Inadequate or overpowering sound levels	• Unannounced or surprise elements
• Improper overhead rigging	• Unfamiliar technology
• Lack of technician support	• Unqualified providers
• Pyrotechnics safety	• Unsafe installation practices

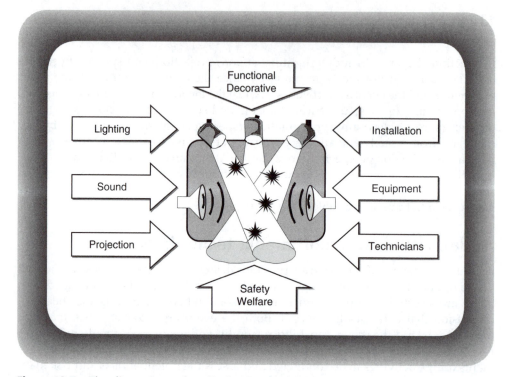

Figure 10.5 The dimensions of audiovisual considerations

are sufficient and the proper permissions have been acquired. Projection equipment is used to make images and action visible from a distance, as well as to emphasize audible messages with visual reinforcement. Various projectors are able to magnify and display images and content on a broad variety of screens, from television monitors to screens the size of a building (or even the sides of a building).

These elements must be examined from a safety viewpoint regarding their installation requirements, the equipment used to create them, and the technicians who will operate them. Installation and operation should always be assigned to professionals. The equipment can be potentially dangerous if mishandled (or tampered with), the installation and rigging of the equipment can be precarious if not done properly, and technical equipment can break down leaving the event in the dark and silent. Sufficient and accessible power sources must be provided to operate the equipment, and contingency plans must be devised to overcome outages or failures. Redundant equipment may be advisable. Sufficient time must be allotted for proper installation, rehearsals, and dismantling to prevent accidents.

Special effects

Special effects are the techniques and theatrical tricks that focus attention, add emphasis, and insert an element of surprise into the event program and environment. As illustrated in Figure 10.6, special effects can include lasers, pyrotechnics, drops, launches, explosions, blasts, fog, and/or scentscaping, and the event organizer will evaluate and select the effects, techniques, and technology to enhance the program. However, from the risk management perspective, many special effects are inherently dangerous and most are potentially hazardous if mishandled and should

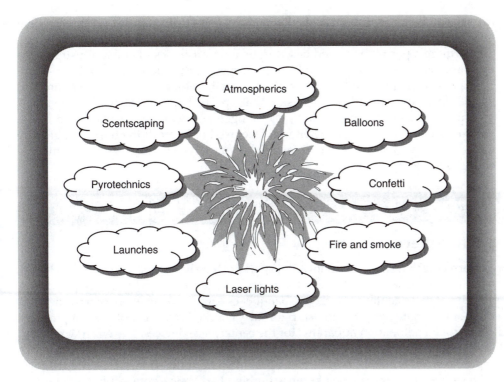

Figure 10.6 Typical special effects employed for events

only be acquired from qualified providers. Additional costs or logistics for site preparation, delivery, installation, and clean up must also be considered. Silvers (2004a, p. 263) cautions that '*everyone in the show needs to know*.' This caveat indicates the need to fully apprise all performers, providers, and production personnel of the scope and specifications of all planned special effects and demonstrates the 'duty to warn' principle for all involved in an event production.

Laser lights and strobe lights can add exciting theatrical effects to an event program – BUT lasers can cause eye damage and both laser and strobe lights can trigger epileptic seizures and signs alerting audience members that such effects will be used must be posted. Confetti cannons can propel large confetti or small trinkets over 100 feet and confetti drops can shower guests with color and glitter – BUT the items or material propelled can get into people's eyes, damage property, or contaminate food and/or beverages if badly timed or aimed (Silvers, 2004a).

Fog machines can fill the air with a misty smoke-like fog and dry ice will provide a fog that clings to the ground, providing a mystical or eerie atmosphere – BUT the materials used to create these and other atmospheric effects can cause burns (e.g., liquid nitrogen and dry ice) and could deplete the oxygen in the adjacent space or disperse particulates into the air, which may affect asthmatics, and the fragrances used in these and scentscaping effects can affect those with allergies (Rossol, 2000). Even the ubiquitous balloon has potential hazards ranging from the helium tanks used for inflation to the flammability and electricity conductivity of foil balloons (Monroe, 2006).

Indoor or outdoor pyrotechnics and aerial displays provide an exciting introduction, emphasis, or finale – BUT they can be fire hazards (burning people and property) and are strictly controlled in most jurisdictions. These restrictions regulate where the pyrotechnics may be detonated, how large they may be, how far away from the audience they must be, and what level of security and fire watch personnel must be provided (NFPA 1123, 2000; NFPA 160, 2001; NFPA 1126, 2001). They typically require a permit be issued based upon a pyrotechnics plan that illustrates the proposed use is 'safe and compatible with respect to the audience, performers, support personnel, pyrotechnicians, activity, stage, ceiling height, ventilation and venue' (Explosives Regulatory Division, 2003, p. 10). Some jurisdictions and venues may prohibit pyrotechnics of any sort altogether, including displays and close-proximity pyrotechnic or flame effects. One need only recall the horrific nightclub tragedy in West Warwick, Rhode Island in February 2003 to realize the consequences of mishandling pyrotechnics.

Consider this... 10.5

Sparkling centerpieces

Pyrotechnic centerpieces that shoot off a shower of sparks on cue have become a popular close proximity effect used at banquets (although these devices are prohibited in many jurisdictions). The provider of these centerpieces at one banquet encountered an ancillary hazard. He had procured the appropriate permits and had rigorously checked the safety of the equipment and the radio-controlled detonation apparatus for the centerpiece devices. The effect went off perfectly as he ignited the centerpieces on cue, providing an exciting climax for the event. Not long after the pyrotechnics went off, however, the provider heard the sirens of the fire trucks approaching the venue. He was confused because nothing had gone wrong with the devices at the banquet; everything was fine. He went outside to determine what caused the fire fighter response and saw his car completely engulfed in flames. Being the conscientious provider he was, he had brought several extra centerpiece appliances in case one of the centerpieces was damaged. But he had forgotten to disconnect the detonator on those extra devices and when he triggered the centerpieces for the banquet, the radio signal also ignited the ones in his car.

Summary

Crafting an event experience is blend of creativity and practicality, of art and discipline. The list of options and possibilities available to the event designer is vast and expanding exponentially as exciting techniques, technologies, and theatrical innovations enter the meetings and events marketplace everyday. This array of artistic choices must be managed through a disciplined approach in order to select the most effective activities and attributes for the environmental, experiential, and operational dimensions of that occasion, as well as the safety of their usage.

The event environment may be shaped and developed with décor, staging, presentation equipment, production elements, and furnishings. It must serve the needs of the event audience by providing the ambiance, equipment, shelter, and services that facilitate the appropriate learning, communication, entertainment, or celebratory event experience while ensuring the health, safety, welfare, and comfort of those in attendance (including those there to create, operate, or participate in the event). Provision of proper signage provides the cues and assistance to ensure the event experience will be as designed or preferentially desired, and should be used to prevent accidents, confusion or disorientation, inappropriate behavior, and access to restricted or hazardous areas.

Virtually all events include food and beverage service in some fashion, varying according to scope and function type. Any type or level of food and beverage service must be considered from a sanitation perspective to protect the health of those consuming these products, and the capabilities and credentials of the providers of these products must be confirmed. The event risk manager must employ the necessary strategies and policies to mitigate the risks associated with serving alcohol, as well as make certain that the appropriate and sufficient liability insurance is secured or in place for the event organization, the host, and the purveyor.

Entertainment, attractions, activities, and theatrical features add to enjoyment levels but must be assessed for appropriateness and potential liabilities, as well as the logistical requirements that will need to be incorporated throughout the operational plans. Magic (or a magical experience) does not just happen; it always requires some level of infrastructure that, in itself, poses potential hazards, vulnerabilities, and liabilities. The risk manager must work with the event organizer or designer to approach these choices as a risk technician rather than a risk taker.

Key safeguards

- Scan the program agenda for potentially controversial or high-demand components.
- Temporary structures or staging elements require special attention to ensure their stability and compliance with safety regulations.
- Confirm that all exit and safety signage has not been obscured by décor or decorations.
- Require a floor or site plan that is accurate in scale for every event.
- Never allow alcoholic beverages to be self-service.
- Amateur and professional speakers and entertainers should be held to the same high safety and accountability standards.
- Ensure appropriate sound amplification systems and sufficient functional, task, and safety lighting are provided.
- Invest in redundant equipment for critical production equipment and a technical director or producer for large or complex productions.
- Every special effect comes with potential hazards and should always be installed and operated by professionals.

Chapter review challenge

1 Review the programming choices made in the events described in this chapter and discuss the consequences (positive or negative) of these choices in terms of the effects they had on the event audiences and the event organizations.
2 Research food handler training programs and prepare a report that outlines the sanitation factors and safety precautions they cover.
3 How do food service risks differ between an on-premise event and an off-premise event?
4 How do you determine what 'suitable' entertainment is?
5 In what ways are production elements components of both a décor plan and a safety plan?

Practical risk management exercise

You have been retained by the CEO of the We Own Everything Corporation (WEOC) to develop a single alcohol management policy for its events department, which coordinates approximately 500 events annually throughout the nation. These events include management meetings, conferences, product launch events, company picnics, awards banquets, training programs, incentive travel programs, and customer hospitality events at numerous trade shows and sports events that the corporation sponsors. The CEO does not wish to prohibit the serving of alcohol at the corporation's events, but wants a policy that can be uniformly applied and enforced at all the corporate events so that there will be consistency in its approach to the serving of alcohol and will reflect sound risk management strategies that limit its liability.

Your job is to research regulatory requirements and best practices in alcohol management and write a 10-point policy that would be suitable for all of the events organized by the events department (e.g., any event hosted by the WEOC where alcohol is served shall use the services of a bartender certified through an alcohol server training program for the dispensing of alcohol), and justify your recommendations citing a minimum of three reference resources.

Key terminology

Alcohol Beverage Commission (ABC): The state-level authority (in the U.S.) that regulates the sale of alcohol.

Alcohol server training: Specific training provided to individuals who sell and serve alcohol that covers the legal responsibilities specified in the liquor laws of a jurisdiction.

Atmospherics: Theatrical fog effects, sometimes used for reflecting lighting effects.

Attraction: An appealing activity, feature, location, or item.

Designated driver program: An initiative wherein an individual within a group agrees to abstain from drinking alcohol so that the others may be assured of having a sober driver.

Dram shop laws: The laws (in the U.S.) that assign liability to an individual or establishment that serves alcohol to an intoxicated person.

Food borne illness: An illness caused by the consumption of a contaminated food.

Green room: A room or lounge for use by entertainers or speakers prior to and after a performance.

Hazard Analysis Critical Control Point (HACCP): A food safety assurance system that highlights potential problems in food preparation and service.

Pictographic icon: A representative image or symbol used to communicate a concept, for example the icons used on signs to indicate the location of toilets or emergency exits.

Program agenda: The chronological sequence, running order, or integrated list of event activities.

Pyrotechnics: The art and science of the use of chemicals, flash powders and explosives, usually ignited electronically, to make flashes, smoke, loud bangs or reports, and other special effect fireworks.

Scentscaping: The use and placement of fragrances to establish a mood.

Soundscaping: The use and placement of sound effects to establish a mood.

Waiver of indemnity: A written statement intentionally relinquishing responsibility for protection from loss or damage against an individual or other party.

Wayfinding: The science of personal navigation through a space, often reliant upon directional signage and environmental cues.

Online resources

Alcohol Server Awareness Program	www.state.vt.us/dlc/education/asap_on.html
American Pyrotechnics Association	www.americanpyro.com/Safety%20Info/safety.html
Entertainment Industry Glossary	www.bytecraftentertainment.com/glossary.phtml
Entertainment Services and Technology Association	www.esta.org/
Event Design Magazine	www.eventdesignmag.com/
Guide to Meeting Technology	www.pcma.org/convene/Templates/Special/
Meeting Manager's Food and Beverage Guide	www.pcma.org/templates/food_bev/
Production Services Association (U.K.)	www.psa.org.uk/
Special Effects Safety	www.effectspecialist.com/safety.htm
Technical Production Services Association (South Africa)	www.tpsa.co.za/
Wayfinding	www.signweb.com/index.php/channel/6/id/1433

Chapter 11
Site management

Know everything about the space and the place

This chapter will examine how to:

- Evaluate potential event sites in order to maximize its strengths and opportunities and minimize its weaknesses and threats
- Determine an event site's hazards and vulnerabilities in relation to the event's audience and activities
- Assess and control the risks associated with the inherent and imported infrastructure of the event site
- Incorporate the logistical needs and site constraints into the operational plan

Introduction

Every event occurs somewhere. An event site is the stage on or place in which the event experience will take place. The event site must accommodate the event attendees as well as the people, products, and services that will be brought together on-site to produce the event project. The management of the site must consider all the roles, responsibilities, applications, and maneuvers associated with these logistical and functional requirements and expectations as well as the experiential dimensions of the event's program as designed.

Event organizers will be considering event sites from a capacity, capability, and marketing perspective. However, any potential event site or venue has strengths, weaknesses, opportunities, and threats that must be addressed from a risk management perspective to ensure it serves the event audience, the event goals and objectives, and the event experience. The event organizer and risk manager must assess the spatial, infrastructural, and logistical attributes of the event and event site in order to assure feasibility. The predictive character of these attributes is shown in Table 11.1.

Site selection

The scope of site selection encompasses the sourcing, inspection, selection, and contracting of locations and facilities that will serve the needs of the event project, and

Table 11.1 Typical event rating attributes

Attribute	Predictive significance and elements
Nature of event	Will predict expected behavior and event intensity • Purpose/type of the event; emotional qualities; spectator or participatory; public or private • Ingress/intra-event movement/egress patterns; expected queuing • Risk of disorder; level of conflict or controversy; probability of accidents or incidents; previous casualty rates
Attendance volume	Will predict movement capacity and services capability requirements • Crowd size and density; movement flow capacity • Admittance criteria: free; purchased (ticket or registration); by invitation only • Tipping points for services or inspections
Audience profile	Will predict expected reaction behavior and response capabilities • Demographics; mix of ages and groups; physical and cognitive ability • Travel distance/complexity; familiarity with event or venue • Affiliation, membership, invitation; solitary or in a group
Event timing	Will predict impact on demand for services and infrastructure • Starting and ending times; daylight or night; peak travel/traffic times • Seasonal/weather factors • Competitive, consecutive, or concurrent event demand on services
Event duration	Will predict level of service requirements • Tipping points for services (e.g., toilet usage, on-site medical provision, labor calls) • Ticketing and seating policies; variable attendance volumes • Availability of on-site welfare services; overnight accommodations
Event location	Will predict capacity and infrastructure requirements • Geographic location, density; indoor/outdoor; urban/rural/remote; on-road/off-road; proximity of definitive care; private or public property • Purpose-built or multi-purpose venue; untried or temporary venue; temporary structures or staging; infrastructure capabilities; environmental controls • Spatial dimensions; layout configuration and complexity; expansive or numerous sites; distribution and concentration of activities
Event frequency	Will predict quality of historical data and organizer familiarity/experience • First time; one-time/one-off • Recurring in same locale; recurring in different locales; recurring (signature) • Rate of recurrence
Event attractions	Will predict spatial and demand levels or inherent risk factors • Hazardous or high-demand activities; food and alcohol service; special effects • Staging and equipment; operation and technician support • Move-in/move-out, installation, and maintenance

Sources: HSE (1999), NFPA 101 (2000), SFPE (2002), and Silvers (2007)

the old real-estate adage 'location, location, location' is equally applicable to selecting the best location and venue for an event as it is for selecting a site for a new business. Events of all types have been staged indoors and outdoors, in purpose-built and temporary facilities, in museums and along city streets, at amusement parks and country clubs, on town squares and vacant lots, in convention centers and empty warehouses, and in stadiums and private homes. Locations can range from urban to remote and from local to distant and exotic destinations.

The spatial capacity, costs, capabilities, features, suitability, and accessibility of a site will be used to determine feasibility. Selection will be based upon availability, affordability, and desirability from both a legal standpoint (see Chapter 3) and an operational standpoint. Once the event site has been acquired through a permit, build, or contract/lease arrangement, the event organizer and risk manager must become thoroughly familiar with the facility and its vicinity in order to be fully prepared for the production of the event. This includes the assessment of any and all hazards or vulnerabilities to ensure that risks may be mitigated.

Site selection criteria

Site selection is a pragmatic and sometimes intuitive process wherein the qualities and qualifications of the potential site are investigated, verified, and evaluated against the requirements and resources of the event. As with all procurement decisions (see Chapter 7), specifications must be established based on the needs assessment and weighted selection criteria must be developed according to priorities and the goals and objectives of the event project. Final site selection decisions may be made by the event organizer alone or in consultation with board members, clients, committees, executive directors, managers, and/or procurement departments. Use of pre-defined and weighted criteria helps prevent or remove any appearance of personal preference, favoritism, inducements, corruption, or political impropriety. Typical site selection criteria are shown in Table 11.2, and these criteria will vary in weight and applicability with each event according to its type, scale, and scope.

Consider this... 11.1

Vocation or vacation

Although site selection for many meeting and conference events takes into consideration the prestige, luxurious features, or popular appeal of a destination in order to make it attractive to potential attendees (sometimes including a conscious effort to induce linkage with a family vacation), this criteria may backfire and become a political liability. Expensive or exotic meeting sites often come under public scrutiny when taxpayer money or budget money from non-profit agencies or public corporations is used to fund participation. Government officials and company or agency executives or employees taking trips to resort areas and glamorous hotel properties for meetings or conferences are often accused of squandering public dollars or misusing agency funds. This criticism, usually unfounded, illustrates that it is imperative to consider the target audience's potential political vulnerabilities when establishing site selection criteria.

It is widely recommended that a physical inspection of a potential event site be conducted prior to selection to qualify and quantify all standards and conditions. Additional venue-specific criteria may be assessed according to the event project's special needs, as shown in Table 11.3. It is important to note that although a venue's facilities, features, and personnel may be an asset or a liability, these may change

Table 11.2 Typical site selection criteria

Capacity	Cost	Capabilities
• Function space adequacy • Housing quantity • Occupancy capacity • Spatial dimensions (e.g., gross square footage/meters, ceiling height)	• Contractual concessions • Cost of services • Equipment rental rates • Facility/space rental rates • Hosting support • Housing rates • Taxes • Union/labor charges	• Equipment availability • Personnel availability • Security and first aid • Shipping/receiving • Special activities • Staff experience • Support services • Technical facilities
Conditions	Compliance	Convenience
• Competitive events • Crime rates • Emergency response adequacy • Facility condition • Function space quality • Safety record • Surrounding vicinity	• Alcohol licensing • Emergency plans • Fire safety • Health and safety standards • Security methods • Special needs compliance	• Airlift to destination • Ease of access • Parking facilities • Proximity to off-site venues • Transportation availability • Vicinity amenities • Visibility
Configuration	Constraints	Cachet
• Building features • Décor elements • Flexibility • Proximity of event elements • Venue arrangement	• Legal limitations • Facility ownership • Policies • Regulations and restrictions • Renovation expectations • Union/non-union labor	• Atmosphere • Climate • Destination desirability • Property amenities • Style or image • Theme match

Table 11.3 Typical venue-specific inspection criteria

• Airwall acoustics • AV requirements • Catering • Communications • Construction • Electrical outlets • Entrances and exits • Exhibit space	• Floors and surfaces • Floor load capacity • Fencing/perimeters • Food/beverage outlets • Function rooms • Guest rooms • Lighting • Loading docks	• Obstructions • Offices • Seating areas • Stages • Storage areas • Toilet facilities • Ventilation system • Walkways/hallways

Sources: Berlonghi (1990), Connell (2002), Krug (2000), and Morrow (1997)

Table 11.4 Typical risk management site inspection criteria

• Adjacent area exposures	• First aid training (e.g., CPR, AED use, Heimlich maneuver)
• Backup generators in case of a power failure	• Health department rating
• Elevator inspections	• History of incidences
• Emergency exits (e.g., well-marked, battery lighted)	• Locks and key type and issuance procedure
• Evacuation plan	• Nearest medical facility
• Event-specific security requirements	• Political unrest
• Fire extinguishers (e.g., placement, visibility, inspection currency)	• Restricted access to guestroom floors
• Fire safety systems (e.g., smoke detectors, sprinkler systems)	• Security (e.g., cameras, patrols, personnel)
• First aid capabilities and equipment	• Shelter-in-place capability
	• Weather perils

Sources: Berlonghi (1990) and Silvers (2004a)

over time, which is likely to affect events that book space years in advance such as large meetings, expositions, and some incentive events. It is also important when considering a multi-use facility such as a hotel or convention center to determine other potential concurrent users to identify possible conflicts.

Using a comprehensive site inspection checklist customized specifically for each event (including key risk management categories as shown in Table 11.4) will facilitate the comparative evaluation of individual or numerous potential sites. In addition, having such a checklist not only helps the organizer assess the suitability of the product or service under consideration, and thereby make decisions on what might or might not be additionally necessary to bring things up to their standards; such documentation shows attention to the important risk management issues, thereby reducing potential liability for 'recommending incompetence.'

Advancing the event production

Once the event site has been selected and contracted, the event organizer and risk manager should concentrate on becoming completely familiar with the venue and its vicinity in order to determine the resources and services that will be used to produce the event, as well as those resources capable of mitigating or responding to unfavorable conditions and incidents (see Table 11.5). This is sometimes referred to as advancing the production (Moxley, 1995), and is particularly important if the event site is in a locale in which the organizer or risk manager does not reside. Telephone numbers, addresses, and driving directions should be collected for all those businesses that would be pertinent to the event project. It is also advisable to procure local and regional maps for any event destination and spend some time driving around the immediate vicinity of the event site or venue in order to familiarize oneself with the 'lay of the land.'

Contact should be made with all appropriate local authorities during this advancing process to determine any special conditions or restrictions applicable to the event production or personnel. For example, in certain cities there may be curfews, in some locations chewing gum or smoking in public is a criminal offense, and in

Table 11.5 Local resources that might be needed during an event

- Auto mechanics
- Banks and ATMs
- Clothing stores
- Convenience or grocery stores
- Doctors, dentists, medical facilities
- Dry cleaners or laundry
- Equipment rental services
- Gasoline stations
- Lodging options (ancillary)

- Office equipment and supplies
- Pharmacies
- Places of worship
- Post office
- Rental cars
- Restaurants (including take-away/carryout)
- Shipping services (e.g., FedEx)
- Taxicab (or water taxi) services
- Veterinarians or animal hospitals

Table 11.6 Typical site hazards and vulnerabilities

- Air pollution
- Animals (domestic, farm, or wild)
- Attractions (high-demand)
- Barriers
- Chemicals storage
- Cliffs, drops, or steep inclines
- Construction zones
- Crowd movement obstructions
- Darkness
- Décor features/equipment
- Dust pollution
- Equipment installations
- Fall hazards

- Ingress/egress (locations, legibility, and capacity)
- Insects
- Laser usage
- Lighting
- Neighboring land use
- Noise levels/vibration
- Noxious vegetation
- Overhead rigging
- Parking areas
- Pedestrian/vehicle crossings
- Perimeters
- Power lines
- Rodents, snakes, spiders

- Seating and sight lines
- Severe weather exposures
- Sanitation systems
- Slip/trip hazards
- Storage areas
- Temperature extremes
- Temporary structures
- Terrain and landscaping
- Uneven/rough surfaces
- Utility hook-ups
- UV radiation
- Walkway/path condition
- Water quality
- Waterways

Sources: Emergency Management Australia (1999), FEMA (2001), Silvers (2004a)

some countries there are restrictions on the amount of currency one may bring into or take out of the country (Moxley, 1995). These restrictions are well known and second nature to the residents and, therefore, may not come up in regular site negotiations, but they may have a significant impact on the event operations and in-bound audience.

Assessing site hazards and vulnerabilities

During an event, the event site will be filled with people, activities, equipment, and probably excitement. A pre-event inspection of the site should be conducted to determine potential hazards and vulnerabilities associated with the site and anticipated activities and equipment, followed by similar inspections during set-up and throughout the event to monitor conditions. The initial inspection should reveal areas or items that must be addressed in the site layout and services provision planning, including but not limited to those shown in Table 11.6. It is advisable to document pre-existing conditions by photograph or video just prior to set up and directly after move-out to document any damage caused by the event operations.

As opposed to the event organizer or designer, who will typically be focusing on the attributes and creative possibilities of the venue, the risk manager will be focusing on any and every aspect of the event site with an eye to what could go wrong. Although such negativity may be uncomfortable to others on the event team, this pessimistic perspective is necessary and risk managers may need to conduct their inspections separately or temper the delivery of their reports or observations (but not the content) so that these concerns are properly addressed rather than dismissed. After all, most site hazards and vulnerabilities may be eliminated or mitigated with simple site planning tactics.

Site planning and development

Architect Louis Sullivan's maxim 'form follows function' is a truism particularly pertinent to site planning for a meeting or event. As discussed in Chapter 10, the planned and likely choreography of the event experience will help shape the proper development and layout of the site wherein the event project takes place. Everything the guest or attendee will do and everything needed for them to do it must be arranged within the space given, and must be done in such a way that ensures the safety of all those occupying that particular space.

Getz (1997) specifies that the key site planning principles include capacity, crowd management, queuing, traffic, and legibility, and stresses the importance of considering access, movement, flow, shelter, comfort, and storage when developing the composition and configuration of the event site. Bowdin, Allen, O'Toole, Harris, and McDonnell (2006) highlight the importance of merging the schedule (e.g., peak flow times) and the product portfolio (i.e., the scope of event elements and services) in site planning. Silvers (2004a) underscores the importance of identifying and incorporating spatial and proximity requirements. Fire safety and crowd management engineers study intra-event movement and egress flow capacity, and retail anthropologists and marketing consultants study consumer movement patterns. All this and more must be factored into development of a safe and effective layout that meets the needs of the event occupants and operations based upon the type of event, the features of the facility, the proposed activities, and the size of the audience.

Activity determines site capacity and configuration

What is supposed to happen within the site and when it is supposed to occur guides decisions on where activities and equipment should be placed. Getz (1997) proposes that activities may be characterized as assembly (static audience), procession (linear attraction movement with static or linear audience movement), linear-nodal (linear attraction movement with audience congregation at nodes), open space (free movement with paths), and exhibition (planned circulation). The distribution of activities and fixed or variable movement times must be integrated into the design of the layout to decrease queuing and congestion and reduce counter or cross flows, thereby enhancing flow capacity (SFPE, 2002). The physical dimensions of the activities and the movement of the audience will determine maximum occupancy capacity, not just the square footage (or meters) of the floor space.

The risk manager should make certain that a minimum of 15 square feet (1.4 square meters) of net floor area is allotted per person in any site plan for egress capability and circulation space (NFPA 101, 2000). Sufficient aisle widths must be provided based on the expected crowd density and movement. Theater-style seating should have the chairs ganged (hooked together) to preserve row and aisle width integrity for maintaining egress flow capacity comparable to seating permanently fixed to the floor (e.g., in actual theaters or auditoriums). Sight lines must be assessed to ensure that ceiling heights can accommodate stage and screen heights based on flat floor seating capacity (Jewell, 1978) and that there is not movement toward the center causing congestion or crushing (Standards South Africa, 2004). Activities and concessions (e.g., attractions, food stations, bars, etc.) should be positioned away from entry points and queuing areas should not obstruct entrances or other activities (Silvers, 2004a; Standards South Africa, 2004). Attraction priority and timing may also be important in the site layout design because high-demand activities and mass movements will require additional space allotment.

Site development

Most purpose-built facilities are fully equipped to meet the needs of most events; yet, many events still require the importation of equipment and services necessary to make a site capable of serving the requirements of the event operations and program. Outdoor or temporary venues will often require the importation of a partial or complete infrastructure including temporary structures, tenting, and mobile facilities in order to be fully functional. The event organizer and risk manager must anticipate the needs of the event audience and providers, and examine the venue's resources in the context of event project as conceived.

The overall site plan must consider and should segregate the audience areas (front of house) and the purely operational areas (back of house), and visual and physical barriers should be devised for restricted back of house areas (Jewell, 1978), including operational equipment installations sited within audience areas. Barriers should also be devised for potentially hazardous site features. For example, ditches along the entrance/exit path for an outdoor festival held at a rural sports field were fenced off using bright orange storm fencing to demarcate the route and prevent the crowds exiting after dark from straying too close to the drop off. Perimeters must be defined and controlled, event components and equipment must be positioned and protected, and medical and welfare services must be acquired and properly situated.

Temporary structures and staging must be built, sited, and installed in compliance with applicable construction and engineering codes, which may entail an inspection by local authorities. Attention must be paid to acquiring the proper equipment according to spatial and load capacity, as well as its positioning within the site plan, including the quality (e.g., gradient, load capacity) of the surface where its installation is intended. Tents, marquees, towers (e.g., AV or camera), platforms, and portable seating typically require adherence to specific codes regarding fabrication, stability, anchoring practices for wind tolerance (e.g., staking or water weights), and usage (NFPA, 1995). Stage configurations should accommodate and segregate backstage facilities and may require barriers to prevent performer falls or crowd surges. Fire codes may govern how close tents may be sited together and the condition of their surroundings, the type and height of guard railings, or even the need for smoke detectors under expansive stages or grandstands.

Site diagrams

Once all the event components and their spatial and proximity requirements have been determined, a diagram should be prepared that is comprehensive and accurate in scale in order to verify the configuration and circulation efficacy of the proposed layout. This diagram may be referred to as a site plan, floor plan, or site map, and should include all the architectural (indoor) and/or topographical (outdoor) features as well as the event-specific attractions and logistical features (Bowdin et al., 2006). The site diagram should be reviewed by the appropriate stakeholders (e.g., suppliers and authorities) to ensure that the crowd movement and logistical requirements have been properly addressed and that the layout facilitates the event experience as envisioned (see Appendix M: Site plan worksheet).

Site diagrams are an important part of the site development process in that the proposed distribution of activities, services, and equipment may be assessed and adjusted prior to the move-in, thereby saving time, money, and effort. Depending on the nature of the site or facility, the site diagram may need to include external features or the surrounding vicinity. Analysis of the diagram may reveal unforeseen health and safety hazards, security vulnerabilities, logistical nightmares waiting to happen, and gaps in infrastructural planning. Alternate forms of the diagram may be devised as communication tools such as travel access instructions, wayfinding maps, and seating charts.

Infrastructure management

Infrastructure may be defined as the utilities and technical support necessary to allow the event to operate at a given site, and its management encompasses the confirmation, acquisition, or enhancement of inherent or imported equipment and services to ensure sufficient transportation systems, parking facilities, utilities, sanitation and waste management systems, and emergency response services are in place to meet the functional needs of the event project. Just as a city planner looks at the needs of residents to determine the city services necessary to conduct the business of everyday living, so too must the event organizer look at the needs of the temporary municipality created for the event.

Varying levels of capacity and capability will be needed based on the type and scope of the event program, and varying levels will be found at purpose-built properties, unique venues, temporary facilities, and completely undeveloped sites. The assessment of transportation systems and parking needs will be affected by the location of the event in relation to the location and size of its audience. The requirements for essential utilities and waste management services will be determined by the activities to be conducted at the event. The provision of sanitation and emergency services will typically be calculated based on the nature and size of the audience and the duration of the event (see Chapter 4).

Transportation and traffic issues

The transportation and traffic issues surrounding an event will depend on the audience size and market area; event site, time, and duration; and the type and scope of the event. The most common issues include modes of travel, traffic congestion, road

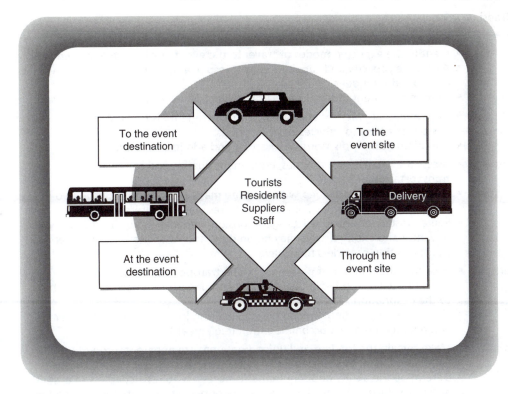

Figure 11.1   The scope of event travel

capacity, routes, non-patron impacts, and traffic and pedestrian safety. Travel and transportation could involve flying, driving, sailing, or taking a train to a destination; driving or riding to a venue at a destination; as well as getting around a destination or an event site in a variety of conveyances (see Figure 11.1). Travel will be necessary for virtually any event but the type of event and its target market will typically dictate the extent of travel and specific transportation issues that the event organizer and risk manager should consider, some of which are shown in Table 11.7. A traffic management plan should be developed in cooperation with the appropriate transportation, law enforcement, and public safety agency stakeholders and should address the following (Latoski, Dunn, Wagenblast, Randall, and Walker, 2003):

- Site access and parking
- Pedestrian access
- Traffic flow
- Traffic control
- En-route traveler information
- Traffic surveillance
- Traffic incident management and safety.

Conventions and conferences often include attendees from outside the vicinity of the event site and issues such as air lift (e.g., the number of carriers and daily flights), taxi service capacity, and ground transportation operators for airport transfers, group transfers, or continuous shuttle services will be required for the high percentage of

Table 11.7   Transportation issues to be considered

Conveyances	• Identify the expected modes of travel to the event destination and event site • Assess the capacity and capabilities of transportation services for in-bound and out-bound attendees • Determine potential for high-occupancy vehicle incentives
Credentials	• Determine necessity for and types of access credentials for vehicles and passenger access to vehicles • Coordinate timely distribution of access and admittance credentials
Ground operators	• Assess the capacity, capabilities, equipment quality, and compliance of transportation providers • Ensure drivers are provided with accurate maps and directions, have two-way communication capability, and adhere to regulatory requirements • Some jurisdictions have strict regulations on who may drive a particular type of vehicle, how long drivers may be on duty, and what licenses the drivers and transportation providers must have
Group transfers	• Ascertain the number of passengers to be transported, the whole group/partial group flexibility of arrival and departure times, and travel time to the destination • Determine the loading, unloading, and waiting locations for the transfer equipment, and driver accommodation (e.g., meals)
Loading areas	• Make certain the loading and unloading areas are apparent, properly illuminated, and well staffed • Determine the ability and requirements necessary to restrict access to ensure ancillary vehicular traffic does not endanger pedestrian traffic within loading area
Public transport	• Identify the proximity and accessibility of existing public transport options • Determine the need and potential for public transit service expansion, express service, and/or charter service
Roads and routes	• Evaluate the necessity and possibility of arranging for specific routes, road or lane closures, or traffic redirection • Determine any 'user pays' costs that would be incurred for police or transportation authority interventions and services • Determine timing restrictions or regulated routes for mass movement or heavy vehicle transit • Establish emergency access and alternate routes to be included in contingency plans
Scheduling	• Determine typical high-demand congestion times and locations and compare to the arrival/departure times and routes for the event • Evaluate and mitigate the traffic congestion impact of event arrival/departure times on the facilities and activities in the immediate vicinity of the event site
Shuttles	• Determine the need for shuttle services for individual or group transfers for destination arrivals and departures, multi-venue housing or attractions, satellite parking lot arrangements, or intra-event movement at expansive event sites • Calculate the arrival/departure demand volume and locations to establish timed or continuous routes
Signage	• Determine the need and sources for static and variable message signage for en-route traveler information • Ensure content and volume of directional signage is sufficient, especially for travelers unfamiliar with the destination

Table 11.8 Transportation and traffic contingency plan checklist

- Absence of trained or volunteer personnel
- Blockage of transport access
- Delayed event
- Demonstration or protest
- Dignitary motorcade transit roadblocks
- Equipment breakdown or no-show
- Emergency evacuations
- Event cancellation
- Flooded access routes or parking areas
- Illegal street vendor activity
- Major traffic incident/accident
- Overcrowding
- Road construction
- Route obstructions
- Security threat
- Security or itinerary delay of participants
- Security or itinerary delay of VIPs
- Severe weather outbreak

Sources: Latoski et al. (2003) and RTA (2002)

visitors. Fair and festivals will typically include local residents and in-bound tourists, which would suggest that the roads and routes for private and rental cars and the capacity of public transportation should be carefully considered. Incentive events and high-level meetings may need to consider prestige or upscale transportation services such as chartered flights to remote locations or limousine service for VIPs and dignitaries. Expositions and trade shows will need to consider the truckloads of exhibits arriving at the exhibition hall and arts and craft fairs will need to consider the individual exhibitors arriving with their displays and inventory in individual vans and vehicles. Sports and other spectator events will need to consider travel demand management techniques such as enhancement of public transport, development of alternatives to (and incentives against) single-vehicle travel, and alternative or altered routes.

Obviously street-use or on-road events such as parades, street fairs, or marathons will have a different set of considerations and traffic impact than events held in high-capacity purpose-built venues, and events that occur on the weekend will likely have different traffic conditions than those held during the week. It is the responsibility of the event organizer to assess the potential impact the event will cause on existing traffic and the impact the existing traffic will have on the event, including the entire duration of the event's operations from move-in through move-out, and then identify the stakeholders and strategies necessary to mitigate negative consequences. In addition, the risk manager should evaluate the incidents, conditions, or scenarios that might require transportation or traffic contingency plans, such as those shown in Table 11.8. Unimpeded access routes should be restricted and protected for emergency vehicles (e.g., police, fire, ambulances, etc.); exclusive and/or priority ingress and egress routes should be planned for busses, shuttle services, service vehicles, and preferential parking services; and in all cases, vehicular and pedestrian traffic should be segregated.

Consider this... 11.2

Half a good time was had

A special off-premise event was planned for the delegates at an international convention held during a major hot air balloon festival, a signature event of the destination. The event organizer of this special event for the convention had procured a special hospitality tent within the festival's corporate village featuring a fantastic gourmet breakfast buffet for the 800 guests who were to be transported to the festival field in deluxe motor coaches very early in the morning to avoid the heavy traffic problems associated with this very popular event. At the appointed pick-up time, 6:00 a.m., only 10 of the 20 coaches that were contracted from a local DMC for the single group transfer showed up at the headquarters hotel.

The event organizer was not able to reach anyone at the DMC and did not know the individual transportation providers the DMC had contracted the coaches from (no single provider had enough equipment), therefore she could not contact them to find out where the remaining coaches were. Considering the signature nature of the event and the early morning hours, it was impossible to locate additional coaches. The event organizer loaded and sent the coaches off, instructing the drivers to return immediately to pick up the second half of the guests, which, due to the traffic, took more than two hours. By this time, many of the remaining 400 guests had given up on going and those that did wait for the transfer missed the mass ascension of the hot air balloons and most of the buffet due to the delay and the additional hour to return to the festival grounds.

Needless to say the convention organizers were very disappointed with the event and the event organizer was compelled to refund 50 percent of the fee paid as well as cover the cost of refreshments for those waiting at the hotel for the second transfer, resulting in a significant financial loss for the event project. Even though the cause was the fault of the DMC, the event organizer was only able to recover the cost of the 10 coaches that did not appear from them, representing only 5 percent of the cost of the event.

Parking considerations

Hundreds or thousands of vehicles must be accommodated with parking places and spaces, even if for only a short period of time whilst loading or unloading occurs. As illustrated in Figure 11.2, the event organizer and risk manager, in conjunction with public safety authorities and/or specialist consultants as appropriate, should conduct a parking demand analysis to determine the number and types of vehicles expected and the arrival and departure patterns of those vehicles to develop a parking plan that allocates, designates, and segregates parking areas according to zones of need and the capabilities and restraints of the parking options.

Parking will be required and designated areas should be considered for event patrons, participants, performers, exhibitors, providers, staff and volunteers, the media, and emergency services. Lot and space assignment factors may include general public parking (free or paid), reserved/VIP parking, disabled parking, valet parking, bus parking, recreational vehicle parking, taxi/limousine staging, and remote park-and-ride, satellite, and/or overflow parking lots (Latoski et al., 2003). Parking area features such as lighting, paving, and security should be reviewed and deficiencies should be addressed. Parking occupancy monitoring tactics and 'lot full' decision criteria should be established and procedures for directing traffic to alternate or overflow parking areas must be devised (e.g., diversion messages via signage or media announcements).

Access routes and vehicle processing issues (e.g., fee payment, credential/permit checking, traffic direction, etc.) should be considered from a safety and efficiency perspective to ensure that ingress and egress flow is properly managed and motorist frustration does not incite violation of the parking controls. Where and when possible,

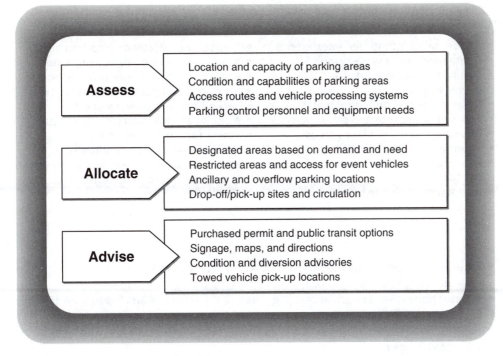

Assess
- Location and capacity of parking areas
- Condition and capabilities of parking areas
- Access routes and vehicle processing systems
- Parking control personnel and equipment needs

Allocate
- Designated areas based on demand and need
- Restricted areas and access for event vehicles
- Ancillary and overflow parking locations
- Drop-off/pick-up sites and circulation

Advise
- Purchased permit and public transit options
- Signage, maps, and directions
- Condition and diversion advisories
- Towed vehicle pick-up locations

Figure 11.2 The elements of parking management

segregated access routes and entrances should be linked to designated parking areas, and traffic flow should be facilitated by stewarding personnel and barrier equipment. Regulations should be established (or may exist and require compliance) to preserve parking for nearby residents and businesses, maintain routes for non-event traffic flow, and safeguard critical event-specific access routes for emergency and essential service vehicles such as ambulances, law enforcement and fire vehicles, portable toilet pump-out and garbage removal vehicles, and utility repair and public works vehicles (FEMA, 2001; Latoski et al., 2003). Ad hoc parking areas should be controlled (or prohibited) to prevent egress traffic flow conflicts.

All parking instructions and restrictions should be publicized to event patrons and non-patrons as appropriate according to the level of parking demand, lot designations, and the traffic demand caused by event parking. This may include en-route signage and maps included in registration and promotional materials and on web sites. Signage should indicate any restrictions before vehicles enter, including 'No Responsibility' waiver language and towing policies and pick-up locations, and pedestrian signage should be provided to guide patrons from the parking area to the event site. Maps may be drawn to scale or superimposed on aerial photographs, which may vary in version according to the stakeholder or user, and should include the following information (Latoski et al., 2003):

- Parking areas or lot designations (including number, letter, or color-coded designation, and class of vehicle or user restrictions).
- Lot-specific access point directions, costs, and hours of operation.
- Restricted off-site and on-street parking areas (including residential neighborhoods and tow-away zones).

Table 11.9   Typical utility service risks for events

- Accidental or intentional interference
- Contamination of water supply
- Damaged equipment due to power surges
- Defective or deficient equipment
- Exposed or unprotected power sources
- Fuel usage in unventilated areas
- Improper electrical installation
- Improper storage of compressed gas tanks
- Inadequate drainage systems
- Inadequate telecommunications access
- Insufficient heating or cooling system
- Insufficient power outlets or distribution
- Insufficient amperage or water pressure
- Lack of back-up power sources
- Noise or air pollution from generators
- Power failure or interruption
- Unrestricted access to equipment
- Unsafe proximity of electricity and water
- Unsecured/unprotected cords or cables
- Ventilation obstruction or corruption

- Shuttle bus service routes and embarkation/disembarkation points (with lot-specific designations, e.g., 'Blue Line' buses for the blue lot, etc.).
- Information on street regulations (e.g., one- or two-way), road closures, and names of and connections to major freeways, arteries, roadways, streets, etc.
- Landmarks, headquarter hotel locations, public transit stations, and private or restricted property.

Parking should be controlled for virtually all events. Failure to plan for and provide parking may increase the event's liability. Uncontrolled parking may violate city ordinances, damage public or private property, cause dangerous traffic congestion, or jeopardize emergency response. All parking services should be procured from experienced, licensed (if applicable), and properly insured providers, and all parking facilities should be evaluated for vehicular and pedestrian convenience, accessibility, safety, and regulatory compliance.

Essential utilities

The public utility services that most people take for granted in their daily lives such as electric power, gas, and a clean water supply are expected in the venues used for events as well, as are sufficient heating, air conditioning, and ventilation systems and telecommunications capabilities. However, given the broad range of developed and undeveloped sites used for events and the variety of activities included in them, these everyday necessities must be carefully assessed for every event and at every event site to ensure sufficient capacities, reliable capabilities, and the proper quantities and distribution of power, fuel, and water according to the needs of the event. The typical risks associated with utility services are shown in Table 11.9, and various jurisdictions will have regulatory codes and specifications that must be adhered to regarding utility usage and installations.

Electrical power is needed for virtually every event and for most activities at an event. From the lights used to illuminate and decorate to the equipment used to make music or make coffee, there will be a demand for access to dependable electricity in varying levels throughout the event site. Moxley (1995) advises that one must know how much power is needed, where it is needed, and where it will come from, and cautions that the power output must be controllable to prevent damage to electronic equipment. The event organizer should determine the power needs by collecting electrical needs estimates from all providers requiring electricity and plot this out in the site plan with the venue's engineer or power provider to ensure the loads (the amount of electricity to be pulled) are properly distributed to the locations where it is needed to prevent overloaded electrical circuits, which may require the acquisition of or augmentation with portable generators in order to mitigate the lack or reliability of power sources.

The risk manager should confirm that a back-up power source is in place for safety and emergency lighting and sound systems should a power failure occur. All electrical equipment, connections, cords, cables, and wires should be checked to ensure they are properly secured to prevent damage, tripping hazards, or unauthorized access. All temporary electrical installations should be done by professionals and may need to be inspected and approved by local government inspectors. The location and operation of controls for lighting, sound, and other electrical systems should be identified in order to ensure they can be turned on or off in an emergency situation, including those used by entertainers so that the stage lighting or sound system may be used or disabled as agreed upon in the emergency action plan.

Natural gas, propane, petrol, and numerous other liquid fuels and gases are used at events for cooking, fueling heaters or power generators, filling helium balloons, and adding the fizz to carbonated drinks. The equipment using these fuels must be safe and in good working condition, must be installed properly according to regulatory requirements, and only operated in well-ventilated areas in order to mitigate any noxious or obnoxious fumes they may emit. All compressed gas containers must be securely anchored in an upright position to prevent damage or becoming a projectile. All fuel containers and storage areas should have restricted access achieved with suitable barriers, and all refueling and maintenance functions should be carefully controlled. The risk manager should make certain all fuel sources have emergency shut-off valves and operators know how and when to use them.

Potable water will be required for drinking, food preparation, cleaning, hand washing, misters or other evaporative cooling equipment, first aid services, equipment cooling (e.g., lasers), and/or decorative treatments. Non-potable water may be required for toilet facilities, fire suppression, or dust abatement. Temporary and outdoor event sites are of most concern and the importation of water will need to be considered if connection to a safe and suitable source is not sufficient or available. Temporary water supplies must be transported and stored in approved and protected containers, and should be tested for bacteriological safety (HSE, 1999). Drainage must also be considered for used or excess water to prevent flooding or slippery surfaces, and sullage and other waste or contaminated water must be disposed of properly.

Heating, ventilation, and air-conditioning (HVAC) systems need to be considered from a comfort perspective as well as a health and safety perspective. For temporary sites and outdoor venues, heating will be important in cold weather for the prevention of hypothermia and cooling will be critical in hot weather for the prevention of heat exhaustion; portable equipment is available for both. Ventilation systems must be carefully considered whenever any fuels or special effects are used, including the permissions and procedures for increasing or disabling and reconnecting the system for smoke or pyrotechnic effects. The event organizer and risk manager should be familiar with the environmental controls in any facility used to ensure access is available to manipulate the heating and cooling of the event space according to the needs of the event, and to ensure access is restricted to prevent unauthorized operation or tampering. In addition, the configuration of ventilation system should be assessed and monitored to ensure it is not obstructed by staging, décor, or stored materials or equipment.

The telecommunications capabilities of the event site will need to be assessed based on the nature and demands of the event and its attendees. Given today's climate of constant connectivity, attendees and exhibitors at meetings and trade shows will require good wireless connection to the Internet and for cellular phone service, which can be problematic in some locations or buildings. WiFi (wireless fidelity) hotspots, a high-frequency limited-range wireless network area for connecting to the Internet, are becoming plentiful in many areas, but caution should be exercised regarding the protection of the data transmitted over such networks. Hard wired or wireless inter-com systems may be needed for stage productions or language translation services, special equipment for the hearing or sight impaired may be required, high-speed telephone lines for Internet access or digital broadcasts may be needed, and public telephones may need to be installed at large public gatherings or remote locations. Telecommunications equipment and services may be available at or through the venue, and attention should be paid to the installation costs and usage fees charged, as well as the ability to quickly respond to maintenance and repair needs. And, of course, all installations should be completed by trained professionals and monitored to ensure cables, wires, and connections do not become trip hazards.

In addition to all installation and operation issues, the event organizer and risk manager need to consider the maintenance and servicing of any and all utilities at the event site. This may include special routes and access points and times for refueling, refreshing, repair, repositioning, and replacement or removal of equipment. As with most topics covered in this book, the organizer and risk manager are not expected to be experts in these areas, but they are expected to know when specialists are needed, who those specialists are, and how to quickly contact them. Become familiar with the venue's engineering and maintenance departments and personnel, as well as the tech-nicians for any outside providers, and know whom to call for assistance. Also, keep in mind that many of the utilities to be provided for the event need to be installed and operational during the move-in and move-out of the rest of the staging, décor, and other equipment and services.

Managing the logistics

The event experience has been designed and defined. The event site has been meas-ured and mapped. The proper infrastructure has been assessed and acquired. The product and service providers have been contacted and contracted. The performers and personnel have been procured and prepared. Now, all that is left is to bring everything and everyone together and implement the event itself, translating 'the program into the reality of an event' (Getz, 1997, p. 88). This assembly of people, provisions, and equipment typically occurs within a short and intense period of time, which requires careful planning and rigorous supervision of the logistics.

The action plan for installing and implementing the event, and, as illustrated in Figure 11.3, management of its logistics encompasses the analysis, sequencing, and supervision of the tasks, providers, and materials necessary for the on-site activities associated with the event project within the physical constraints of the event site. The event risk manager must scrutinize the action plan to ensure that everything

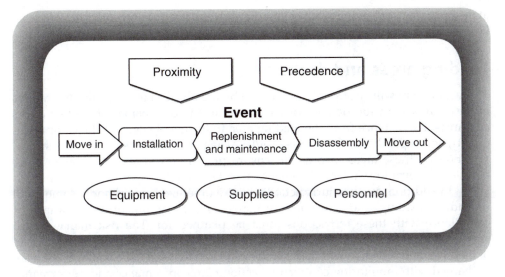

Figure 11.3 Overview of event logistics

necessary is included and all aspects of the plan are well thought out and safe. This is best accomplished by becoming involved in its preparation.

Coordinating flow and task sequencing

The science of logistics is employed in military, industrial, and project management contexts as a way to coordinate and optimize the time-related flow and positioning of resources, services, supplies, and support in the necessary and proper sequence. The action plan for positioning and sequencing will be dependant upon the scope of the event, the proximity and precedence order requirements of the activities and event equipment, and the physical limitations of the event site. Bowdin et al. (2006) emphasize the need to manage the flow of the people and equipment into, around, and out of the site based on the subcontractors' needs and time constraints. Tum, Norton, and Wright (2006) highlight the importance of calculating demand and matching resources to that demand. Given that time and space are finite, the event organizer must allocate the flow of materials and activities in such a way that the demand for these fixed capacity levels is chronologically and spatially managed.

The spatial and temporal specifications for each product or service must be collected from each in-house or subcontracted provider, and these must be analyzed to determine the most efficient routing, unloading and loading locations, timing, and task sequencing based on precedence order (what must precede something else) and proximity needs (where something must be placed). For many events, the precedence order for this action plan may be accomplished with simple common-sense logical thinking for putting first things first (e.g., largest items in first, first in/last out, etc.), but for large or complex events, use of a precedence diagraming software for the blending of the work breakdown structure and the production schedule may be required that illustrates the full scope of activities (i.e., what needs to happen) and the logical relationships among them, such as mandatory and external dependencies (i.e., this can not be started until that has arrived or has been completed) (PMI, 2000). Large or small, straightforward or complicated, the action plan's objective is to prevent workers from trying to occupy the same space or use the same installation equipment at the same time, or leaving work crews idle and frustrated waiting for critical tasks to be completed.

Loading areas and docks

This action plan will be strongly influenced by the physical features and limitations of the event site, including the capacity, location, and dimensions of loading docks and areas, the distance from the loading area to the event site, and the complexity, quality, and capabilities of the access routes. The risk manager should focus special attention on these areas in order to ensure proper consultation has taken place between the event organizer, the venue, and the providers, performers, or participants. In addition, as some jurisdictions require unionized labor handle some or all unloading, loading, and movement of materials and equipment within a facility, compliance with these restrictions must be planned for. The risk manager also should confirm that all contractors and subcontractors have been properly advised of their role and schedule within the action plan and that someone on the event team is charged with monitoring contractors' action plan conformance and performance during the move-in and move-out time periods.

Many purpose-built facilities have loading docks, but there may be restrictions on when deliveries may be made and how long vehicles may occupy spaces. The entrance to the loading area or dock may have height restrictions or there may be disparate levels between the dock's edge and the vehicle's opening requiring special ramps. Temporary or outdoor sites may require development or designation of loading areas, as well as additional parking areas for delivery vehicles throughout the duration of the event. Marshaling areas may be required for events expecting large numbers of delivery vehicles, such as expansive productions or exhibitions, in order to position vehicles while waiting access the dock area, or staging areas where unloaded equipment may be temporarily stored after unloading and before installation.

The route from where equipment or material is unloaded to its final destination on the event site must be assessed. The distance between the loading area and the event site may be lengthy and may require intermediate equipment such as fork lifts, flat dollies, or hand trucks for moving heavy props or other equipment. If an outdoor event, the route may be dirt or grass and may require plywood be laid down to ease the movement of wheeled cases or hand trucks. The route may involve doorways and/or passageways with sharp turns that can not accommodate the size of equipment, which will require alternate routes or disassembly of the item prior to move-in. The event location may be on a different floor than the loading area and although freight elevators may be available at purpose-built facilities, these elevators may not have the dimensional or weight load capacity for the equipment being delivered. Moxley (1995) advises that one must know all the options for getting from the loading area to the event site at a venue, no matter how extreme the final solution may be. This may include using construction cranes to hoist equipment to a rooftop, using the escalator in the public lobby to move a large piece of staging or décor, or walking live animals up the levels of a contiguous parking garage.

Move-in through move-out

The risk manager should confirm that the logistics of the action plan includes and chronologically choreographs the entire duration of the use of the event site, from the delivery of the first item to the removal of the last item and the cleaning and restoration of the site to its original (or better) condition. This often starts with the pre-con meeting at which all key role players review the chronological details in the context of a common picture of what each must accomplish, and ends with the post-con at which the results are reviewed and residual problems are resolved (Connell, 2002).

The two periods that are often insufficiently addressed in terms of logistics are the times during the event when maintenance and replenishment activities must take place and during the dismantling and move-out period. For multi-day or multi-venue events, the delivery of supplies will often be required (e.g., replenishing inventories for exhibitors or food provisions for concessionaires) and maintenance activities will need to be conducted (e.g., portable toilet pump-out or equipment replacement or repositioning). Not only will storage areas need to be established (and often protected with security); the timing and routing will need to be integrated into the action plan and the site plan. Although these activities may often be scheduled prior to each day's opening, this may not be sufficient or feasible and arrangements for intra-event movement of deliveries must be made.

The closure phase, during which the event is dismantled and the equipment is moved out and reloaded onto all the respective provider's vehicles, is often the most haphazard and risky. The excitement is over, the workers are often tired, and the event personnel just want to go home and relax. Consequently, disassembly and repacking is chaotic, equipment is lost or damaged, congestion develops at the loading areas, frustration and tempers flare, and worker injuries occur. The risk manager should ensure that the move-out is as carefully choreographed, staffed, and monitored as the move-in, and that cleaning services are procured and properly conducted.

Summary

The event site and the space available within that site can become an asset or a liability, and it is critical to remember that everything at an event requires sufficient space to minimize risk, particularly from a safety and emergency egress point of view. Site selection and inspection should be done using sensible procurement and assessment criteria, and once the site has been acquired, complete familiarity with it must be achieved.

An event site could be considered a virtual, temporary, and self-contained metropolis. Confirming or importing the necessary infrastructure for a fully functional event site requires a thorough assessment of the various needs, constraints, and options associated with bringing an event to life. This assessment must be conducted with many points of view considered, including those attending, those supplying goods and services, those operating attractions and equipment, and those participating in the event, as well as those who may be affected by the event occurring in their vicinity.

The risk manager should review the scope of the travel and transportation pertinent to the event based on its type, scope, purpose, audience, and location to determine the necessary operational safeguards and infrastructure. A written parking plan should be included in the event's evidentiary documentation and the audience should be advised of parking options and restrictions in the event promotions and publicity. Essential utilities such as power, fuel, water, and telecommunications must assessed for accessibility, reliability, quantity, and quality, and any deficiencies must be mitigated with ancillary services as appropriate.

Bringing the event to life on site and then closing it down involves the coordination of dozens to hundreds to thousands of tasks, personnel, and materials, all of which must be scheduled and positioned in a logical manner. Failure to properly sequence all this activity and equipment movement can result in a logistical collapse that could threaten the safety of the event personnel and audience, as well as turn its operations into an expensive and torturous nightmare. The application of good procurement practices, common sense, attention to detail, and, if necessary, project management software will increase the probability of successful site management.

Key safeguards

- Include weather, economic and political conditions, and the site's vicinity, support services, and safety in site selection decisions.
- Spatial decisions must consider dimensions, proximity, and flow capacity.
- Assess and control the transportation impact of and vehicular access to and within the event site.
- Designated ingress routes and entrance gates should be linked with parking area designations.
- Access to utility areas and equipment should be restricted to prevent mishaps, injuries, and accidental or intentional interference.
- Contingency plans should be in place for the loss or interruption of any critical utility.
- Know whom to call for immediate on-site plumbing or electrical maintenance and repair.
- Incorporate reserve time into the operations action plan for unforeseen logistical problems.

Chapter review challenge

1 Review the 'event location' factors in Table 11.1 and discuss the possible strengths and weaknesses of each.
2 How does a venue's surroundings impact the choice of one site over another and why?
3 Why is an accurate site diagram important for effective risk management?
4 What are the infrastructure considerations for using a totally undeveloped site, and how might these differ for a purpose-built facility such as a hotel ballroom or convention center?
5 In what ways could a logistical collapse occur and what would the consequences likely be of such a collapse?

Practical risk management exercise

Read the following case study and prepare a report that analyzes the site selection and infrastructural issues, answering the questions posed at the end.

An Intergalactic Reception

As a tactic to generate publicity and press coverage that would distinguish Albuquerque and New Mexico from the surrounding Southwestern states and communities, a one-night festival-style event was created for the convention and visitors bureau to capitalize on the science fiction/science fact assets of the destination. Not only is New Mexico home to the legendary Roswell Incident; Albuquerque is home to Lovelace Medical Center where the first astronauts were tested as humorously depicted in the film *The Right Stuff*. In addition, New Mexico has the Alamogordo Space Center and the Los Alamos and Sandia National Laboratories, and boasts the highest per-capita ratio of science fiction authors in the U.S. The event was an all-volunteer effort with all the goods, services, and exhibits donated in support of the bureau, including sponsorship by a local television station.

The Albuquerque Intergalactic Reception featured a UFO landing strip; a dozen exhibits including the UFO Museum from Roswell, roving lunar robots from Sandia National Lab's Robotics Department, hands-on zero-gravity activities, and a full-scale model of the Mercury I Space Capsule; a science fiction book fair with book signings by several New Mexico writers; a portable inflatable planetarium; telescopes provided by the university's astronomy club; food concessions and a beer garden; a disk jockey on a stage playing science fiction movie themes; an inflatable Moon Walk bouncy cage for children; a 'Milky Way Mercado' of souvenir vendors; and a special appearance by the star of a popular science fiction television program who signed autographs at the television station's sponsor tent.

The site was the uppermost level of the five-level parking structure adjacent to the convention center because it was the largest and highest open space in the downtown area, and the parking authority wanted to promote the parking structure so more residents would use this facility. The first three levels of the parking structure were available as free parking for event-goers and the fourth level was reserved for parking the event vehicles. All the staging, tenting, equipment, and exhibiting companies were notified in writing that the access to the event site was through the parking structure levels, which had a seven-foot clearance.

Set-up day arrived and so did the truck delivering the portable toilets, which was too tall for the seven-foot clearance and the toilets had to be stationed on the ground floor of the parking structure next to the elevator because 'tipping' them was not an option, and directional signage had to made to inform attendees of their new location. Despite the event organizer's clear communication to all the parties involved regarding clearance limits and access to the event, the portable toilets were just the tip of the iceberg. The convention center's food concessionaire had to revise its catering operations that day because it realized its colorful concession wagons could not fit within elevator, nor could they withstand rolling them throughout the five levels of the parking structure route. The model of the space capsule had to be stationed on the street next to the parking structure because it could not fit under the seven-foot clearance. The emergency medical technicians (EMTs) contracted to oversee the event had to walk up the five levels with their emergency gear because their ambulance was too tall for the seven-foot clearance. The first beer truck could not make it in because it was too big for the seven-foot clearance.

Nevertheless, the event was a success, attracting more than 2000 men, women, assorted aliens, and especially children, and generating more than $300 000 worth of national and international publicity coverage. And everyone on the event team, from participants to providers, soon made the low clearance into the running joke.

If anything went awry, they just slapped their cheeks and cried 'seven-foot clearance!' to lighten the load with a little laughter.

1 What were the strengths and weaknesses of using the top level of the parking structure as the event site?
2 What infrastructure was required to accommodate the event elements and the event audience?
3 What were the operational challenges associated with the location and the access to the site?
4 How would you have solved the seven-foot clearance issue?

Key terminology

Ad hoc parking area: A temporary or unsanctioned parking area charging fees operated by an individual not connected with an event.

Amperage: The volume of electricity flowing through an electrical circuit.

Floor plan: A graphical diagram of an event site or space drawn to scale including its dimensions, entrances and exits, the positioning of all equipment and staging, and event activities.

Flow capacity: The volume and rate at which people are able to move through a given space.

Ganging chairs: The fastening together of unsecured chairs via built-in hooks or other means.

Ground transportation: Transportation services at a site or destination, including taxicabs, buses, shuttles, automobile rental, and limousine services.

HVAC system: The heating, ventilation, and air-conditioning system in a building or structure; also known as a climate control system.

Infrastructure: The facilities, utilities, and technology, transportation, communication, and sanitation systems necessary to make a site functional.

Intercom: A closed circuit intercommunication system.

Marshaling area: A holding area adjacent to the main event area where trucks, equipment, and/or participants are arranged in their proper order or await access.

Move-in/move-out: The date and time set for the delivery, installation, dismantling, and removal of equipment and supplies at the event site; also known as bump-in/bump-out or load-in/load-out.

On-road event: An event or event component that takes place on a public road, street, or highway, such as a parade or marathon.

Portable generator: A gas-powered source of electrical power that may be moved to an event location or site.

Portable seating: Seats that are not permanently fixed in a venue and may be arranged in a variety of configurations, including chairs, bleachers, benches, etc.

Potable water: Water from a government-approved source that is safe to drink.

Precedence order: The sequence in which activities are to be performed based on dependency and proximity requirements.

Queuing: The formation of waiting lines when arrival rate exceeds the service rate.

Shuttle service: The transport of people, usually by coach or van, over an often short route between two points.

Site development: The importation of the equipment and services necessary to make a site capable of serving the requirements of the event operations and program.

Site inspection: The visit to and careful investigation of the premises of a potential facility or location, typically to determine suitability.

Site plan: A schematic drawing of an area, property, or specific facility to be used for an event; see floor plan.

Tipping point: The threshold at which the condition or nature of something changes.

Traffic flow: The volume and pattern of movement of vehicles or people.

Transfer: The movement of people or equipment from one location to another.

Transportation provider: The individual or company that provides destination management services, valet parking services, ground transportation services, and bus, van, and limousine services to an event.

User pays: A policy that the costs for services provided by a public entity (e.g., police, traffic control, etc.) are charged to the event because such services are specifically for the benefit of those organizing and/or attending the event and not the public at large.

Valet parking: A service in which motor vehicles are parked by attendants for guests who are met at the entrance to a facility and given a claim check for their vehicle.

Ventilation: The supply and circulation of fresh air and removal of contaminated air.

Water weights: Large water-filled barrels used as an anchoring method for a tent.

Online resources

APEX Site RFP Templates	www.conventionindustry.org/apex/panels/RFPs.htm
Conworld.net	www.conworld.net
Destination Marketing Association International	www.iacvb.org
Parking Management	www.vtpi.org/tdm/tdm28.htm
Portable Generator Hazards	www.usfa.dhs.gov/downloads/pdf/fswy24.pdf
Room capacity calculator	www.eventageous.com/planning_guides/peoplecalc.htm
Site Selection (Expoweb)	www.expoweb.com/Site_Selection/
Traffic Management	http://ops.fhwa.dot.gov/program_areas/sp-evnts-mgmt.htm
Unique Venues	www.uniquevenues.com/meeting-facilities.html

Chapter 12
Attendee management

Behavior is predictable and malleable

This chapter will examine how to:

■ Determine appropriate admittance and credentialing systems to facilitate and control access to the event and event areas
■ Develop entry and exit strategies according to the anticipated arrival and departure modes and crowd movements to and through an event
■ Formulate crowd management and crowd control plans based on predictable and projected crowd behavior
■ Incorporate customer service, care, and comfort into the crowd management plans

Introduction

The alpha and omega of every meeting or event is the person attending the event, and everything so far discussed in this book leads to and must focus on that person – the audience member, contributor, delegate, dignitary, exhibitor, guest, media, performer, or speaker – and the assembly of these people in a particular place at a particular time. Everything created and coordinated to bring these people together has been selected and arranged to meet their needs and manage their expectations according to the goals and objectives of the event and the facilities and resources available. The program has been designed and the site has been laid out in such a way to ensure the desired experience is delivered in a safe and effective manner. The final step is anticipating and accommodating all the physical factors associated with this assembly based upon the numbers, behavior norms, and attributes of the event being held, as illustrated in Figure 12.1, and the characteristics of the attendees (as shown in Table 9.2).

The risk manager should focus on the plans for the arrival of these people, their likely movement flow and congregation within the event, and the tactics for controlling and sculpting their projected and preferred behavior patterns. And make no mistake; behavior can be sculpted with proper planning. From admission systems to queue configuration and seating plans to site cleanliness, cues on the rules of behavior can be communicated in creative and compelling ways. The typical assembly risks are shown in Table 12.1, which should be carefully examined in the context of blending movement, behavior, and customer service.

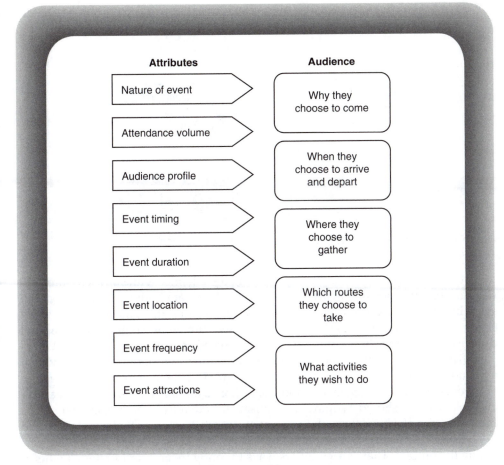

Figure 12.1 Factors associated with an assembly

Table 12.1 Typical risks associated with an assembly

- Arrival and departure modes
- Congestion and overcrowding
- Cross- or counter-flow crowd movement
- Equipment failures
- Exceeding occupancy limits
- High demand attractions
- High density crowds
- Inadequate communication
- Inadequate facilities
- Inattention to crowd behavior
- Incorrect distribution of attractions
- Ineffective registration/ticketing systems
- Inefficient seating systems
- Lack of admittance controls
- Public disorder/panic
- Unclear or incomplete instructions
- Uncontrolled queues
- Undesirable circumstances

Attendee and participant management

Attendee management (encompassing all those in attendance) seeks to direct and control the attendee's actions and interactions with the event from arrival through

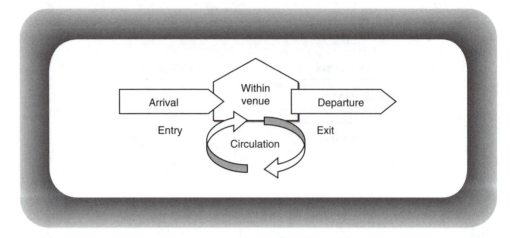

Figure 12.2 Dimensions of human movement within an event

departure. Effectiveness relies upon supplying the attendee with sufficient information, means, and methods to access the event, participate in the event, and exit the event in a safe and successful manner. As shown in Figure 12.2, the attendee's interaction with the event experience encompasses numerous spatial and temporal dimensions that must be accommodated with procedural and operational strategies.

Sufficient space must be allocated, entry procedures and portals must be evident and understandable, and enough information must be provided to ensure navigating the event experience is achievable and frustration is minimized. The event organizer and risk manager should examine and envision the attendee's routes and interactions from the point of arrival through the point of departure in order to devise tactics that will ensure the desired actions are feasible and facilitated at each point of service within the process. There are countless ways to configure and control these points of service and interactions, which vary according to the style and scope of the event and event audience, and offer numerous creative opportunities and strategies for crafting a safer and more satisfying event experience for the attendee.

Admission control and credential systems

Unless the meeting or event is free, open to the public, and in a venue that has no perimeter barriers or occupancy limits there will be some form of admission system.

Admission systems include numerous entry controls, from signing a register to collecting tickets to checking badges or other credentials. The nature of the event, its activities, and its audience may indicate the need for a layered system that includes a variety of high- and low-tech entry controls and credentials (Garber, 2004).

Credentials establish an individual's access rights to an event or certain areas or activities at an event. Many public and civic events sell tickets that permit entry and the savvy ones also sell passes that permit special access to desirable locations, attractions, or services. Concerts and other entertainment events often use different colored tickets for different seating sections. Festivals will often use colored wristbands for each event day or to indicate whether the wearer may purchase alcohol or have access to special exhibits or events. Some events require the issuance of credentials with photo ID, such as laminated passes on lanyards for political events or for the media at a sports event. Meetings and conferences typically use a registration system (sometimes called attendee management systems) to pre-qualify or register individuals who will attend, and the attendee's or delegate's credential, their badge, may serve as a name tag as well as a lead retrieval system for the accompanying trade show. Social or life-cycle functions often have a guest book to sign or perhaps an invitation to show at the entrance.

Clarity regarding entry and credential acquisition procedures is critical for the attendee and clarity regarding admission authorization is critical for the security personnel charged with checking credentials prior to admission. The prospective attendee must be advised of exactly how and where to acquire the admission credential as well as the procedures for using that credential, including what will occur during the admittance process (e.g., going through a security checkpoint such as a turnstile or magnetometer). This will include instructions regarding entrance routes and times, segregated or restricted entrances, seating designations, prohibited items or activities, and any other information needed in order to gain admittance in an efficient manner. Security or stewarding personnel and ushers must be thoroughly briefed on the various types of credentials to be used and their specific meanings (e.g., seating assignment, access privileges, permissions or prohibitions, etc.) to ensure the efficacy of the admittance control system.

Name badges all look alike to the security or stewarding staff person that has not been shown what is acceptable or applicable, which suggests that it is advisable that the various credentials provided should be distinctively differentiated in some manner such as color coding and/or title (e.g., green for full access, red for exhibitor, blue for Tuesday only, etc.). Ticket differentiation may include ticketing to different entrances, time of arrival, or reserved seating. Of note: festival seating and general admission seating – either no seats are provided or seating is first come/first serve – has been shown to cause serious crowd rushes and crushes at high occupancy entertainment events and has been prohibited for such events in many jurisdictions.

The need for credentials expands for larger or more complex events and the need for controlling access (see Table 12.2). Access to various areas of an event and event site should be based on 'zones of need.' Limited access to various event activities, individuals, equipment, or materials should be based on specific conditions, such as a specific work assignment on a specific day or at a specific time or the purchase of the right to such access. The risk manager must determine what must be protected and from whom, then employ the appropriate access controls and security precautions to prevent unauthorized access to restricted areas, times, people, or items. Strategies to prevent exceeding occupancy limits must also be reviewed, particularly for high demand activities or attractions such as popular sessions at a conference or special tents at a fair.

There is a difference between public and private areas at an event. These are often designated as front of the house (FOH) and back of the house (BOH) in a public assembly facility (Jewell, 1978), as illustrated in Figure 12.3. In some cases, areas or items that must be protected are in the FOH areas, in which case, additional attention must be paid to the security of those areas or items. Controlling access is not only a means of protecting event assets and individuals from nefarious activity, although that is an important factor. It is also a matter of safety because BOH or restricted access areas often contain equipment and technicians performing tasks that could cause injury to the unauthorized individual or that individual could create or instigate hazardous conditions for those working on and others attending the event.

Table 12.2   Controlled access needs and strategies

Access restrictions	*Admission controls*
• Restricted activities • Restricted areas • Restricted date or time • Restricted equipment • Restricted information • Restricted materials/people • Restricted occupancy limits	• Identification credentials • Perimeter barriers and patrols • Portals and pathways • Pre-registration and ticketing • Seating plans • Security checks and checkpoints • Turnstiles and head counts

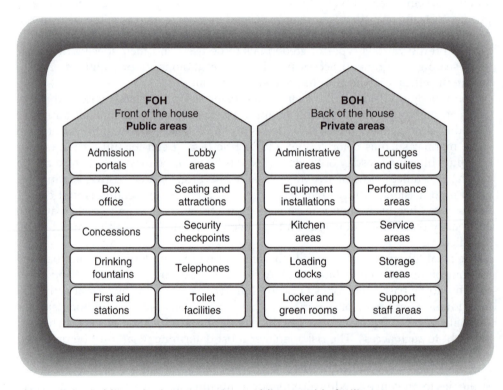

Figure 12.3   Public and private areas in a public assembly facility

The risk manager should review the admission control and credential systems devised for any gaps or vulnerabilities, including confirmation that they have been thoroughly integrated into the site, marketing, and operational plans. As noted in Chapters 3 and 8, information gathered during the registration or admittance credentialing process must be protected from misuse according to privacy compliance requirements, and, for international events, precautions and protocols may be required to ensure the prospective attendee is genuine. As noted in Chapter 9, all cash value credentials (i.e., tickets, purchased passes, etc.) must be protected from loss, theft, or counterfeit. All controlled area access credentials must also be protected from being compromised or counterfeited.

Consider this... 12.1

Foreign visas

Attendees at international meetings and events must often acquire a visa in order to enter the country in which the event is being held. The visa, granted by the country's government, provides verification that the specific non-citizen is eligible to enter the country for a specific purpose and for a specific time period. The necessity and procedure for obtaining a visa varies from country to country, each with their own requirements and restrictions, and can include intense scrutiny of the applicant. The U.S., for example, may require the collection of digital fingerprints and a face-to-face interview at its embassy or consulate in order to issue a visa (they will be screening applicants according to a set of keywords on the Technology Alert List or specific nationalities or backgrounds on a Watch List).

International attendees to a U.S. meeting, for example, are sometimes asked to provide a 'Letter of Invitation' from the sponsoring organization, which some events will post as a downloadable document on their Web site for the convenience of their attendees. However, this practice may be problematic as some individuals use the pretext of conference attendance as a way to enter a country for other purposes. Many meeting planners now require the payment of the registration fee prior to issuing the invitation letter.

Some countries may require a special type of visa for anyone receiving speaking fees or honoraria for lectures and presentations. Some countries have visa waiver programs that only require passports (or machine readable passports with digital photo or biometrics chip requirements) for nationals from specific countries. It is strongly advised that event organizers consult with their government (e.g., the U.S. State Department) regarding visa rules and requirements and educate their attendees about immigration procedures. It may be possible to list the event with the government and provide a roster (and updates) of conference participants that can be posted on an intranet for the country's embassies and consulates to facilitate the visa approval and processing procedure.

Arrival and departure modes

The audience or attendees or guests will arrive at a certain point in time through certain portals and will depart at a certain point in time through certain portals. They will also move through the event space in a variety of ways, planned and perhaps unplanned. In order to manage this human movement or 'pedestrian traffic flow,' the risk manager must understand and anticipate this traffic flow, including arrival and departure modes, queuing, and human behavior patterns in both normal conditions as well as emergency conditions, as illustrated in Figure 12.4. Arrival and departure modes may be defined as trickle or dump.

- *Trickle mode*: The attendees or guests arrive and/or depart at various times throughout the duration of the event.
- *Dump mode*: Most of the attendees or guests arrive and/or depart all at the same time.

Obviously, the type, scope, and schedule of the event and the size and characteristics of the audience will shape the plans to accommodate these individuals. A consumer gate show (exposition) expecting 10 000 people will likely have a surge of arrivals at its opening but will have attendees trickling in and out throughout its hours of operation.

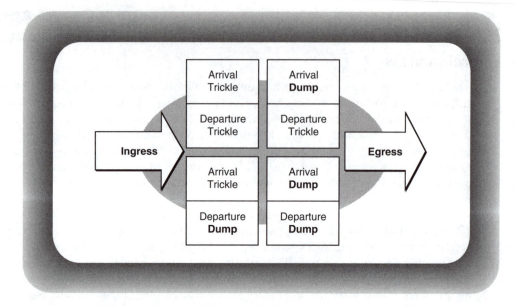

Figure 12.4   Typical arrival and departure patterns

Table 12.3   Typical arrival and departure concerns

Arrival issues	Departure issues
• Admission controls • Crowd characteristics • Flow capacity • Layout • Queue duration • Queue pressure	• Crowd emotions • Flow capacity • Means of egress – normal • Means of egress – emergency • Re-admittance policies • Time of day

A concert expecting 10 000, on the other hand, will be very different, with everyone arriving within a short period of time and departing en masse. The risk manager should carefully examine the arrival and departure issues shown in Table 12.3 in order to evaluate the physical and procedural strategies for accommodating the number of event attendees.

The size and layout of the entrance to an event, as well as the arrangement of attractions near the entrance (preferably limited), will facilitate the proper traffic flow into the event. The number and location of entrances must be reviewed to ensure they are appropriate for the type and scope of event, as well as the arrival mode. Depending on the event's size and scope, barricades, fencing, or rope and stanchion 'bank maze' queues may be needed to help control the flow of pedestrian traffic and direct people entering or departing the event site or to activities within the event site.

Entrances should 'look' like an entrance; decorations and/or signage should be used, including clearly labeled segregated entrances as well as clearly marked no-entry and exit-only portals (Au, Ryan, Carey, and Whalley, 1993). Entrances must be allocated enough space and configured in a manner that accommodates and facilitates the designated service processing system (e.g., registration, ticket sales and collection, credential checking, etc.), processing rates, and the volume of people expected. A separate desk, table, or counter should be set up to handle guests with service difficulties or deviations so the majority of the guests can proceed without waiting for the problem to be resolved (Goldblatt, 2002; Silvers, 2004a). In addition, the risk manager should confirm that entrances and entry procedures are equipped to accommodate patrons with special needs such as sight, hearing, and mobility impairments.

Accommodating the arrival and intra-event movement of special guests (e.g., dignitaries or celebrities), performers, and participants may require special attention and facilities. Exclusive entry (and exit) routes and entrances may need to be established and protected with barriers and/or personnel, and may need to be kept secret and hidden from view altogether. The intra-event movement of these people may need to be regulated and/or escorted to ensure such movement does not cause crowd crushes or hazardous crowd flow obstructions. For example, one country western singer is rolled into his stadium concerts inside a specially equipped packing case that looks like the other equipment cases to prevent crowd crushes by fans as he gets from the performer entrance to the stage area.

The manner and means of exiting an event (egress) must accommodate the audience as efficiently as the arrival. If there is an emergency evacuation, all available means of egress must be clearly identified and used by the audience. The number, location, and character of emergency exits will be determined by the local fire codes, but these must be reviewed by the risk manager to ensure the proper safety and emergency precautions are incorporated into the event plans, such as making an opening announcement regarding the use of the closest available exit in case of an emergency, and that sufficient human resources are allocated and positioned to facilitate this mass egress.

The time of day, crowd emotions, and the policies permitting or prohibiting re-admittance to the event must be examined to determine departure risks. The inclusion of exterior lighting equipment may be required to illuminate exit routes and parking areas if the event ends after dark. Extra security personnel may be necessary to patrol these areas or to control exuberant or antagonistic audience members. Mass exodus may also put undue pressure on transportation facilities and routes, which must be carefully evaluated based on the departure characteristics.

Crowd management and control

A crowd is a large number of individual persons gathered together at a certain time, within a certain space, and for certain and often similar reasons. Managing a crowd requires developing the hard and soft systems that will regulate and shape the movement and behavior of the individuals within the crowd in such a way that safety and order are maintained. Crowd management and crowd control are synergistic rather than synonymous (Fruin, 1984, 1993), as illustrated in Figure 12.5, and typical strategies are shown in Table 12.4.

The systematic planning for the orderly movement and assembly of people begins with a needs assessment to determine what portals, facilities, and space allotments are necessary to accommodate the size and type of gathering anticipated. This is followed by an analysis of the anticipated behaviors that must be controlled through

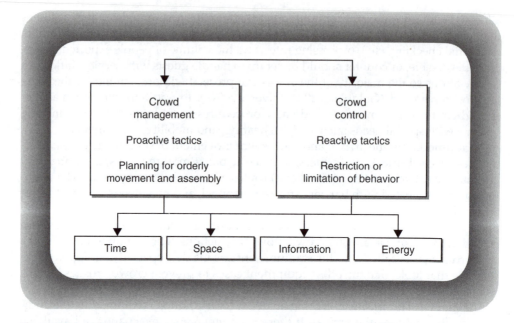

Figure 12.5   The dimensions crowd management and crowd control

Table 12.4   Factors included in typical crowd management and control strategies

Crowd management	Crowd control
• Adequate facilities • Adequate ingress and egress • Adequate space and flow • Supervision and monitoring • Understanding of audience and activities	• Admission controls • Barriers, layouts, and controlled perimeters • Communications • Restriction of behavior • Security and stewards

policies, procedures, personnel, and equipment. Tactics are then developed, implemented, and monitored throughout the duration of the event, and evaluated after the event in order to capture lessons learned. If using a purpose built facility that has accommodated a similar event, the facility should have guidance regarding crowd management tactics that have proven to be effective. If, however, the event size, type, or site is unusual or initial, guidance should be sought from comparable events and/or locations, and, if appropriate, from security or crowd management specialists.

Crowd size and density is a significant factor in crowd management. Most of the deadliest event disasters involved large crowds, with most of the injuries and fatalities due to crowd compression and the subsequent loss of footing or inability to move (Fruin, 1993). Abbott and Abbott (2000) note that the dangers of overcrowding are panic, violence, injury, and liability (i.e., foreseeability and duty of care). Fruin (1984) contends that understanding the crowd flow principles of time, space, information, and energy (force) is central to the prevention of critical crowd densities and triggering rapid crowd movements that could precipitate unsafe conditions.

- *Time*: arrival and departure demand rates; processing and movement speeds; event schedule and attraction timing; time period in which the exceeding of capacity occurs.
- *Space*: size and configuration of the area occupied; movement and escape pathways and patterns; per-person space allotment; route and service point capacities.
- *Information*: information upon which the crowd reacts, including sights, sounds, perceptions, and speculation; communication between the staff and the crowd; communication between crowd monitors and control or response personnel; lack of communication from front to back within the crowd.
- *Energy*: critical crowd density force; intensity of psychological and physiological stresses; immobility or compressive power due to pressing forward, pushing, leaning, or collapses; pressure exerted within the mass and/or against a barrier.

Crowd behavior will be shaped by the unity, intensity, and volatility of the crowd and their objectives (Emergency Management Australia, 1999), as well as the audience preparation activities, control procedures, and monitoring actions conducted by the event organizers. Crowd control measures should be devised that include a progression of triggers or thresholds for implementation ranging from orderly assembly to crisis situations involving unlawful or unsafe behavior (Abbott and Abbott, 2000), beginning with the limiting of the number of tickets sold to prevent overcrowding in the first place.

Consider this... 12.2

Deadly rumor

August 31, 2005: It was reported that 841 people died and more than 350 were injured when the rumor of a suicide bomber within the midst of a Shiite religious procession of hundreds of thousands of worshippers caused a panicked stampede on the two-lane Al-Aaimmah Bridge over the Tigris River in Baghdad, Iraq. Some were injured or suffocated in the crush; some jumped into the river and were injured or drowned; others fell into the river and drowned when a railing on the bridge collapsed. Most of the dead were believed to be women and children. The rumor that incited the stampede was not an intentional terrorist act, but its effect was in part caused by tension resulting from a terrorist bombing earlier that day near the Shiite shrine where the worshippers were headed and from repeated sectarian attacks by extremists against large religious gatherings. In addition to this climate of fear and 110-degree heat, the crush was exacerbated by the extreme density of the crowd and the blockage of pilgrims jammed against the checkpoint at the bridge's western edge.

Crowd movement

The traffic flow during and within the event must be carefully considered. Pedestrian traffic flows should do just that, flow. Anything that impedes that flow can be hazardous. The larger and denser the crowd, the more dangerous these movements become. As discussed in Chapter 10, wayfinding and one's orientation within an event site not only facilitates the delivery of the event experience as designed and desired; it is critically important to the flow of people and the control of hazardous

Table 12.5 Tactics for minimizing hazardous crowd movements

Avoidance of	Provision of
• Bottlenecks and pinch-points • Combined arrival and departure conflicts • Converging dispersion or egress routes • Cross, counter, or reverse flows • Improper barrier design or capacity • Locked or blocked exits • Overly restrictive or constrictive crowd movement • Steep slopes, ramps, or stairs	• Adequate space for congregation and circulation • Ample and accurate information • Capacity regulation through monitoring • Metered inflow • Multiple dispersion routes and exits • One-way systems to separate flows • Staggered attraction start times • Staff for diversion to alternate routes • Sufficient processing points

Sources: Au et al. (1993), Emergency Management Australia (1999), Fruin (1993), and Wertheimer (1980)

conditions. People need to be able to see where they are and where they are going. People also need sufficient space to be able to move about.

The occupancy capacity will be determined by the local fire codes, but the event layout and program of activities may cause dangerous mass movements at certain times in pursuit of certain activities. The thoughtful positioning and timing of event activities and attractions can reduce congestion in certain areas and build traffic in others. The use of event personnel to add the 'human' connection may facilitate more controlled movements through the event space, particularly during an emergency when people must either evacuate an area or make space for responders to reach a specific area.

Hazardous crowd movements may occur due to flight response or craze competition motivations (Fruin, 1993) causing crowd collapses, crazes, crushes, panics, or surges, and may also include such things as mixing vehicles and pedestrians, moving animals or attractions through crowds, and cross flows within dense crowds (Au et al., 1993; Emergency Management Australia, 1999; FEMA, 2001; HSE, 1993; Silvers, 2004a). Au et al. (1993, pp. 5–10) identify hazards to be included in a risk assessment as overcrowding, crushing, impact/collision, pile-up, trampling, surging, pushing, swaying, rushing, falling, and tripping; and the possible consequences include anxiety, physical discomfort, minor or major injury, and death. High density movements may be expected at mass arrival and departure times, but should be carefully monitored to ensure pressure is not building to a point at which movement is constricted too much. Still (2005) notes that one must also understand that at high densities the movement flow rates are affected and regulated by the slowest members of the crowd (the 'little old lady factor'). Typical strategies for managing crowd movement are shown in Table 12.5.

The risk manager should also pay particular attention to queue management because these waiting lines can instigate or amplify dangerous crowd conditions. The crowd density, pressure, size, and duration of a queue will have an impact on the person waiting, and may become a source of anything from grumbling to hazardous crowd movements. The beginning of a queue should be readily apparent and queues should not obstruct traffic or other event elements. Shape the queue with appropriate barrier equipment (e.g., rope and stanchions, temporary fencing, etc.) or marshalling personnel. Although once an orderly queue has been established it typically becomes self-perpetuating (Au et al., 1993), personnel may be required to direct people to the shortest queue. Avoid queues on, exiting on, or blocking stairs or escalators, and ticket or registration queues should be positioned a sufficient distance from entrances and in such a way that they are separated from traffic or other hazards (Au et al., 1993). Metering tactics such as inviting bar mitzvah or wedding dinner guests to partake of the buffet by table number, using color-coded and/or numbered boarding vouchers for group transfers, and time-of-arrival ticketing for entertainment attractions can assist in managing the size of queues.

Crowd behavior

Crowd behavior is potentially very different than individual behavior because at a certain critical mass and under certain conditions or catalysts the individual loses the ability to control their movement or suspends social responsibility and the crowd can become a cohesive and collective entity in pursuit of a common goal, which may be benign or malevolent and can become dangerous if it exceeds the spatial and/or safety capacity of the environment. This is typically influenced by the nature of the event, the agenda or activities, the size and density of the multitude, and urgency or emergency conditions (real or imagined). Dangerous crowd behavior can spread like a wildfire or rush like a raging river. There are, however, tactics that can control these negative conditions, including the removal of fuel for the fire or providing an alternate spill-off route for the river's flow.

Crowds and their behavior have been studied by psychologists, sociologists, and engineers in economic, social, political, and physical contexts ranging from civil disorder to special events and from railroad stations to shopping malls. Beginning with the collective behavior work of French crowd psychologist Gustave Le Bon in the 1890s all the way to the present day with fire safety engineers and crowd safety experts conducting crowd simulations that focus on public assembly facilities and transportation networks, the nature and movement of crowds reveals that their behavior is based upon the environmental conditions, the individual crowd member's motives and emotions, and the forces facilitating or obstructing the individual's attempts to attain desired outcomes.

In contrast to Le Bon, who proposed that a crowd's behavior was irrational, herd like, and hypnotically homogenous, Berk (1974) posits that collective behavior ranging from collective expression to collective disorder is grounded in rational and conscious thought, often instigated due to legitimate motives, and, when closely examined, does not represent a homogenous or single mind set. Rather, it is composed of individuals participating in group problem solving wherein a lack of time or information and heightened emotion may undermine decision accuracy but not rationality. However, Gladwell reminds us that 'once we're part of a group, we're all susceptible to peer pressure and social norms' (2002, p. 171). It must also be remembered that, after all, an event is a 'collective experience' that often relies upon and encourages shared actions and emotions. In other words, the individuals in a crowd have not lost their mind; they have made their own decisions, which results in commonality rather than absolute unity, and the collective behavior may be cooperative or competitive (e.g., for scare resources).

Gladwell (2002), citing the work of criminologists, also suggests that criminal or undesirable behavior is, in part, a result of physical conditions that reflect (and project) the social context – if broken windows or graffiti remain unattended to, the message is that no one cares or is in control. Veno and Veno (1992) contend that behavior is affected by example; successive minor incidents empower individuals to defy regulations or social norms because authority has been de-legitimized and a new 'norm' has been established. It is the little problems – indications that things are not under control – that gives permission to act in ways that are not acceptable. This includes addressing undesirable behavior that may occur, which, without timely and visible intervention, may lead others to exhibit the same infractions (e.g., throwing objects onto a sports field or climbing a perimeter fence to gain access to an event) in the belief they will not be penalized. The lack of response allows escalation of a situation, as shown at the Puerto Rico Day parade in New York City in 2000 at which more than 50 women suffered various and increasing degrees of molestation whilst the police stood by without taking action (Tarlow, 2002).

Frustration and boredom are often cited as instigators of undesirable behavior (see for example, Au et al., 1993, Doukas, 2006, and Veno and Veno, 1992). Frustration–aggression theories, stating that frustration (particularly unexpected frustration) increases the likelihood of aggression, hypothesize that destructive behavior often results when an individual is prevented from achieving a desired goal. (Boredom may be seen as a type of frustration.) The level of aggression is based upon the individual's tolerance level when severe restrictions or controls are imposed (Veno and Veno, 1992). The aggressive behavior may be in response to such strictures or emotional triggers such as elation, fear, or anger, and may be exaggerated by impairments such as drug or alcohol intoxication and lack of accurate information. Aggressive behavior may also result from physical discomfort due to environmental conditions such as heat, cold, noise, etc., and may become more likely if others are displaying aggressive behavior and are either rewarded or go unpunished. The risk manager should seek ways to minimize frustration and closely monitor and quickly respond to crowd conditions that indicate frustration (Au et al., 1993).

Crowd control

In order to control a crowd, one must first understand the factors that shape and influence the crowd, establish policies and procedures that limit undesirable behavior or conditions, continually monitor the status of crowd conditions, and implement response plans should conditions cross a pre-established threshold. For example, if a queue exceeds a certain limit another ticket window will be opened, or if certain spectators or audience members are exhibiting undesirable behavior they will be ejected from the event. Typical crowd types and response strategies are shown in Table 12.6, most of which center on observation, supervision, and communication, and should be based on the hierarchy of tactical steps as discussed in Chapter 5 and shown in Figure 12.6.

In the event that crowd conditions become unmanageable, event organizers will likely turn to law enforcement personnel to control a situation (Beene, 1992). Their approach will begin with a situation assessment followed by a hierarchy of actions as shown in Figure 12.7. Understanding their approach may influence the risk manager's response plan development, as well as facilitate the effectiveness of law enforcement in the event that they are called in. Once law enforcement has been called in, however, the event must typically surrender all authority to the police. If the event itself is controversial (e.g., a protest march), expects eruptions (e.g., highly-contested sports events),

Table 12.6 Typical crowd types, characteristics, and response strategies

Type	Characteristics	Response strategies
Casual	Tranquil; neutral; compliant; self-directed and self-controlled; ambulatory with minimal or short-lived high density constriction points	• Monitor for changes in crowd densities at control points; signs of frustration or confusion; opportunistic criminal behavior (e.g., pickpockets, purse snatchers, etc.) • Activate ancillary routes or services for constricted points; provide accurate information; activate law enforcement to apprehend and arrest criminals
Cohesive	Cooperative; gathered for shared spectator or participatory experience; sometimes organized (e.g., demonstrations, rallies, marches); often high density by design	• Monitor for critical crowd densities; signs of frustration, boredom, or heightening of emotions; escalation of rhetoric or actions promoting unsafe or violent behavior • Activate ancillary routes or services for constricted points; provide accurate information; establish and publicize firm rules for behavior; deal with infractions in a timely and reasonable manner
Expressive	Exuberant; spontaneous emotional releases; displaying horseplay or frolic behavior; often high density by desire	• Monitor for altercations; signs of frustration, boredom, or heightening of emotions; unsafe crowd movements; unsafe physical activity • Act to diffuse situations; remove instigators of of unacceptable behavior; provide accurate information and instructive advisories
Aggressive	Competitive (e.g., rivalries or vying for limited resources or desired object); verbally antagonistic or hostile; intense social tensions; vicious pranks; antisocial behavior (sexual assault, etc.)	• Monitor for escalation of rhetoric or actions promoting unsafe or violent behavior; signs of intoxication; rushing, looting, or destructive behavior; possible weapons (conventional or impromptu) • Establish, publicize, and enforce firm rules for behavior and distribution of desirable objects; separate rival factions; limit or eliminate availability of alcohol; prohibit display of weapons; provide accurate information and cautionary advisories
Explosive	Crazed (tumultuous but not malevolent); panicked (escape, emergency); violent; disorderly (defiantly unlawful); angry and destructive (riot)	• Monitor for critical crowd densities; escalation of emotional urgency; rushing, pushing, and shoving behavior; emergency conditions • Consider temporary delay or cancellation of event; activate contingency or evacuation plans; provide accurate information and escape routes; activate law enforcement for response to unlawful acts and/or for crowd dispersal

or is of such a scope that the very size of the crowd is a liability (e.g., festivals or large concerts), it is critically important that law enforcement be included very early in the planning stages so that their needs and expertise can be incorporated into the overall event plans.

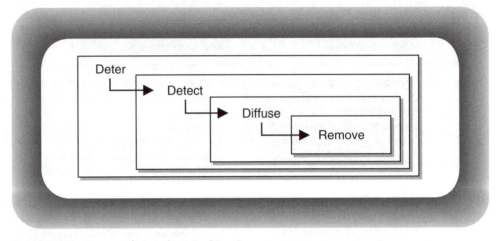

Figure 12.6   Stages of crowd control tactics

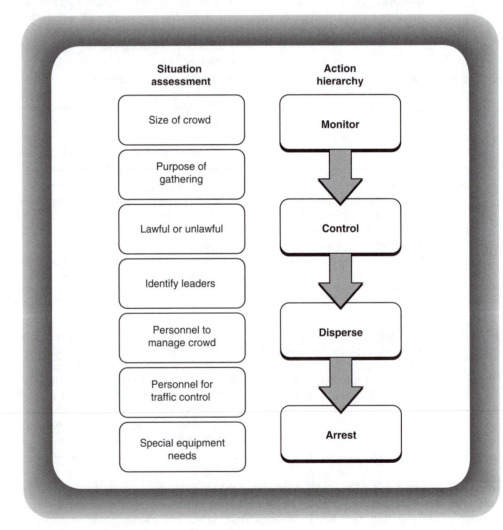

Figure 12.7   Dimensions of police crowd control

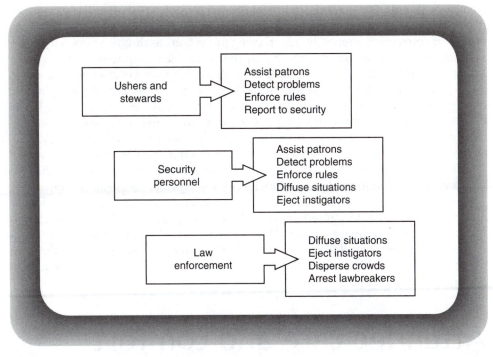

Figure 12.8 Typical hierarchy of responsibility and authority for crowd control personnel

Crowd control personnel are a key component of any crowd control strategy and they must be properly equipped, trained, and deployed. Crowd control personnel may range from ushers and stewards to professional security forces and law enforcement personnel. It is important to establish clear guidelines regarding the hierarchy of command and control as well as the duties and authority that each level of personnel will have, such as shown in Figure 12.8. It is widely recommended that ushers and stewards not be assigned with adversarial or physical intervention duties, only reporting situations that require such tactics to security personnel or law enforcement.

As with all event personnel, providing assistance and guidance to the event patron should be a primary responsibility of crowd control personnel. Doukas (2006) notes employing preventative tactics and assisting crowds is often far more effective than trying to control them. The actions and attitudes of staff and security personnel can lead to compliance or defiance with respect to instructions and regulations. Provision of accurate and timely information can often prevent high-risk actions or de-escalate crowd tension or anxiety as well as communicate the 'house rules' and behavioral norms expected of the event audience, and may cause patrons to take an active role in the crowd control process, empowering them to monitor and report situations, conditions, or behaviors that threaten their safety (Wertheimer, 1980).

Crowd control personnel must be provided with training regarding the crowd management and control mechanisms in place (e.g., admittance systems, rules for behavior, restricted access areas, etc.), the crowd monitoring activities to be carried out, and the procedures to be used regarding response to incidents and conditions, as well as specific training and procedures for diffusing and/or physical intervention of aggressive, abusive, or violent behavior. They should also be provided with high visibility clothing that identifies them as authorized to conduct these activities

(WorkSafe Victoria, 2006). Keep in mind that crowd control personnel must be protected in compliance with occupational health and safety regulations, and may need to be provided with protective equipment (e.g., hearing protection), as discussed in Chapter 4.

Monitoring activities will require appropriate surveillance equipment and vantage points. Stewards and ushers will likely be strategically placed in amongst the crowd and can observe conditions and individual behavior problems, but observing crowd density problems will usually require an elevated vantage point. As discussed in Chapters 5 and 8, a communication network and procedures must be established to ensure that emerging crowd problems are properly transmitted within the appropriate chain of command. It must also be remembered that the very nature of a crowd (i.e., its size and composition) can make such things as communication and changes in action slower and more difficult (Emergency Management Australia, 1999).

Crowd control is not an imperative exclusive to large-scale events with immense audiences. One need only recall the tragedy involving the band Great White's performance at the Station nightclub in West Warwick, Rhode Island that had an attendance of approximately 300, of which one-third perished, to recognize that the need for crowd control is dictated by time, space, and volatility or urgency; not just an enormous number of people.

Attendee care and comfort

Crowd management and control is greatly enhanced when its focus remains on the customer – the attendee. Effective interactions between the attendee and the event organization are reliant upon physical (tangible) as well as behavioral (intangible) strategies that ensure an appropriate level of assistance and courtesy is delivered, which, in turn, increases the effectiveness of crowd control strategies. Au et al. (1993) and others advise that the attendee must not be relied upon to recognize potential hazards associated with their actions; they don't realize the impact their actions could have on others or their immediate environment. Therefore initial interventions should be polite and instructive rather than abrasive. This customer service attitude can reduce instances of inappropriate behavior or incidents causing or escalating hazardous conditions. Anticipating the attendee's physical and emotional needs within the context of the event and event venue is necessary for development of the tangible and intangible features that underscore this preventative approach.

Care and welfare

The event organizer will be able to reduce frustration, confusion, and anxiety – common causes of crowd control problems and customer dissatisfaction – by providing space, services, and amenities that demonstrate attention to the care and welfare of the event patron, such as those shown in Table 12.7. These are in addition to the facilities and services required to ensure health and safety such as toilets and first aid stations. The risk manager should confirm that the positioning and signposting of these public amenities is acceptable and adequate, ensuring that they are accessible without obstructing crowd movement.

Meeting and waiting areas, places where patrons can congregate while waiting for others in their group, should be allocated sufficient space and be positioned far enough away from entrances or exits to make certain they do not interfere with the

Table 12.7 Typical public amenities provided by events

• ATMs	• Cyber cafes	• Message centers
• Baby changing stations	• Designated smoking areas	• Misting tents
• Business centers	• Food and beverage outlets	• Shipping centers
• Coat check service	• Information booths	• Stroller rentals
• Concierge services	• Lost and found centers	• Tourist desks
• Courtesy phones	• Meeting/waiting areas	• Welcome centers

ingress and egress flow. Information booths should be centrally located and highly visible, and must be staffed with personnel who are completely familiar with the event venue and the event's policies and procedures. Lost and found centers, including those for lost children, should have protocols established for receiving and returning property or children as well as communications capability to make announcements or advisories as appropriate. Sub-contracted services must be acquired according to proper procurement policies, and appropriate liability insurance coverage for both in-house and outsourced services must be confirmed.

Accommodations and hospitality

Event organizers will have varying levels of responsibility for arranging for housing and specific guest services depending upon the type of the event and the scope and nature of the attendees. Some events such as meetings and conventions require the booking of hotel rooms for attendees, with some or all of the rooms to be paid for by the event organization. For example, incentive events or corporate events with mandatory attendance may be paying all housing costs, conferences with voluntary attendance may be paying for only staff and speaker housing yet reserving sufficient rooms for self-paying attendees, and conventions or large sports events may be contracting room blocks with various hotel properties due to the large attendance or the need to segregate opposing factions or individual groups.

The risk manager should confirm that the contracts associated with this housing include guarantees based upon reliable attendance projections, attrition procedures and costs are clearly specified, the appropriate room pick-up monitoring is taking place (Connell, 2002), and that restrictions on what charges the organization will cover are clearly communicated to the room occupant as well as the hotel (Silvers, 2004a). Housing is sometimes handled in-house or contracted out to a housing bureau, and housing forms will need to be included in the registration process and materials (Krug, 2000). It is advised that the event organization avoid taking any responsibilities regarding room sharing, making the matching of roommates a self-selection process.

Reception areas, ready rooms, dressing rooms, and lounge facilities may need to be acquired for participants such as speakers, entertainers, sports teams, sponsors, dignitaries, or officiates. The accessibility and proximity of these facilities should be carefully considered from logistical, hospitality, and political perspectives. Food, beverage, equipment, and other amenities may be desired or contractually required, special access routes and admittance controls may be needed, and specific distances from or between certain facilities may be necessary.

Hospitality functions and suites, typically hosted by sponsors of the event, may be included in or in conjunction with the event. The event organization may be intimately involved in the scheduling and placement of such ancillary events or the events may occur without direct involvement by the main event's organizer. However, since these functions and suites are meant to attract the main event's attendees, there will be a perceived affiliation that might create a level of liability for the main event. Therefore, it is advisable to establish clear policies and procedures that limit such liability (e.g., co-location, alcohol service, or activities). This will need to be incorporated into sponsorship agreements to ensure client entertainment activities at the event meet the same standards as the main event's and are incorporated into risk assessments.

Customer service

Anticipating needs and the courteous and conscientious delivery of the services to meet those needs is the foundation of good customer service. In addition, managing expectations (i.e., establishing and clearly communicating what the customer can expect) will increase the probability of customer satisfaction. This is applicable throughout the attendee's interaction and involvement with the event from the admissions procedures to the event attractions to the departure and any post-event contact. The risk manager should confirm that the systems are in place to deliver quality customer service because dissatisfaction can lead to image degradation, disruptive behavior, or lawsuits.

For example, if attendees at a training conference require the tracking and recording of continuing education credits for credential maintenance, attendance tracking software and hardware (e.g., badge scanning equipment) may need to be in place. If exhibitors at a trade show have been promised a mailing list of attendees for their pre- and post-event marketing activities, registered attendees need to be advised that this will occur (and perhaps given the option for non-inclusion). If seating at a convention's gala banquet needs to be assigned (to prevent a rush for seats or the age-old and dangerous practice of guests tipping a chair against the table to indicate it has been saved for someone), perhaps a ticket exchange table needs to be provided so that attendees exchange a reservation coupon or ticket in their registration package for a table assignment based upon a first come/first serve basis.

Advising the attendee of what to expect and the prohibition of certain items or behaviors will facilitate a positive experience for them and will lessen the risks for the event. Preparing all personnel that will have contact with the attendee, from call centers to ticket collectors, with methods and materials or devices for providing timely and useful assistance will facilitate an effective level of control and excellent level of service. Then, when the inevitable problems do occur, both sides in this human exchange will be more amenable and predisposed to cooperation rather than confrontation.

Summary

A key characteristic of events of all types is the assembly of a group of people. This can be a joyous and exciting experience or a frightening and dangerous situation depending on how well that assembly is managed. The type, scope, and purpose of the event, as well as the characteristics and objectives of the audience, will define the strategies and tactics to be used to ensure the appropriate behavior of and the orderly movement to and through the event by the assembled crowds.

Most events will require some sort of access or admittance control: a ticket, a badge, a pass, or simply being counted to get an accurate attendance. In recognition that controlling access is an important loss prevention as well as crowd safety strategy, many events utilize equipment and features to control access into the event site, as well as specific seating plans and credentials to limit access to certain areas within an event site. Understanding crowd capacity, characteristics, and cues will allow the risk manager to effectively supervise and monitor crowd conditions and implement the appropriate crowd control responses.

The event risk manager must analyze the physical and behavioral factors that could influence a crowd and incorporate the appropriate crowd controls necessary to mitigate negative outcomes. The risk manager should make every attempt to preempt the possibility of undesirable behavior or hazardous conditions by clarifying the desirable behavior and safe conditions, and then implementing the appropriate plans and operational procedures that support these and eliminate permission-givers for deviant behavior. The appropriate layout and accessibility must be designed into the site, the appropriate personnel must be trained and positioned properly, and the appropriate messages must be communicated to the audience both before the event and during the event.

The way in which the event organization prepares and provides facilities for the attendee will influence not only the attendee's behavior; it will shape the event experience and attendee's level of satisfaction with that experience. It is very rare that attendees come with intent to disrupt the event or create unsafe conditions, although that is a possibility, but they often do not realize what effect they can have on the safety and security of the rest of the audience. It is not their job to make sure disorder or hazardous conditions are prevented; it is yours. However, the attendee can become a partner in managing these risks if their needs and behaviors are anticipated and shaped with clear and carefully designed systems and interactions.

Key safeguards

- Ensure that there are sufficient entry and exit portals and they are kept completely clear of all obstacles.
- Confirm sufficient means of egress including exit route capacity and clarity, exit door functionality, and exit discharge area safety.
- Restrict unsafe or unauthorized viewing areas or vantage points.
- Use appropriate crowd barriers to define queuing systems.
- Prevent mass crowd movements between attractions whenever possible.
- Establish, communicate, and enforce rules and prohibitions regarding behavior and conditions for entry to ensure a positive influence on crowd behavior.
- Continually monitor crowd conditions and behavior.
- Make certain crowds are given accurate information and timely advisories.
- Infuse all attendee systems, controls, and interactions with customer service.

Chapter review challenge

1 How is crowd management affected by the site layout?
2 Identify the various credentials used by events and discuss how they might be employed in various types of events.

3 Conduct a SWOT analysis of the arrival and departure patterns shown in Figure 12.4 and identify strategies you might use to mitigate the weaknesses and threats.
4 In what ways do time, space, information, and energy affect crowd behavior?
5 Reviewing the factors in Table 12.6, what types of crowds do you think would be typical for the event genres described in Chapter 1 (see Table 1.3)?

Practical risk management exercise

A high level politician and a very famous movie star are getting married and very much want this to remain a private event. The wedding is to take place at a very upscale beach resort property (the place where they met) and the guest list of 200 includes dignitaries and film celebrities from around the world as well as family and friends, most of whom will be staying overnight at the resort. The ceremony will take place on the beach and the reception will be held in a tent in the gardens of the resort property; however, the beach is not private property. Devise an admission system that will control access yet maintain the character of this celebration. Be sure to include a risk assessment that identifies the potential threats and vulnerabilities, justifications for the strategies you have selected, and the methods you will use to prepare the guests prior to the event.

Key terminology

Access control: The establishment of procedures and conditions for restriction of areas of an event site and the screening of individuals to determine their authority or right to enter a restricted area at an event.

Admission controls: The restrictions and procedures established to prevent unauthorized entry of individuals and items/objects into the event site.

Arrival/departure modes: The manner, volumes, and timing in which guests will arrive and depart an event, for example, all at once, in segments, or randomly throughout the event duration; see also trickle mode and dump mode.

Assigned seating: Attendees, guests, or audience members are assigned a specific seat or reserved seating area.

Back of house (BOH): The functional areas of a facility or event site not open to the public.

Bank maze: A queue configuration achieved with rope and stanchion barriers that snakes the line back and forth.

Consumer gate show: An exposition with an admission fee created for members of the public featuring consumer products.

Counter flow: The movement of people in opposite directions.

Credentials: The document or item that verifies identity, authority, and/or eligibility, often designating authorized access to an event or certain area of an event.

Credentialing system: The system or process required for access to an event or a certain area of an event through issuance of identification tag, badge, pass, or other credential.

Cross flow: The movement of people across the path of another movement flow.

Crowd collapse: The falling down or caving in of a crowd due to a sequential loss of footing by individuals.

Crowd control: The tactics used for restriction or limitation of individual or group behavior.

Crowd craze: A competitive rush or push of a crowd in pursuit of or toward a desirable objective or individual.

Crowd crush: The progressive compression of a crowd due to the absence of a portal or escape.

Crowd density: The number and/or concentration of people in a given amount of space, expressed in a number of persons per square foot calculation.

Crowd management: The systematic planning for, and supervision of, the orderly movement and assembly of people.

Crowd panic: The frantic movement of a crowd to escape a real or perceived danger.

Crowd surge: A rapid compression movement of a crowd in a particular direction.

Dump mode: A pattern in which most of the attendees or guests arrive and/or depart all at the same time.

Festival seating: A large floor or lawn area at a venue where no seats are provided for the audience.

Front of house (FOH): The functional areas of a facility or event site open to the public.

General admission seating: Attendees, guests, or audience members are allowed to sit in any available seat they choose; may also be called open seating.

House rules: The rules indicating prohibited behaviors or items at a venue, which may vary at a particular venue depending on the type of event and therefore may cause confusion for an attendee that has come to expect one set of rules.

Housing bureau: An organization providing hotel reservation services for event attendees.

Lead retrieval system: A system by which a badge or other credential is used to actively or passively collect a potential customer's contact information.

Metered inflow: The measurement and control of inflow using admittance controls to prevent congestion.

Point of service: Any point at which there is an interaction between the attendee and the event wherein the attendee is required to do or provide something or requires assistance.

Public space: Space in a facility that is available for public use.

Reverse flow: The movement of people reversing their direction.

Room pick-up: The number of hotel sleeping rooms used by event attendees, including those who have made their reservations independently and through the housing bureau.

Trickle mode: A pattern in which the attendees or guests arrive and/or depart at various times throughout the duration of the event.

Online resources

APEX Housing and Registration Accepted Practices
www.conventionindustry.org/apex/ acceptedpractices/housingregistration.htm

Center for Venue Management Security
www.iaam.org/CVMS/CVMScrowd.htm

Corbin Ball's Favorite Links	www.corbinball.com/bookmarks/
Crowd Dynamics Ltd.	www.crowddynamics.com
Crowd Management Curriculum Project Report	www.iaam.org/CVMS/ IAAMCrowdMgmt.DOC
Crowdsafe.com	www.crowdsafe.com
International Association of Assembly Managers	www.iaam.org
International Ticketing Association	www.intix.org
Safety Rocks	www.safety-rocks.org

Appendix A: Event concept worksheet

Date Prepared: _____ **Prepared By:** _____
Event Title: _____

Host Organization: _____
Mailing Address: _____
Telephone: _____ Email: _____
Attach list of organizations involved and structure of authority

Event Organizer: _____
Mailing Address: _____
Telephone: _____ Cell: _____
After Hours: _____ Pager: _____
Fax: _____ Email: _____

Purpose of Event: _____

Type of Event: _____

History of Event: _____

Event Date(s): From: _____ To: _____
Site Preparation Start Date: _____ Vacate Site Date: _____
Event Times: Start: _____ Finish: _____

Attach complete schedule of proposed event activities

Event Location(s):
Site Address: _____
Contact Name: _____ Telephone: _____
Site Details: ☐ Indoor ☐ Permanent ☐ Single Venue ☐ Normal Use
☐ Outdoor ☐ Temporary ☐ Multiple Venue ☐ Atypical Use
Attach proposed site layout diagram or map

Event Audience:
Expected Number: Total: _____ Per Day: _____
Admission: Public: ☐ Free ☐ Ticketed ☐ By Registration
Private: ☐ By Invitation ☐ Ticketed ☐ By Registration
Audience Profile: _____

Event Activities: _____
Attach complete list of proposed event components, features, entertainment, and attractions

Appendix B: Risk register worksheet

Date Prepared: _____ **Prepared By:** _____

Risk Number: _____ **Risk Category:** _____

Risk Type: ☐ Property Damage/Loss   ☐ Bodily Illness/Injury/Death   ☐ Liability

Identified Risk: _____

(Description)   _____

_____

Probability:	Remote	Unlikely	Possible	Likely	Certain
Occurrence	☐	☐	☐	☐	☐
Consequence:	Insignificant	Minor	Moderate	Significant	Catastrophic
Humans	☐	☐	☐	☐	☐
Property	☐	☐	☐	☐	☐
Operations	☐	☐	☐	☐	☐
Business	☐	☐	☐	☐	☐
Image	☐	☐	☐	☐	☐

Extent of Harm/Damage: _____

Urgency: _____

Causal Influences: _____

Cost Implications: _____

Schedule Impacts: _____

Dependency Impacts: _____

Response Selected: _____

Corrective Action: _____

Contingency Plan: _____

(Description) _____

Monitoring Tactics: _____

Implementation Trigger: _____

Implementation Impacts: _____

Responsibility Assigned To: _____ **Contact #:** _____

Appendix C: Site inspection checklist

General location and vicinity:

Adjacent area concerns	OK	Risk	N/A	Remarks
Neighboring land use	☐	☐	☐	_____
Noise-sensitive/intensive facility proximity	☐	☐	☐	_____
Road, rail, or waterways	☐	☐	☐	_____
Construction zones	☐	☐	☐	_____
Severe weather and other natural perils	☐	☐	☐	_____
Surrounding attractions	☐	☐	☐	_____
Competitive events	☐	☐	☐	_____
Local holidays/religious celebrations	☐	☐	☐	_____
Transportation availability	☐	☐	☐	_____
Vicinity amenities	☐	☐	☐	_____
Crime rates	☐	☐	☐	_____
Political unrest	☐	☐	☐	_____
Street people presence	☐	☐	☐	_____
Youth gang activity	☐	☐	☐	_____
Other	☐	☐	☐	_____

Venue:

Venue profile concerns	OK	Risk	N/A	Remarks
History of incidences	☐	☐	☐	_____
Safety record	☐	☐	☐	_____
Health department rating	☐	☐	☐	_____
Proximity to off-site venues	☐	☐	☐	_____
Adjacent facilities (e.g., overflow hotels)	☐	☐	☐	_____
Distance from transport, medical facilities	☐	☐	☐	_____
Renovation/construction expectations	☐	☐	☐	_____
Facility ownership	☐	☐	☐	_____
Facility personnel	☐	☐	☐	_____
Legal limitations	☐	☐	☐	_____
Policies, regulations, restrictions	☐	☐	☐	_____
Other	☐	☐	☐	_____

Venue concerns	OK	Risk	N/A	Remarks
Vehicular access	☐	☐	☐	_____
Parking facilities (condition, security)	☐	☐	☐	_____
Pedestrian/vehicle crossings	☐	☐	☐	_____
Perimeter fencing, barriers	☐	☐	☐	_____
Entrances and exits	☐	☐	☐	_____
Walkways, hallways, stairwells	☐	☐	☐	_____
Floors and pathways (uneven, rough)	☐	☐	☐	_____

	OK	Risk	N/A	Remarks
Wayfinding and advisory signage	☐	☐	☐	_____
Lighting	☐	☐	☐	_____
Loading docks and freight access	☐	☐	☐	_____
Storage areas	☐	☐	☐	_____
Toilet facilities	☐	☐	☐	_____
Seating condition and sight lines	☐	☐	☐	_____
Noise levels	☐	☐	☐	_____
Hanging objects, overhead rigging	☐	☐	☐	_____
Utility hook-ups and power lines	☐	☐	☐	_____
Exposed equipment or machinery	☐	☐	☐	_____
Fall hazards (edges, ledges, balconies)	☐	☐	☐	_____
Temporary structures	☐	☐	☐	_____
Other	☐	☐	☐	_____

(Inspect all function and back of house areas pertinent to the event)

Environment concerns	OK	Risk	N/A	Remarks
Grounds and gates (maintenance, control)	☐	☐	☐	_____
Landscaping (obstruction, hiding places)	☐	☐	☐	_____
Cliffs, drops, steep inclines, uneven terrain	☐	☐	☐	_____
Infestations (insects, rodents, snakes)	☐	☐	☐	_____
Noxious vegetation	☐	☐	☐	_____
Building overhangs	☐	☐	☐	_____
Culverts, drains, sewer openings	☐	☐	☐	_____
Other	☐	☐	☐	_____

Health concerns	OK	Risk	N/A	Remarks
Sanitation system and practices	☐	☐	☐	_____
Food service facilities and practices	☐	☐	☐	_____
Overall maintenance and cleanliness	☐	☐	☐	_____
Ventilation systems	☐	☐	☐	_____
Water quality	☐	☐	☐	_____
Air pollution	☐	☐	☐	_____
Other	☐	☐	☐	_____

Security standards	OK	Risk	N/A	Remarks
Security (cameras, patrols, personnel)	☐	☐	☐	_____
Security response time, procedures	☐	☐	☐	_____
Locks/key type, issuance procedure	☐	☐	☐	_____
Restricted access to guestroom floors	☐	☐	☐	_____
Guest rooms	☐	☐	☐	_____
Other	☐	☐	☐	_____

Emergency preparedness:

Fire safety	OK	Risk	N/A	Remarks
Emergency exits (well-marked, battery lighted)	☐	☐	☐	_____
Fire safety systems (smoke detectors, visual and audible fire alarms)	☐	☐	☐	_____
Suppression systems (sprinkler systems, fire blankets)	☐	☐	☐	_____
Fire extinguishers (placement, visibility, inspection currency)	☐	☐	☐	_____

| Fire alarms alert fire department directly | ☐ | ☐ | ☐ | _____ |
| Other | ☐ | ☐ | ☐ | _____ |

Emergency response adequacy	OK	Risk	N/A	Remarks
Emergency action plan in place, practiced	☐	☐	☐	_____
Evacuation plan instructions	☐	☐	☐	_____
Independent power source for emergency lighting and communication systems	☐	☐	☐	_____
Backup generators in case of power failure	☐	☐	☐	_____
Shelter-in-place capability	☐	☐	☐	_____
Emergency responder proximity and response time (fire, ambulance, police)	☐	☐	☐	_____
Other	☐	☐	☐	_____

Medical care	OK	Risk	N/A	Remarks
First aid capabilities and equipment	☐	☐	☐	_____
First aid trained personnel	☐	☐	☐	_____
Nearest medical facility	☐	☐	☐	_____
Provision of 24-hour on-call doctor	☐	☐	☐	_____
List of local doctors, dentists, etc.	☐	☐	☐	_____
Other	☐	☐	☐	_____

Compliance:

Venue compliance	OK	Risk	N/A	Remarks
Fire safety inspections	☐	☐	☐	_____
Emergency plans	☐	☐	☐	_____
Elevator inspections	☐	☐	☐	_____
Food and alcohol service licenses	☐	☐	☐	_____
Building and electrical codes	☐	☐	☐	_____
Disability accessibility compliance	☐	☐	☐	_____
Other	☐	☐	☐	_____

(Secure copies of permits, inspection certificates, or other compliance instruments)

Event compliance	OK	Risk	N/A	Remarks
Labor union jurisdictions	☐	☐	☐	_____
Liquor laws	☐	☐	☐	_____
Noise ordinances	☐	☐	☐	_____
Smoking ordinances	☐	☐	☐	_____
Sanitation codes	☐	☐	☐	_____
Traffic/street closure ordinances	☐	☐	☐	_____
Temporary structure construction codes	☐	☐	☐	_____
Security mandates	☐	☐	☐	_____
Special effect codes (lasers, pyrotechnics)	☐	☐	☐	_____
Insurance coverage requirements	☐	☐	☐	_____
Disability accessibility compliance	☐	☐	☐	_____
Other	☐	☐	☐	_____

(Identify pertinent regulations and acquire necessary compliance applications)

Appendix D: Security plan worksheet

Date Prepared: _____   **Prepared By:** _____

Event Date(s):   From: _____   To: _____

Event Times: Start: _____   End: _____

Event Location: _____

Audience profile: _____
_____

Event activities: _____
_____

Specific Risk Factors: _____
_____

Security functions:

Access/intrusion control: _____

Admissions control: _____

Crowd control: _____

Property protection: _____

Surveillance: _____

Personnel protection: _____

Emergency response: _____

Security Deployment:

☐ Admission points   ☐ Exhibit areas   ☐ Registration areas

☐ Alcohol service areas   ☐ Exit points   ☐ Restricted areas

☐ Cash collection points   ☐ Food service areas   ☐ Roving patrol

☐ Concessions   ☐ Lounges and VIP areas   ☐ Seating areas

☐ Delivery areas   ☐ Parking areas   ☐ Stage/backstage areas

☐ Equipment installations   ☐ Perimeters   ☐ Storage areas

☐ Event offices   ☐ Personnel escort   ☐ Utility and HVAC controls

    ☐ Other

Security Schedule:	Operational hours	Overnight hours
Site preparation:	_____	_____
Move-in:	_____	_____
Installation:	_____	_____
Event:	_____	_____
Dismantle:	_____	_____
Move-out:	_____	_____
Site renovation:	_____	_____

Security Personnel:

- [ ] Contracted – uniformed
- [ ] Contracted – plainclothes
- [ ] Law enforcement – uniformed
- [ ] Law enforcement – plainclothes
- [ ] Private
- [ ] Volunteer

Security Systems and Devices:

Electronic surveillance: _____

Intrusion alarms: _____

Emergency alarms: _____

Lighting systems: _____

Appendix E: Sample instructions for security personnel

The following instructions are examples for informational purposes only. Instructions provided to security personnel should always be confirmed and aligned with law enforcement or the authority having jurisdiction. Contracted security personnel should be provided instructions by their own company only to ensure the contracted company retains liability for their actions.

Disorderly behavior

- Politely inform the individual of the house rules and ask them to desist without causing embarrassment to the individual
- Advise the individual that they will be ejected if behavior does not stop or reoccurs
- If individual does not comply, *ask* the individual to leave the venue by following you out
- If individual refuses, *ask* them again
- If individual refuses, *tell* them to leave the venue by following you out
- If individual refuses, audibly call for back-up on your radio
- If individual still refuses when back-up arrives, gently but firmly place your hand on the individual's shoulder and begin to escort the individual out of the venue with the minimum amount of force possible
- Use only the amount of force or restraint as you are authorized and trained to exert
- Always be polite and show bystanders (witnesses) that you have attempted a peaceful intervention
- Do not hesitate to call law enforcement personnel to the scene

Bomb threat

Written Threat

- Alert the proper authorities
- Save all materials, including any envelope or other container

- Avoid unnecessary handling to retain possible evidence such as fingerprints, hand writing, paper, and postmarks
- If the threat message was hand delivered, describe the messenger or any other suspicious persons in the area

Telephone Threat

- Take the caller seriously; assume the threat is real
- Remain calm; note the date and time of the call
- If on a digital phone, look for and note the originating number
- Keep the caller on the line as long as possible; signal another person to listen in if possible
- Ask the caller to repeat the message; record every word spoken by the caller
- Ask the caller for the location of the bomb, what type of device it is, what it looks like, when it is set to go off, what will cause it to detonate, and why it was placed
- Ask the caller for his or her name, address, and present location
- Listen closely and note the caller's voice gender (male, female, disguised) and estimated age, voice quality (calm, excited, nasal, deep/high tenor), unique speech attributes (accents, speech impediments, diction), threat language (educated, irrational, abusive, taped or read from a script)
- Listen for and note background noises that might be clues to the caller's location (street traffic, office or factory machinery, music, animals, PA announcements, etc.)
- Immediately after the caller hangs up, report the information to the police department, fire department, and other appropriate authorities
- Do not use any wireless communication device (cell phone, two-way radio) as it can trigger the bomb
- Remain available for law enforcement personnel to interview you

Appendix F: Emergency plan worksheet

Date Prepared: _____ Prepared By: _____

Event Title: _____

Event Venue: _____

Venue EAP: ☐ Readily available   ☐ Copy provided   ☐ Adequate
                        ☐ Venue and event EAP consistent and integrated
                        ☐ Roles and responsibilities clearly identified and coordinated

Range of emergencies

☐ **A threat assessment and venue evaluation was conducted on:**
(Specify date and by whom it was conducted, e.g., event risk manager, venue management)

☐ **The following have been identified as potential threats for this area/facility/event:**

Biological
☐ Disease (influenza epidemic/pandemic,
West Nile virus, SARS-type disease,
plague, smallpox, anthrax, foot, and mouth
disease, rabies)
☐ Infestation (animal or insect)
Geological
☐ Earthquake
☐ Landslide, mudslide, avalanche
☐ Tsunami
Meteorological
☐ Extreme temperatures (heat, cold)
☐ Fire (forest, range, urban, urban/wild-land
interface)
☐ Flood (river, flash flood, tidal surge)
☐ Snow storms (blizzards, ice, hail, sleet)
☐ Wind storms (hurricane, tornado, dust
storm)

☐ Other _____

Accidental
☐ Fire
☐ Food contamination
☐ Hazardous material (Hazmat) spill or
release (chemical, radiological, biological)
☐ Transportation accident (rail, aircraft,
watercraft, vehicles)
☐ Water control structure failure (dam, levee,
reservoir)
Intentional
☐ Bombs, bomb threats
☐ Workplace or civil violence
☐ Terrorism (conventional/explosive, chemical,
radiological, biological, cyber)
Technological
☐ Communications systems interruptions/
failure
☐ Energy/power/utility failure
☐ Equipment failure
☐ Mechanical failure

☐ **If such an emergency would occur it would have this impact on our operations:**
(Specify impact for each identified threat, e.g., closure, rescheduling, relocation, data protection, etc.)

☐ **Of the identified threats, we are prepared to address the following:**
(List emergencies; indicate how all others will be addressed, e.g., reliance on emergency management authorities)

☐ **The response we will take is:**
(Specify response for each threat prepared to address, e.g., immediate evacuation, shelter-in-place, cancellation, device-appropriate response, etc.; specify event cancellation procedures)

Reporting procedures

☐ **The preferred method for personnel to report emergencies is:**
(Specify, e.g., dialing 911, dialing an internal emergency number, pulling a manual fire alarm, contacting JOC by radio, etc.)

☐ **The method for reporting emergencies to external responders is:**
(Specify instructions and contact numbers for emergency responders, e.g., fire, police, ambulance, health department, etc.)

☐ **The internal reporting protocol is:**
(Specify procedures according to the type of emergency, e.g., coded announcements, notifying security, activate alarm systems, phone tree, etc.; establish notification flowchart for persons responsible for emergency actions)

☐ **The crisis communications plan is as follows:**
(Specify the designated spokesperson(s), protocols for media inquiries, protocols for inquiries from the public/victim's family, etc.)

Notification & warning systems

☐ **The methods for alerting personnel of actions to be taken include the following:**
(Specify the type of warning system, e.g., smoke detector alarms, bells, flashing lights, radio contact, phone trees, public address announcements, etc.)

☐ **The distinction of alarms for different alerts is as follows:**
(Specify the various alarm types and their meanings regarding actions to be taken according to each type of emergency, e.g., coded announcements, sequence of horn blasts, sirens, etc.)

☐ **The following systems have an independent or auxiliary power source:**
(Specify all independent systems and alternative systems that would be employed for others if power source were damaged)

Evacuation policy & procedures

☐ **The following protocol for declaring an evacuation is:**
(Specify the conditions and person or position designated to authorize an evacuation, e.g., chain of command, condition thresholds, etc.)

☐ **The following protocol for issuing an all clear is:**
(Specify the person or authority authorized to allow re-entry into the facility or resumption of operations, e.g., fire department official, manager on duty, etc.)

☐ **The evacuation actions for different types of emergency include:**
(Specify different actions for evacuation to internal or external locations, e.g., internal location for tornado and external location for fire, and the actions to be taken by individuals evacuating, e.g., turning off equipment, closing doors, etc.)

☐ **The escape route assignments for the facility include:**
(Specify any variable escape routes according to different locations within a facility)

☐ **Evacuation routes and exits are clearly marked in the following manner:**
(Specify the types of escape route diagrams used and the location(s) where they posted and/or published)

Emergency shutdown procedures

☐ **In the event of an evacuation, the following utilities shall be shutdown:**
(Specify the utilities, e.g., gas, electric, etc., their locations, and the shutdown instructions)

☐ **In the event of an evacuation, the following systems and/or equipment shall be shutdown:**
(Specify the systems and/or equipment, e.g., computers, machinery, etc., their locations, and the shutdown instructions)

☐ **In the event of an emergency, the following personnel shall perform shutdowns before evacuation or monitor critical operations:**
(Specify the personnel, by name or job, assigned with shutdown responsibilities, e.g., utilities, systems, equipment, etc., or are to remain)

Shelter-in-place procedures

☐ **The following conditions requiring a shelter-in-place have been identified:**
(Specify the potential threats, e.g., storm, biohazard, quarantine, identified for the area/facility/event that you are prepared to accommodate)

☐ **In the event of a shelter-in-place emergency, the following shelter location(s), equipment, and supplies have been prepared:**
(Specify the locations of special shelters, e.g., tornado shelter, and list the equipment and supplies maintained; specify the duration of emergency these supplies can accommodate)

☐ **In the event of a shelter-in-place emergency, the following personnel shall have the following responsibilities:**
(Specify the personnel, by name or job, assigned with performing shelter-in-place duties, e.g., ventilation covering, equipment activation, etc.; specify employee requirements for providing and maintaining personalized supply kits)

Accounting procedures

☐ **In the event of an evacuation, personnel are to gather at the following designated assembly areas:**
(Specify the location(s) where evacuees are to gather after evacuating the facility)

☐ **After an evacuation the following procedure for accounting for all personnel is:**
(Specify the method for ensuring everyone is accurately accounted for, e.g., head count, manifest, roster, etc.)

☐ **In the event that personnel cannot be accounted for, the following procedure for identifying and reporting last known locations is:**
(Specify the methods and protocol that shall be followed to determine last known location, e.g., area monitors, radio logs, work schedules, session registrations, etc.)

Rescue & medical responsibilities

☐ **The following emergency equipment is provided for personnel use:**
(Specify the types and location of common emergency equipment that personnel are authorized to use, e.g., portable fire extinguishers, fire blankets, eyewash stations, etc.)

☐ **In the event of an emergency, the following personnel are assigned to perform rescue or medical duties:**
(Specify the personnel, by name or job, and duties of personnel responsible for rescue and medical assistance; specify qualifications for said personnel, e.g., first aid or CPR certification)

☐ **In the event of a medical emergency, the following first aid equipment is provided:**
(Specify the types and locations of common first aid equipment, e.g., first aid kit, AED, etc., and instructions for their usage and maintenance)

☐ **In the event of a medical emergency, the following on-site medical facilities are provided:**
(Specify the on-site medical facilities, e.g., first aid room/station/tent, vehicles, equipment, service providers, etc.)

☐ **In the event of a medical emergency, the following off-site medical facilities have been identified:**
(Specify the nearest or designated medical facility or facilities where medical assistance can be provided, including contact information; specify the ambulance services that may be used to transport casualties, including contact information)

Personnel training

☐ **Personnel are provided orientation and training on emergency roles, responsibilities, and procedures in the following manner:**
(Specify how and when orientation and training activities are conducted, e.g., upon hiring, when new equipment or procedures introduced, etc.; specify schedule and locations, e.g., monthly or on-site safety meetings, etc.)

☐ **Practice drills are conducted as follows:**
(Specify schedule of practice drills for evacuation, shutdown procedures, medical emergency, etc.)

☐ **Additional specialized training and retraining is delivered as follows:**
(Specify scope and schedule for specialized training for procedures or equipment, and for training reinforcement activities, e.g., annual retraining sessions)

Key contact lists

☐ **The following personnel have been assigned duties in conjunction with this plan:**
(List the names and contact information for personnel including alternates assigned specific duties and the duties they have been assigned)

☐ **The following individuals may be contacted to clarify plan aspects and procedures:**
(List the names and contact information for personnel that can answer questions about the plan and the procedures included within it)

☐ **The following individuals may be contacted during off-hours emergencies:**
(List the names and contact information for personnel that should be notified of emergencies occurring outside normal hours of operation and can make decisions regarding response activities to be taken)

☐ **The following vendors may be contacted to obtain emergency supplies, equipment, or services:**
(Specify those vendors from whom emergency supplies should be procured, e.g., portable power generators, transportation equipment, food or water supplies, etc.; specify payment procedures)

Appendix G: Disaster preparedness supply kits

On-site event disaster preparedness supply kit

Event organizers should have an on-site disaster supply kit in the event that an event-specific or community-wide disaster occurs during a meeting or event. The following list may be used to create this kit, which may be packed in a large box or container and should be stored on-site in the event office or JOC. Check your disaster preparedness supply kit prior to each event and at least once a year to replenish outdated or missing items.

- ☐ First aid kit (see below)
- ☐ Toilet paper, paper towels, moistened towelettes
- ☐ Hand sanitizer (no-water cleanser)
- ☐ Eye wash
- ☐ Battery-operated radio, extra batteries
- ☐ Flashlight, extra batteries
- ☐ Duct tape
- ☐ Re-sealing plastic bags (assorted sizes)
- ☐ Whistle
- ☐ Chalk and markers
- ☐ Matches in a waterproof container
- ☐ Work kit: gloves, goggles, dust masks
- ☐ Tool kit: pliers, screwdriver, hammer, nails, adjustable wrench, all-purpose knife
- ☐ Emergency contact list (see Appendix J)

Personal disaster preparedness supply kit

Disaster preparedness is a personal responsibility as well. This list may be used to prepare a personal disaster preparedness supply kit, which should be placed in an easy-to-carry container(s) and stored in an accessible location within the home or workplace where it can be accessed quickly in an evacuation or shelter-in-place situation. Check your disaster preparedness supply kit at least once a year to replenish outdated or missing items.

Water

One (1) gallon of water per person per day; at least a three-day supply of water for each person in the household (replenish with fresh water every six months)

- If you have questions about the quality of the water, purify it before drinking. You can heat water to a rolling boil for one (1) minute or use commercial purification tablets to purify the water.
- Chemical sterilization. In some situations, boiling may not be an option. The alternative is to treat the water chemically. Plain household chlorine bleach may be used. Be sure the label states that hypochlorite is the only active ingredient. Bleach containing soap or fragrances is not acceptable. With an eye dropper, add eight (8) drops of bleach per gallon of water (16 if the water is cloudy), stir and let stand. After 30 minutes the water should taste and smell of chlorine. At this time it can be used. If the taste and smell (and appearance in the case of cloudy water) has not changed, add another dose and let stand. If after one half hour the water does not have a chlorine smell, do not use it.

Food

At least a three-day supply of nonperishable food that requires no refrigeration, preparation, or cooking and little or no water (replenish every six months or according to expiration date)
☐ Ready-to-eat canned meats, fruits, and vegetables
☐ Canned juices, milk, soup (if powdered, store extra water)
☐ High-energy foods–peanut butter, jelly, crackers, granola bars, trail mix
☐ Foods for infants, elderly persons, or persons on special diets
☐ Comfort/stress foods–cookies, hard candy, sweetened cereals, instant coffee, tea bags

Kitchen items

☐ Mess kits or paper cups, plates, and plastic utensils
☐ Manual can opener
☐ All-purpose knife
☐ Small pot/pan for heating food or water
☐ Household liquid bleach to treat drinking water
☐ Sugar, salt, pepper
☐ Aluminum foil and plastic wrap
☐ Re-sealing plastic bags

First aid kit

One for home and one for each car
☐ First aid manual
☐ Sterile adhesive bandages in assorted sizes
☐ 2-inch sterile gauze pads (4–6)
☐ 4-inch sterile gauze pads (4–6)
☐ Hypoallergenic adhesive tape
☐ Triangular bandages (3)
☐ 2-inch sterile roller bandages (3 rolls)
☐ 3-inch sterile roller bandages (3 rolls)
☐ Tube of petroleum jelly or other lubricant
☐ Tongue blades (2)
☐ Needle
☐ Moistened towelettes
☐ Latex gloves (2 pairs)
☐ Cotton balls
☐ Thermometer
☐ Sunscreen
☐ Scissors
☐ Tweezers
☐ Aspirin or non-aspirin pain reliever
☐ Anti-diarrhea medication

- ☐ Assorted sizes of safety pins
- ☐ Antibacterial ointment
- ☐ Cleaning agent/soap
- ☐ Antacid (for stomach upset)
- ☐ Laxative
- ☐ Vitamins

Tools and supplies

- ☐ Battery-operated radio and extra batteries
- ☐ Flashlight and extra batteries
- ☐ Plastic storage containers
- ☐ Aluminum foil
- ☐ Medicine dropper
- ☐ Pliers
- ☐ Duct tape
- ☐ Paper, pencil
- ☐ Needles, thread
- ☐ Candles
- ☐ Plastic sheeting
- ☐ Matches in a waterproof container
- ☐ Work gloves
- ☐ Compass
- ☐ Signal flare(s)
- ☐ Whistle
- ☐ Fire extinguisher: small canister, ABC type
- ☐ Shutoff wrench to turn off household gas and water
- ☐ Tube tent
- ☐ Camping shovel

Sanitation

- ☐ Toilet paper, towelettes
- ☐ Soap, liquid detergent, hand sanitizer
- ☐ Personal hygiene items
- ☐ Feminine supplies
- ☐ Paper towels
- ☐ Plastic garbage bags, ties (for personal sanitation uses)
- ☐ Plastic bucket with tight lid
- ☐ Disinfectant
- ☐ Household chlorine bleach

Clothing and bedding

Include at least one complete change of clothing and footwear per person
- ☐ Sturdy shoes or work boots
- ☐ Rain gear
- ☐ Blankets or sleeping bags
- ☐ Hat and gloves
- ☐ Thermal underwear
- ☐ Sunglasses

Household documents and contact numbers

- ☐ Personal identification, cash (including change) or traveler's checks, and a credit card
- ☐ Copies of important documents; be sure to store these in a watertight container

- ☐ Birth certificates
- ☐ Marriage certificate
- ☐ Driver's license
- ☐ Social security cards
- ☐ Passport
- ☐ Wills
- ☐ Deeds and titles
- ☐ Inventory of household goods
- ☐ Insurance papers
- ☐ Immunizations records
- ☐ Bank and credit card account numbers
- ☐ Stocks and bonds
- ☐ Emergency contact list and phone numbers
  - ☐ Establish an out-of-state contact
- ☐ Map of the area and phone numbers of places you could go
- ☐ An extra set of car keys and house keys

Special items

Include items for family members with special needs, such as infants and elderly or disabled persons.

- ☐ Prescription drugs and medications
- ☐ Denture needs
- ☐ Contact lenses and supplies
- ☐ Extra eye glasses

Appendix H: Sample change order form

Project/Contract Number: _____   Change Order Number: _____

Date Prepared: _____   Prepared By: _____

Contact #: _____

Client name: _____

Event Title: _____

Change Requested By: _____

Change Requested: _____
(Description)   _____
                       _____
                       _____
                       _____

Change will result in:	Increased	Decreased	Unchanged
Time:	☐	☐	☐
Cost:	☐	☐	☐
Labor:	☐	☐	☐
Materials:	☐	☐	☐
Services:	☐	☐	☐

The total estimated cost for the above change will be: $ _____

Approved and accepted by:
As the duly authorized representative of the purchaser for this project, I hereby affirm that I approve and accept financial responsibility for the changes listed above.

Client _____   Date: _____
       Signature

Printed name: _____

Position: _____

Company: _____   Contact #: _____

Appendix I: Radio protocol

Common terminology

This is	Identifies caller or receiver
Base	Call sign for the communication center or dispatch
Over	Transmission finished, awaiting response
Out	Call finished, talk group is clear for next user
Say again	Asks caller to repeat last transmission
Say all after	Asks caller to repeat parts of message after a specific word (e.g., 'Say all after northbound')
Say all before	Asks caller to repeat parts of message before a specific word (e.g., 'Say all before southbound')
Stand by	Asks caller to wait a moment
Standing by	Confirms the Stand By message
Copy	Tells caller the message is received and understood
Roger	Tells caller the message is received and understood
Priority	Used to interrupt talk in emergencies
All clear	Indicates emergency radio priority is lifted and may return to normal
Affirmative	Response to a question is Yes
Negative	Response to a question is No
Inbound	Indicates you are approaching the other party
Outbound	Indicates you are heading away from the other party
ETA	Indicates estimated time of arrival; may need to use the phonetic alphabet (e.g., Echo – Tango – Alpha)
I spell	Indicates you will spell the next word or group of words phonetically
Radio check	Request for response to test the performance of the radio

International Phonetic Alphabet

Alpha	Hotel	Oscar	Uniform
Bravo	India	Papa	Victor
Charlie	Juliet	Quebec	Whisky
Delta	Kilo	Romeo	X-ray
Echo	Lima	Sierra	Yankee
Foxtrot	Mike	Tango	Zulu
Golf	November		

Appendix J: Sample contact list

Date Prepared: _____   Prepared By: _____

Event Title: _____

Event Date(s): _____

Event Location:_____
                 Include physical and mailing address

Operational: Include office, cellular, pager, home/hotel phone and room numbers
Event organizer: _____
Risk manager: _____
Key staff members: _____
Venue: _____
Venue manager: _____
Key vendors: _____
Housing hotel(s): _____
Emergency:
Nearest emergency room: _____
Address: _____
Nearest walk-in clinic: _____
Address: _____
Nearest pharmacy: _____
Address: _____
Event EAP staff: _____
Venue EAP staff: _____
Venue security: _____
Airlines: _____
24-hour travel agency: _____
Ground transportation: _____
Emergency suppliers: _____
Emergency Responders:
Police: _____
Fire: _____
Ambulance: _____
Other: _____

Keep an 'In Case of Emergency' (ICE) list of contact names and numbers for all staff, volunteers, and attendees (as appropriate) on site and on file in the office. Dispose of properly after the event.

Appendix K: Sample incident report form

Injured Person/Property Owner Information				
Last (family) name	First (given) name	MI	Date of birth	Male ☐ Female ☐
Address:			Telephone:	
City:	State:	Zip:	ID number:	
Event affiliation: Attendee ☐ Participant ☐ Employee ☐ Volunteer ☐ Other: _____				

Incident Information		
Date of incident:		Time of incident:
Location of incident	Type of incident	Classification of incident
Specify exact location:	☐ Accident (physical) ☐ Accident (vehicular) ☐ Assault ☐ Theft ☐ Property damage ☐ Other:	☐ Event or facility related ☐ Not event/facility related ☐ Minor injury or illness ☐ Serious injury or illness ☐ Non-injury ☐ Other:
Describe how the incident, injury, or property damage occurred: (*use separate sheet if necessary*)		
Property damage description:		
Victim's primary injury and/or condition:		
Disposition: ☐ Care not needed ☐ Refusal of care ☐ Medical attention on site ☐ Referral to hospital/clinic ☐ Report only	☐ EMS transport ☐ Patient-requested EMS transport ☐ Released to personal vehicle	☐ Police summoned ☐ Police report filed Report Number: Officer's Name:

Witness Information		
Name	Address	Telephone Number

Report Prepared Information		
Date Prepared:	Preparer's Name:	
Preparer's Position:		Telephone Number:
Preparer's Signature:		

Office Use Only	
Incident Number:	Incident Date:
Event Name:	Event Date(s):
Event Venue:	Date Report Received:

Appendix L: Stakeholder analysis worksheet

Date Prepared: _____   Prepared By: _____

Stakeholder/Group: _____   Ref. Code: _____

Contact Name: _____   Contact #: _____

Nature of Stake:

Impact of stakeholder on project: _____

Impact of project on stakeholder: _____

Key Issues: _____

Potential Impact:	Insignificant	Minor	Moderate	Significant	Extreme
	☐	☐	☐	☐	☐

Risk classification: _____

Stakeholder Status:

Level of Attitude:	☐ Champion	☐ Supporter	☐ Neutral	☐ Critic	☐ Opponent
Level of Power:	☐ High	☐ Medium	☐ Low		
Level of Interest:	☐ High	☐ Medium	☐ Low		
Level of Urgency:	☐ High	☐ Medium	☐ Low		

Threat or Opportunity Level

Motivation to act: _____

Opportunity to act: _____

Resources to act: _____

Communications Plan

Response Strategy: _____

(Description) _____

Key Messages: _____

Modes: _____

Mediums: _____

Schedule: _____

Monitoring Tactics: _____

Responsibility

Assigned To: _____   Contact #: _____

Appendix M: Site plan worksheet

☐ Venue overview including names of all streets or areas that are part of venue and the surrounding area
☐ Moving route (e.g., parade); show direction of travel and street or lane closures
☐ Location of topographical or terrain features or hazards (outdoor site)
☐ Location of architectural features or obstructions (indoor site)

☐ Ingress routes for attendees, participants, staff, and vendors
☐ Parking areas/facilities; parking area designations
☐ Internal service routes for vendors

☐ Location of perimeter fencing, barriers, and/or barricades
☐ Location of admission/entrance points; exit points (if different)
☐ Location of loading docks/areas
☐ Location of emergency exits

☐ Ingress, egress, and internal routes for emergency services
☐ Location of removable perimeter fencing/barricades for emergency access
☐ Location of joint operations center (JOC)

☐ Location of all attractions, exhibits, booths, activities, seating areas
☐ Location of all tents, stages, platforms, and other temporary structures
☐ Location of décor items or furnishings
☐ Location of sound, lighting, projection, and special effects equipment/installations

☐ Location of hospitality areas/lounges
☐ Location of storage areas
☐ Identification of all restricted-access areas

☐ Location of catering areas/food concessions or booths and cooking areas
☐ Identification of all concessions using cooking/compressed gas or open flame cooking
☐ Location of all alcohol service areas (e.g., bars, beer gardens)

☐ Location of power/water outlets
☐ Location of portable generator(s)
☐ Location of trash containers/dumpsters

☐ Location of all sanitary facilities/portable toilets
☐ Location of on-site first aid facilities/medical services/ambulances
☐ Identification of all components that meet disability accessibility requirements

References

Abbott, J. and Abbott, S. M. (2000). Event management: minimizing liability through effective crowd management techniques. In *Conference Proceedings of Events Beyond 2000: Setting the Agenda* (eds J. Allen, R. Harris, L. K. Jago and A. J. Veal). Australian Centre for Event Management, 105–119.

AIRMIC, ALARM and IRM (2002). *A Risk Management Standard*. The Association of Insurance and Risk Managers (AIRMIC), the National Forum for Risk Management in the Public Sector (ALARM), and the Institute of Risk Management (IRM). Available at: http://www.theirm.org/publications/documents/Risk_Management_Standard_030820.pdf (accessed October 2005).

Alexander, D. (2002). *Principles of Emergency Planning and Management*. Oxford University Press.

Association for Wedding Professionals International (AFWPI) (2006). *Statistics for the Wedding Industry*. Available at: http://www.afwpi.com/wedstats.html (accessed April 2006).

Au, S. Y. Z., Ryan, M. C., Carey, M. S. and Whalley, S. P. (1993). *Managing Crowd Safety in Public Venues*. HSE Books. Available at: http://www.hse.gov.uk/research/crr_pdf/1993/CRR93053.pdf (accessed April 2006).

Augustine, N. R. (1997). *Augustine's Law*, 6th edn. American Institute of Aeronautics and Astronautics.

Awerdick, J. H. (1996). On-Line Privacy. In *The Internet and Business: A Lawyer's Guide to the Emerging Legal Issues* (ed. J. F. Ruh). The Computer Law Association, Inc. Available at: http://www.cla.org/RuhBook/chp4.htm (accessed December 2005).

Ball, C. (2005). *RFID (Radio Frequency Identification) in Action*. Available at: http://www.corbinball.com/articles_technology/index.cfm?fuseaction=cor_av&artid=2481 (accessed December 2005).

Beene, C. (1992). *Police Crowd Control: Risk-Reduction Strategies for Law Enforcement*. Paladin Press.

Berk, R. A. (1974). *Collective Behavior*. Wm. C. Brown Company Publishers.

Berlonghi, A. (1990). *The Special Event Risk Management Manual*. Bookmasters, Inc.

Berlonghi, A. (1996). *Special Event Security Management, Loss Prevention, and Emergency Services*. Bookmasters, Inc.

Biz/ed (2005). The Psychology of Shopping. Available at: http://www.bized.ac.uk/current/leisure/2004_5/140305.htm (accessed October 2005).

Bowdin, G. A. J., Allen, J., O'Toole, W., Harris, R. and McDonnell, I. (2006). *Events Management*, 2nd edn. Elsevier Butterworth-Heinemann.

Briggs, S. (2001). *Successful Tourism Marketing: A Practical Handbook*, 2nd edn. Kogan Page.

British Columbia Provincial Emergency Program (BCPEP) (2005). *Community Disaster Recovery: A Guide for BC Local Authorities and First Nations*. Government of Canada. Available at: http://www.pep.bc.ca/Community/Community_Recovery_Planning/Community_Disaster_Recovery_Guide-2005_09_21.pdf (accessed March 2006).

Broder, J. F. (2000). *Risk Analysis and the Security Survey*, 2nd edn. Butterworth-Heinemann.

Building Owners and Managers Association (BOMA) (2001). *Security Survey Checklist*. Available at: http://www.boma.org/emergency/security%20checklist.pdf (accessed July 2003).

Bureau of Labor Statistics (2006). Public Relations Specialists. *U.S. Department of Labor Occupational Outlook Handbook*. Available at: http://www.bls.gov/oco/ocos086.htm (accessed February 2006).

Cain, S. (2006). *The Threat of Hurricanes, Floods, Fires, Earthquakes and Tsunamis Pose Difficult Questions for Meeting Planners, Hotel and Convention Center Managers*. Hotel Online Special Report. Available at: http://www.hotel-online.com/News/PR2006_1st/Feb06_PlannersRisks.html (accessed February 2006).

Canadian Standards Association (1996). *Principles in Summary*. Canadian Privacy Code. Available at: http://www.csa.ca/standards/privacy/code/Default.asp?articleID=5286&language=English (accessed December 2005).

Cetron, M., DeMicco, F. and Davies, O. (2006). *Hospitality 2010: The Future of Hospitality and Travel*. Pearson Prentice Hall.

CIC (2005). *Meetings Industry Is 29th Largest Contributor to the Gross National Product*. Convention Industry Council. Available at: http://www.conventionindustry.org/aboutcic/pr/pr_091305.htm (accessed October 2005).

Clarkson Centre for Business Ethics (1999). *Principles of Stakeholder Management*. Available at: http://www.rotman.utoronto.ca/ccbe/publications.htm (accessed September 2006).

CNN.com (2003). At least 96 killed in nightclub inferno, 21 February.

Connell, B. (ed.) (2002). *Professional Meeting Management*, 4th edn. Professional Convention Management Association.

Crowd Dynamics (2005). *Crowd Disasters*. Crowd Dynamics Ltd. Available at: http://www.crowddynamics.com/Main/Crowddisasters.html (accessed April 2005).

Crown, The (2005a). *Emergency Response and Recovery*. HM Government. Available at: http://www.ukresilience.info/ccact/errpdfs/emergresponse.pdf (accessed February 2005).

Crown, The (2005b). *Emergency Preparedness*. HM Government. Available at: http://www.ukresilience.info/ccact/eppdfs/emergprepfinal.pdf (accessed February 2005).

Defense Acquisition University (2002). *Risk Management Guide for DOD Acquisition*, 5th edn. DAU Press.

Doukas, S. G. (2006). Crowd Management: Past and Contemporary Issues. *The Sport Journal*, 9(2). United States Sports Academy. Available at: http://www.thesportjournal.org:80/2006Journal/Vol9-No2/Doukas.asp (accessed January 2007).

Doyle, M. (2005). Getting Serious About Security. *Corporate & Incentive Travel*, (23)1, 40–44.

Dubin, A. (2006). *Big Oscar Parties Mean Big Money*. BiZBash Media. Available at: http://www.bizbash.com/content/editorial/e5833.asp (accessed March 2006).

Emergency Management Australia (1999). *Safe and Healthy Mass Gatherings, A Medical, Health and Safety Planning Manual for Public Events*. Australian Emergency Manuals Series, Manual 2. Commonwealth of Australia. Available at: http://www.dhs.sa.gov.au/pehs/publications/ema-mass-gatherings-manual.pdf (accessed May 2002).

Essex, D. (2006) RFP checklist: Security information management. *Government Computer News*, (25)8. Available at: http://www.gcn.com/print/25_8/40435-1.html?CMP=OTC-RSS (accessed April 2006).

Event Solutions (2005). *Event Solutions Black Book 2005*. Event Publishing, LLC.

Explosives Regulatory Division (2003). *Pyrotechnics Special Effects Manual*, 2nd edn. Minister of Public Works and Government Services Canada.

Federal Emergency Management Agency (FEMA) (2000). *State Capability Assessment for Readiness (CAR)*. Federal Emergency Management Agency. Available at: http://www.fema.gov/doc/preparedness/state_car2000.doc (accessed March 2006).

Federal Emergency Management Agency (FEMA) (2001). *Special Events Contingency Planning*. Federal Emergency Management Agency.

Federal Emergency Management Agency (FEMA) (2004). *Standard Checklist Criteria for Business Recovery*. Federal Emergency Management Agency. Available at: http://www.fema.gov/ofm/bc.shtm (accessed February 2006).

Federal Emergency Management Agency (FEMA) (2005). *Effective Communication*. Federal Emergency Management Agency. Available at: http://www.training.fema.gov/emiweb/IS/is242.asp (accessed August 2006).

Finn, N. (2006). Emmy's Taxing Goody Bags. *E! Online*, 14 August 2006. Available at: http://www.eonline.com/News/Items/0,1,19761,00.html (accessed September 2006).

Fischer, R. J. and Green, G. (1998). *Introduction to Security*, 6th edn. Butterworth-Heinemann.

Foltz, M. A. (1998). *Designing Navigable Information Spaces*. Massachusetts Institute of Technology. Available at: http://www.infoarch.ai.mit.edu/publications/mfoltz-thesis/node8.html (accessed July 2004).

Foster, J. S. (2000). *Is Your Web Site Legal? Conducting a Web Site Audit*. Available at: http://www.corbinball.com/articles_legal/index.cfm?fuseaction=cor_ArticleView&artid=440&sectionCode=art_legal (accessed December 2005).

Foster, J. S. (2002). *Meetings & Liability*, version 2.0. Foster.

Frame, J. D. (2003). *Managing Risk in Organizations*. Jossey-Bass.

Fruin, J. J. (1984). Crowd Dynamics and Auditorium Management. *Auditorium News*. Available at: http://www.iaam.org/CVMS/IAAMCrowdDyn.doc (accessed December 2005).

Fruin, J. J. (1993). The Causes and Prevention of Crowd Disasters. *First International Conference on Engineering for Crowd Safety*. Elsevier Science Publishers. Available at: http://www.crowdsafe.com/FruinCauses.pdf (accessed March 2002).

Garber, N. (2004). Security Counsel. *Special Events Magazine*, 23(3), 61–63.

Getz, D. (1997). *Event Management and Event Tourism*. Cognizant Communication Corporation.

Gifford, R. (2002). *Environmental Psychology: Principles and Practice*, 3rd edn. Optimal Books.

Gindin, S. E. (1997). Lost and Found in Cyberspace: Informational Privacy in the Age of the Internet. *San Diego Law Review*. Available at: http://www.info-law.com/lost.html (accessed December 2005).

Gladwell, M. (2002). *The Tipping Point: How Little Things Can Make a Big Difference*. Little, Brown and Company.

Gladwell, M. (2005). *Blink: The Power of Thinking Without Thinking*. Little, Brown and Company.

Glaesser, D. (2006). *Crisis Management in the Tourism Industry*. Butterworth-Heinemann.

Goldblatt, J. (2002). *Special Events, Twenty-First Century Global Event Management*, 3rd edn. Wiley.

Government Accountability Office (GAO) (2005). Congressional Report on Information Security: Radio Frequency Identification Technology in the Federal

Government. United States Government Accountability Office. Available at: http://www.gao.gov/new.items/d05551.pdf (accessed December 2005).

Grieve, S. (2003). *Criminal Liability For Event Organisers: Le Race 2001 Case*. Available at: http://www.lawlink.co.nz/resources/lerace.pdf (accessed December 2004).

Grieve, S. (2004). *Criminal Liability For Event Organisers: The Court Of Appeal Decision In The "Le Race 2001" Case*. Available at: http://www.lawlink.co.nz/resources/lerace2.pdf (accessed December 2004).

Guardian, The (1985). Hideous images linger after carnage of 'celebration' day. 13 May. Available at: http://www.guardian.co.uk/fromthearchive/story/0,12269,1214220,00.html (accessed November 2005).

Haddow, G. D. and Bullock, J. A. (2003). *Introduction to Emergency Management*. Butterworth-Heinemann.

Hanna, J. A. (1994). *Emergency Preparedness Guidelines for Mass, Crowd-Intensive Events*. Emergency Preparedness Canada, Minister of Public Works and Government Services.

Hansen, B. (1995). *Off-Premise Catering Management*. Wiley.

Harvard Business Essentials (2004). *Crisis Management*. Harvard Business School Press.

Hazards Magazine (1997). *Mapping Out Work Hazards*. Available at: http://www.hazards.org/diyresearch/riskmapping.pdf (accessed November 2002).

Health and Safety Executive (HSE) (1996). *Working with animals in entertainment, Entertainment Sheet No 4*. Health and Safety Executive. Available at: http://www.hse.gov.uk/pubns/etis4.htm (accessed April 2002).

Health and Safety Executive (HSE) (1998). *Fairgrounds and Amusement Parks, Entertainment Sheet No. 5*. Health and Safety Executive. Available at: http://www.hse.gov.uk/pubns/etis5.htm (accessed April 2002).

Health and Safety Executive (HSE) (1999). *The Event Safety Guide: A Guide to Health, Safety and Welfare at Music and Similar Events*. Health and Safety Executive.

Health and Safety Executive (HSE) (2001). *Safe use and operation of play inflatables, including bouncy castles, Entertainment Sheet No. 7*. Health and Safety Executive. Available at: http://www.hse.gov.uk/pubns/etis7.htm (accessed April 2002).

Heller, R. (1998). *Communicate Clearly*. DK Publishing, Inc.

Henderson, J. C. (2007). *Tourism Crises: Causes, Consequences and Management*. Elsevier Butterworth-Heinemann.

Hilliard, T. (2004). *Contract and Liability Issues for Event Professionals*. ISES EventWorld Conference for Professional Development, Chicago.

Hodge, M. A. (2005). Security Essentials for Event Planners. *Special Events Magazine*, 24(1), 76–78.

Hoyle, L. H. (2002). *Event Marketing, How to Successfully Promote Events, Festivals, Conventions, and Expositions*. Wiley.

Hudson, A. (2003). Bug devices track officials at summit. *The Washington Times*. Available at: http://www.washingtontimes.com/national/20031214-011754-1280r.htm (accessed January 2004).

Hurley, L. (2004). Rewriting the Rules. *Special Events Magazine*, 23(12), 8.

IACVB (2005). *Delegate Spending, ExPact2004 Frequently Asked Questions*. Destination Marketing Association International. Available at: http://www.iacvb.org/iacvb/view_page.asp?mkey=andmid=242 (accessed October 2005).

IAEM (2004). Security Approach for Convention and Trade Shows. *The Safety & Security Newsletter*, March 2004. International Association for Exhibition Management Center for Exhibition Safety & Security. Available at: http://www.iaem.org/content/membersonly/cess/1stQtr2004Newsletter.htm (accessed March 2004).

ICCA (2005). *UN recognises meeting and exhibition planning as a distinct economic activity.* International Congress and Convention Association. Available at: http://www. iccaworld.com/npps/story.cfm?ID=830 (accessed October 2005).

ICCA/COPE (2005). *Secure Event Management: Advice and checklists for better protected international meetings.* International Congress and Convention Association. Available at: http://www.iccaworld.com/cnt/docs/COPEbrochure.pdf (accessed October 2005).

IEG (1996). *IEG's Complete Guide to Sponsorship.* IEG, Inc.

IEG (2005). *Sponsorship Spending Worldwide.* IEG, Inc. Available at: http://www. sponsorship.com/learn/worldwidespending.asp (accessed October 2005).

IFEA (2005). *Overview.* International Festivals and Events Association. Available at: http://www.ifea.com/about/(accessed October 2005).

Jewell, D. (1978). *Public Assembly Facilities, Planning and Management.* Wiley.

Jeynes, J. (2002). *Risk Management: 10 Principles.* Butterworth-Heinemann.

Joyce, K. M. (2005). Riding the Tide. *PROMO Magazine.* Available at: http:// promomagazine.com/mag/marketing_riding_tide/index.html (accessed October 2005).

Kaatz, R. (1989). *Advertising & Marketing Checklists.* NTC Business Books.

Kendrick, T. (2003). *Identifying and Managing Project Risk.* AMACOM.

Kennedy, D. S. (1991). *The Ultimate Marketing Plan.* Bob Adams, Inc.

Kennedy, J. (2006). *Data Leakage: A Real Business Continuity Issue.* Available at: http://www.continuitycentral.com/feature0361.htm (accessed July 2006).

Kopecky, C. (2004). Dealing with disaster: use force-majeure provisions and event-cancellation insurance to address risks of unpredictable and uncontrollable events. *Texas Meetings and Events,* Winter 2004, 66–7.

Kotler, P., Bowen, J. and Makens, J. (1996). *Marketing for Hospitality and Tourism,* 2nd edn. Prentice Hall.

Krantz, M. (2005). *The Value of Meetings.* Meetingnews.com. Available at: http://www. meetingnews.com/meetingnews/search/search_display.jsp?vnu_content_id=10012 63570 (accessed October 2005).

Krug, S. (ed.) (2000). *Convention Industry Council Manual: A Working Guide for Effective Meetings and Conventions,* 7th edn. Convention Industry Council.

Kwasnik, B. H. (1999). The Role of Classification in Knowledge Representation and Discovery – 1. *Library Trends,* Summer 1999. Available at: http://www.findarticles. com/p/articles/mi_m1387/is_1_48/ai_57046525 (accessed September 2006).

Lagauskas, V. (ed.). *IFEA's Official Guide to Parades.* International Festivals Association.

Latoski, S. P., Dunn, W. M., Wagenblast, B., Randall, J. and Walker, M. D. (2003). *Managing Travel for Planned Special Events.* U.S. Department of Transportation, Federal Highway Administration. Available at: http://www.ops.fhwa.dot.gov/ program_areas/sp-events-mgmt/handbook/handbook.pdf (accessed November 2005).

Lawrence, P. (2006). Why Design? *Fast Company.* Available at: http://www. fastcompany.com/resources/design/lawrence/032006.html (accessed March 2006).

Lewis, J. P. (1997). *Fundamentals of Project Management.* AMACOM.

Lynch, K. (1960). *The Image of the City.* MIT Press.

Lynch, P. (2004). *Criminal Nuisance Prosecutions in Recreation: Cause for Concern?* Available at: http://www.rivers.org.nz/article/CriminalNuisance (accessed May 2005).

Management Sciences for Health and United Nations Children's Fund (MSH and UNICEF) (1998). Stakeholder analysis. *The Guide to Managing for Quality.* Available at: http://erc.msh.org/quality/ittools/itstkan.cfm (accessed September 2006).

Martinez, L. (2005). Playing it safe, the inflatables industry gets serious about safety. *Special Events Magazine*, (24)9, 46–47.

Masterman, G. and Wood, E. H. (2006). *Innovative Marketing Communications: Strategies for the Events Industry*. Elsevier Butterworth-Heinemann.

McSwane, D., Rue, N. and Linton, R. (2003). *Essentials of Food Safety & Sanitation*, 3rd edn. Prentice Hall.

Meeting Professionals International (MPI) (2005). *The Power of Partnership: Capitalizing on the Collaborative Efforts of Strategic Meeting Professionals and Procurement Departments*. Available at: http://www.gccoe.mpiweb.org (accessed July 2006).

Middleton, V. T. C. with Clarke, J. (2001). *Marketing in Travel and Tourism*, 3rd edn. Butterworth-Heinemann.

Mileti, D. S. and Sorensen, J. H. (1990). *Communication of Emergency Public Warnings*. Federal Emergency Management Agency. Available at: http://www.emc.ornl.gov/EMCWeb/EMC/PDF/CommunicationFinal.pdf (accessed November 2005).

Monks, J. G. (1996). *Shaum's Outline of Theory and Problems of Operations Management*. McGraw-Hill.

Monroe, J. C. (2006). *Art of the Event: Complete Guide to Designing and Decorating Special Events*. Wiley.

Moody, A. (2005). Do You Really Know Who is Working for You? Background Checks: Why You Need Them. *Event Solutions Magazine*, 10(3), 52–53.

Morrow, S. L. (1997). *The Art of the Show*. IAEM Foundation.

Moxley, J. (1995). *Advance Coordination Manual*. Zone Interactive.

Murray, E. (2006). Climate conference strip show storm. *The Sydney Morning Herald*, 7 September. Available at: http://www.smh.com.au/news/national/climate-conference-strip-show-storm/2006/09/07/1157222252074.html# (accessed September 2006).

Nadler, L. and Nadler, Z. (1987). *The Comprehensive Guide to Successful Conferences and Meetings*. Jossey-Bass.

National Assessment Institute (1998). *Handbook for Safe Food Service Management*, 2nd edn. Prentice-Hall.

National Fire Protection Association (NFPA) (1995). *NFPA 102 Standard for Grandstands, Folding and Telescopic Seating, Tents, and Membrane Structures*, 1995 edn. National Fire Protection Association.

National Fire Protection Association (NFPA 101) (2000). *NFPA 101 Life Safety Code*, 2000 edn. National Fire Protection Association.

National Fire Protection Association (NFPA 1123) (2000). *NFPA 1123 Code for Fireworks Display*. National Fire Protection Association.

National Fire Protection Association (NFPA 1250) (2000). *NFPA 1250 Recommended Practice in Emergency Service Organization Risk Management*, 2000 edn. National Fire Protection Association.

National Fire Protection Association (NFPA 160) (2001). *NFPA 160 Standard for Flame Effects Before an Audience*. National Fire Protection Association.

National Fire Protection Association (NFPA 1126) (2001). *NFPA 1126 Standard for the Use of Pyrotechnics before a Proximate Audience*. National Fire Protection Association.

National Fire Protection Association (NFPA) (2002). *NFPA 1221 – Standard for the Installation, Maintenance, and Use of Emergency Services Communications Systems*, 2002 edn. National Fire Protection Association.

National Fire Protection Association (NFPA) (2004). *NFPA 1600 Standard on Disaster/Emergency Management and Business Continuity Programs*, 2004 edn. National Fire Protection Association.

National Fire Protection Association (NFPA) (2005). *NFPA 730 Guide for Premises Security*, 2006 edn. National Fire Protection Association.

New Zealand Ministry of Civil Defense and Emergency Management (MCDEM) (2003). *Safety Planning Guidelines for Events*. Available at: http://www.civildefence.govt.nz (accessed February 2004).

O'Connor, M. C. (2005). *RFID Takes a Swing at Ticket Fraud*. Available at: http://www.rfidjournal.com/article/articleview/2060/1/1/ (accessed December 2005).

Office of Critical Infrastructure Protection and Emergency Preparedness (OCIPEP) (2006). *A Guide to Business Continuity Planning*. Government of Canada. Available at: http://www.publicsafety.gc.ca/prg/em/gds/bcp-en.asp (accessed March 2006).

O'Toole, W. (2006a). *Event Project Management System*, CD ROM. www.epms.net.

O'Toole, W. (2006b). *Creativity*. www.epms.net.

O'Toole, W. and Mikolaitis, P. (2002). *Corporate Event Project Management*. Wiley.

OSHA (2002). *Emergency Action Plan Checklist*. Evacuation Plans and Procedures eTools. U.S. Department of Labor Occupational Safety & Health Administration. Available at: http://www.osha.gov/SLTC/etools/evacuation/docs/eap_checklist.pdf (accessed May 2005).

OSHA (2005). *What is an emergency action plan?* Evacuation Plans and Procedures eTools. U.S. Department of Labor Occupational Safety & Health Administration. Available at: http://www.osha.gov/SLTC/etools/evacuation/eap.html (accessed May 2005).

Pine, B. J. and Gilmore, J. H. (1999). *The Experience Economy*. Harvard Business School Press.

Privacy International (1998). *Privacy and Human Rights: An International Survey of Privacy Laws and Practice*. Global Internet Liberty Campaign. Available at: http://www.gilc.org/privacy/survey/ (accessed September 2006).

Project Management Institute (PMI) (2000). *A Guide to the Project Management Body of Knowledge, PMBOK® Guide*, 2000 edn. Project Management Institute.

Ransom, M. (2001). The Three Tenors Concert – An Incident. *Events & Installations Contractor*.

Regester, M. and Larkin, J. (2002). *Risk Issues and Crisis Management*, 2nd edn. Kogan Page Ltd.

Reiss, C. L. (2001). *Risk Identification and Analysis: A Guide for Small Public Entities*. Public Entity Risk Institute.

Risk & Reliability Associates (2003). *Risk & Reliability – An Introductory Text*, 4th edn. Available at: http://www.r2a.com.au/publications/4th_Edition/0-risk-paradigms.html (accessed October 2004).

Roads and Traffic Authority Transport Management Centre (RTA) (2002). *Traffic Management for Special Events, Version 6*. Roads and Traffic Authority, New South Wales. Available at: http://www.rta.nsw.gov.au/trafficinformation/downloads/tmc_specialevents_dl1.html (accessed May 2002).

Rogers, C. (2004). Guest Room: Large-scale Security. *Special Events Magazine*, 23(9), 20.

Ronan, P. (2004). *Safety at Sport and Recreational Events Bill*. Draft legislation. Department of Sport and Recreation South Africa.

Rossol, M. (2000). *The Health & Safety Guide for Film, TV & Theater*. Allworth Press.

Safetyinfo.com. *Fire Extinguisher Training Outline* (accessed December 2002).

Salt Lake Organizing Committee (SLOC) (2000). *Team 2002™ Volunteer Training Manual*. Salt Lake Organizing Committee.

Shock, P. J. and Stefanelli, J. M. (2001). *On-Premise Catering*. Wiley.

Shuster, R. D. (2003). Security strategies for special events. *Special Events Magazine*, 22(2), 40–44.

Silvers, J. R. (2004a). *Professional Event Coordination*. Wiley.

Silvers, J. R. (2004b). Global knowledge domain structure for event management. In *Conference Proceedings, 2004 Las Vegas International Hospitality and Convention Summit* (ed. Z. Gu). University of Nevada Las Vegas.

Silvers, J. R. (2005). The potential of the EMBOK as a risk management framework for events. *Conference Proceedings, 2005 Las Vegas International Hospitality and Convention Summit*. University of Nevada Las Vegas.

Silvers, J. R. (2007). Analysis of the international EMBOK model as a classification system. *Conference Proceedings, 2007 Las Vegas International Hospitality and Convention Summit*. University of Nevada Las Vegas.

Silvers, J. R. and Nelson, K. (2005). *Introduction to Financial Management for Meetings and Events*. Silvers.

Silvers, J. R., Bowdin, G. A. J., O'Toole, W. J. and Nelson, K. B. (2006). Towards an International Event Management Body of Knowledge (EMBOK). *Event Management*, 9(4), 185–198.

Skinner, B. E. and Rukavina, V. (2003). *Event Sponsorship*. Wiley.

Smith, P. G. and Merritt, G. M. (2002). *Proactive Risk Management: Controlling Uncertainty in Product Development*. Productivity Press.

Society of Fire Protection Engineers (SFPE) (2002). *Engineering Guide to Human Behavior in Fire, Review Draft*. Available at: http://www.sfpe.org/sfpe/pdfsanddocs/DraftHumanBehaviorGuide.pdf (accessed January 2003).

Somerson, I. (2003). *Mitigation of Civil Liability/Injury – Event Management*. Available at: http://www.experts.com/showArticle.asp?id=105 (accessed November 2005).

Sonder, M. (2004). *Event Entertainment and Production*. Wiley.

Sorin, D. (2003). *The Special Events Advisor: The Business and Legal Guide for Event Professionals*. Wiley.

Special Events Magazine (2004). Tent-handling practice that killed 3 is common, experts say. *Eventline newsletter*. Available at: http://specialevents.com/newsletter/Tent_handling_practice_that_killed_3_is_common_20041026/ (accessed October 2004).

Standards Australia (1999). *Risk Management AS/NZS 4360: 1999*. Standards Association of Australia.

Standards South Africa (2004). *SANS 10366:2004: Health and safety at live events*, 1st edn. Standards South Africa.

Still, K. (2001). *Optimising Emergency Egress from Offices*. CrowdSafe.com Library. Available at: http://www.crowdsafe.com (accessed March 2002).

Still, K. (2005). *Lincoln Workshop Programme 2005*. Crowd Dynamics.

Tarlow, P. (2002). *Event Risk Management and Safety*. Wiley.

Tassiopoulos, D. (ed.) (2005). *Event Management: A Professional and Developmental Approach*, 2nd edn. Juta Academic.

Thomsett, M. C. (1990). *The Little Black Book of Project Management*. AMACOM.

TIA (2005). *Domestic Research: Travel Market Segments*. Travel Industry Association of America. Available at: http://www.tia.org/Travel/TravelTrends.asp (accessed October 2005).

Tratos, M. G. (2004) *Areas of Law That Every Entertainment Attorney Ought To Know Something About*. Available at: http://www.quirkandtratos.com/article_ent_know.htm (accessed December 2004).

Tricker, R. (2001). *ISO 9001:2000 for Small Businesses*, 2nd edn. Butterworth-Heinemann.

Tum, J., Norton, P. and Wright, J. N. (2006). *Management of Event Operations*. Elsevier Butterworth-Heinemann.

United States Copyright Office (2006). Available at: http://www.copyright.gov/ (accessed February 2006).

United States Patent & Trademark Office (2006). Available at: http://www.uspto.gov/ (accessed February 2006).

U.S. Army (1985). *Civil Disturbances Field Manual No. 19-15*. Department of the Army.

Van der Wagen, L. and Carlos, B. R. (2005). *Event Management for Tourism, Cultural, Business, and Sporting Events*. Pearson Education, Inc.

Veno, A. and Veno, E. (1992). Managing public order at the Australian Motorcycle Grand Prix. *Crowd Violence at Australian Sport: ASSH Studies in Sports History No. 7*. Australian Society for Sports History Incorporated.

Wahle, T. and Beatty, G. (1993). *Emergency Management Guide for Business & Industry*. Federal Emergency Management Agency. Available at: http://www.fema.gov/pdf/library/bizindst.pdf (accessed October 2004).

Weiss, J. W. and Wysocki, R. K. (1992). *5-Phase Project Management: A Practical Planning and Implementation Guide*. Perseus Books.

Wertheimer, P. L. (1980). *Crowd Management, Report of the Task Force on Crowd Control and Safety*. City of Cincinnati. Available at: http://www.crowdsafe.com/taskrpt/toc.html (accessed August 2003).

Wiener, L. (2006). When is a gift taxable? *U.S. News and World Report*, 28 August 2006. Available at: http://www.usnews.com/usnews/biztech/articles/060828/28webtax.htm (accessed September 2006).

WorkSafe Victoria (2006). *Crowd Control at Venues and Events*. Victoria State Government, Canada.

WTTC (2005). *2005 TSA World Report*. World Travel and Tourism Council. Available at: http://www.wttc.org/2004tsa/frameset2a.htm (accessed October 2005).

Wujec, T. (1995). *Five Star Mind*. Doubleday.

Yates, J. F. (2003). *Decision Management: How to Assure Better Decisions in Your Company*. Jossey-Bass.

Index

absolute risk, 4, 22
Academy of Television Arts and Sciences, 228
access control, 113, 200, 202, 291, 308
accessibility, 63–4
  admission procedures, 295
  electronic marketing, 218
  evacuation assistance, 143
  food service special needs, 252
  legal compliance, 16, 58, 70
  signage, 250
  site development, 247, 248
  toilet facilities, 92
  workforce planning, 170
accounting, 15, 130, 141, 162, 181
act of God, 61, 77. See also force majeure
activities, program, 6, 15, 71, 241–5
  ancillary, 229, 256
  site planning implications, 248, 249, 270–1
activities, sales. See sales management
activity, project. See also critical path
  activity architecture, 15, 160–1
  activity definition, 159, 214
  task sequencing, logistics, 281, 284
activity log, 199, 200
ad hoc parking area, 277, 286
admission control, 290–3, 294, 296, 308
advanced life support, 151
advancing the event, 268–9
advertising, 218–19
aggressive hospitality, 117
agreements. See legal documents
AIDA, 217, 233
Alcohol Beverage Commission (ABC), 253, 262
alcohol management, 15, 56, 250, 252–4, 261, 290
  server training, 253, 262
  in crowd management, 300, 301
  legal compliance, 71, 228, 267
ambush marketing, 208, 213, 227, 229–30, 234
American Red Cross, 140. See also International
  Federation of Red Cross and Red Crescent
  Societies
American Society of Composers, Authors, and
  Composers (ASCAP), 68
Americans with Disabilities Act (ADA), 63, 77
amperage, 278, 286
analogous estimating, 161, 182
anti-discrimination liability, 58, 63–4, 170
antitrust, 58, 228, 234
arrival/departure patterns, 83, 274, 276, 293–5,
  308
Asia-Pacific Privacy Charter, 67

assembly occupancy, 86–7, 101
assigned seating, 306, 308
Association for Wedding Professionals
  International, 10
attendee management, 16, 289–95. See also crowd
  management; crowd control
  accommodations and housing, 305–6
attendee management systems, 178, 182. See also
  admission control
  privacy issues, 68–70, 199, 203
  site design issues, 250, 265
atmospherics, 259, 262
attraction, definition, 262. See activity, program
attrition, 61, 166, 182, 305
audiovisual technology, 66, 249, 257–8
Australasian Mechanical Copyright Owners
  Society (AMCOS), 68
Australasian Performing Right Association
  Limited (APRA), 68
Australian Capital Territory (ACT) Occupational
  Health and Safety Council, xvii
Australia Privacy Act, 67
automated external defibrillator (AED), 147,
  151, 268

back of house, 271, 291, 292, 308
bank maze, 294, 308
basic first aid, 148, 150, 151
basic life support, 151
Belgian Society of Authors, Composers and
  Publishers (SABAM), 68
blog, 68, 69, 216, 217, 218, 234
bodyguard. See personal security
bookkeeping, 75, 162, 163, 167, 178, 182
bottom-up analysis, 165, 182
bounce back coupon, 234
brainstorming, 36, 37, 50, 159, 205, 241
brand, 216, 234
  brand management, 16, 213
  branding as a marketing strategy, 215, 216,
  218, 249
  protection as property, 65, 66, 221, 227,
  229, 231
break-even analysis, 165, 182
briefing. See pre-con
Broadcast Music Incorporated (BMI), 68
budget, 15, 162, 163–5, 180, 182
  as a risk management tool, 36, 45
  control, 177
  time-phased, 166
bump-in/bump-out. See move-in/move-out

call sign, 197, 210
Canada Labour Code, 94
Canadian Musical Reproduction Rights Agency
   Ltd. (CMRRA), 68
Canadian Privacy Code, 67
capacity, definition, 101
cardiopulmonary resuscitation (CPR), 147, 151,
   152, 268
cash flow, 15, 162, 164, 166, 180, 182, 230, 234
cash handling, 6, 16, 162, 166, 231
caterers, food safety, 92–3, 250–1
cause/effect analysis, 39, 40, 50, 181
certificate of insurance, 61, 77, 112
change management, 33, 177
change order, 33, 182
   as documentation, 46, 60, 200
   as control measure, 45, 162, 163
chart of accounts, definition, 182
civil protection. *See* emergency management
Clarkson Principles of Stakeholder Management,
   204–5
clearance, 78, 87
closed circuit TV (CCTV), 117, 125
code of conduct, xvii, 73–4, 99, 253
collective behavior. *See* crowd behavior
commercial sponsor, definition, 234. *See*
   sponsorship
common law, 68, 78
communication, 6, 12, 13, 33–4, 45, 184–8, 208–9
   crisis communications, 130, 139, 224–5, 233
   in contingency plans, 108
   in crowd management, 296, 297, 301
   in emergency management, 83, 130, 136, 141, 148
   in evacuations, 143, 145–6
   in marketing, 212, 214, 215, 216
   in stakeholder management, 204, 207–8
   in security, 114, 120–1
   nonverbal, 188
communications management, 16, 188–98
   equipment, 194–5
   on-site communications, 192–4
   protocols, 196–8
   system development, 190–2
communication block, 185–6, 210
communication channels, 168, 169, 185, 210
compliance management, 6, 16, 28, 70–2, 76. *See*
   also accessibility; alcohol management; food
   safety; intellectual property; life safety;
   music licensing; occupational health and
   safety; privacy rights; public health;
   sanitation
   as site selection criteria, 267
   compliance instruments, 46, 61, 70–2, 77, 78, 177
   laws, codes, and regulations, 56, 58–9
Composers & Authors Society of Singapore
   (COMPASS), 68
concessionaires, 16, 234
   food service, 92, 251, 252
   merchandise, 231–2, 233
   site planning for, 283

confidential information, 68, 69, 140, 171, 202,
   203. *See also* proprietary information
consequence management, 140
constituent. *See* stakeholder management
constituency, definition, 210
constraint analysis, 39, 50
consumer gate show, 293, 308
contact list, 46, 137, 139, 150, 188, 195, 198, 200
content design, 11, 15, 242–4
contests and giveaways, 221
contingency plans, 43, 44, 51, 104, 106–8, 123
   in emergency management, 6, 131, 134
   sponsorship, 233
   transportation, 274, 275
   utility failure, 258, 284
continuity plans, 104, 108, 203
continuous improvement, 14, 17, 27, 36, 179
contracts, 15, 16, 59–62, 76, 78, 305. *See also*
   liability; due diligence
   as a communication tool, 185, 186, 187
   as documentation, 36, 46, 198, 200, 204
   catering, 250, 251
   entertainment, 255, 256
   in codes of conduct, 73, 74, 75
   in financial management, 162, 163, 164, 165
   in human resources management, 68, 173
   in procurement management, 174, 176–8
   insurance, 110, 111
   merchandise and concessionaire, 231–2
   sponsorship, 227–9
contract rider, 60, 78, 111, 255, 256
contractual security, definition, 125
Cooper-Zobott, Beth, 189
Copyright Agency Limited (CAL), 68
cost avoidance, 164, 173, 227
costing and pricing. *See* pricing
counter flow, 83, 270, 289, 298, 308
craze marketing, 213, 220, 234
creativity, 14, 65, 215, 240, 260
credentialing system, definition, 308
credentials, access, 118, 290–3, 308
   for emergency responders, 139
   transportation and parking, 274
crisis, definition, 127
crisis communications, 130, 139, 224–5, 233
crisis management. *See* emergency management
critical path, 38, 51, 160–1
cross flow, 83, 270, 289, 298, 309
cross promotion, 16, 217, 218, 221, 234
crowd behavior, 297, 299–300, 307
   human behavior in evacuations, 144–5
   life safety evaluation factor, 83
crowd collapse, 298, 309
crowd control, 113, 295, 296, 297, 300–4, 307, 309
crowd craze, 298, 301, 309
crowd crush, 220, 295, 298, 309
crowd density, 289, 296, 297, 309. *See also* flow
   capacity
   evacuation factor, 144–5
   life safety evaluation factor, 83

medical services factor, 148
program design factor, 245, 246, 248
crowd management, 16, 270, 295–304, 309
crowd manager, 87
crowd movement, 295, 297–9, 301, 307
program design factor, 245, 248
site planning factor, 270
crowd panic, 121, 289, 298, 309
crowd surge, 271, 298, 309
cryptographic controls, 200, 210
cultural diversity, 63–4, 188
customer service, 117, 172, 231, 288, 304, 306, 307

debriefing. *See* post-con
decibel (dBA), 98, 101, 257. *See also* noise level
decision management, 16, 20, 179
decision making authority, 31, 167
decision points as milestones, 160, 164
emergency action plan component, 136
procurement, 175, 176
decision tree analysis, 39, 51
decriminalizing risk, 20, 33, 171
design, 15, 239–40
designated driver program, 253, 262
disability. *See* accessibility
Disability Discrimination Act (DDA), 63, 78
disaster, definition, 127
disaster management. *See* emergency
management
documentation, 13, 28, 71, 76, 188, 198–202.
See also legal documents; risk documentation;
underlying documents
disaster recovery, 141
emergency management, 149
evidentiary nature, 46, 58, 187, 268
security, 118, 122
dram shop laws, 253, 262
drill, 137, 138, 150, 152
due diligence, 27, 34, 57, 63, 116, 129, 227, 232
dump mode, 293, 309. *See also* arrival/departure
patterns
duty of care, 28, 35, 51, 53, 56–7, 89, 129, 131,
146, 296
duty to warn, 57, 95, 98, 170, 259

early bird, 219, 230, 234
e-commerce, 187, 210, 218, 230
electrical power. *See* utilities
emergency, definition, 127
emergency action plan, 135–7, 150, 152
emergency management, 6, 16, 128–30, 152. *See
also* contingency plans; crisis
communications; evacuation; means of
egress; medical services; spokesperson
communications management role, 187, 192,
193, 198
mitigation, 129–32
preparedness, 134–8
public relations role, 223–5
recovery, 140–2

response, 138–9, 152
security personnel role, 112–13, 121, 143
site factors, 83, 267, 268, 274, 275, 276–7
emergency medical services. *See* medical
services
emergency medical technician (EMT), 148, 152
emergency telephone number, universal, 139
encryption, 69, 203, 210
entertainment, 15, 254–6. *See also* activities,
program
environment design, 15, 246–50
décor and furnishings, 248–9
layout configuration 247
ergonomics, 101
Escritório Central de Arrecadação e Distribuição
(ECAD), 68
Estrin, Bob, 96
ethics, 14, 16, 20, 72–6, 117, 175, 204
European Agency for Safety and Health at
Work, 94
European Union Data Protection Directive, 67
evacuation, 16, 142–6, 152, 295. *See also*
emergency action plan; emergency
management; life safety
behavior and movement factors 144–5
event, 6, 7, 14, 22
event genre (types), xix, 7–10
scope of industry, 10–11
event management, 22. *See also* change
management
core values, 14
legal obligations, 56
phases, 13–14
process, 12–13
role, 11
scope of duties, 14–16
Event Management Body of Knowledge
(EMBOK), 12–17, 22
event marketing, 11, 22
event organizer, definition, 22
event spend, 10–11, 22
event tourism, 11, 22
exemption, 63, 67, 70, 72, 76, 78
exposure, 22, 39. *See also* duty to warn; insurance;
occupational health and safety
exposure avoidance. *See* risk avoidance

fault tree analysis, 39–40, 41, 49, 51
Federal Emergency Management Agency, 140, 226
festival seating, 291, 309
financial management, 15, 45, 157, 162–7
fire retardant, 84, 101
fire safety, 58, 72, 81–7, 267, 268
fire detection systems, 85
fire suppression system, 83, 85, 86, 101
first aider, 148, 152
floor plan, 70, 72, 95, 100, 247, 248, 272, 286. *See
also* site plan
flow capacity, 83, 101, 143, 144
in site planning, 265, 270, 284, 286, 294

flowchart, 160, 182, 193, 198, 210
food and beverage management, 15, 250–4, 261.
    See also alcohol management; food safety
food-borne illness, 89, 92–3, 122, 262
food poisoning. *See* food-borne illness
food safety, 6, 92–3, 122
force majeure, 61–2, 78. *See also* act of God
franchise agreement, 78
front of house, 271, 291, 292, 309
frustration-aggression theory, 300

ganging chairs, 271, 286
gap analysis, 36–7, 51, 106
gas cylinder storage, 85, 87–8, 90, 252
gastrointestinal illness. *See* food-borne illness
general admission seating, 291, 309
German Society for Musical Performing
    Rights and Mechanical Reproductions
    Rights (GEMA), 68
green room, 171, 245, 262
ground transportation, 189, 273, 286, 287
guidelines, definition, 182

handicap accessible. *See* accessibility
Hazard Analysis Critical Control Point (HACCP),
    93, 94, 251, 262
hazard mapping, 37, 51, 95, 101
hazardous/toxic waste, 90–1, 101, 221. *See also*
    waste management
Health and Safety at Work Act of 1974, 94
health and safety management, 16. *See also* crowd
    management; fire safety; life safety;
    occupational health and safety; public health
Heimlich maneuver, 147, 150, 152, 268
Hilliard, Tyra, 62, 66
house rules, 303, 309
housing, 16, 256, 267, 274, 305
housing bureau, 309
human resources management, 6, 15, 157,
    167–73, 180
    workforce planning, 168, 169–72
    workforce relations, 172–3
HVAC system, 114, 119, 279–80, 286

incident, definition, 125
    as a trigger, 32
incident log, 122
incident response and reporting, 121–3
    as a security function, 113, 118, 119, 303
    medical incident procedures, 149
incident reports, 122, 125
    as evidentiary documentation, 46, 199, 200
    food service, 93
indemnification, 61, 62, 110, 111, 112, 125
influence diagram, 41, 42, 51
information management, 15, 199–204
    acquisition and distribution, 200–2
    control, 202–3
    crowd management role, 297, 301
    data organization, 201–2

medico-legal issues, 149
    retention and preservation, 203–4
    systems technology, 179–80
infrastructure, definition, 286
    as a risk factor, 6, 142
    communications infrastructure, 34
    security infrastructure, 113
infrastructure management, 16, 272–80, 283
in-kind, 178, 228, 234. *See also* sponsorship
instructions, definition, 182
insurance, 4, 6, 16, 104, 108–12, 123, 148. *See also*
    certificate of insurance; liability; loss
    prevention
    contract clause, 56, 61
    risk assessment component, 28, 36
    risk response technique, 44
insurance broker, 29, 109–12, 123
intellectual property, 16, 58, 61, 65–7, 68, 78, 222.
    See also proprietary information
intercom, 280, 286
Internal Revenue Service (U.S.), 228
International Confederation of Authors and
    Composers Societies (CISAC), 68
International Events Group, 228
International Federation of Red Cross and Red
    Crescent Societies, 148, 153
International Festivals and Events Association
    (IFEA), 10, 11, 73
International Phonetic Alphabet, 210, 331
International Songwriters Association (ISA), 68
International Special Events Society (ISES), 74
interoperability, 188, 209, 210
intranet, 202, 210, 293
intrusion detection alarm, 113, 117, 119, 125
invoice, 60, 175, 182, 183
Irish Music Rights Organization (IMRO), 68
Ishikawa, Kaoru, 39

Japanese music copyright association
    (JASRAC), 68
joint operations center (JOC), 120, 193

labor union. *See* union jurisdiction
laws, codes, and regulations, 55, 58–9, 62–3. *See
    also* compliance management
lead retrieval system, 200, 291, 309
lease agreement, 78, 266
legal documents, 59–62, 76. *See also* contracts;
    rights and interest records
liability, 56. *See also* alcohol management; due
    diligence; duty of care; duty to warn
    ancillary and recreational program, 256
    human resources, 171, 173
    insurance coverage, 109–12
    procurement, 176, 178
    statutory, 62–9
license, 61, 70–2, 78, 115, 230, 233
licensing agreement, definition, 78.
    See merchandise management
life safety, 81–9

lighting, decorative. *See* environment design; production design
lighting, safety, 6, 88, 98, 257, 269, 279
lighting, security, 114, 117, 118, 267, 279
lighting, emergency, 85, 87, 136. *See also* evacuation
liquidated damages, 61, 78
loading areas, 282
load-in/load-out. *See* move-in/move-out
logistics, 16, 130, 280–3
loss prevention, 103–5
loyalty program, 217, 234

magnetometer, 118, 125, 291
manifest, 200, 202, 203, 210
manual, definition, 210
manual handling procedures, 95, 97, 101
marketing, 15, 212–13
    marketing plan management, 213–18
    message and medium, 216–17
    target market, 215–16
marshalling area, 282, 286
materials management, 15
    collateral materials, 221–2
material safety data sheets (MSDS), 98
means of egress, 82, 83, 100, 101, 143, 247, 249, 294, 295, 307
Mechanical Copyright Protection Society (MCPS), 68
media kit, 223, 234
media plan, in emergency response, 136, 139
medical services, 146–9
    capability assessment, 147
    incident procedures, 149
    level of services, 147–8
    site considerations, 148–9
Meeting Professionals International (MPI), 73
merchandise management, 16, 71, 213, 217, 231–2
metered inflow, 298, 309
MICE (meetings, incentives, conventions and exhibitions), 10, 22
milestone, 45, 46, 51, 158, 160, 161, 164
move-in/move-out, 95, 96, 158, 245, 257, 275, 280, 282–3, 286
multi-attribute utility theory (MAUT), 176, 177, 182
music licensing, 67, 68, 78, 254, 255

naming conventions, 198, 202, 211
National Collegiate Athletic Association, 142
National Occupational Health and Safety Commission, Australia, 94
needs assessment, xviii, 11, 22
    in crowd management, 295
    in disaster recovery, 141
    in financial management, 180
    in site selection, 266
    in workforce planning, 170
negligence, 56, 57, 78, 87, 103, 109, 115, 116, 125
Nelson, Gloria, 171
911. *See* emergency telephone number, universal

Ninow, Errol, 131
noise level, 89, 186, 246, 247, 257, 269
    as occupational hazard, 95, 98
nonverbal communication, 188
Norwegian Performing Right Society (TONO), 68
notice, 61, 66, 93, 112, 192, 211, 221

occupational health and safety, 6, 93–9, 101, 251, 304
Occupational Health and Safety Act of 1993, 94
Occupational Safety and Health Administration, 94, 136
Occupiers Liability Act of 1957, 86
official spokesperson. *See* spokesperson
Olympic Winter Games, the 2002, 76, 115, 118, 198
on-road event, 275, 286
operations manual. *See* production book
organizational chart, 169, 182
organizational structure, building the, 168–9
outboarding, 229, 234

paramedic, 148, 151, 152
parking, 276–8
participant management, 16, 289–95
peer security, 116, 125
penetration, market, 217, 221, 234
performing rights organizations. *See* music licensing
Performing Right Society (PRS), 68
permission marketing, 218, 234
permit, 61, 70–2, 78
personal protective equipment, 97, 304
personal security, 116, 125
phone tree, 193, 211
pictographic icon, 250, 262
point of service, 290, 309
policy, administrative, 162–3, 170, 175, 182
policy, insurance. *See* insurance
portable generator, 107, 279, 286
portable seating, 271, 286. *See also* ganging chairs
post-con, 181,182, 283
potable water. *See* water, potable
precedence order, logistics, 281, 286
pre-con, 181, 182, 283
premium, insurance, 112, 125
pricing, 15, 162, 163, 165, 253
Principles for Computerized Data Files. *See* United Nations, Principles for Computerized Data Files
privacy rights, 67–70, 199, 202–3
probability/severity matrix, 41, 42, 51
procedure, definition, 182
procurement, management, 15, 173–8, 180, 181, 182
    as administrative practices, 157, 162, 163, 170
    as ethical practices, 74, 75
    of security services, 116
production book, 16, 198, 209, 211
production design, 15, 257–60
    audiovisual and multimedia technology, 257–8
    special effects, 258–60

production schedule, 36, 158, 161, 171, 180, 182, 281
pro forma, 163, 164, 182
program agenda, 161, 245, 261, 262
program design, 15, 239–40
    structure and sequencing, 245
project management, 157, 183
promotion management, 16, 218–22
    advertising, 218–19
    collateral material, 222
    contests and giveaways, 221
    promotional events, 219–21
proof of purchase, 221, 234
proprietary information, 59, 75, 167, 199. *See also* confidential information; intellectual property
proprietary security, 116, 121, 125
protestors, rights of assembly, 114
public health, 89–93, 99, 140, 149, 208
publicity, 68, 69, 217, 222
publicity stunt, 213, 217, 223
public relations management, 16, 222–7, 234. *See also* crisis communications
    role in communications management, 120, 121, 141
    role in stakeholder management, 207
public space, definition, 309
public service announcement (PSA), definition, 234
pyrotechnics, 56, 70, 71, 84, 138, 257, 258, 259–60, 263

queues, 83, 265, 286
    crowd management, 289, 294, 298–9, 300, 307
    signage, 250
    site planning factor, 270, 271

radio discipline, 196–7
radio frequency identification (RFID), 69–70
receiving hospital, 147, 152
Red Crescent. *See* International Federation of Red Cross and Red Crescent Societies
Red Cross. *See* International Federation of Red Cross and Red Crescent Societies
registration system. *See* attendee management
regulations, definition, 78. *See* laws, codes, and regulations
regulatory official, definition, 78
relational database, 202, 211
relations diagram. *See* influence diagram
relationship management. *See* stakeholder management
request for proposal (RFP), 116, 120, 123, 160, 163, 176, 183
residual risk, 31, 39, 51
response capability, definition, 152
reverse flow, 298, 309
rider. *See* contract rider
rights and interest records, 203
risk, definition, 4, 22

risk analysis, 33, 38–41, 46, 51
risk assessment, xvii, 27–8, 51
    in emergency management, 130, 131–2
    in insurance procurement, 110, 123
    marketing activities as a tool, 214, 215
    risk assessment meetings, 37, 88
    stakeholder and supplier involvement, 47, 48, 249
risk avoidance, 4, 30, 43, 51
risk categories, 35, 51
risk communication, 33–4
risk control, 12, 31–3, 44, 45, 51
    control measures, 104–5
    fallacy of control, 33
risk deflection. *See* risk transference
risk documentation, 27, 34–5, 44–7, 51
risk factors, 6, 22, 113
risk financing, 108
risk identification, 31, 35–8, 51
risk management, 4, 17, 22
    process, 25–35
    tools and techniques, 35–47
risk manager, role of, 17–20, 22
risk mapping. *See* hazard mapping
risk monitoring, 31, 44–5, 51
risk planning, 25–7, 51
risk reduction, 30, 43, 51, 95, 257
risk register, 30, 51
risk resilient, 17, 22, 123
risk response, 28–31, 42–4, 52, 104, 257
risk retention, 4, 30, 43, 52, 108
risk transference, 30, 44, 52. *See also* insurance
room pick-up, 305, 309

safety culture, 98–9, 171
safety meetings, 88, 99
safety patrol, 105
St. John Ambulance, 148, 153
sales management, 16, 230–2
    merchandise, 231–2
    sales platforms, 230–1
sampling, 229, 234
sanctioning, 62, 78
sanitary facilities. *See* toilets
sanitation, 16, 58, 91–2, 95, 251, 269. *See also* waste management
scentscaping, 259, 263
schedule development, 15, 161–2, 177
scenario/tabletop exercise, 37, 52
scope creep, 158, 160, 183
scope management, 157–8
screening, 116, 125, 293, 308
search and rescue, 138, 152
secondary risk, 30, 31, 39, 52
security, 16, 112–23
    as hazard detection resource, 45, 85, 88
    as site selection criteria, 267, 268
    communications, 120–1
    deployment, 118–19, 125
    equipment, 117–18

personnel, 115–17
  role in crowd management, 291, 295, 296, 303
  role in emergency management, 112, 114, 121, 143
  role in information protection, 179, 200, 201, 202
segmentation, 215–16, 234
sewage, 90, 101
shelter-in-place, 137, 152, 268
shuttle service, 165, 253, 274, 275, 278, 286
signage. *See also* wayfinding
  as sponsorship benefit, 227, 228
  for medical services, 148
  in communications plan, 195
  in site design, 246, 247, 260, 261
  safety warning signs, 88, 91, 98, 121
  transportation and parking, 274, 276, 277
simulation, 138, 152
site development, 270–1, 287
  medical service considerations, 148–9
  site planning principles, 270
site diagram. *See* site plan
site inspection, 36, 45, 83–4, 88–9, 266–8, 287
site management, 16, 264, 265. *See also*
    accessibility; assembly occupancy;
    compliance instruments
site map. *See* site plan
site plan, 36, 287. *See also* floor plan
site selection, 57, 264–70
  selection criteria, 266, 267
situation analysis, 215
Society of Authors, Composers and Editeurs of
    Music (SACEM), 68
Society of Composers, Authors and Music
    Publishers of Canada (SOCAN), 68
Society of European Stage Authors and
    Composers (SESAC), 68
Society of Fire Protection Engineers, 144
Society of Italian Authors and Composers
    (SIAE), 68
soundscaping, 257, 263
South African Music Rights Organisation
    (SAMRO), 68
spam, 217, 234
special effects, 58, 70, 98, 242, 258–60, 261, 265.
    See also pyrotechnics
special needs. *See* accessibility
specifications guide. *See* production book
speculative risk, 4, 22
spokesperson, 139, 188, 193, 211, 225, 226–7, 233
sponsorship, spending, 10–11
sponsorship management, 16, 175, 219, 227–30, 233, 234
stakeholder, definition, 28, 52
stakeholder analysis, 33, 205–8
stakeholder management, 15, 204–8
  Clarkson Principles of, 204–5
  involvement in risk assessment, 28, 29, 47
  role in communications, 190–2, 207–8
  public relations as a facet of, 223

statement of work, 158, 159, 183
statutory, definition, 78. *See* laws, codes, and
    regulations
stewards, 115, 125, 145, 277. *See also* security
strategic alliance. *See* sponsorship
suitcasing, 213, 229, 234
sullage, 90, 101, 279
SWOT analysis, 37–8, 52
systems management, 15, 178–80, 181. *See also*
    decision management
  communication systems, 83, 190–2, 193, 209
  data management systems, 201–2
  risk management systems, 27

tabletop exercise. *See* scenario/tabletop exercise
target market, 215–16, 234
telecommunications, 134, 194, 278, 280, 283
telemarketing, 217, 218, 235
temporary structures, 87, 88, 246, 261, 271
ten-codes, 196, 197, 211
termination clause, 61, 78
terrorism, 61, 110, 121, 128, 132–4, 218, 297
threat assessment, 131–2, 133, 152, 206
thresholds. *See* triggers and thresholds
timeline, definition, 183
time management, 6, 15, 158–62. *See also* activity,
    project
tipping point, 265, 287. *See also* triggers and
    thresholds
toilets, 58, 90, 91–2, 249, 262, 304
tort, 56, 68, 78, 104
traffic, pedestrian, 293, 294, 297. *See also* crowd
    movement
traffic, vehicular, 58, 71, 192, 205, 206, 276–7, 299.
    See also transportation and traffic
traffic flow, 273, 287
training, emergency response, 137–8
transfer, 287
transportation and traffic, 16, 62, 64, 133, 134, 192,
    272–6, 283, 284, 295
transportation provider, definition, 287
Transportation Security Administration (TSA),
    189
trauma center, 150, 152
Travel Industry Association of America, 10
trickle mode, 293, 309. *See also* arrival/departure
    patterns
triggers and thresholds, 27, 31, 32, 35, 106,
    160, 297

underlying documents, 163, 182, 183
union jurisdiction, 58, 167, 173, 183, 256, 267
United Nations, International Standard
    Industrial Classification of All Economic
    Activities, 10
United Nations, Principles for Computerized
    Data Files, 202
unrelated business income tax (UBIT), 228, 235
user pays, 274, 287
utilities, 16, 62, 137, 272, 278–80, 283, 284, 286

valet parking, 276, 287
variable message sign, 121, 187, 211, 274
ventilation, 98, 247, 260, 267, 278, 279, 287
Verhelst, Ray, 65
vetting, 114, 125
vicarious liability, 67, 78
vital records, 130, 141. *See also* Rights and Interests records
voice procedures. *See* radio discipline
volunteers, definition, 183. *See* human resources management

waiver, 65, 67, 68, 78
waiver of indemnity, 44, 70, 256, 263

walk-through, 45, 52, 89, 100
waste management, 72, 90–1, 101. *See also* infrastructure management
watch list, 45, 293
water, potable, 89, 91, 92, 148, 254, 279, 286
water weights, 271, 287
wayfinding, 83, 144, 246, 249–50, 263, 297. *See also* signage
wishful listening, 186, 188, 211
work breakdown structure, 34, 38, 52, 158, 159, 281
workforce planning, 167, 169–72
workforce relations, 172–3
Wünsch, Ulrich, 214